A PHILOSOPHER AMONG ECONOMISTS

Selected Works of John M. Brewster

A PHILOSOPHER AMONG ECONOMISTS

by

John M. Brewster

edited by

J. Patrick Madden

and

David E. Brewster

J. T. Murphy Co., Inc.
200 W. Fisher Avenue
Philadelphia, Pa. 19120

Printed in the United States of America

J. T. Murphy Co., Inc.
200 W. Fisher Avenue
Philadelphia, Pa. 19120

Library of Congress Catalog Card No. 74-628881

FIRST PRINTING

1970

FOREWORD

John M. Brewster succumbed to a heart attack on May 23, 1965. On that day we lost an able colleague, a devoted public employee, and a valued friend. "We," in this instance, includes American farmers, employees of the Department of Agriculture, and agricultural economists and other social scientists everywhere. John Brewster made a unique and lasting contribution to our literature. He thought deeply, and wrote prolifically. He enriched the thinking of many of us who were privileged to know him and to work with him.

Although John was a prolific writer, he was too busy to bring his thoughts together in book form, as many of us had urged him to do. Many of his best articles were never published or were published in places hard for scholars to find. This volume of his selected writings has been brought together both as a memorial to a stimulating mind and as a means of making his ideas available to scholars everywhere.

We hope that this collection of John's work does justice to the man himself. However, if he were here, we know that he would not be satisfied. He was never completely satisfied with his own writing. He kept rewriting and all the while developing, testing, and refining his ideas. His restless search for truths and for better ways to express his thoughts led him into unexplored paths. He shed light into the dark corners of his field of intellectual interests. He transformed vague ideas into a clear philosophy.

The book was made possible by the dedicated and unselfish efforts of a committee of John Brewster's contemporaries and by the financial support of the Farm Foundation, Chicago. Without both this book could not have been published. The Committee was headed by Frederick V. Waugh and included Wilhelm Anderson, Kenneth L. Bachman, Willard W. Cochrane, James O. Howard, David L. Miller, and Harry C. Trelogan. J. Patrick Madden acted as secretary and did much of the work of selecting, editing, and arranging this volume, while employed by Economic Research Service. David E. Brewster gave enormous help in editing and in making available unpublished works from his father's library. Others too numerous to name gave their time and efforts generously to this project. My special thanks go to all these people who have labored long to prepare this book and to the Farm Foundation for its encouragement and support.

The committee and I wish to dedicate this volume to the memory of John M. Brewster—a great intellect, teacher, and friend—with the hope that its publication and use will stimulate others to equally fruitful careers.

M. L. Upchurch
Administrator
Economic Research Service

CONTENTS

Part I.

John M. Brewster: A Biographical Note

John Brewster belonged to a generation that lived through America's conversion from a rural to an urban society. As a boy he knew the small farms with horse drawn implements—farms just emerging from the frontier. For 10 years after he left the farm he lived and worked as a student, first at the College of Emporia and later at Chicago and Columbia Universities. And for the last 30 years of his life he worked in Washington, D.C., as a researcher for the Department of Agriculture.

Millions of Americans followed the same path from farm to city, or one much like it. But Brewster kept alive his early experiences to an unusual degree; and they provided the basis for much of his writings. He remembered the loss of livestock or a bad crop year not simple as an incident from the past, but as a lesson in the way men react to adversity and as illustrations of the hopes and values men hold dear and fall back upon in hard times. He never forgot—or lost— the language and mannerisms of the farmer, any more than he forgot those of the men he knew during his university days. Consequently, he seemed to personify many of the contrasts of rural and urban America, of the past and the present.

Brewster had a deep faith in the value and durability of American democracy. The story of the American people and their conquest of a continent held a great interest for him; and while he could be extremely critical of contemporary society, he was always critical with an eye toward improvement. Given his concern with social improvement, Brewster's long association with the government does not appear unusual. Yet it seems a bit strange that a man educated for a career in philosophy, instead spent his most productive years as an economist in the Department of Agriculture. To explain how this came about we must take a look at John Brewster's background.

John Monroe Brewster was born in 1904 in the hilly, scrub oak section of Oklahoma between Grove City and Southwest City, Mo. He came from people who for generations had pushed the frontiers of farming across the continent. Until he was fourteen he worked with his father on farms in Oklahoma, Kansas, Colorado, and Utah. For the most part, these farms were small—sometimes rented and always worked with horses rather than tractors. By modern standards the Brewster family had little and what they had came hard. Education facilities for John and his brothers were often poor. John himself was taught for 2 years by his mother before he ever went to school.

In 1919, the family moved by covered wagon from Utah to Lakin, Kans., where they stayed for a year before moving back to Oklahoma. John remained in Lakin to finish high school, after which he went on to the College of Emporia where he majored in English and psychology and minored in history and political science.

He graduated from Emporia in 1927, then spent a semester at the University of Chicago. After a year of teaching high school in Cicero, Ill., he returned to the University of Chicago in 1929 with a fellowship. Brewster enrolled in the philosophy department's Ph.D. program, where he worked under George Herbert Mead, a social philosopher who had a lasting influence on him. Called by John Dewey "the most original mind in philosophy in the America of the last generations," Mead traced his intellectual lineage back to the American pragmatists Charles S. Peirce and William James. Like Peirce, Mead was well trained in mathematics and the sciences; and like James and Dewey, he believed that philosophy could have significant relevance to men's daily problems—that there was no real division between men's thoughts and their actions.

Despite Mead's strong influence, Brewster was not himself a pragmatist. He thought highly of this school of philosophy for the insights it provided into the way individuals work together in society; and he agreed that consciously or unconsciously men act on beliefs and "first principles" whether or not these principles can be shown to have a metaphysical truth. But he was not ready to agree with William James that "what is true is what works." What impressed Brewster about the pragmatists was not their metaphysics, but their social awareness and social commitment.

In 1931, Mead took a position at Columbia University where his old friend John Dewey was teaching. Brewster decided to go with him, and took a job as lecturer in logic and history. In April of 1931, Mead died unexpectedly, just a few months before he was to leave for Columbia. Mead's death was a blow to Brewster both emotionally and academically. It meant that Brewster had to change advisors midway through his doctoral program. And there was the added problem at Columbia of teaching a full course load while completing the University's course requirements and writing a dissertation.

At Columbia Brewster continued the study of mathematics that he had begun at Chicago, and he intensified his reading in American history. These years also marked the beginning of his writing career. From 1935 to 1937, he collaborated with Charles W. Morris, Albert M. Dunham, and David L. Miller in editing *The Philosophy of the Act,* a volume of Mead's unpublished works. And in 1936, two issues of the *Journal of Philosophy* carried Brewster's dissertation, "A Behavioristic Account of the Logical Function of Universals."

In 1936, when Brewster received his doctorate from Columbia, jobs were scarce and teaching positions in particular were rare indeed. A degree in philosophy was no guarantee of employment. Franklin Roosevelt's New Deal government was hiring men, however, so Brewster was drawn to Washington.

In the spring of 1936, Assistant Secretary of Agriculture M. L. Wilson, seeking for a way to create a better climate of opinion between Washington and the farmer, established the Division of Program Study and Discussion in the Department of Agriculture. Formally organized in 1936 under the direction of Carl F. Taeusch, the Division drew on the talents of such men as John Kenneth

2

Galbraith, John D. Black, Kimball Young, and Ralph Barton Perry in an effort to bring to the people what amounted to a socio-economic justification of New Deal farm policy.

A clear thinking and imaginative man, Taeusch recognized the need for philosophers in the new division, and Brewster was one of the men he picked to form the core of his staff. Brewster's job was to develop educational materials for farmers' discussion groups. These materials dealt with farm surpluses, soil conservation, and farm income. Brewster also became one of the program's most popular lecturers. His farm background gave him an appreciation for the problems of a farming population that had been thrust into the machine age almost overnight. His training in philosophy helped him to understand the interrelations between farmers' attitudes and their actions. And his exposure to Mead's ideas of social action gave him the conviction that society could and should act to alleviate national problems.

With the exception of a year's teaching at Kansas State College from 1947 to 1948, Brewster was with the Department of Agriculture for the rest of his life. In the early forties the immediate crisis of the Depression died as America entered the Second World War, and the men who came to Washington to work with Taeusch moved into other work. Most of Brewster's work between the end of the New Deal and the close of the fifties dealt with the economic aspects of agriculture. During this time he did several highly influential studies on oilseed processing; the relation of resources to income in family farming; and the effects of technological advance on American farming. But he also continued to work with the problems of beliefs and values he had begun to explore while in Taeusch's division, and during the fifties he made several attempts to formulate what he considered to be the central American creeds.

In 1958, he got the chance to work with these problems as leader of the Farm Size and Resource Requirements Section in the Economic Research Service. The difficulty of formulating agricultural policy in economic terms was great but as Brewster saw it, this was only a part of the picture. Policies needed to be applied to people and accepted by them. It was essential that the attitudes of farmers and of American society as a whole be identified and analyzed for the policymakers.

In 1959, Brewster's first papers on this subject appeared—"Value Judgements as Principles of Social Organization" and "Role of Rural Beliefs and Values in Agricultural Policy." The ideas presented in these two studies were developed further in a number of speeches and articles throughout the early sixties. They received their fullest expression in "The Cultural Crisis of Our Time," a long treatment of American value systems that appeared in 1963. This work brought Brewster his greatest recognition.

In 1964 Brewster shifted his attention to cultural attitudes as they are a factor in the economic growth of under-developed countries. The result of this work was a posthumously published article, "Traditional Social Structures as Barriers to Change." It drew on research Brewster did in Taiwan while helping to set up a study of the Island's agricultural system.

3

Brewster's long and fruitful career in the Department of Agriculture brought him many friends and honors. In 1954 he received the Department's Superior Service Award, and in 1964 he earned the Distinguished Service Award, the highest award given by the Department. Despite these decorations, the real picture of the man emerges through his writing. The essays that follow speak more eloquently of John Brewster than any biographical sketch.

Brewster was always extremely conscious of his farm background. When he wrote—especially when he wrote of beliefs and values—he first looked at his own past and the ideals he himself held. The next step was to examine the society around him, both in its past and present aspects; then came the job of formulating and testing hypotheses. But the original impetus behind the research came from within the man, from the farming background where he spent his early years.

Brewster was at his best when drawing on a number of disciplines in an effort to throw new light on problems that could not be dealt with adequately within the framework of any one field. Other men had better backgrounds than he in some aspects of the humanities and social sciences, but few were able to command and utilize as wide a variety of knowledge. His ability in this respect is what gives these essays their value and their originality.

Part II.

Beliefs and Values in American Democracy--
Origins and Emerging Problems

"The Cultural Crisis of Our Times," which opens this section, contains Brewster's most complete treatment of American beliefs and values. In addition, it is here that he draws the all-important distinction between policy problems and crisis problems and identifies what he considered to be the three central crises facing America in the early sixties. His analysis of racial discrimination is certainly relevant today. And his theoretical framework helps illuminate other current crisis problems and policy problems as we move into the 1970's.

The other three papers in this section are previously unpublished manuscripts that predate "The Cultural Crisis" by about 10 years. They contain the seeds of many ideas that Brewster was later to develop in his other writings. All three were left in a relatively unpolished form that could be entirely corrected only by a thorough rewriting, rather than the editing they have received. Despite these drawbacks, however, the manuscripts present several important ideas that should not be lost sight of.

Chapter 2, "Views of Man and Society in the American Tradition," discusses the advantages, purposes, and problems of democracy. What is the nature of America's commitment to democracy? What implications does this commitment have for our society? What must a democratic society's attitude be toward the dissenter, especially the dissenter whose ideas are considered destructive to the social structure as it stands? These are questions that demand the continued attention of Americans in a day when the value and effectiveness of our institutions are being critically examined both from within and from without.

Chapter 3, "Additional Economic and Philosophic Aspects of the Spirit of Enterprise," is a portion of an unpublished manuscript, "The Spirit of Enterprise as the Product of the Theologian and the New World." In this chapter Brewster discusses several important aspects of the enterprise creed. Above all, he distinguishes the enterprise creed from Max Weber's spirit of capitalism and Thorstein Veblen's instinct of workmanship, and contrasts the creed with the economic and traditionalistic views of man. In addition, his chapter casts some new light on the origins of Veblen's attitudes toward the American society of his day.

Chapter 4, "Origins and Implications of the American Dream," is taken from an unpublished manuscript, "The Romantic and Messianic Aspects of the American Dream." This chapter contains Brewster's most thorough treatment of the effects of America's great economic potential on our thinking about ourselves and our role in the world.

The beliefs and values discussed in these four chapters play an important part in a number of the papers found elsewhere in this book.

CHAPTER 1. THE CULTURAL CRISIS OF OUR TIME

Introduction

This paper is about American culture, not about culture in general. In these terms, our topic presupposes that our culture is in a crisis. But is it? More importantly, what is culture anyway? And what is the difference between policy problems and problems of cultural crisis? People are not afraid of policy problems; they regard them as challenges for creative response because they are confident they can resolve them in line with the basic belief directives of their traditions. But even the most gifted and courageous people are uneasy at the very suggestion that they are up against problems of cultural crisis. What, then, is the substantive difference between these two kinds of problems? On this question, the literature is vague, despite the fact that there is much talk and writing about the so-called cultural crisis of our time.

And it is even more vague on the most fundamental question of all: What is culture? I would assume that in a very vital sense it has to do with the heritage of belief systems that are the foundations of the organized ways of life and work which distinguish one civilization from another. In line with this assumption, what are the key American belief systems that are now supposed to be in a crisis? Furthermore, since these belief systems have not always been in a crisis, what were they like before they were in a crisis? And what happened to put them in a crisis?

As we size up our assignment, we are faced with four major tasks. First, we must come to grips as best we can with the meanings of certain terms, the key one being "culture." What does it mean? Often it means somewhat different things to different people. We mean by it the heritage of belief systems which people use in guiding their striving for individual and collective significance—for assurance that they are the kind of persons they most prize, respect, and feel obligated to be. This striving is the cultural constant of history, shared alike by primitives on the islands of the sea and the sophisticates of Madison Avenue. But people differ as day from night with respect to specific beliefs they hold concerning what ways of living and making a living and what types of persons are most worthwhile. Thus, the cultural variables of history are the specific belief systems which people use in guiding their striving for significance. The cultural constant is the striving for significance.

This view raises three questions. What is the nature of the striving for significance and what are its salient characteristics? What precisely do we mean by the expression "beliefs and values"? Why do we hold that the belief systems which people use in guiding their striving for significance constitute the very essence of cultures? The first section of the paper deals with these questions.

Background paper for the Second Quadrennial Town and Country Convocation of the United Church of Christ, Aug. 27-29, 1963, Heidelberg College, Tiffin, Ohio. Reprinted by permission of the United Church Board for Homeland Ministries, St. Louis, Mo.

For two reasons, we use 1920 as the approximate take-off date of the alleged crisis in our culture. First, it is commonly recognized that crises in cultures are turning points in history. They occur when new conditions of living and making a living lead people to alienate themselves from their belief heritage, and in this way transmute their striving for significance into anxiety over the shape of things to come. Second, it is commonly said that the end of World War I is approximately the dividing line between the normal and crisis phases of American culture. For in marked contrast to the present era, the America from Jamestown and Plymouth Rock to the end of World War I, was a nation of confident optimism that conquered a virgin continent and replaced the age-old system of "domestic manufacturers" with a vast industrial plant. Much contemporary discussion holds that in the period since 1920 our 19th century heritage of belief systems is increasingly sinking. And there is anxiety because people are unable to return to the Garden of Eden and they have no compass to the Promised Land. My own guess is that 20th century America runs the danger of being trapped in a pessimism as unrealistic as the optimism of 19th century America.

This brings us to our second major task: identifying the key belief systems that 20th century America received from 19th century America. Unless this identification is made, talk about the cultural crisis of our time is fruitless because we do not know what the culture is that is supposed to be in crisis. Section two of the paper deals with this problem.

Our third task is to specify what major conditions of living and making a living forged the belief systems of 19th century America into the confident optimism that guided the course of Empire through the American wilderness. The third section of the paper deals with this identification. Until this is done, we have no way of determining which of the new conditions in 20th century America may be generating problems of cultural crisis, and which are generating policy problems.

Our fourth section spells out the way in which fast changing 20th century conditions of life may be generating problems of cultural crisis, as distinct from policy problems.

Then, with a bare minimum of detail the final section will bring into clear focus the inter-connected concepts that make up the theory of cultural change which has guided our analysis, point up the way we have applied the theory to American culture and list the main findings to which it helped lead.

I. Culture as the Belief Systems People use in Guiding Their Striving for Significance

Turn now to our first task, which is showing why we equate the essence of any specific culture with given belief systems which a people use in guiding their striving for significance.

Nature and Essential Attributes of the Striving for Significance or Worth

Men the world over strive for an ever finer image of themselves in their own eyes and in the eyes of others, whether actual or ideal. But what is the nature of this good which energizes men and nations?

It is the most spiritual of all treasures. You can get no photograph of it, neither can you weigh it, nor store it in barns or vaults; it has no abode in earth or stone—yet we seek it above all else, both individually and collectively. And no evil is so terrifying as the anxiety over being so devoid of meritorious qualities as to be undeserving of favorable valuation by anyone, including oneself. As William James observed:

> No more fiendish punishment could be devised...than that one should be turned loose in society and remain absolutely unnoticed by all the members thereof. If no one turned round when we entered, answered when we spoke, or minded what we did, but if every person we met 'cut us dead,' and acted as if we were non-existing things, a kind of rage and impotent despair would ere long well up in us, from which the cruelest bodily tortures would be a relief; for these would make us feel that, however bad our plight, we had not sunk to such a depth as to be unworthy of attention at all.[1]*

Few would disagree that Hitler and Eichman were among the most evil men of all time. Read their unspeakable deeds in William Shirer's *Fall of the Third Reich*. Yet so great is the terror of being devoid of meritorious qualities that the last thing Hitler did before blowing his head off was to affirm his faith that history would pass a favorable judgment on his life and work. He could neither live nor die without his inward assurance of a favorable judgment in history. The same was true of Eichman, who sent 6 million Jews to the gas chambers. Going to the gallows, his last words were, "I have been correct. I did my duty. I had to follow my flag and the laws of war."

This striving for assurance of significance or worth we might call the status motivation, except that the status hunger is usually equated with the mere desire for popularity—a favorable image of ourselves only in the eyes of others. But this is only half the truth; the need for favorable valuation in his own eyes is no less urgent than the need for a favorable image of his personality in the eyes of his human world. And the means of meeting the two needs do not always coincide. For the individual often finds himself in situations where what he feels that he must do to achieve a satisfying image of himself in the eyes of his group (or groups) is opposite to what he must do in order to merit a favorable image of himself in his own eyes.

These are the serious situations in life. We are often popular with others, but unpopular with ourselves; eating ourselves out with self-blame at the very moment others are praising us to the skies. The aspiration for high standing is never fully gratified until one finds a line of action which fulfills his need for being the person he feels obliged to be, both in his own eyes and in the judgment of others. And the same principle applies to any group with which the individual identifies himself.

---

*Footnotes are listed by chapter at end of book beginning on p. 283

The potency of this need for assurance of significance is evident on every hand. From the individual standpoint, it moves families from slums to suburbs so their children can have a decent chance to rise to higher levels of distinction. It has led soldiers to certain death and saints to martyrdom. It sets the tone and shapes the style of the whole man, influencing the kind of dress he wears, the car he buys, the house and home he seeks, the career, friends and associates he chooses; the way he works and plays, cuts his hair or eats his dinner; how he bears his troubles and the courage he displays under stress and strain; and the stand he takes on vital issues. Virtually everything one does he does with a view to enhancing the prestige of his person, and above all avoiding damage to the treasured image that he and others have of himself. There is seemingly no interest, however particular (say flowers for his girl friend) or however general (say what should be done about the national debt) which is not impregnated by the striving for significance.

From a collective standpoint, the striving for significance is the need of each to be a valued agent of the needs and aspirations of a larger whole, such as the business community, the nation, the world, and even the generations to come. For success in mere individual rivalry goes only a short way toward gratifying the need for assurance of meritorious qualities. Far greater fulfillment is achieved through identification with a group, actual or ideal, which one views as superior to other groups. Being first on one's team is gratifying, but this is nothing as compared with being first on a team that excels all others. Loyalty, even to the point of giving one's life for his group, is thus a striking aspect of the striving for significance. In fact, the individual often tends to stave off personal defeat within his group (or groups) by outdoing his rivals in professions of loyalty to his group against outsiders.

In the modern world, this collective aspect of the need for significance reaches its zenith in the life of nations. Thus Churchill braced his countrymen for the Battle of Britain with the challenge to so bear themselves that "if the British Empire and its commonwealth lasts for a thousand years, men will still say: 'This was their finest hour.' "[2]

In launching the Battle of France, Hitler spurred his armies with the image of themselves as builders of a Reich that would last a millennium. "We have been naught, we will be all," runs a favorite Communist hymn. The need to be accepted and prized as equals, second to none in dignity and worth, provides the dynamics of the Afro-Asian drive for nationalism and the American Negro's struggle for recognition in him of those human rights which our Constitution invests in every citizen. At the heart of our national songs and other poetic expressions of American character is the hunger of the Nation for a favorable "judgment of history"—a potent expression of the collective aspect of the aspiration of the human animal for high standing in his universe.

Belief Systems as Guides to the Striving for Significance

The guides people use in directing their quest for significance we call "belief systems." But what does this expression mean?

Beliefs are *concepts* of ways of living and making a living which people feel obliged to follow so as to be the type of person they most prize. *While concepts include beliefs, mere concepts of given ways are not beliefs.* For example, I can have a concept of proficiency in scalping and head-hunting as a way of living and making a living. In my case, this concept is not a belief because I feel no need of engaging in such practices in order to prove myself a worthwhile person. For many primitive tribes, however, this concept is an intensely motivating belief. Similarly, millions of people in master-servant societies have the concept of free elections, speech, and assembly. But for them this concept is not a belief because they feel no need to follow these practices in order to prove themselves worthwhile persons. On the other hand, in our society men have valued these practices more than life itself because of their deep-seated need of proving themselves self-masters, subject to the arbitrary power of no one.

To be emphasized is the fact that concepts of given ways of life and work are beliefs only to the extent that people value such ways as essential for being the kind of people they most prize. It follows that *values are the relative weights (degrees of desirability or importance) which people assign to their various beliefs.* They are concepts of ways of living and making a living which they feel obliged to follow for the sake of proving themselves the kind of people they most prize. This means two things.

First, beliefs and values are as interdependent as the sides of a coin. Neither exists without the other. We cannot stick beliefs in one jug and values in another jug. For there are no beliefs without concepts of practices which are *valued* in some degree as valid evidence of prized personal and social qualities. Conversely, without concepts of given ways of life there are no values, as there is nothing to value.

Second, while beliefs and values are interdependent, they are not identical. For often people share the same beliefs and yet have different values because they attach different weights to these beliefs. For example, most people may feel a commitment to telling the truth, and also a commitment to protecting the sick against anxiety over a fatal illness. But they may attach such different degrees of importance to the action claims of these commitments that some feel obliged to tell the patient the full truth, whereas others feel obliged to forego truth telling for the sake of protecting the patient from worry over his condition.

Again, people may share the belief that all deserve the same treatment because of their equal dignity and worth, and also the belief that all deserve differential status in line with differences in their efficiencies in their performance as teachers, messenger boys, administrators, and the like. Yet some may give such importance to the action claims of their equalitarian belief as to favor a very high progressive income tax, whereas others may place such a high premium on the claims of their inequalitarian belief as to oppose fiscal measures that tax the dollars of the well off appreciably more heavily than the dollars of the less well off.

Clearly these people have sharp disagreement over what specific tax rules all should be obliged to observe. But resolution of this disagreement merely calls for a re-evaluation of the relative importance of their equalitarian and

11

inequalitarian beliefs to a point where both parties can agree on a tax rule that meets the demands of both beliefs. Thus their different viewpoints constitute a policy problem and not a crisis problem. For, throughout their negotiations, there runs the commitment of both parties to reappraise the relative importance of their common belief directives so as to reach an agreement on a tax measure that enables both parties to continue living in line with both their equalitarian beliefs that all men should be treated alike at least in some respects, and also with their belief that at least in some respects they should be treated differently.

Thus people's disagreements over what ought and ought not to be done constitute solvable policy problems, provided they share the same beliefs and differ only with respect to the relative importance they give to their belief demands. For, under this circumstance, disputing parties guide their search for solutions of their differences with the conviction that no proposed action is acceptable which requires either party totally to forego allegiance to any of their convictions. Thus, the bonds of people with common beliefs are stronger than differences in their values; that is, stronger than the different premiums they place on the action demands of their beliefs. Put in another way, disagreements of such people over what ought to be done leads them to make compromise with each other rather than fight one another.

Policy problems arise, then, when people have the same beliefs but different values—different weights for the action claims of their common beliefs. In sharp contrast, crisis problems arise when people confront each other with diametrically opposite beliefs concerning what ought and ought not be done. Thus, their sense of obligation to find a way of living harmoniously with one another is transformed into hostility and resentment, each feeling that right action can be achieved only if the other is overcome. Suppose, for example, one party is totally committed to the belief in natural inequality and the other totally committed to the belief in natural equality. The driving power of such opposite beliefs is so total as to render people wholly incapable of ever reaching a mutually satisfactory agreement, whether on tax rules or anything else.

The terms "truth" and "falsity" do not apply to beliefs. For there is no scientific procedure whereby a knowledgeable and devoted democrat, such as a Lincoln, can prove to a knowledgeable and devoted aristocrat, such as an Aristotle or a Calhoun, that his democratic (equalitarian) beliefs are true, and that their aristocratic (inequalitarian) beliefs are false. The same principle applies to any other system of beliefs.

Belief Systems as the Essence of Culture

The relationship between institutions and individuals makes clear that belief systems and values are the foundations of institutions, and hence the essence of any given culture. Institutions, such as free elections, congresses, monogamy and private property, are but approved uniform ways of living and making a living. As overt ways of life, institutions lie outside any given personality, but they also have a locus *inside* each personality. As the *"insides"* of individuals, institutions are *concepts* of ways of living and making a living that persons feel obliged to follow, and this feeling is their need and desire of proving themselves the kind of individuals and society they deem most worthwhile. But, as already shown, such concepts are the sets of beliefs which people use in guiding their behavior as they strive for significance or worth (to themselves and others). Thus, institutions, as activities *outside* particular individuals are but the overt expression of institutions as concepts of ways of life each individual feels obliged to follow in meeting reciprocal responsibilities. In these terms, the foundations of any given civilization are its belief systems.[3]

Clash of Diametrically Opposite Beliefs as Turning the Striving for Significance into Destructive Anxiety

Situations sometimes arise in which parties approach each other under the guidance of diametrically opposite beliefs. The weaker party is forced to conform with the belief demands of the stronger party. The effect is so catastrophic as to turn the weaker party's confident striving for significance into destructive anxiety, such as anxiety of despair over the emptiness and meaninglessness of life; the anxiety and aloneness arising from the separation of the individual from a secure place in a human world; the anxiety of guilt over having failed to make wiser choices at the fork-roads of life.[4]

Consider, for example, the Tasmanians, a primitive people on one of the islands in the South Pacific. Before the white man came, they guided their quest for significance with the belief that proficiency in head-hunting was the only kind of action in which people could earn a decent image of themselves in either their own eyes or in the eyes of others, including their deities. Then came the Westerners who, in line with the demands of their beliefs, suppressed the bloody practice. But their action did not detach the Tasmanians from their traditional beliefs as a highwayman separates a traveler from his purse. After the prohibition even as before, the older belief represented for the Tasmanians the only conceivable way of living and making a living in which they could envision themselves as being the kind of people they most prized and felt obliged to be. The prohibition simply generated within them the additional conviction that they were devoid of abilities they needed for achieving a human world which prized them and in which they could prize themselves as worthwhile persons. As a result, the Tasmanians literally were torn apart by their traditional sense of obligation to prove themselves worthwhile people through proficiency in head-hunting and their new conviction that they were devoid of all capacities for being the kind of people they most prized and felt obliged to be. Whipsawed by the positive and negative power of their old and new convictions, the Tasmanians simply disintegrated from the inside out.

> They grew apathetic, indifferent to work and the future, and at the same time so proficient in abortion that the tribe was committing suicide by depopulation. [5]

Thus, by forcing upon the Tasmanians new conditions of living and making a living which alienated them from their traditional belief system, the Westerners turned the hitherto confident striving of the natives into soul-killing anxiety over the worthlessness of life.

Except for its extremely acute form, the destructive anxiety thus generated in these primitive people is not unlike that which is commonly held to

13

impregnate our modern epoch. Thus, in speaking of Western culture, as a whole, Tillich has observed that the anxiety of the modern period has only two historic parallels: (1) The tremendous anxiety over the threat of fate and death associated with the breakup of the Greco-Roman social structures, and (2) the anxiety of guilt and condemnation associated with the dissolution of the religiously guided medieval civilization.[6] Such anxieties are dangerous, since they drive people to destructive ways of escaping its torment, including the drive to identify their wills with the will of dictatorial leaders in an effort to overthrow their whole existing civilization so as to achieve a human world that prizes them and in which they can be the kind of persons they most prize.

After careful review of literature in various fields on American culture, Nisbet brought the same point to focus in saying that the characteristic terms of modern lexicons are words such as "disorganization, disintegration, decline, insecurity, breakdown, instability . . ." "Not the free individual," says Nisbet in another place, "but the lost individual; not independence but isolation; not self-discovery but self-obsession; not to conquer but to be conquered; these are the major states of mind in contemporary imaginative literature."[7] In sharp contrast, the key words in much of 19th century writing were "individual, change, progress, reason, and freedom . . ." These words were both the outcome of thought and the elicitors of thought. Men were fascinated by their referents and properties.[8]

II. Twentieth Century Heritage of Nineteenth Century Belief Systems and Values

Our guess is that the allegedly massive anxiety complex of present day American people exists more in the "modern lexicons" than in the people. Yet the sharp contrast in language makes clear that the very first step in an analysis of the alleged cultural crisis of the 20th century must be an identification of the belief systems which 20th century America received from her 19th century fathers. We find these to be a sense of individual and collective destiny, a compelling image of the best of all conceivable forms of political economy that rested on a tripod of democratic, work, and enterprise belief systems.

The Sense of Destiny

In the belief systems of 19th century America, the brightest star was a magnificent sense of destiny, commonly called the American Dream. This Dream had three component directives that have long constituted America's most comprehensive guides to national and individual purpose. The first component is a vision of good government awaiting only a little time for plain people to make their voice heeded by the rich and the powerful. The second component is the vision of an economic realm of peace and plenty, awaiting only a little time for diligent industry to bring forth its bounty. The third component of the Dream is the feeling that destiny has assigned America and all her citizens an auspicious part to play in furthering the age-old prophetic hope of a world-wide realm of law and justice.

This sense of world mission contained a deeply motivating belief concerning the sure method of its achievement. This belief was that if America spurned aggressive designs on anyone, aspired to live within her own borders, scrupulously avoided entangling alliances, practiced industry, conquered the continent, and day by day bettered conditions of common life under free institutions, then, the sheer attractiveness of her example would induce people of other lands to bring to earth their dreams and visions in similar fashion. Thus with only minor exceptions, America's historic image of her world-role has been that of a tutor and not the master of mankind in his pilgrimage to perfection.

A Compelling Belief Concerning the Best of all Possible Forms of Political Economy

At only a slightly lower level of veneration, the 19th century American belief systems included a compelling conviction concerning the best possible form of political economy. In this conviction no conceivable form of national organization so perfectly relates men to each other with reciprocal rights and duties as a politico-economic order which divides society as a whole into two distinct spheres. The first is a large private sector characterized by an absence of collective restraints on individual action. The second is a relatively small public sector of popularly controlled government that "helps people help themselves," but abstains from policies and programs which limit the nature-given right (power) of proprietors to run their businesses as they choose, or which penalize the industrious with a tax system or other measures that transfer any appreciable degree of their earned income to others.

This image of the good world ran to the very bottom of the 19th century convictions. It is caught up in Jefferson's famous saying "that government is best which governs least." And the same spirit reached a crescendo in the closing lines of Jackson's veto of the Bank Renewal Bill in 1832:

> Equality of talents, of education, or of wealth cannot be produced by human institutions. In the full enjoyment of the gifts of Heaven and the fruits of superior industry, economy, and virtue, every man is equally entitled to protection by law.... If [government] would confine itself to equal protection and as Heaven does its rains, shower its favors alike on high and low, the rich and the poor, it would be an unqualified blessing.

The Three Undergirding Belief Systems

Powerful commitment to this proprietor image of the best of all possible forms of political economy rested on a tripod of belief systems: the democratic ethic, the work ethic, and the enterprise ethic. As the discussion proceeds, it will become apparent that devotion to the proprietor image of the good world emerged from the fact that in 19th century America, the work beliefs had no other status than that of a mere tool for justifying the action demands of enterprise beliefs. With this ultimate finding in mind, we begin our investigation with a consideration of the democratic belief system.

1. *The democratic belief system:* This system centers in two beliefs, (a) all men are of equal dignity and worth, and (b) none, however wise or good, is good or wise enough to have arbitrary power over any other. These belief demands include a guide to freely determined collective behavior. This guide is the conviction that Nature and Nature's God invests each man with an equal right or power to be a participant in deciding on what rules all must observe for the sake of their mutual well-being. Being such a participant is the democratic meaning of freedom; each liberated from subservience to anyone and yet subject to common rules. Saying the people hold this belief is only an alternative way of saying they have an intense need for ways of life, such as free elections, and freedom of speech and assembly, which invest each man with the power (right) to be a participant in shaping the rules which each must observe.

Three general characteristics of the democratic belief system are instructive. First, in contrast to the Ancient Hebrew from whom stems the basic humanism of Western society, the Ancient Greek from whom stems our scientific tradition would give devotees of this belief system a rough trouncing. For the Greek would rightly point out that having dignity and worth means that one is prized—valued—both for his own sake and as an agent of collective purposes. Hence, to say that all men have a status of equal dignity and worth means that there must be at least one person who prizes himself and every other with exactly the same degree of affection, respect and esteem. Obviously there is no such person. Furthermore, there is no specific human trait, whether reason, skill, or will, which all men possess in the same degree and in virtue of which they deserve to be prized to the same extent.

Thus the wise Greek held that the first equalitarian premise of the democratic ethic is sheer nonsense. And the second premise is in exactly the same boat. As discoverer of theoretical reason, the Greek held that intelligence is of higher worth than any other human trait. But men vary without assignable limit with respect to the wisdom to know what rules all must observe for the sake of their mutual well-being. As it is absurd for the inferior to manage the superior, the realistic Greek took as axiomatic that the principle of natural inequality is the first law of men's nature and that this law invests the wisest with a natural and moral right to have arbitrary power over the less wise. In Aristotle's blunt words:

> . . . the lower sort are by nature slaves, and it is better for them as for all inferiors that they should be under the rule of a master. For he who can be, and therefore is, another's and he who participates in rational principle enough to apprehend, but not to have, such a principle is a slave by nature.[9]

Thus, in line with his presupposition that the human animal is merely a creature of Nature, the Ancient Greek logically concluded that the second equalitarian premise of the democratic creed makes as little sense as the first.

The reverse is true of the Ancient Hebrew. This is not because he was wiser than the Greek; he simply used a different point of departure in reflecting on the nature of the human animal. For in Biblical literature the cardinal presupposition is that men are not merely creatures of Nature but also children of a Creator-Father-God, who has the same compassion for every human being, irrespective of differences in IQ or any other human trait. It follows that all men are of equal dignity and worth because there is at least one person who prizes each member of the whole human race with exactly the same concern that he does every other. And all men fulfill their need for significance best when each emulates the Father's attitude toward himself and every other. Thus, in looking at men from the perspective of Nature, it was as obvious to the Hebrew as it was to the Greek that they differ without assignable limit with respect to any specific skill or ability. But in looking at men from a Divine perspective, it was equally obvious to the Hebrew, as it was not to the Greek, that men do not derive their value or worth from specific abilities or skills which they may possess in varying degrees, but solely from the fact that all have an equal place in the Father's concern. Differences in abilities or skills do not endow people with a natural or moral right to differential dignity or worth, any more than do differences in the color of their hair or the size of their bank account.

Thus, in viewing human nature from a Divine perspective as well as a Nature-perspective, the Hebrew, in contrast to the Greek, was able to make a clean-cut separation between persons and specific abilities, and to see that persons rather than abilities were the proper object of affection, respect, and esteem. In so seeing, he rightly inferred that differences in IQ's and other abilities have no more moral significance than monkey wrenches and mink coats. This being the case, no amount of wisdom, however great, can ever be enough to give any individual or group a natural or moral right to arbitrary power over any other.

Thus the central premises of the modern democratic creed make sense from the standpoint of the presuppositions of the Ancient Hebrew, whereas the reverse was true of the Ancient Greek.

This brings up the second observation. The Greek realist rejected both premises of the democratic creed, saying each was equally absurd. But, by and large, the same is not true of the modern realist. For he takes different attitudes toward each of the democratic premises, saying that people really don't believe the first premise; they just pay lip service to it for fear of the unpopularity they would elicit if they expressed their true sentiments. For in his "realistic view," it is inconceivable that anyone could have any factual ground saying derelicts and Einsteins deserve a status of equal dignity and worth.

But the realist takes a back seat to none in affirming the second judgment of the democratic creed. To prove it, he offers as "self-evident" the proposition that if even the wisest and best were given arbitrary power, they would use it to enhance their own power and privilege at the expense of others, generally under the delusion that they were actually upholding an impartial justice for all. The fact remains, however, that the tough-minded realist is a poor logician. For the central beliefs of the democratic creed are like the sides of a coin; they stand or fall together, since consistent reasoning will not permit one to deny either premise without forcing him to deny the other.

The third observation concerns an important difference in the types of situations in which each of the democratic beliefs takes over as the dominant guide to feeling, thought, and practice. By and large, the first belief comes to the front on all occasions of memorial and dedicatory character. And rightly so. For these are the moments when a people most want to express gratitude for their goodly heritage, bind themselves to each other with high visions of their destiny, and feel most keenly the need of strength for trial and battle. In such moments, people use the first premise of their democratic creed as the most appropriate vehicle of their sentiments. For unlike the second premise, the first lifts to full view the inherent nobility of each without the slightest hint of anything base or mean.

The same is not true, however, when people turn from memorial and dedicatory occasions to the rough and tumble of everyday life. There, they are ever barking their shins on the fact that each individual or group tends to assert its own dignity at the expense of others.

This does not mean that the aspiration for a status of equal dignity and worth is any less potent in the world of sharp elbows than in the world of memorial and dedicatory festivities. But it does mean that if people are to further this aspiration in the rough and tumble of life, they had best keep a sharp eye on the fact that even the wisest and best are not so wise or so good but that ere long they will use superior power to enhance their own position at the expense of others. Usually they will do so under the delusion that they are in fact best serving the common good. Only in keeping a clear eye on this propensity, can people achieve proficiency in checkmating it, thereby ridding their actual world as much as possible from the arbitrary power of anyone. Thus, as the first premise of the democratic creed best meets the need of pulpit and platform, so the second premise best fits the realities of smoke-filled rooms.

To be specific, Jefferson is more recognized than any other American as the voice of "America's better self."[10] Yet, he declared that:

> ... free government is founded in jealousy and not in confidence ... In questions of power then let no more be heard of confidence in man ...[11]

In similar fashion, Hamilton, the chief architect of the Constitution, translated the substantive meaning of the second premise of the democratic ethic into the following guide of statecraft:

> Political writers ... have established it as a maxim that, in contriving any system of government, and fixing the several checks and contracts of the Constitution, every man ought to be supposed a knave; and to have no other end, in his actions, but *private interest*. By this interest we must govern him; and by means of it, make him *cooperate to the public good*, notwithstanding his insatiable avarice and ambition. Without this, we shall in vain boast of the advantages of any Constitution.[12]

Finally, the substance of the second premise of the democratic ethic was a leading presupposition of the Founding Fathers in their day-by-day drafting of the Constitution—a fact which James Bryce expressed in these words:

> [The American Constitution] is the work of men who believed in original sin, and were resolved to leave open for transgressors no door which they could possibly shut.[13]

The two central beliefs of the democratic ethic thus combine into a constructive balance an otherwise unrealistic optimism concerning the goodness of the human animal, and an equally unrealistic pessimism concerning his depravity. They are thus a continual reminder that, while individuals and groups in their capacity for goodness are little lower than the angels, they are at the same time never more than an eyelash above the pit, owing to their capacities for cruelty and all manner of evil. It is questionable if any people ever excelled the insight of 19th century America into this double-sided potential of individuals and groups—an insight that inevitably stems from giving equal attention and devotion to each of the key components of the democratic belief system.

2. *The system of work beliefs:* Going hand in hand with the 19th century system of democratic beliefs was the driving power of a remarkable system of work commitments. The key component is the conviction that striving for excellence in all employments is the proper way of earning one's own highest respect and esteem and also the respect and esteem of others. In this motivation, what counts is not what one does, but how well he performs his social role in the community, whether it be growing corn, butchering hogs, making mousetraps, writing songs, composing sermons, and the like. No socially approved employment is any "higher" or any "lower" as a chance for people to prove their worth.

Thus, the specific employment that happens to engage one is not important as long as it contributes to the welfare of the community of which he is a member. What counts is how he uses it to develop his potential, both for his own sake and for the sake of furthering the aspirations of his community, his country, and even his world for a greater abundance in all spheres of life—economic, scientific, religious and cultural. The spirit of this conviction has never been expressed more truly than by Hiram Goff, a New England shoemaker, in his conversation with his minister, John Jessig. To strike up pleasant chatter Goff remarked:

> I believe in honest work. Work is the law of nature and the secret of human happiness.

His minister replied:

> I am glad to see a man who can use the humblest vocation to the glory of God, as you are doing.

This made the shoemaker's hair stand on end. Said he:

> There ain't no such thing in this wide world, pastor, as a humble vocation. Listen, you are a minister by the grace of God . . . I am a shoemaker by the grace of God. You'll carry up to the judgment seat a fair sample of the sermons you preach, and I'll carry up a fair sample of the shoes I've been making. . . . If your sermons are your best, and my shoes are my best, He'll say, 'John and Hiram, you have used your talents about equally well. It's just as necessary for people to have good shoes as it is good sermons.'[14]

Stemming from peculiar interpretations of the so-called Protestant Ethic, much contemporary sociological opinion equates the American work ethic with an ox-like submissiveness to monotonous routines that tend to dehumanize people by treating them as a mere means, or as "cogs in a machine." This is a caricature of our historic work ethic.[15]

For no error is so pernicious and no absurdity so absurd as the easy equation of this ethic with the belief that people prove themselves the kind of persons they most feel obliged to be through the excellence with which they devote themselves to the brute strain of an ox or the inanimate strain of a "cog in a machine." The heart of this fantastic belief is a hair-shirt concept of work that has never been indigenous to our people. This sort of thing they have detested with bitterness.[16]

What has always been indigenous to them is the belief that they fail in being the persons they feel obliged to be unless they strive to use their ingenuity, intelligence, initiative, and imagination in finding new ways of liberating life from drudgery and brute strain so as increasingly to experience themselves as the active bearers of their own creative powers and richness.

In terms of our actual work ethic, it is difficult to envision a higher responsibility than that of doing all we can to replace factory-type processes, which incarnate machines in human flesh, with technologies where men and not machines are in the saddle. The new and growing electrical technologies, usually called automation, are headed in this direction.[17]

The conviction that increasing excellence in all employments is the proper way of earning high standing clearly includes a further commitment to a peculiar brand of "practical idealism" that has long distinguished our people. As Santayana observed the typical American is "an idealist working on matter."[18] This fact accounts for his skittishness toward either visionary idealism or crass materialism. Few things get on his nerves more than the preaching of "ideals" that are without tangible promise of such materialistic outcomes as conquering disease or unlocking the secrets of photosynthesis. For the mandates of his work beliefs permit him neither to live by bread alone nor to accept poetic pieties as a substitute for bread. They prevent him from dividing his life into a sphere of idealism, on the one hand, and a sphere of materialism on the other. Instead, they prompt him to weave the more humane aspirations of the race for a better lot into a forward march of material progress.

Thus, the relationship between "idealism" and "materialism" is like the sides of a coin. The one is inconceivable without the other, although neither is identical with the other. Accordingly, if one calls the usual American a materialist, he scowls. Call him an idealist, and he wonders if you think he is soft-headed. Call him a practical idealist, and he dilates with good feeling. Add that he is a self-made man, and he bursts with pride.

His "practical idealism" is thus only another name for his work belief that, in their productive potential, men possess ample means for achieving the good world of their dreams through an ever greater mastery of nature, both human and physical. In this feeling is rooted his deep respect for and preoccupation with quantity—a respect that leads to a virtual worship of bigness. Nourished by this respect, the mind is most at home with what can be rolled between the fingers and the thumb; and imagination is most nimble when working "with the clearest and least ambiguous terms known to his experience," which are "number, measure, contrivance, economy, and speed."[19]

Commitment to increasing excellence in all employments clearly includes commitment to the Innovator-Personality Ideal as the type of character most deserving of emulation, respect, and esteem. For, of all types of people, innovators are characterized by the strong need and great capacity for identifying themselves with long range purposes in the confidence that with their own initiative, insight, and creative industry, they can lift themselves from even

20

the lowest to the highest stations through generating new forms of thought and practice which others come to recognize, want, and accept as superior to their own. Such people best practice the belief in increasing proficiency in all employments as the badge of highest distinction.

It is questionable if any people have ever placed so high a premium on innovator personalities as 19th century America. Then, as now, she prizes such strivers not only as excellent providers of mankind's victuals, but as more solid pillars of the community, thinkers of bigger thoughts, dreamers of vaster dreams, wiser judges of right policy and safer keepers of the public conscience than other breeds of men, owing to their closer touch with the eternal verities. In glancing at the heroes of our folklore, it is astonishing to see how frequently the brightest stars are those who have found new ways of turning into fortunes such lowly matters as making chewing tobacco, or butchering hogs, and then turned the fortunes into endowments of great universities, hospitals, churches, and other feats of philanthropy.

It is instructive to observe that, in generating devotion to the Innovator Character Ideal, the urge to excel brings into a constructive balance the destructive passion of the conformist for perfect "togetherness" and equally destructive individualism of the total nonconformist. This is why. The need of innovators for a prized image of themselves in the eyes of their peers is not less urgent than that of the conformist, but they do not permit this need to drive them to surrender their own individualistic views and sentiments concerning what is true or false, good or bad, right or wrong with the thinking and practice of their group on specific issues. Instead they so prize their own exceptional views and sentiments that they resist the pressure for total conformity, even at the cost of rejection and ostracism. This was so especially true of 19th century America that in his study of American democracy in the 1830's, DeTocqueville asked what was the "philosophical method of the American?" And he answered that:

> ... in most of the operations of the mind, each American appeals only to the individual effort of his own understanding. America is therefore one country where the precepts of Descartes are least studied, and are best applied.... Every one shuts himself up in his own breast, and affects from that point to judge the world.[20]

In similar fashion, the Innovator Personality shares the strong need of the total nonconformist for a prized image of himself in his own eyes but he does not permit this need to drive him to be different simply for the sake of being different. For his stronger need is to be different in ways that make society's ways into his own image, at least to some extent. To do this, he feels obliged to evaluate and check his unique views and sentiments from the standpoint of the claims of his group (or groups) as well as from his own individualistic standpoint.

Western society has reaped high dividends from this sense of responsible individualism, which is the very heart of the Innovator Personality. For, there is hardly an implement of modern life, a piece of art, or a law of science which does not run back to where it once had no other home than the mind of some innovating personality—a constructive dissenter who checked and disciplined his exceptional sentiments and views by placing himself in the mind and feeling of his peers until he succeeded in developing his own views to a point where others would eventually accept them as superior to their own. The whole paraphernalia of social life, by and large, is thus a collection of memorials to Innovating Personalities who placed their bets on their capacities to make the world over into their own image. The McCormick reaper, the Singer sewing machine, the Newtonian world machine, the Darwinian theory, Mendel's law, the Babcock cream tester, the Oliver plow—the list is endless.

The belief that being increasingly proficient is the individual's highest responsibility to himself and his society includes the further conviction that society owes three reciprocal debts to the individual. These debts are the obligations to (1) provide all its members with opportunity or access to the means (e.g. public schools) necessary for developing his potential to the fullest extent possible, (2) offer opportunities for productive roles in keeping with his abilities, and (3) give each a fair return for his contributions.

In technical terms, the first two of these debts are called distributive justice and the third is commutative justice. Both are caught up in what the plain man calls "the justice of equal opportunity." Guided by these directives, it is as natural for the individual to resent the unfairness of a society which fails to do its best to discharge all of these debts as it is for society to resent the unfairness of the individual who seeks a living and a favorable valuation of himself, but is unwilling to earn these goods through superior industry. Thus, the 19th century system of work beliefs placed society under duties to the individual which were not less binding than those which it placed on the individual to himself and society.[21]

We need to observe, however, that while the work beliefs system thus placed the individual and society under reciprocal obligations, there is no automatic harmony or adjustment between its directives to distributive justice on the one hand, and commutative justice on the other. For example, distributive justice obligates society to provide all its members with opportunities to develop their capabilities to the fullest extent and also offers them productive opportunities in keeping with their abilities. But meeting this debt might require severe limitations on income inequalities which many might regard as incompatible with fair return to individuals for their contributions.

The 19th century belief demand for increasing proficiency in all employments was more than a mere equation of scientific and technological advance with productive excellence. It was also an audacious faith—the conviction that if men infuse their muscle power with ever-increasing brain power, there is no limit to the extent to which they can break down the walls of Fate, become increasingly the masters of Nature, both physical and human, and in this way achieve the Biblical vision of man's dominion over this surrounding universe. This confidence pervaded all walks of American life: plain people, businessmen, and intellectuals, both scientific and literary. Several observations bear out this point.

Such everyday sayings as "we do the difficult today; the impossible will take a little longer," are clearly motivated by the belief that increasingly scientific and technically excellent work is an automatic generator of the

22

increasingly satisfactory world. One can scarcely imagine anything more infuriating to a young Cyrus McCormick than the suggestion that the binder he was trying to develop might destroy more human values than it would create. The same principle applies to early American farmers, who became "tinkerers" long before the birth of agronomists and agricultural engineers, and out of whose "tinkering" in the early 1800's came all the basic farm machines and implements that entered into the technological revolution of American agriculture in the late 1900's.

The same confidence in mixing brain and brawn as the sure generator to a better life for all led to equating the businessman's highest social duty with adopting the most profitable practices which scientific and technological advance can make available; otherwise he fails to be the helper he feels obliged to be in meeting the needs of society for an ever greater abundance of want-satisfying goods.

This same confidence led scientific workers to equate their highest social duty with a monk-like devotion to their laboratories, and rendered them indifferent to any concern of government with the tremendous social consequences of their discoveries. For example, at the height of her World War I effort, England requested her great physicist, Ernest Rutherford, to do research for the armed services. He rejected the request saying his independent experiments suggested a discovery which would "eclipse the importance of the war," namely the artificial disintegration of the atom.[22]

About the same time in the United States, Edison was given responsibility for mobilizing civilian science and technology for war effort. He showed the same indifference to problems of public policy as Rutherford with his suggestion to the Navy that it bring in at least a physicist in case it became necessary to "calculate something."[23] In the same spirit, Robert Hook, in the late 1600's, admonished his fellow natural scientists that they should:

... improve the knowledge of natural things ... by Experiment (not meddling with Divinity, Metaphysics, Moralls, politicks, Grammar, Rhetoric or Logick).[24]

This historic belief that the duty of scientific workers as discoverers of new knowledge relieves them of all responsibility concerning society's utilization of the new knowledge they produce is absurd except for the 19th century confidence of all classes that an ever greater mixture of brain and brawn is an automatic generator of an increasingly satisfactory world.

Workers in the social sciences were caught up in the same confidence. For example, in the 1930's, Kimball Young, a distinguished sociologist, declared:

... collective conflicts as well as individual conflicts, can be successfully and hygienically solved ... by the rational reconditioning of attitudes on ... an intellectual symbolic plane to the facts of science.[25]

John Dewey expressed the same confidence this way:

Just as soon as we begin to use the knowledge and skills we have to control social consequences in the interest of shared abundant and secured life, we shall cease to complain of the backwardness of our social knowledge. We shall take the road which leads to the assured building up of social science just as men built up physical science when they actively used the technique of tools and numbers in physical experimentation.[26]

All that stands in the road, said Dewey:

> . . . is a lot of outworn traditions, moth-eaten slogans and catchwords, that do substitute for thought, as well as our entrenched predatory self-interest. We shall only make a beginning in intelligent thought when we cease mouthing platitudes.[27]

Sharing the same confidence as farmers, businessmen, physical and social scientists, and plain people, in the capacities of men to bring their actual conditions in line with their aspirations through scientific and technical advance, literary intellectuals sang the wondrous achievements the future held in store for men of this faith. *In Thou Mother With Thy Equal Brood,* Walt Whitman sang it thus:

> Brain of the New World, what a task is thine
> To formulate the Modern. . .
> Out of thyself, comprising science, to recast poems, churches, art,
>
> . . .
>
> By vision, hand, conception, on the background of the mighty past, the dead,
> To limn with absolute faith the mighty living present . . . . . . thou shalt face
>   thy fortunes, thy diseases, and surmount them all,
> Whatever they are today and whatever through time they may be,
> They each and all shall lift and pass away and cease from thee,
> While thou . . .
> Shalt soar toward fulfillment of the future. . . .[28]

In *Locksley Hall,* Tennyson sang the same faith thus:

> For I dipped into the future, far as human eye could see,
> Saw the Vision of the world, and all the wonder that would be;
> Saw the heavens fill with commerce, argosies of magic sails,
> Pilots of the purple twilight, dropping down with costly bales
>
> . . .
>
> Till the war drum throbbed no longer, and the battle flags were furled
> In the Parliament of man, the Federation of the world.
> There the common sense of most shall hold a fretful realm in awe,
> And the kindly earth shall slumber, lapped in universal law.
>
> . . .
>
> Science moves, but slowly slowly, creeping on from point to point;
>
> . . .
>
> Yet I doubt not through the ages one increasing purpose runs, And the thoughts of men are widened with the process of the suns.[29]

3. *Enterprise belief system:* Finally, the beliefs systems of 19th century America included a set of directives which we call the enterprise belief system. This system is distinguished by commitment to capital accumulation as the exclusive test of work ethic virtue. As a result of this commitment, the remarkable system of work beliefs had no status in 19th century America except as tools for justifying the overriding enterprise commitment to a proprietary form of political economy. Why this is true is explained in the rest of this section.

What is the proper test to use in reaching accurate decisions on whether or not people are actually sensitive to the work belief demand for increasing proficiency in all employments? Saying that people have differing degrees of sensitivity to this demand is only an alternative way of saying they have different degrees of work ethic virtue. Some may have not such virtue at all. Therefore, if people are deeply committed to the claims of work beliefs, they must have strong convictions concerning what test to use in judging the extent to which individuals are actually responsive to such claims. What precisely should the test or tests be?

The answers of 19th century America to this important question were clear and unequivocal. Their answers constitute three key components of the enterprise belief systems. They are as follows:

First, in the 19th century increasingly successful proprietorship—capital accumulation—was the correct test of work ethic virtue—the striving for increasing excellence in all employments as the badge of highest distinction. According to this test, the American way is equated with starting out in life with little except one's bare hands and moving up the ladder of proprietorship with his own initiative and industry. No one ever expressed this conviction more eloquently than Abraham Lincoln:

> What is the true condition of the laborer? I take it that it is best for all to leave each man free to acquire property as fast as he can. Some will get wealthy. I don't believe in a law to prevent a man from getting rich; it would do more harm than good. So while we do not propose any war on capital, we do wish to allow the humblest man an equal chance to get rich with everybody else. When one starts poor, as most do in the race of life, free society is such that he can better his condition; he knows that there is no fixed condition of labor for his whole life. I am not ashamed to confess that twenty-five years ago I was a hired laborer, mending rails, at work on a flatboat—just what might happen to any poor man's son. I want every man to have a chance—and I believe a black man is entitled to it—in which he can better his condition—when he may look forward and hope to be a hired laborer this year and the next, work for himself afterward, and finally to hire men to work for him. That is the true system.[30]

In the 1870's, Frothingham, an outstanding religious thinker of his day, expressed the same belief this way:

> The chief agency of Providence is wealth. . . .Though the rich man be a miser he is none the less, though unintentionally, a providence.[31]

In their detailed second study of Middletown (actually Muncie, Indiana) in the 1930's, the Lynds found that the plain man expressed the same conviction in these words:

> "Any man who is willing to work hard and be thrifty and improve his spare time can get to the top. That's the American way, and it's as true now as it ever was" . . . The Captains of industry are social benefactors because they create employment. Capital is simply the accumulated savings of these people with foresight. . . ." "Where'd all our jobs be if it wasn't for them?"[32]

This 19th century belief in capital accumulation as exclusive proof of work ethic virtue included the corollary conviction that failure to achieve a proprietary status proves a life-long dislike for work of any kind. And this dislike includes aversion to responsibility and initiative, lack of ambition, and a preference for being bossed by others instead of directing oneself. Such people seek ever larger rewards for work, but their distaste for work is so strong that the promise of reward is not enough to overcome it. They will put forth adequate effort only if directed and coerced by the threat of job insecurity. As Samuel Insull, the great utility magnate of the 1920's, declared: ,. . . the greatest aid to the efficiency of labor is a long line of men waiting at the gate."[33]

In the enterprise belief system of the 19th century no conviction was so ironclad as the belief that failure of people to meet their own total security needs proved such lack of work ethic virtue as to make them undeserving of social acceptance. This test of the absolute minimum of work ethic virtue was commonly equated with Heaven's first law. For example, the 1870's Henry Ward Beecher expressed the equation this way:

> There may be reasons of poverty which do not involve wrong; but looking comprehensively through city and town and village and country, the general truth will stand, that no man in this land suffers from poverty unless it be more than his own fault—unless it be his sin.[34]

Guided by this belief, he chastised railroad employees striking against drastic wage cuts in 1877 with these words:

> It is said that a dollar a day is not enough for a wife and five children. No, not if the man smokes or drinks beer. It is not enough if they are to live as he would be glad to have them live. It is not enough to enable them to live as perhaps they would have a right to live in prosperous times. But is not a dollar a day enough to buy bread with? Water costs nothing; and a man who cannot live on bread is not fit to live. What is the use of a civilization that simply makes men incompetent to live under conditions as they actually exist. . . .[35]

In the 1930's researchers found the plain man expressing his devotion to the same creed in these words:

> . . .society should not coddle the man who does not work hard and save, for if a man does not "get out" it is his own fault . . . . the strongest and best should survive, for that is the law of nature, after all . . . . it is a man's own fault if he is dependent in his old age. . . . it "undermines a man's character" for him to get what he doesn't earn.[36]

In line with these tests of work ethic virtue, the overriding enterprise conviction was the belief that the best type of society is a proprietary form of economy in which democratic government owes people three main debts.

First, its central responsibility is to make available to people whatever public services they cannot provide for themselves but which they must have in order to become increasingly successful proprietors, and in this way meet the demand of their belief in capital accumulation as the proper test of work ethic virtue.

Few if any governments have excelled 19th century America in meeting the work belief that society owes all its members an equality of opportunity for productive work. This is abundantly illustrated in the passage of numerous laws that gave farmer entrepreneurs opportunities to acquire public lands on increasingly favorable terms; set up the system of land grant colleges, experiment stations, and extension service; and established agricultural credit institutions such as the Federal Land Banks and the Bank for Cooperatives. The same responsiveness is also illustrated in the adoption of policies that gave industrial entrepreneurs huge tracts of land, timber stands, and mineral deposits, a virtual monopoly of rapidly expanding domestic markets through a system of increasingly protective tariffs against world competitors, and an abundant supply of relatively cheap labor through extremely liberal immigration policies.

Second, government is obliged to abstain from making rules that tax the dollars of high income more heavily than the dollars of others; otherwise it will penalize the industrious and reward the indolent, thus suffocating the very work ethic virtue which it is obliged to foster by the national belief in proficiency in all employments as the proper way of earning high standing. A typical modern expression of this reasoning runs thus:

> The government has adopted the role of the "welfare state" and declared its will to attain the "four freedoms," "full employment," and other grandiose objectives. This it proposes to do largely by redistributing the income of its people. By heavily progressive income taxation, it deprives its successful citizens of their product and gives it to the less successful; thus it penalizes industry, thrift, competence, and efficiency and subsidizes the idle, spendthrift, incompetent, and inefficient. By despoiling the thrifty, it dries up the source of capital, reduces investment and the creation of jobs, slows down industrial progress, and prevents society from attaining its highest level of consumption.[37]

Third, government was obliged to abstain from rules that limit the entrepreneurial freedom of proprietors to run their businesses as they choose; otherwise government will stifle the very striving for distinction which it is obliged to foster by the national work belief that innovators are the type of people most deserving respect and emulation.

In elegance of design and power of underlying convictions, this national pattern of life and work is something wonderful to behold. It commanded deeply felt allegiance. Those who would lay unclean hands on this palladium of the Republic commonly found they had called down on their heads the righteous wrath of an aroused enterprise conscience–a wrath never more cogently expressed than by William Graham Sumner in his little monograph of 1884 on "What the Social Classes Owe to Each Other." Here is a sample of his hard-hitting words:

> ...God and Nature have ordained the chances and conditions of life on earth once for all. The case cannot be reopened. We cannot get a revision of the....rules of right living. They consist of labor and self-denial repeated over and over again in learning and doing.....class distinctions simply result from the different degrees of success with which men have availed themselves of the chances which were presented to them...If there be liberty, some will profit by the chances eagerly and some will neglect them altogether. Therefore, the greater the chances the more unequal will be the fortunes of these two sets of men. So it ought to be in all justice and right reason. The yearning after equality is the offspring of envy and covetousness, and there is no possible plan for satisfying the yearning which can do ought else than rob A to give to B; consequently all such plans nourish some of the meanest vices of human nature, waste capital, and overthrow civilization.[38]

There is no question but what Sumner was here voicing convictions deep and strong in the conscience of the 19th century America. No one ever really answered him.

In making capital accumulation the exclusive test of work ethic virtue, the 19th century enterprise belief system further equated the businessman's highest social responsibility with profit maximization. No other demands could take precedence over this one. Suppose, for example, a businessman is confronted with a choice between a present production practice which yields a 5-percent profit on each dollar he invests in labor, and a new practice which will yield 10 percent. Unless he chooses the new practice, he not only fails in his duty to do the best he can by his business, but he also fails in his social duty to help the community obtain an ever greater abundance of want-satisfying goods. Carrying out this duty may require him to discharge the workers whose labor is no longer needed in his business.

If it was asked what happens to the displaced workers, he answered that some other businessman had jobs for them. All they needed to do was look. Put in another way, the belief was that the competitive striving of businessmen to outdo each other in giving the consumer the most for his dollar automatically generated plenty of work opportunities at fair pay for all who were willing and able to work. Therefore, saying that one business was laying off men as a result of adopting a labor-saving practice was only an alternative way of saying some other businesses were opening up new jobs somewhere else.

One is struck by the spiritual kinship of the 19th century scientist and the 19th century businessman. Because of his unquestioning belief that new knowledge automatically leads to an increasingly satisfactory world, the 19th century scientist felt he would fail in duty to serve the needs of mankind if he took time out to help public leaders decide on which of the many possible uses society should make of the knowledge he was discovering. Similarly, because of their unquestioning faith that competition in giving the consumer the most for his dollar automatically generated an abundance of work opportunities for everyone, the 19th century businessman felt he would fail in his social duty unless he installed the higher-profit making methods which scientists were making possible with their new discoveries.

The doctrine of automatic harmony—like peace, "it's wonderful!" It lifts from the back of the human animal any burdensome concern with the harm he may inflict on others by headlong pursuit of his own individualistic interest.

III. Conditions Accounting for Rise of
19th Century Belief System

We need to ask what major conditions led to the development of the 19th century belief systems which we inherited. We must identify these conditions, else we have no way of determining which conditions in 20th century America are generating crisis problems and which are generating policy problems. Two major factors are especially relevant to our problem: (1) the carry-over of certain Old World belief systems; (2) and an expanding system of family businesses in a virgin continent of opportunities.

Heritage of Conflicting Belief Systems

Our 19th century belief systems stemmed in no small measure from a set of prior belief systems which the builders of early America carried over from the Old World. This carry-over included a central belief of the Medieval landlord civilization concerning the superior standing of proprietors. It also included a revolutionary interpretation of the ethical significance of work that was first generated by the religious reformers of the 16th and 17th centuries. And, finally, it included an equally revolutionary belief of the Natural Rights philosophers that natural or moral law places no limits on the amount of property men could acquire as a fair reward for work. The builders of early 19th century America were both creatures of and fugitives from an older Medieval landlord civilization. As creatures, they shared the age-old belief that proprietorship is unquestioned proof of highest merit. In this belief proprietors were regarded as the kind of people who deserved highest respect and emulation because they were the exclusive owners of the managerial wisdom which enables people to be their own rulers, endowed with an equal right to a voice in making the rules which all the members of their group must observe for the sake of their mutual welfare. This belief included the corollary conviction that non-proprietorship—wage and tenantry status—was unquestioned proof of inferior character—persons whom nature had made so lacking in self-directing capacities as to be wholly dependent on the directives of their superiors.

In terms of these beliefs, political democracy was conceivable only if there were a situation in which the great bulk of the population could be proprietors; otherwise a democratic way of making the rules, which all must observe, was sheer nonsense. At the Constitutional Convention, James Madison stated this belief in these blunt words:

> In future times a great majority of the people will not only be without landed [sic], but any other sort of property. These will either combine under the influence of their common situation; in which case, the rights of property and the public liberty, will not be secure in their hands: or which is more probable, they will become the tools of opulence and ambition, in which case there will be equal danger on another side.[39]

But while the builders of earlier America were creatures of the Medieval landlord civilization, they also were creatures of the great religious reform movements of 16th and 17th century Europe. Therefore, they held some beliefs which were diametrically opposite to those of the older Medieval landlord civilization. For that older order rested in part on the belief that dependence on economic work (producing subsistence goods) is proof that people are so lacking in self-directing ability as to be dependent on superiors for their life directives, whereas the reverse is true of those exempt from economic employments. Medieval proprietors were thus lords who lived without work, and those who produced subsistence for the whole community were known as serfs, villeins, and the like.

The religious reformers upended this belief with the opposite belief that striving for excellence in all employments is the proper way of earning high standing.

The revolutionary interpretations of the ethical significance of work came about in substantially the following manner.

In their break-away from the Mother Church, the religious reformers of the 16th and 17th centuries had to face up to the question of what occupation is most truly appropriate for the upright man. According to the traditional view, such employment was boxed up in the monasteries where every moment of the 24-hour day was organized into a systematic series of routines that were known as the Holy Callings. As long as the reformers left this view unchallenged, it was impossible for them to complete their break with the Mother Church. They completed the break by taking the position that all employments, whether composing sermons, painting pictures, making mouse traps, or growing corn, are equally appropriate opportunities for people to prove themselves deserving of highest standing.[40]

This expanding concept of God's work to include all occupations released an avalanche of productive aspirations that literally reshaped the world. Vast energies that hitherto found release in building great cathedrals now found new expressions of the heavenward urge in sailing the seven seas, turning deserts into gardens, conquering pests and disease, breeding scrub stock into fine herds, transforming hovels into firesides of good cheer, and building new social worlds, new churches, new schools, new governments—new ways of living and of making a living in all spheres of human endeavor. These were the new songs of salvation.

In this concept, no amount of riches ever exempts one from the responsibility for further expression of his powers in productive employment. And no greater incentive to proficiency is conceivable. For, whether it takes a religious or a secular form, this belief diverts the insatiable striving for evidences of personal worth from the "easy ways" into a ceaseless striving for professional excellence, even beyond one's actual abilities. For any amount of earnings one can ever generate from his work will always fall short of the amount he needs for the sake of showing he has all the initiative, genius, imagination, knowledge, and other virtues which entitle him to as much approbation and esteem as he would like to deserve and enjoy. Thus no achieved level of proficiency, however high, can ever release him from the felt obligation to strive for a still higher level. If he succeeds in making two blades of grass grow where only one had grown before, his thirst for a still finer image of himself then obliges him to find a way of making three blades grow where only two had grown before. Energized by this directive, people seldom find any rest and would be bored if they did. Always they are on the move and never are they so taut as when everything gets quiet and there is nothing to do except sit.

In line with this directive, people found themselves producing in excess of their customary needs. To put this excess product of their work to proficient use, they exchanged it for money, which they invested in additional land, shops, stores, and the like. In this way they expanded their possessions beyond the amount they could work with their own labor, and also beyond what they needed for their own subsistence. This subjected them to the charge of depriving others of their natural and moral right to as much property as they needed for making a living. Why? Because the older landlord civilization rested in part on the belief that natural or moral law limited the amount of capital which individuals could accumulate to the amount necessary to support their customary level of living. If they sought to exceed this limit, it was assumed that greed and miserliness led them to acquire riches at the expense of others. This older culture would have been shocked by James Madison's axiom, widely shared by the Founding Fathers, that the chief object of good government is the protection of men in their "different and unequal faculties of acquiring property."[41] Thus, in acquiring capital in excess of their customary needs as a result of following work beliefs, people found themselves in serious conflict with the pre-capitalistic conviction that they were enriching themselves at the expense of others.

The Natural Rights philosophers, especially John Locke, got them out of this bind.[42] By reasoning from widely accepted premises of his time, he showed that limitation on the right to acquire capital applied only to primitive societies in which a money economy was totally absent. But then he went on to show that the moment men agree to use money as the equivalent of all forms of property, their natural or moral right to acquire capital expands to the limit of their abilities to produce.

Virgin Continent and Expanding Economy of Family Businesses as Means of Transforming Old World Heritage of Conflicting Beliefs Into Belief Systems of 19th Century America

Thus the builders of earlier America held the Medieval landlord belief that proprietorship is the badge of kingly capacity. But in two basic respects they had alienated themselves from the older landlord civilization. First, they had completely separated themselves from its conviction that participation in economic work is the badge of dependency on superiors for their life directives. And they had accomplished this separation through identifying themselves with the religious reformers' revolutionary belief that striving for increasing excellence in all employments is the noblest of motivations. Therefore the builders of earlier America would have literally exploded with resentment and hostility had they been forcibly contained within the older landlord systems of master-servant institutions.

Second, the builders of earlier America had also completely separated themselves from the undergirding conviction of the older landlord society that natural or moral law limited the amount of capital which people could acquire to the amount needed to support their customary wants. They had accomplished this separation through identifying themselves with the opposite belief of the Natural Rights philosophers that natural or moral law imposes no limit on the amount of capital people may acquire as a fair reward for their industry. Trying to squeeze the tall pines into a match box would be easier than forcing them to guide their lives in line with the older natural-law ceiling on capital accumulations.

Thus, as both creatures of and fugitives from their feudal heritage, the builders of earlier America faced a baffling problem in social organization. Here it is. The new system had to be one that would enable people to accomplish three things: It had to free them from the feudal beliefs that economic work, tenantry, wage status, and unlimited capital accumulation were proofs of inferior character. Second, it had to bind them to the belief that striving for excellence in all employments is the noblest of motivations and that the test of devotion to this work belief is capital accumulation. Finally, the new social order had to enable people to live in line with the carryover of their feudal belief that proprietorship proves possession of kingly self-directing capacities.

The social organization that met all these requirements was finally

31

achieved within a proprietary political economy that rested on a tripod of democratic, work, and enterprise belief systems. I would place the date of this achievement around 1840 when aristocratic trappings ceased to be an asset to candidates for political office. This was over 200 years after the landings at Jamestown and Plymouth Rock.

The principal means of accomplishing this great cultural achievement was a rapidly expanding economy of predominantly family businesses in a virgin continent of work opportunities. Why this is true is explained as follows:

For an ever-increasing number of people in town and country alike, the 2 billion acres of virgin continent in the New World permitted combining in each skin the managerial and labor roles which their feudal past had distinctly segregated into lords and serfs. This re-combination of roles generated a tremendous character transformation.[43] On the one hand, by investing them with proprietorship, it enabled working people to identify themselves with the dignity, approbation and self-esteem which the ages had hitherto posited in the lords of the land.[44] To such people, no premise is so self-evident as the democratic belief that all men are of equal dignity and worth; that none, however wise or good, is good or wise enough to have arbitrary power over any other; and therefore, that all by nature have an equal right to a voice in making the rules which all must observe.

Thus, by combining into the same skin the proprietary and labor roles, the expanding system of family businesses in the New World enabled people to transform their ancient belief in proprietorship as proof of self-governing capacity into a profound commitment to political democracy. This new commitment in turn generated powerful demands for land reforms that would accelerate the growth of family businesses as the basis of political democracy. Daniel Webster expressed this demand in these words:

> A republican form of government rests not more on political constitutions, than on those laws which regulate the descent and transmission of property. Governments like ours could not have been maintained, where property was holden [sic] according to the principles of the feudal system; nor, on the other hand, could the feudal constitution possibly exist with us. Our New England ancestors brought hither no great capitals from Europe. . . . They left behind them the whole feudal policy of the other continent. . . . They came to a new country. There were, as yet, no lands yielding rent, and no tenants rendering service. The whole soil was unreclaimed from barbarism. They were themselves . . . nearly on a general level in respect to property. Their situation demanded a parcelling out and division of the lands, and it may be fairly said, that this necessary act *fixed the future frame and form of their government*. The character of their political institutions was determined by the fundamental laws respecting property.[45]

In the great land policy debates of the 1840's, Thomas Hart Benton expressed the same logic with uncommon clarity and eloquence:

> Tenantry is unfavorable to freedom. It lays the foundation for separate orders in society, annihilates the love of country, and weakens the spirit of independence. The farming tenant has, in fact, no country, no hearth, no domestic altar, no household god. The freeholder, on the contrary, is the natural supporter of a free government; and it should be the policy of republics to multiply their freeholders, as it is the policy of monarchies to

multiply tenants. We are a republic, and we wish to continue so: then multiply the class of freeholders; pass the public lands cheaply and easily into the hands of the people; sell, for a reasonable price, to those who are able to pay; and give, without price, to those who are not. I say give, without price, to those who are not able to pay; and that which is so given, I consider as sold for the best of prices; for a price above gold and silver; a price which cannot be carried away by delinquent officers, nor lost in failing banks, nor stolen by thieves, nor squandered by an improvident and extravagant administration. It brings a price above rubies—a race of virtuous and independent laborers, the true supporters of their country, and the stock from which its best defenders must be drawn.[46]

The economy of family businesses did more than transform the age-old feudal equation of kingly qualities with proprietorship into a profound commitment to democratic government. It also enabled people to re-enforce their new democratic beliefs with the driving power of their belief in excellence in all employments as the badge of distinction.

Caught up in their conquest of a formidable continent, pioneering farmers quickly acquired a common sense that turned them against every vestige of the old belief that exemption from economic employments was evidence of superior character. Confirmed in this rebellion by such commonplaces as the uselessness of white gloves and lace wristlets in living and making a living, they became increasingly suspicious of the alleged superior political wisdom of those whom Hamilton called "the rich and well-born;" more and more they equated such wisdom with those whom Jackson called "the humble members of society."

Thus the burning concern was over symbols that indicate highest merit—calloused hands or silver buckles. In line with their work ethic directives, pioneering farmers came to look on their own industry as proof of civic and moral superiority over those who lived without work. This proof strengthened their legs so that they could stand up against the last vestiges of old beliefs and demand a government that recognized humble origins as indices of merit.

The presidential campaign of 1840 marks the high point of this battle of symbols. For in that year the aristocratic Whigs concluded that they could win another national election only by throwing off their broadcloth in favor of log cabins and hard cider. They thereby hoped to hang the onus of aristocracy on the Jacksonian democrats. Typifying the lead scouts in this battle, Webster shouted that "The man that says that I am an aristocrat-Is a Liar; and he who makes this charge and then will not come within the reach of my arm, is not only a liar but a coward."[47] This delightful horseplay marks the traceless disappearance from the American scene of the age-old belief that exemption from the heat and grind of life is in and of itself somehow evidence of superior wisdom to know what ought and ought not be done.

As the expanding economy of family businesses thus led people to use their work beliefs to re-enforce their democratic beliefs, so it likewise led them to use the same work beliefs to justify a system of enterprise beliefs. A useful point of departure in developing this point is the observation that the earlier economy of family businesses was a nationwide organization of producers and distributors in which the Government in effect spoke thus to each family: The business is yours to do with as you please. No one is going to boss you except yourself. Anything you make over and above your production and family living costs is yours to plow back into the business if you want to. Such increases in your business assets are the rewards you will get if you choose to apply yourself and use good judgment in doing the right thing at the right time. On the other hand, if you waste your time and substance in too much fishing or fox-hunting and if you make poor decisions, such as planting corn in June instead of May, or if you let your buildings run down and you pile up debts, which you don't pay, and your creditors close you out without a roof over your head, then all these mishaps will be considered the just deserts of not doing right by your business, just as whatever you make over and above your production and family living costs will be considered the just deserts of doing right by your business. In short, if you take care of your business, your business will take care of you.

Thus, the Nation staffed its expanding system of producing and distributing units with family capitalists, but they were not Marxian "money-bags." For the typical capitalist was a parent, a citizen, and a churchman who felt obliged to be an increasingly useful parent, citizen, and churchman. He could do so only through producing more than he consumed and turning the surplus into a bigger business that would enable him to achieve his goals.

There is thus no mystery in the fact that the ways of life and work in this earlier economy led people to see in capital accumulation an exclusive test of work ethic virtue. For, with natural resources so abundant as to be "dirt cheap" and technologies so primitive as to require little or no cash costs, it was clear that anyone had an inherent dislike for work if he failed to become a proprietor, even if he started with only his bare hands. For the same reason, it was clear that people lacked the bare minimum or work ethic virtue if they failed to produce at least enough to meet their own security needs.

Again, by combining the ownerships of labor and capital within the same skin, this economy prevented large inequalities of wealth—so much so that people did not feel that some boys had less chance in life because they came from poor families. This being true, it was plain that Government should abstain from taxing dollars of the well-off more than the dollars of the others. For if it failed to observe this restriction, it would penalize the industrious and reward the ne'er-do-wells, and in this way suffocate the striving for excellence which the national work belief obliged it to foster.

Finally, by combining the ownerships of labor and capital in the same family, this earlier economy virtually limited the workers in a business to the operator and his family. Thus the decisions they made on how to run their businesses affected none but themselves. Therefore, if Government limited the power of proprietors to run their affairs as they choose, it would stifle their striving for excellence.

In this way, the earlier economy led people to use work beliefs in drawing a sharp line between (1) the demands of their democratic beliefs for a voice in making the rules which all must observe, and (2) the demands of their enterprise belief in freedom from collective restraints on individual action. This balance between these opposite meanings of freedom was maintained only through a government that helped people become successful proprietors. But at this point, their work commitment to the Innovator-Personality Ideal stood as a stone wall against any further expansion of the service role of Government. For within an economy of predominantly owner-entrepreneurs any further expansion of the economic role of Government could only result in (1) inequalitarian tax levies which would penalize the industrious and reward the incompetent, or (2) restrictions on entrepreneurial freedom of people to follow their own independent ideas concerning what ought and ought not be done.

IV. Cultural Change in Our Time

The years since World War I have witnessed a series of departures from the political economy which first gave rise to the American belief systems. In that economy the ownerships of labor and capital were combined in the same person. Today these ownerships have been torn apart and resegregated into separate ownership classes, each dealing with the other on a bargaining basis. This transformation of that earlier economy into the modern structure of large corporate businesses, unions, and other groups, has been accompanied by an expanding service role of Government—an expansion which has already gone far beyond the limitations prescribed by the high importance which 19th century America assigned to policy demands of enterprise beliefs.

Suppose American people suddenly said, as they did in the 19th century: We prize entrepreneurial freedom so highly that Government must repeal all laws that limit the power of proprietors to run their businesses as they choose. And suppose they also declared: We are so averse to rules that penalize the industrious that Government must forthwith desist from progressive taxation. If people today insisted on lining up policies in conformity with these 19th century premiums on enterprise beliefs, the service role of present day Government would collapse like a house of cards.

I have defined the essence of cultures as the belief systems which people use in guiding their decisions on ways of life and work which they feel most obligated to follow as means of fulfilling their striving for significance to themselves and others.

Cultural Change as Altering Relative Importance of Belief Systems So As to Satisfy Their Competitive Action Demands with New Rules of Life and Work

The question thus arises if the vast differences in the organizational structure of 19th and 20th century America mean that present day America has discarded the essential culture of 19th century America? No. They mean that the genius of American people is their capacity for adjusting their beliefs so as to meet the demands of new conditions. And these new conditions are principally ones brought about as a result of their work belief in scientific and technological advance as a badge of excellence. Thus, my position is that 20th century America is as much guided by the democratic, work, and enterprise belief system as 19th century America. The only difference lies in the relative importance they assign to the demands of these belief systems. Today American people place even higher premiums on the claims of their work and democratic beliefs than ever, but a lower premium on the claims of enterprise beliefs. This alteration has enabled them continually to modify old rules so as to enrich democratic and work ethic values through increasingly rapid rates of scientific and technological development. My reasons for this position are as follows:

First, two important facts lead me to conclude that American people are more sensitive than ever to the claims of their work beliefs. The first pertains to what they most want for their children. The second is the disdain they have for proposals to remedy the problems generated by technological advance through slowing down investment in education and research.

Never before in our history have parents, teachers, and the whole educational system been so anxious to use the best child-rearing practices they know in an effort to instill in each child the motivation to discover, prize, develop, use, and enjoy his unique capabilities to the fullest extent possible in whatever employments best suit his talents and interests. Never before have the "elders" been so concerned with "internalizing" in each youngster their own belief that the best interests of himself and others alike oblige him to find a life work that will bring out the best there is in him. Never before, so far as I can gather, have American people been so concerned as now that society provide all its members with abundant opportunities for productive work and fair returns. Nor have they ever been more concerned with "internalizing" into their children their belief that the people most deserving respect and esteem are the innovators—the kind who make their mark by mastering the thought and practice of their society, and use this knowledge in developing their own independent ideas to a point where others prize them as superior to their own.[48]

That American people are now more sensitive to their traditional work beliefs than ever is also evident in their impatience with proposals that would remedy their problems through slowing down the rates of scientific and technological advance. Nowhere is this attitude more pronounced than among farm people who have been burdened for over 40 years with the price-depressing surpluses—a burden which arises from the fact that farm people, in line with traditional work beliefs, are increasing their productive capacities so rapidly that they expand their total output of foods and fibers faster than population growth generates additional market outlets. Conceptually the whole trouble could be remedied by throttling the new know-how that is streaming from our laboratories at an ever-hastening pace. But, as I have said, any suggestion to get out of their trouble by doing this is greeted with disdain.

I am unable to find any time in our history when American people have been so sensitive as now to the action claims of their democratic belief that all are of equal dignity and worth; that none, however wise or good, is wise or good enough to have arbitrary power over any other; and therefore, that all are entitled to a voice in making the rules which all must observe. To be sure, America today as always falls far short of meeting the demands of this belief system, and we shall return to some of these shortcomings later. But this is not the point; the issue is whether or not American people are less sensitive to the demands of this belief system now than formerly. I can find no reason to suppose they are.

While people as a whole attach even more importance than before to their democratic and work beliefs, they attach less importance to their enterprise beliefs than formerly. In this way, they continually meet the demands of all their belief systems under changing conditions with revised rules of living and working with each other. Several observations bear out this generalization.

First, American people have long since discarded the 19th century enterprise belief in capital accumulation as the exclusive test of work ethic virtue. Consider, for example, a plant scientist who spends a lifetime in developing a new cotton variety that is well suited to irrigated deserts of the West, and receives the modest return of approximately $8,000 per year for his service. Then comes the entrepreneur who takes over the new variety and becomes a millionaire through producing and marketing it on a big scale. It overburdens the common sense to hold that the wide difference in their incomes has the slightest bearing on whether the plant scientist is any less dedicated than the entrepreneur to workmanlike excellence, or that he is any less a useful agent of society's needs and aspirations. Similar examples could be multiplied manyfold.

This does not mean that capital accumulation has been totally discarded as a test of work ethic virtues. Most assuredly it is a test if one is a businessman. For his employment is one in which the amount of profit he makes from a given investment is a true measure of the excellence with which he performs his social role. But one would not use capital accumulation as a test of the excellence with which a minister, a physician, a teacher, a physicist, or a musician performs his social role. In the earlier economy of predominantly owner-entrepreneurs, business was about the only social role open to most people. In that situation, it made sense to use capital accumulation as an exclusive test of work ethic virtue. But this is no longer true in today's economy, with thousands of careers open to people. In keeping with this fact, the whole movement for "professional standards" is an expression of the need of various occupational groups to specify many yardsticks as valid tests of work ethic virtues. We have not thrown away the old yardstick of capital accumulation, but we say it is no longer an exclusive test. Relatively speaking, it is much less important than it once was.

The older economy of predominantly family businesses generated the enterprise belief that meeting one's own total security needs was an accurate test of the absolute minimum of work ethic virtue necessary for social acceptance. This test made sense in the older economy where the ownerships of labor and capital were combined within the same skin. For under this circumstance, one's security depended solely on his own decisions as to whether he would work or loaf, spend or save for future needs.

But this is no longer true in our present day economy of corporate businesses where ownership of capital and labor are segregated into different classes. For, under this circumstance the individual's security depends not only on his willingness to work or save; it also depends on whether the business community offers him an opportunity to work and on how well it invests and manages his savings. Businessmen may invest one's savings in the best of faith but fail to make any earnings from them. Because of this new dependence of the individual on others for work and investment opportunities, people may feel more committed than ever to earning high standings as proficient doers, and yet wind up the victims of greater insecurity than they would in the earlier economy of owner-entrepreneurs where ownerships of labor and capital were combined in the same family.

Faced with this fact, American people threw away neither work beliefs nor their enterprise beliefs. Instead, they corrected the inadequacy of the older test by recognizing that responsibility for the security needs of the individual is a joint obligation of both society and the individual. This enabled them to meet the demands of all their beliefs with a new rule according to which people help each other meet their security needs through a collective saving procedure, known as the social security system.

The earlier economy of mainly family businesses generated the belief that Government was obliged to refrain from unequal taxation; otherwise it would penalize the industrious and reward the improvident, and in this way stifle the work of ethic virtue which it is obliged to foster. The high importance of this enterprise belief made sense in the early 19th century. For in combining the ownerships of labor and capital within the same person, the economy of that period prevented inequalities of personal incomes from becoming so great that some had appreciably better chances in life than others because their families were rich.

But the same is not true today. For the present economy of large corporate businesses generates incomes that range from as low as $1,000 per year to over $500,000. These wide differences in incomes amount to vast inequalities in the power to acquire the housing, the clothing, the food, the schooling, the health care without which it is impossible to develop one's productive potential to the fullest extent possible. The more scientific and technologically advanced we become, the sharper becomes the conflict between the work ethic belief that society owes to all its members an equality of opportunities and the older enterprise belief that just Government must abstain from policies which shift income from the prosperous to the relatively disadvantaged. For the more advanced we become, the higher is the minimum number of dollars it takes to enable each individual to acquire the goods and services he must have for developing his skill and knowledge in line with the requirements of society's employment opportunities.

Clearly, if American people continued to attach the same degree of importance to the demands of enterprise beliefs as they did in the 19th century, they would do so at the expense of opportunities which are demanded by their work beliefs. As new conditions increasingly generated this value conflict, the Nation did not throw away either its enterprise beliefs or its work beliefs. Rather it altered their relative importance so as to meet the demands of both with a new rule that taxes the high incomes more heavily than the low incomes.

Finally, ways of life and work in early 19th century led to the belief that Government was obliged to refrain from making rules limiting the entrepreneurial freedom of proprietors to run their businesses as they choose. This belief made sense then. For, by combining the ownerships of labor and capital within each family, the economy of that day limited the numbers of workers in a business mainly to the operator and his immediate family, plus some occasional hired help. Under this circumstance, imposing any collective restraint on individual operators to run their businesses as they chose would have been an act of sheer arbitrary power. But this ceased to be true as family businesses were transformed into modern corporations with ownerships of labor and capital divided into different classes. Under this circumstance, the complete power of management to make the rules of work and pay ran into conflict with the demands of democratic beliefs that all members of a group have an equal voice in making the rules which all must observe.

This led to violent outbreaks such as the Haymarket Riots. But at length American people remedied the trouble by altering the relative importance of its enterprise belief system so as to adopt a new procedure according to which the power to make the rules of work and pay is a joint power. Consequently, the legal representatives of both capital and labor must work out their work and pay rules with each other at the bargaining table. After establishing this new collective bargaining procedure, American people were as much committed to both enterprise and democratic freedom as they were before. This new law merely signified that 20th century America was not willing to buy entrepreneurial freedom of proprietors to run their businesses as they choose at the expense of the democratic freedom of each party to a voice in making the rules which all must observe.

Crisis Problems

The type of cultural change thus far considered is one in which new conditions throw into conflict the relative importance people have hitherto assigned the demands of their various beliefs. Such conflicts are policy problems. For, as long as disputing parties share the same beliefs they are bound to each other by the sense of obligation to work peacefully with each other in searching for new and mutually satisfactory rules. They achieve this objective through reappraising the relative importance they have hitherto attached to their beliefs. Thus, disagreements over what ought to be done are solvable policy problems if people share the same beliefs and differ only as to their relative importance. For the bonds of common convictions of disputing groups are thus strong enough to withstand the differences in values they place on the competitive claims of their beliefs.

In sharp contrast, crisis problems arise when a group of appreciable size and influence alienate themselves from the ties of hitherto common beliefs and turn in anger and resentment against their existing social order. And they accomplish this alienation through forsaking old beliefs and accepting new ones diametrically opposite to those which they and their society have previously used as guides in making common rules.

We wish to consider five manifestations of this alienation process in American belief systems: (1) The Negro's rebellion against discrimination reflects crisis in our democratic beliefs. (2) The Radical Right reflects a crisis in our enterprise beliefs. (3) The present economy, even though it increases income per capita as rapidly as ever, tends to generate a crisis in work beliefs in apparently laying more and more people on the shelf. (4) The seriousness of these crisis spots in our culture is worsened by the fact that they feed on each other. (5) Finally, people at the 20th century have rejected the unrealistic optimism of 19th century America, but in doing so they are in danger of becoming trapped in an equally unrealistic pessimism.

Negro's Rebellion Against Color Discrimination as Crisis in Democratic Beliefs

Since the landing of the first boat-load of slaves at Jamestown in 1619, white and black Americans have related themselves to each other under common rules that rested on the belief that black skin proves possession of inferior character—people who are so lacking in self-directing capacities and other virtues as to deserve a subservient social role.

Under the guidance of the belief, white people of America have long felt obliged to fill their statute books with rules that subordinate the Negro to a second class status in all spheres of life. With these rules backed up by police power, white people may demand, for example, that people with black skin not live in houses next to whites, not attend the same theaters, not go to the same schools and churches as whites, not use the same public facilities that whites use, and not belong to unions that whites belong to.

That such discriminatory demands rest totally on the belief that mere black color proves inferiority is evident in many ways. For even though a person with black color may be world-renowned as an artist, a diplomat, a poet, a musician, or a novelist, he is nonetheless ordered by law and custom not to eat here, not sit there, not to buy or rent a house in this locality, not to go to such and such theaters, and not join this or that union. And the same rules would apply to Shakespeares and Newtons if their pigmentation were black.

In recent years the Negro has alienated himself from the old belief in color as proof of his inferior character. He had done so by identifying himself with the democratic belief that all men, irrespective of their color, deserve equal access to society's jobs, schools, votes, and public services.

Under the guidance of this democratic belief, the "I" component of the Negro self identifies itself as a first class citizen and turns in aversion against the older concept of himself as an inferior type of character (the "me" component of the self). And he likewise turns in aversion and anger against the whole social order that condemns him to his old second-class status—rules that stem from the 300-year action demands of the belief that a black skin proves inferior character.

Beliefs, as we have explained, are concepts of types of character and ways of life and work which people most prize and feel obliged to achieve. So, it is by shifting from their old beliefs into diametrically opposite beliefs, that people acquire new and tremendously moving visions of the kind of persons and civilization that merit their deepest allegiance. The process by which this revolutionary change in their motivations is accomplished is called alienation—

the type of behavior in which the "I" component of the self gets a new "me" through separating itself from old beliefs and identifying itself with opposite ones.

In thus alienating themselves from their concept of themselves as second-class citizens through identifying themselves with the democratic belief in their deserts to first class status, 20 million Negroes in all regions of the country are bringing all the pressure they peaceably can on Government and private bodies to do away with the whole legalized structure of social practice that has long consigned them to a menial social role.

Ralph J. Bunche, American Negro who is Under Secretary of the United Nations, expressed the driving spirit of this rebellion against second-class status in these words:

> The fact has to be faced by the whole country and people, North and South, that there is a real social revolution in progress, involving the unshakable determination of the Negro to escape from second-class status.
> It involves the Negro's complete release from the fear of the white man that gripped him, particularly in the South, only a couple of decades ago.
> It involves a new realization by the Negro of what he can do by organized collective effort and a very great impatience.
> As a Negro myself, I have to say that no government, national, state or local, has ever done enough so long as the problem of racial repression persists. That's because there is a built-in impatience among those who suffer the disabilities of racial discrimination. The individual who is deprived must always feel that the measures taken by governments are inadequate. And they are.
> The impatience and determination on the part of the Negro will grow stronger day by day and the pressure on the Government to do more and do it faster will be ever increasing until the decisive breakthrough is achieved.[49]

As shown by a series of recent reports by observers in ten widely scattered States, the Negro's revolt is nationwide.[50] Chicago, Los Angeles, Jackson, Detroit, Birmingham—everywhere the story is the same. The Negro has stepped out of the old concept of himself as an inferior character and into the new democratic concept of himself as of equal dignity and worth. And he will never return to the older degrading image of black skin as a sign of subservience.

Will the 160 million white Americans forego discriminatory practices which 20 million black Americans reject in resentment because they have totally identified themselves with the democratic beliefs of the 160 million white Americans? This is the crisis problem in American democratic culture that we are up against. Three factors contribute to its seriousness.

First, removing a discriminatory practice piecemeal will not turn the Negro's resentment into gratitude for past achievement. "Gradualism"—token desegregation reforms—will not be enough. For the more a person separates himself from an inferior image of his worth by identifying himself with the image of equal dignity, the more he feels himself wronged by each remaining barrier to equal treatment, and the more determined he is to remove it.

Second, past discriminatory practices have become capitalized in real estate and other assets, so that if the "color line" moves into a new area, white proprietors stand to lose a high percentage of the value of their investment. This may be due to panic selling, but the threat of loss is there, nonetheless. It is thus understandable that white people's sympathy for the Negro's demand for

41

equality of opportunity tends to be counteracted by their enterprise belief in the right of each to sell or rent his property to whomever he pleases. Resistance to moves of Government to restrict discriminatory use of this entrepreneurial freedom in buying or renting houses is typified by the recent statement of the National Association of Real Estate Boards. The statement opens thus:

> Today, the rights and freedoms of the individual American property owner are being eroded. This endangers the rights and freedoms of all Americans. It is self-evident that the erosion of these freedoms will destroy the free enterprising individual American.

The Association then proceeded to draw up "The Property Owners Bill of Rights." It read as follows:

> It is our solemn belief that the individual American property owner, regardless of race, color, or creed, must be allowed, under law, to retain:
> 1. The right of privacy.
> 2. The right to choose his own friends.
> 3. The right to own and enjoy property according to his own dictates.
> 4. The right to occupy and dispose of property without governmental interference in accordance with the dictates of his conscience.
> 5. The right of all equally to enjoy property without interference in giving special privilege to any group or groups.
> 6. The right to maintain what, in his opinion, are congenial surroundings for tenants.
> 7. The right to contract with a real estate broker or other representative of his choice and to authorize him to act for him according to his instructions.
> 8. The right to determine the acceptability and desirability of any prospective buyer or tenant of his property.
> 9. The right of every American to choose who in his opinion are congenial tenants in any property he owns—to maintain the stability and security of his income.
> 10. The right to enjoy the freedom to accept, reject, negotiate, or not negotiate with others.

The bill then concludes.

> Loss of these rights diminishes personal freedom and creates a springboard for further erosion of liberty.[51]

Third, while the rebellion of the Negro is in line with the Nation's work ethic and democratic directives, his substantive demands cannot be met within an economy that fails to provide enough productive opportunities for all. What the Negroes are demanding are better schools, better jobs, better houses—a chance to get out of the ghettos. But as Lippman observes:

> The hard truth is that while the Negroes are making these demands, the country is in fact short of good schools, good housing, and good jobs. This makes the Negro problem part of the generalized national problem. By law and with good will, segregation will be wiped out in airports, bus depots, lunch counters, movie theaters, public parks and the like, without substantial difficulties. But it is not possible to desegregate all the schools and universities and provide equal educational opportunities for Negroes and Whites. There are not enough good schools. The same is true of housing and jobs. The basic fact is that the pie, which is supposed to be divided equally, is too small.[52]

Unless the pie is made much bigger, the substantive grievances of the Negro cannot be redressed. With each new gain in doing away with most distasteful grievances, such as discrimination in the use of public facilities and accommodation the pressure of discontent will increase until an abundance of good schools, good houses, and good jobs are available for all.

In this country, minority groups have always had access to either of two distinct types of pressure to get the majority to comply with their demands. One type is destructive; the other, constructive.

The destructive type is an individualized conformity pressure wherein a minority group masquerades its policy views as majority beliefs and at the same time equates its opposition with subversives or innocent dupes of subversives. Then they are able to use majority aversions to alien "isms" in destroying their opponents. For this type of conformity pressure:

> ... launches an inquiry into private motive and intention as well as public statement and deed. It deals in oaths, and the thorough investigation of past behavior and associations; it revels in the discovery of secret sympathies and "front" organizations. It ultimately seeks to uncover and root out all possibilities of dissent, both public and private... It insists that a particular school teacher be fired, a certain textbook be dropped, a particular speaker be forbidden the right to use a certain hall, etc.[53]

Clearly the Negro is not resorting to this individualized type of conformity pressure. Instead, he is using a generalized type of pressure. For the leverage of his pressure is the power of the majority's own democratic beliefs. Exertions of this generalized conformity pressure are constructive. For they are simply efforts of injured minority groups to get the majority to desist from practices which are incompatible with their own professed beliefs. Such pressures reveal anomalies in our social structure and help uncover aspects of our culture that endanger democratic values.

This is the type of conformity demand which minority groups, the various immigrant nationalities, for example, have used in breaking down unfair majority practices and achieving acceptance of themselves in the majority circle of American life. This is the type of conformity pressure the Negro is using today in his rebellion against segregation. His sit-ins, his freedom rides, his attempts to register for school and votes, his endurance of police dogs, his passive resistance when he is knocked to the ground and kicked in the face, or when his respected leaders are shot in the back—in all these ways he is exerting a powerful pressure on the conscience of the Nation to bring its practice in line with its own democratic directive to fair play.

But the cost of using this constructive type of conformity pressure is very high for the Negro. For it is not easy not to strike back when, as a result of commitment to democratic ways of life, you are protesting against laws and customs that consign you to an inferior status because of your color. But the Negro is more than willing to pay this cost. As Lippman observed:

> A new generation of Negroes has emerged, one which has lost the fear of being arrested and jailed, and has steeled itself to use the weapon of the weak, which is to be prepared to suffer more pain than the oppressor will dare to inflict. When an aggrieved people reach this point, they have acquired a force which government must reckon with and people must respect.[54]

Thus there is indeed a serious crisis in democratic culture. But there is ground for confidence that the crisis can and will be resolved in terms of a richer democratic culture than ever. The basis for this confidence is as follows:

First, the alienation of whites and Negroes from common beliefs is not total by any means. Were this the case, white people would have alienated themselves from their own democratic beliefs. And they would have done so through completely identifying themselves with the conviction (1) that black color proves inferior character, and (2) that the Negro's rebellion against his inferior status is actually a revolt against the absolute demands of natural or divine law. Only in this way could they achieve sufficient will power to use whatever degree of violence is necessary to force the Negro to accept present segregation practices. This white people as a whole cannot do. For their commitment to discriminatory practices is so counteracted by their democratic convictions that they cannot steel themselves to do the amount of killing and beating that would be necessary to force the Negro to accept his old inferior status. As Lippman observed:

> The rebellion against segregation cannot be suppressed because American people as a whole will not consent to the use of violence which would be necessary to suppress the rebellion. The fire hoses and the police dogs and the mass arrests have shocked the country. Yet they are a mere slap on the wrist compared with what would have to be done to restore law and order on the basis of complete segregation.[55]

Saying American people as a whole will not consent to the use of violence which would be necessary to suppress the rebellion is only an alternative way of saying that they acknowledge the rightness of the Negro's rebellion and feel guilty of being a party to the injustices he has long endured. White people know that if they were in the Negro's place they would be rebelling, too.

The Negroes as a whole are aware that many white people are sympathetic to their struggle. Ralph Bunche expressed this awareness in these words:

> ... the unshakable determination of the Negro to escape from his second-class status ... is aided ... by much more understanding, and even active support, from many more white people, South as well as North, than ever before and by the fact that white populations, in Southern as well as Northern communities, do not react violently to racial events as they once did.[56]

This knowledge tends to check the Negro's impulse to violence and at the same time arms him with a will and capacity to suffer "more pain than the oppressor will dare to inflict." This is the weapon of the weak, but it is a weapon which Government must reckon with and people must respect.

My guess and my confidence are that, with the help of white people's recognition of the incompatibility of their discriminatory practices with their own democratic beliefs, this weapon of the weak will prevail. If it does, democratic culture will be vastly enriched by the disappearance from American culture of the conviction that a certain color proves inferior character.

But it is also possible that white people might so alienate themselves from their democratic beliefs as to steel themselves to use whatever violence is necessary to force the Negro to submit to current segregation practices. Should this happen, democratic culture would receive such a set-back as to become a mockery to ourselves and the whole wide world. For reasons stated, I am convinced this will not happen. Yet it could. Therein lies the central crisis of our time.

The "Radical Right" as Reflecting a Crisis in Enterprise Beliefs

As the Negro's rebellion against color discrimination is a crisis problem in democratic beliefs, so the extreme pressure of the Radical Right for a return to the 19th century Garden of Eden has all the earmarks of a crisis problem in enterprise beliefs. As previously explained, American people as a whole in this century give higher importance than ever to the claims of their democratic and work beliefs, and less importance to the claims of all their traditional enterprise belief systems. In this way, they have been able to expand the service role of Government increasingly beyond the limitations prescribed by enterprise beliefs in the 19th century.

But a growing minority may be unable to change the relative importance of its beliefs as rapidly as the majority. In this event, a point sooner or later will be reached at which such a minority will feel that any further devaluation of their enterprise beliefs is tantamount to surrendering the beliefs themselves. Such surrender is impossible. For it would turn the striving for a significant life into unbearable anxiety over a life without meaning or purpose. Under such a circumstance, the striving for significance leads people to save the meaning and purpose of life by turning the demands of their beliefs into moralistic absolutes. This happens, for instance, if people equate 19th century enterprise restrictions on Government with "true Americanism." This equation alienates them from the existing social order because it involves the conviction that majority views are in fact alien "isms" and that their spokesmen are subversives or the innocent dupes of subversives.

Four observations indicate that this crisis in 19th century enterprise beliefs systems is being experienced today by the minority which is today called the Radical Right. First, a central premise of this minority is that the American political system and major social and economic groups are in the hands of a Communist Conspiracy. For example, in the July 1960 issue of the *Monthly Bulletin* of the John Birch Society, Robert Welch declared that the " 'key' to the advance of Communism is treason right within our government and the place to find it is right in Washington." In his book *May God Forgive Us,* he wrote that there are "more Communist sympathizers in our government today than ever before." In January 1961, he told his supporters that "Communist influences are now in almost complete control of our Federal Government." In the *Policitician,* a book-length letter circulated to hundreds of persons, Welch named Presidents Roosevelt, Truman, and Eisenhower; Secretary of State John Foster Dulles; CIA Director Allan Dulles; and Chief Justice Warren as "knowing instruments of the Communist conspiracy."[5][7]

Leadership of major economic and social groups as well as the political system is in the hands of conspirators. Thus, in a supplement to the February 1961 bulletin, Welch declared that "Communist influences" were "very powerful in the top echelons of our educational system, our labor-union organizations, and of almost every important segment of our national life." The

National Council of Churches of Christ was Communist-minded. "Treason is widespread and rampant in our high army circles." Even the American Medical Association could no longer be relied upon for support in the fight against socialism.[58]

Second, the expanding service role of Government in recent decades is the work of conspirators who have gotten control of Government positions since the 1930's. In a letter to Khruschev in 1958, Welch declared: "Your hands played the decisive and unseen part" in the American banking crisis of 1933. Communist-contrived American recognition of the Soviets in 1933 was what "saved them from financial collapse." Again the "very idea of American foreign aid was dreamed up by Stalin, or by his agents for him." And again he says the "trouble in the South over integration is Communist-contrived." Communists have concocted "a phony 'civil rights' slogan to stir up bitterness and civil disorder, leading gradually to police-state rule by federal troops and armed resistance to that rule." The civil rights situation has been aggravated by the Supreme Court, which "is one of the most important agencies of Communism." Furthermore, the Federal Reserve System is a "realization" of Point 5 of the *Communist Manifesto* which calls for centralization of credit in the hands of the State. Everywhere, according to Welch, the Communists are advancing their cause—in "the press, the pulpit, the radio and television media, the labor unions, the schools, the courts, and the legislative halls of America."[59]

Third, thus equating modern departures from the policy demands of 19th century enterprise restrictions on Government, the positive program of the Radical Right is a return to the 19th century Garden of Eden through removal of all modern functions of Government. In the international sphere this removal includes withdrawal of the Nation from the United Nations, the North Atlantic Treaty Organization, the International Labor Organization, the World Health Organization, reciprocal trade agreements, all foreign aid programs, and diplomatic relations with the Soviet Union and all other communistic countries. In the domestic sphere, the program calls for a repeal of the National Labor Relations Act, doing away with social security, the graduated income tax, the Rural Electrification Administration, the corporate dividend tax, the Reconstruction Finance Corporation, the Tennessee Valley Authority, the Federal Reserve System, urban renewal, Federal aid to housing, and all programs "regimenting" farmers.[60]

In short, the program demands of the Radical Right are (1) end all foreign aid and divorce ourselves virtually from all 20th century international commitments, (2) abolish most 20th century domestic activities of the Government, (3) abolish the Federal income tax, and (4) stop reapportionment of State legislatures. These policy demands clearly coincide with the 19th century America enterprise demands for an exceedingly limited service role of Government.

Finally, the Radical Right elevates these policy views and sentiments into moralistic absolutes which they call "true Americanism." Then they are able to use the aversions of Americans for alien "isms" to destroy their opponents. In this way, they are able to exert powerful pressure on the majority to conform with their own minority demands. Thus, by quoting a passage out of context, they can give the impression that so and so is a supporter of Mao Tse Tung, and in this way destroy overnight the reputation and employment opportunities of a highly reputable scholar. This kind of attack on one's standing in the eyes of his community is more dangerous than rifle fire. Responsible leaders of majority beliefs cringe before it and run for cover like deer. For a typical example, consider the following report on what is now happening in the Intermountain States:

> But the Birchers are only one of a dozen or more right-wing extremist groups that work together closely, have some interlocking directorates, sow the same seeds of distrust of all government and profess to see a Nation duped by officials alleged to be conscious or unconscious Communist stooges.[61]
> A University of Wyoming professor refused to speak at a seminar on the right wing movement because he was 'not ready to leave Wyoming.' A teacher who is deeply disturbed about right wing influence in the school system declined to talk with me about it even on an off-the-record basis because he feared for his job. An editor who is out of sympathy with the right wing radicals stipulated that he would talk with a visiting reporter if his name were not mentioned.
> . . . .the right wingers are denouncing the 'brain washing' in the public schools, by which they mean any objective discussion of public policies. . . .teachers are known to be carefully watching what they say. Some are staying away from discussion of even mildly controversial issues.[62]

In terms of occupational status, formal education and personality and other relevant traits, what groups in our population are most prone to identify themselves with Radical Right positions? Information on this important question is very inadequate, yet it is much needed both for the sake of sympathetic understanding of the problems of people of the Radical Right, and for achieving feasible measures for resolving these problems. Proper functioning of our democracy is handicapped by the great lack of research information in this important problem area.

Available data indicate that today's Radical Right draws much of its membership as well as its familial and polemical backing from small businessmen in the sense of having limited experience as corporate managers in a complex world. (But they are not necessarily poor. One can own a small trucking or real estate firm, or candy company and still amass millions.) An important research study made in Bennington, Vermont, in 1954, showed the principal political support for McCarthy in the 1950's came mainly from small businessmen. In the 1950's the Radical Right was known as "McCarthyites" just as they are known by other names today. Three findings deserve attention. First, at every level of formal education:

> . . . the small businessmen showed a distinctly higher proportion of McCarthy supporters than did the salaried men of similar education, and among those who had not been to college, the small businessmen were even more pro-McCarthy than the manual workers. And the differences were substantial. For example, among the men who did not finish high school two-thirds of the small businessmen supported McCarthy, as compared with only half of the workers who did and only a little more than a third of the salaried employers who did. Among those who had been to college the differences by occupational group [were] smaller but still substantial; where one in three of

these better educated small businessmen supported McCarthy, only a little over one in five of the salaried employees with this education did.[63]

Second, respondents to questions of the study fell into four major orientations with respect to how they feel about trends toward bigness in Government, business, and unions.

Orientation I was distinguished by "approval of labor unions but suspicion of the power of big companies."

Orientation II was called "nineteenth century liberalism;" others call it the "Radical Right." By whatever name it is called:

> ... The important thing about this orientation is not its intellectual content but rather its emotional tone, its diffused anger, and its generalized suspicion toward modern tendencies of all kinds. ... This nineteenth century liberalism appears both as a wistful nostalgia for a golden age of small farmers and businessmen and also as an expression of a strong resentment and hatred toward a world which makes no sense in terms of older ideas and which is conducted in apparent violation of old truths and values of economic and political life.[64]

Orientation III was called moderate conservatism. [It] is held by people who are reconciled to the continued existence both of big companies and of trade unions; this is the dominant political orientation of both major parties today.[65]

Orientation IV was called "right wing conservatives." People of this orientation are pro-big business and anti-union. With respect to these four orientations, the study revealed that:

> ... the small businessmen ... were distinctly more likely than manual workers or salaried employees to hold nineteenth century liberal views regarding trade unions and large corporations. There small businessmen comprised only one-fifth of the men in these occupational categories in our sample, they contributed a third of the nineteenth century liberals. Moreover, the small businessmen who *held* these views gave McCarthy a very high measure of support.[66]

Finally, men of the "nineteenth century liberal orientation" were the only ones with:

> ... no effective [means] and institutional channels of expression. Right-wing conservatives have substantial power in the business community and the Republican party; labor-liberals are a strong force in the trade unions, some big city machines, and are well represented in the Democratic party; and the moderate conservatives have everything else.[67]

This means relatively small proprietors find themselves in a world which they feel is not only threatening their very existence, but has abandoned all concern for them. Trapped in such a world, we should expect them to prize more highly than ever the 19th century claims of enterprise beliefs, even to the point of equating their opposition with communist stooges and thereupon feeling duty-bound to use whatever means they can to liberate from Government a network of subversives.

Expanding Ranks of Unemployed as Generating a Crisis Problem in Work Beliefs

Rapid scientific and technological advance is begetting a crisis problem in work beliefs by laying increasing numbers of people on the shelf instead of providing them with work opportunities. Several considerations lead to this conclusion.

First, the most baffling characteristic of our dynamic economy is the fact that, while it increases income per capita as fast as ever, it is also generating human obsolescence more rapidly than ever. For the total number of work opportunities it creates is increasingly less than the number of people needing and seeking work.

Here are some key figures. During the 15-year period from 1947 to 1962, the economy created 10 million new work opportunities but population growth created 13 million new workers.[68] Thus, 3 million workers were added to those who had been told the world of productive opportunities has no place for them. Those hardest hit are young people from 14 to 24 years of age; nonwhite workers; workers in declining industries like farming, mining, and many lines of manufacturing; workers in depressed areas (where major industries have virtually disappeared) and unskilled workers generally.[69]

These people are being side-tracked for two reasons. First, the rate at which our economy generates human obsolescence is commonly faster than the rate at which the individual can build into himself, tear out, and rebuild stable habits of life. Typical victims are the miners, locomotive engineers, firemen, conductors, yardmen, and maintenance workers. *Adapt, readapt, and adapt again!* Men can be driven half out of their minds by this harassing demand.

Second, this fast-changing economy is requiring an increasingly higher level of skills than numbers of people now possess or may be able to acquire, even under the most perfect system of education conceivable. It is creating abundant opportunities for professional and technical workers of all sorts especially mathematicians, physicists, chemists, engineers, and the like. For every 100 such workers in 1950 there were 147 in 1960. There were also very sizeable increases in opportunities for clerical, service, and sales workers, and a small increase in opportunities for skilled workers. But opportunities for the less skilled declined sharply—10 percent in industry and 40 percent in agriculture.[70]

Can expansion of educational services raise the skill equipment level of the people as a whole at the same rate as scientific and technological advance raises the skill requirements level of employment opportunities as a whole? Consider this fact:

> ... for the period 1929 to 1957, the improved education of the work force accounted for more than one-fifth of the increase in real national product. This was a larger share than that provided for by the increase in capital investment. Education combined with the advance of knowledge accounted altogether for about two-fifths of the national growth during this period.[71]

Note the implications. Had we not expanded our programs of educational services in past years, we would have had slower rates of scientific and technological advance, a slower increase in total output of goods and services per capita, and the skill requirement level of employment opportunities would have remained in line with the skill equipment level of the people.

Now, suppose we enter upon a vast expansion of educational services so as to raise the skill equipment of our population in line with the rising skill requirement of our economy. Experience shows this would lead to much faster rates of scientific and technological advance than the ones we now have. This would accelerate the current rate of economic growth in terms of total output of goods and services per capita. But would it not also widen still further the gap between the skill requirement level of the economy and the skill equipment level of the population?

As previously shown, the current gap has been caused by past step-ups in investment in the production of scientific and technical skills. This does not mean that greatly improved programs of education are not needed and eminently justified. But there is a question whether the expansion of such programs, although necessary, will be sufficient to provide an effective remedy for the unemployment problem in an economy of rapidly rising skill requirements.

From the standpoint of mere material welfare there is no reason for lamenting the fact that our rapid rates of scientific and technological advance are making obsolete increasing numbers of people. For even though such advance is laying more people on the shelf each year, the fact remains that it is increasing total income per capita as rapidly as ever. This kind of economic progress is headed toward an economic Garden of Eden in which all people can have more and more income without having to do any work. This is precisely what the American people would most want, if, like the Ancient Greeks, they guided the striving for significance with the conviction that the badge of highest distinction is exemption from all employments having to do with material means of life.

Research shows, however, that what American people most want is not a more leisured life, but more abundant work opportunities.[72] For example, in summarizing studies of the attitudes of unskilled industrial workers, who were seemingly little more than cogs in a machine, David Reisman noted that 80 percent of such workers interviewed in one study said they would continue to work even if there was no financial need to do so. "Work may not be an active presence in the life of these workers " said Reisman,

> but its absence would be an active absence. Or, more accurately, it is not so much 'work' that would be missed as having a job: it doesn't have to be, and should preferably not be, hard work, nor need it even be gregarious work, but rather the self-definition ... that comes from holding a job and the punctuation of life provided by regular employment.[73]

And in another place Reisman comments:

> ... my collaborators and I in *The Lonely Crowd* took it for granted that ... current efforts to make work more meaningful ... might as well be given up, with the meaning of life to be sought henceforth, in the creative use of leisure. We failed to see, in the famous Marxian phrase, that "quantity changes into quality" and that there would come a point where addition increments of leisure would prove more stultifying than satisfying and that the mass of men would be incapable of absorbing any more.[74]

Sebastian de Grazia puts the same point this way:

> One is not appalled or indignant on learning that another doesn's work; one simply does not understand, doesn's know where next to turn for conversation, cannot size up the ostensibly human object standing there.

Doctors, psychiatrists, and ministers, "sense the effect of too much time in the hands of young and old alike as time without a purpose to guide it . . .," says de Grazia. "Sunday neurosis, as it is sometimes called, seems fairly widespread as . . . a malady exhibiting a peculiar uneasiness rather than true anxiety on free-time days. The lack of structure to the days opens them up to choice, and choices without a guiding pattern may lead either to temptation or to reflection, which then leads to a feeling of not knowing how to act, or existing without a purpose. Work days roll around to the sound of relief. If the number of characterless free-time days increases, these phenomena should increase too."[75]

From a strictly economic standpoint, then, how unfortunate it is that American people do not share an inherent dislike for work. For then they would want to work only as a means of overcoming their poverty. The richer they got, the more leisure they would want; and hence they would count as a blessing an economy that produced more and more income per capita and at the same time laid more and more people on the shelf. The belief or cultural foundations of such economy would be exceedingly secure if, instead of being "indignant on learning that another doesn't work," American people looked on work as "a curse" as the story books often say they do. As matters stand, however, the belief or cultural foundations of the economy are not secure. They are in a crisis; maybe not a very big crisis, but a crisis just the same.

This means that when more and more people with work beliefs are laid on the shelf the "I" component of the self tends to alienate itself from confidence in its capacity to be the type of person ("me") it most prizes. It accomplishes this alienation with the opposite conviction that it is actually a worthless type of person ("me"), devoid of capacities for deserving the respect and esteem of anyone. Thus, the "I" is troubled. In virtue of its work belief, it feels obliged to prove its worth through the competence with which it performs a productive role in life. In virtue of being laid on the shelf, it is trapped by the conviction that it is devoid of capacity for being of use to anyone. In this way, its hitherto confident quest for significant life is turned into despair over the meaningless-ness of life.

This anxiety can never be assuaged by any amount of "relief payments." No ceremonial magic of high sounding names can ever drown the psychic pain of such payments. They are an index of inability to be a man like other men. This fact cannot be ducked or dodged by any doctored-up "welfare terminology." Laid-on-the-shelf people cannot be role-performing participants in their "own" culture and society. Thus alienated from the productive persons they feel obliged to be, the only way in which they tend to achieve a challenging sense of purpose is through identifying themselves with the conviction that it is the economy and not themselves which deserves to be laid on the shelf. Thereupon they feel their duty is to combat the social order that has disavowed its responsibility ot provide all its members with opportunities for leading a useful life.

This sense of destructive purpose may take the form of juvenile and adult delinquency. Or it may take the form of attachment to some power elite who promises to do away with the existing order and bring to pass a new order that gives all a chance to develop, use, and enjoy their productive potential to the fullest extent possible.

Thus our technologically dynamic economy is both an expression and a generator of crisis in its cultural foundations—the work belief conviction that increasing proficiency in all employments is the mark of superior character. The economy meets the demands of this belief insofar as it continually increases income per capita. But the more it makes people with work beliefs useless, the more it threatens its own security by turning their striving for significance into hostility and resentment over being condemned to a life without meaning, without purpose, without significance.

The Crisis in the Three American Belief Systems as Feeding on Each Other

Twentieth century America is thus experiencing a crisis problem in each of the three great belief systems she inherited from 19th century America. The Negro Rebellion against color discrimination reflects a crisis problem in democratic beliefs. The increasing ranks of unemployed in the midst of increasing affluence reflects a crisis problem in work beliefs, and the Radical Right reflects a crisis in interprise beliefs, especially among small proprietors.

Each of these crises by itself is serious enough. But the larger fact is that their combined danger is greater than the mere arithmetical sum of their separate dangers. This is why. As previously explained, the negro rebellion is not limited to mere demands for riddance of segregation practices in airports, lunch counters, movie theaters, public parks and the like. By law and good will these might be done away. This would not be enough. The Negro seeks more than the removal of these humiliating practices. He seeks better schools, better jobs, better houses. But there are not enough schools, jobs, and houses to provide equal opportunities for Negroes and whites, even if there were no color barriers to opportunities at all. The basic trouble is that the pie that is supposed to be divided equally is too small.

To make the pie bigger requires policies that would expand the rate of economic growth to the point of generating enough new employment opportunities for everyone to have a job who wants one. Thus the measures required to ease the crisis problem in democratic beliefs are also the ones required to ease the crisis in work beliefs.

Such measures, however, intensify the crisis problem in enterprise beliefs. They involve expanding the service role of Government much beyond the limitations imposed by present weights assigned to enterprise beliefs. Thus the Nation tends to wheeze and sputter on dead center for fear that, if it acts to relieve one crisis, it only worsens another. Meantime, the crisis problems keep feeding each other, thus building up more pressure for remedial action, and also more and more fear of doing much of anything except just sit on the lid.

20th Century America as a Swing From an Unrealistic Optimism to an Equally Unrealistic Pessimism

Attention is now directed to a tendency of 20th century people to trap themselves in a pessimism as unrealistic as the unrealistic optimism of the 19th century. By an unrealistic optimism, I mean a confidence in men's capacities to achieve an increasingly satisfactory world that is so boundless as to virtually amount to the belief that they can lift themselves into the kingdom of heaven by their own bootstraps. All that is needed is a little more time, and there is plenty of that.

Such unrealistic optimism is dangerous because sooner or later, it leads people into such monstrous undertakings as the "war to end wars," a war to discharge the white man's burdens, to bring light unto the heathen, and even a titanic struggle to bring forth a new humanity in which each of his own volition "produces according to his ability and receives according to his needs."

Nineteenth century America was loaded with this sort of unrealistic optimism. It is most conspicuous in the directives of the American Dream. For as previously explained, the dictate of the 19th century Dream was that if American people sought no other international goal than to live within their own borders, conquer the continent, and better their conditions of life through diligent industry under free institutions, the sheer attractiveness of their example would incite people of other lands to do likewise. In similar fashion, 19th century America tended to translate their work beliefs into a secular faith that scientific and technological advance is an automatic generator of an increasing prosperous and harmonious world.

But the unrolling events of the 20th century have caused many thinking people to ask if scientific and technological advance is not more a revelation of man's destructive potential than of his capacities for achieving an increasingly just and harmonious life.

For example, men make marvelous gains in new knowledge and then use it in killing over 40 million people in two world wars, in sending 6 million Jews of all ages and both sexes to the gas chambers, and in keeping a shaky world peace with an international "balance of nuclear terror." Within our national borders, in a mad race for progress, we invent and put into use new mining technologies that leave virtually whole States in despair over a bleak future. We develop and use new farm, transportation, and merchandising technologies that uproot half the farm population, undermine the economy of thousands of farm-based towns, and throw millions of rural people into metropolitan jungles, lost, bewildered, afraid, and commonly without any employment at all.

On the world scene, there is a grim struggle to enable hundreds of millions of impoverished people to achieve the far richer life which modern science and technology can put in their reach. Everywhere the chief obstacles to the success of this struggle is the fact that no dominant class of power and privilege has ever been persuaded to step aside by any appeal of scientific evidence that the well-being of millions of disadvantaged people could be vastly improved if they did so.

Where in all this is one to find evidence to support the equation of rapid rates of scientific and technological advance with human capacities to achieve an increasingly satisfactory world? Many feel it is like looking for a needle in a haystack. There is thus no surprise in the fact that highly intelligent and dedicated men during the last 30 years have felt impelled to raise a halting hand against what they consider to be a deceiving faith.

Foremost of these in this country is a distinguished clergyman, Reinhold Neibuhr, whom Schlesinger, the eminent historian, has called the most influential voice of his generation. In the 1920's, Niebuhr's experience in a Detroit parish with social problems created by technological advance led him to conclude that:

> The most persistent error of modern educators and moralists is the assumption that our social difficulties are due to the failure of the social sciences to keep pace with the physical sciences which have created our technological civilization. The invariable implication of this assumption is that, with a little more time, a little more adequate moral and social pedagogy and a generally higher development of human intelligence, our social problems will approach solution.[76]

In this assumption, he declared:

> They completely disregard the political necessities in the struggle for justice in human society by failing to recognize those elements in man's collective behavior which belong to the order of Nature and can never be brought completely under the dominion of reason or conscience. They do not recognize that when collective power, whether in the form of imperialism or class domination, exploits weakness, it can never be dislodged unless power is raised against it.[77]

Becoming specific, he said:

> No class of industrial workers will ever win freedom from the dominant class if they give themselves completely to the "experimental techniques" of the modern educators. They will have to believe rather more firmly in the justice and in the probable triumph of their cause, than any impartial science would give them the right to believe, if they are to have enough energy to contest the power of the strong.[78]

Niebuhr made clear that far more than the unduly optimistic claim for the social sciences was at stake in the issue he was raising. If men of various classes cannot be induced by reason and science to correct the injustice that divides them, there is reason to suppose that, in increasing their destructive potential through scientific and technological advance, they may thereby bring down their whole civilization in ruins. As Niebuhr put it:

> ... the conquest of nature, and the consequent increase in nature's beneficiences to man, have not eased, but rather accentuated, the problem of justice. The same technology, which drew the fangs of nature's enmity to man, also created a society in which the intensity and extent of social cohesion has been greatly increased and in which power is so unevenly distributed, that justice has become a more difficult achievement.[79]

Then he had the courage to draw the implication of this fact in these words:

> Perhaps it is man's sorry fate, suffering from ills which have their source in the inadequacies of both nature and human society, that the tools by which he eliminates the former should become the means of increasing the latter. That, at least, has been his fate up to the present hour; and it may be that these will be no salvation for the human spirit from the more and more painful burdens of social injustices until the ominous tendency in human history has resulted in perfect tragedy.[80]

It is not an easy thing for a man to question the guiding beliefs of his civilization. It is a lonely job. Niebuhr expressed his sense of estrangement this way:

> A social analysis which is written, at least partially, from the perspective of a disillusioned generation will seem to be almost pure cynicism from the perspective of those who will stand in the credo of the nineteenth century.[81]

But expressions of man's destructive potential on a massive scale over the last 30 years have so strengthened Niebuhr's position that it is not uncommon for social scientists themselves to speak now as he spoke some 30 years ago. For example, in summarizing the many types of adjustments that must be made in our school system and other institutions, if we are to avert disastrous consequences of the present wave of automation, a noted economist has this to say:

> Adrift on a furious current of technology, we allow ourselves to be swept along, trusting to blind forces at work to bring us safely to unknown but unquestioned destination. It need hardly be pointed out this belief in the benign impact of technology may turn out to have been the most tragic of all contemporary faiths.[82]

Niebuhr is no anti-intellectual. He is one of those rare geniuses with genius enough to see that the beginning of wisdom, scientific or otherwise, is the gumption to know that there is a tension between the limited capacities of the human animal for meritorious achievement and the infinitude of his aspirations, from which no amount of scientific and technological progress can ever provide escape. Therein lies his peril. Rivals would scarcely be human did they not tend to meet their need for an increasingly favorable image of their worth through the deception that their decisions on what ought and ought not be done are more valid than they actually are. Thereupon the need of each rival for a meritorious image of himself obliged him to overcome the other, by persuasion if possible, by force if necessary, in order that an impartial justice may prevail. In this way they turn their striving for significance into animosities that destroy the more just and harmonious life each feels obliged to achieve. This principle operates in all levels of life, tearing families apart over daughter's questionable boy friends and turning the nations and races against each other over questions of national honor.

Niebuhr had no new recipe for getting people out of this box. Nobody does. But he had the wit to see that the destructiveness of their frailty is worsened by an unrealistic optimism—the deceiving confidence—that, in their capacities for endless scientific and technological advance, they have the wherewithal for getting any closer than they already are to a "just and lasting peace" with each other. For this purpose, the equations of Ptolemy, Newton, and Einstein are equally useless.

In all of Niebuhr's voluminous writings, I have found no suggestion that men could increase their capacity for living peacefully and justly with each other if they abandoned their quest for scientific and technological advance. This is not true of others, especially those whom C. P. Snow has called literary intellectuals. As Snow pointed out, scientific and literary intellectuals today are divided by divergent creeds of life. By and large, scientific intellectuals recognize the falseness of the 19th century belief in scientific and technological advance as an automatic generator of an increasingly satisfactory world. Yet they still have faith in man's ability to use new knowledge to solve the very problems it creates. Thus, "they have the future in their bones."

In contrast, literary intellectuals by and large, turn this faith of scientific intellectuals into the diametrically opposite belief that the more scientifically and technologically advanced the human race becomes, the more dehumanized and cruel is the world it generates. In this existentialist belief, the model of human nature is one in which the unlimited aspirations of the "I" component of the self are stymied by an actual self ("me") that is devoid to the capacities for achieving the significant life which his aspirations oblige him to seek. In terms of this belief, the professional responsibility of literary intellectuals is to use their artistic capacities in interpreting the self resentments, hostilities, anguish, and despairs of personalities with infinite sensitiveness for greatness by hopelessly separated from the persons they feel obliged to be by virtually zero capacities for achievement. Thus, the poets still sing, but not to Walt Whitman's "destined port triumphant" nor to Tennyson's "far off divine event toward which all creation moves." Typically, they sing thus:

> . . .the new barbarian is no uncouth
> Desert-dweller; he does not emerge
> From fir forest: factories breed him;
> Corporate companies, college towns
> Mothered his mind, and many journals
> backed his beliefs. He was born here.
>
> . . .
> . . . this stupid world where
> Gadgets are gods and we go on talking,
> Many about much, but remain alone,
> Alive but alone, belonging—where?—
> Unattached as a tumbleweed.
>
> . . .
> . . . he has fattened on
> His public perch; takes pills for vigor
> And sound sleep, and sees in his mirror
> the jawing genius of a jackass age. . . .[83]

Concerning the painters and sculptors as interpreters of the inner concerns of alienated people in our technological civilization, Paul Tillich has said that modern art is a revelation of the meaninglessness of our existence. "The categories which constitute ordinary experience have lost their power," claims Tillich.

> The category of substance is lost: solid objects are twisted like ropes; the causal interdependence of things is disregarded: things appear in a complete contingency; temporal sequences are without significance, it does not matter whether an event has happened before or after another event; the spatial dimensions are reduced or dissolved into a horrifying infinity. The organic structures of life are cut into pieces which are arbitrarily (from the biological, not the artistic, point of view) recomposed: limbs are dispersed, colors are separated from their natural carriers.[84]

"The creators of modern art have been able to see the meaninglessness of our existence;" Tillich concludes, "they participated in its despair."

Thus in sharp contrast to the 19th century, the intellectual community today divides into opposite camps with respect to the traditional work belief in scientific and technological advance as proof of man's capacities to achieve significance. As C. P. Snow so well said:

> The non-scientists have a rooted impression that the scientists are shallowly optimistic, unaware of man's condition. On the other hand, the scientists believe that the literary intellectuals are totally lacking in foresight, peculiarly unconcerned with their brother men, in a deep sense anti-intellectual, anxious to restrict both art and thought to the existential moment.[55]

As Snow observes the pessimism of the literary intellectuals contains:

> ... a moral trap: ... it tempts one to sit back, complacent in one's unique tragedy, and let others go without a meal.[56]

In contrast:

> As a group, the scientists fall into that trap less than others. They are inclined to be impatient to see if something can be done: and inclined to think it can be done, until it's proved otherwise. That is their real optimism, and it's an optimism that the rest of us badly need.[57]

Snow regards as tragic this separation of the intellectual community by opposing creeds of life. He is right. The human animal is seemingly so constituted that he can reach his full stature only as he is able to gird himself with beliefs that the cosmos is on his side. Whenever he traps himself in the opposite conviction that Nature has denied him the capacities for achieving the dreams and visions he has implanted in him, he empties himself of the motivation to grapple with his problems and responsibilities as well as he is actually able.

It is indeed a tragic thing if people deceive themselves with the unrealistic optimism that in their capacities for scientific and technological advance they have the wherewithal to lift themselves into the kingdom of heaven by their own bootstraps. It is no less a tragedy if they deceive themselves with the equally unrealistic pessimism that if they forsake science and emulate the serenity of the ox, they will increase their capacity to live with each other in peace and justice.

V. Summary

We now need to bring into focus the interconnected concepts that constitute the theory of cultural change which has guided our analysis and also point up how we used the theory in identifying the crisis spots in 20th century American culture.

Theory

The interconnected concepts are as follows:

1. *The striving for significance.* The major premise is that the dominant striving of people the world over is for acting in ways that merit an increasingly favorable image (valuation) of themselves in their own eyes and in the eyes of others, whether actual or ideal. The need for a favorable image of oneself in his own eyes and the need for a favorable image in the eyes of others stand on a similar footing. Were the cost of complete fulfillment of either need the

complete negation of the other, life would be equally unbearable, whichever choice were made. Both needs are thus aspects of one and the same motivation, which we call the *striving for individual and collective significance.*

2. *Beliefs.* In their effort to achieve significance, people use guides or pointers concerning what organized ways of life and work identify them as the *type* of persons and society that deserve high standing. These guides or pointers we call beliefs. Types of persons, types of society, and ways of achieving them are concepts. Therefore, *beliefs are concepts of ways of life and work which people feel obliged to follow for the sake of proving their worth.*

There are no beliefs without concepts, but mere concepts are not beliefs. People may have a concept of proficiency in scalping and head-hunting as a way of life and work. This concept is a belief only when combined with the feeling—the conviction—that proficiency in head-hunting is the proper way of proving oneself the type of person he feels obliged to be. Beliefs are thus the working union between the viscera and the cortex—between the appetitive and conceptual aspects of any motive.

While people of all cultures share the striving for individual and collective significance, they differ as the poles with respect to their beliefs—concepts of what ways of life and work they feel obliged to follow, and which best relate people to each other with reciprocal rights and duties. Thus beliefs are the cultural variables of history.

3. *Values.* Values are the relative weights which people attach to the action demands of given beliefs. For example, most everyone believes in telling the truth but not everyone attaches the same importance to truth telling. Some take it lightly, others would scarcely tell even a white lie.

4. *Interdependence of beliefs and values and prior importance of beliefs.* Since values are relative weights which people assign to the action claims of their various beliefs, it follows that beliefs and values are as interdependent as the sides of a coin. Neither exists without the other. We cannot stick beliefs in one jug and values in another. There are no beliefs without concepts of practices which are *valued* in some degree as valid evidence of prized personal and social qualities. Conversely, without concepts of given ways of life there are no values. Thus beliefs are of prior importance to values. Trying to identify and measure people's values without first identifying their beliefs is fruitless. There is nothing to measure, no point of reference, no significant hypothesis to guide investigations, nothing to sink one's teeth in.

5. *Policy problems and crisis problems as differing in kind.* Changing conditions generate two types of conflict among groups over what rules all must observe. One type constitutes policy problems; the other crisis problems. Changing conditions commonly throw into conflict the relative importance which different groups have hitherto given the action claims of their common beliefs. We call these conflicts policy problems. In such conflicts, the bonds of common beliefs are strong enough to withstand the difference in the values people place on the claims of their beliefs.

In sharp contrast, crisis problems arise when changing conditions lead a sizeable group to alienate themselves from beliefs that bind them to their existing social order. They do so by identifying themselves with new beliefs that turn them against their social order.

Crisis problems are thus disagreements in which each party increasingly tends to equate its own belief demands with moralistic absolutes of Natural or Divine Law. Thereupon the alienated group feels obliged to use whatever means it can, including violence, to overpower opposing groups for the sake of achieving a universally valid justice. This is the process through which one civilization rises and another passes away.

6. *Beliefs and institutions as "inner" and "outer" expressions of same types of activities.* Institutions are types of activities through which people relate themselves to each other with reciprocal rights and duties. As the "outside" of each participant, institutions are the *overt* expressions of the same activities in the form of internal beliefs concerning what ways of life and work people feel obliged to follow.

Take, for example, the pattern of racial discrimination. As activities outside each individual, this institution is clearly the overt expression of the belief that black skin possesses inferior character. If both blacks and whites separated themselves from this belief—this internal expression of discriminatory practices—the overt expression of the same practices would quickly disappear.

The same principle applies to any system of institutions. For this reason we equate the essence of culture with belief systems which people use in relating themselves to each other with reciprocal rights and duties.

Application of Theory to American Culture

Use of these interconnected concepts in determining crisis spots in present day American culture required two first steps. First it was necessary to identify the belief systems which people of 19th century America used in guiding their individual and collective striving for increasingly significant, worthwhile life. It also required identification of the major conditions leading to the development of these belief systems. Without the first step we have no concrete knowledge of what the culture is that is supposed to be in a crisis. Without the second step we have no way of determining which of the new conditions of 20th century America may be generating crisis problems, and which conditions are generating only policy problems.

With respect to the first step, we found that 20th century America inherited from 19th century America five interconnected belief systems. These were a magnificent sense of destiny and a compelling image of the best of all conceivable forms of political economy resting on a tripod of democratic, work, and enterprise belief systems. In outline form, the components of these belief systems are as follows:

The sense of destiny included the two convictions: (1) that America's world purpose was to lead the nations in bringing to pass: A political realm of a government, based on the voice of the plain people; an economic realm of plenty, stemming from diligent industry; a world realm of law and justice, and (2) that the way for America to accomplish this world purpose was to live peacefully within her own borders, and by her industry so to improve the conditions of common life that the attractiveness of her example would induce others to do likewise. Accompanying this sense of destiny was a compelling belief that the best of all possible national organizations is a proprietary form of political economy in which democratic government: (1) provides people with services they cannot provide themselves but need in becoming increasingly successful proprietors; (2) abstains from penalizing the industrious and rewarding incompetent through taxing the dollars of big income people more heavily than the dollars of low income people; and (3) abstains from laws that limit the power of proprietors to run their businesses as they choose.

The overriding commitment to this proprietary form of political economy rested on a tripod of democratic, work, and enterprise belief system, as follows:

(1) *Democratic belief system:* The central components of the democratic belief system were:
    (a) That all men are equal in dignity and worth;
    (b) That none, however wise or good, is wise or good enough to have arbitrary power over any other;
    (c) That each is entitled to a voice in making the rules which all must observe.

(2) *Work belief system:* We found that the work belief system included six major commitments, all stemming from the first. These were the beliefs:
    (a) That striving for excellence in all employments is the proper way of earning one's own highest respect and esteem and the respect and esteem of others. This is just the opposite of the "hair-shirt concept of work."
    (b) That no employment is any "higher" or any lower than any other as a chance for people to prove their worth.
    (c) That of all types of character, the Innovator-Personality is the one most deserving emulation, respect, and esteem.
    (d) That society has three major obligations to all individuals. These are (1) to provide all its members with equal opportunities for developing their potential to the fullest extent possible, (2) to offer opportunities for productive roles in keeping with their abilities, and (3) to give each a fair return for his contributions. In this way, the work beliefs called for a service state.
    (e) That in their productive capacities men and nations have ample means to bring their actual conditions increasingly in line with their aspirations.

(3) *Enterprise belief system:* Finally, the belief systems of 19th century America included a set of convictions which we call the enterprise belief system. The central convictions of this system are:
    (a) That increasingly successful proprietorship—capital accumulation—is the correct test of work ethic virtue—the striving for excellence in all employments is the badge of highest distinction.

(b) That failure to achieve a proprietary status proves a life-long distaste for work of any kind.

(c) That failure of people to meet their own total security needs proves such a lack of work ethic virtue as to make them undeserving of social acceptance.

(d) That these tests of work ethic virtue called for the proprietary form of political economy described above.

(e) That the businessman's highest social responsibility is maximizing profits to his business.

(f) That the competitive striving of businessmen to outdo each other automatically generated plenty of work opportunities at fair pay for all who were willing and able to work.

We found the 19th century belief systems stemmed mainly from two major sets of conditions: (1) the carryover of certain Old World belief systems, (2) and an expanding system of family businesses in a virgin continent of opportunities. These were substantially as follows. The builders of earlier America carried over the central belief of the Medieval landlord civilization, that proprietorship was exclusive proof of capacities for self direction entitling people to a voice in making the rules which all must observe and that tenantry and wage status proved such a lack of self-directing capacities as to make people dependent on superiors for these directives. But they had alienated themselves from the masterservant beliefs and institutions of the Old World. This alienation resulted in part from the revolutionary work beliefs of the religious reformers that striving for increasing excellence in all employments was the hallmark of upright men. It also stemmed from the equally revolutionary belief of the Natural Rights philosophers, especially John Locke, that there was no ceiling on the natural or moral right of men to acquire capital as fair reward for work.

Thus, the builders of early America were confronted with the baffling problem of how to achieve a form of social organization that would resolve these conflicts. They found the answer to this problem in a proprietary form of political economy that rested on a tripod of democratic, work, and enterprise belief systems. The principal means making possible this achievement was an expanding economy of predominantly family businesses in a virgin continent of work opportunities.

For this economy, combining in each skin the proprietary and labor roles which the feudal past has segregated into lords and serfs enabled people to see themselves as "equally kings," and in this way become committed to the democratic belief system.

Furthermore, this economy made clear that the productive work, not aristocratic exemption from work, proves the superior wisdom needed for making political decisions. The day of aristocracy was done.

Finally, the economy of predominantly family businesses led common sense to see work beliefs as mere tools for justifying the enterprise beliefs commitment to a proprietary form of political economy. For with physical resources dirt cheap and ownership of labor and capital combined in the same skin, it was clear that successful proprietorship was a valid test of work ethic virtue.

Therefore, Government was obliged to provide people with services they could not provide themselves but which they needed in becoming increasingly successful proprietors. On the other hand, Government was obliged to abstain from taxing high incomes more heavily than low incomes. For the economy of family businesses prevented inequalities of wealth from becoming so great as to be incompatible with equality of opportunity.

Finally, by combining the ownership of labor and capital in the same skin, the earlier economy limited the number of workers in business establishments mainly to the operator and his family. Thus, decisions on how to run their businesses affected none but themselves.

Therefore, Government was obliged to abstain from placing any limitations on the power of proprietors to run their affairs as they chose. Such limitations would be an act of sheer arbitrary power and stifle the striving for being increasingly proficient doers.

Major Findings Concerning 20th Century Cultural Change

Twentieth century America has witnessed a series of departures from the political economy which first gave rise to the American belief systems. In that economy the ownership of labor and capital was combined in the same person. Today these ownerships have been torn apart and resegregated into separate ownership classes, each dealing with the other on a bargaining basis. In the earlier economy, being an owner entrepreneur was the only career open to most people. In today's economy of large organizations, thousands of types of careers are available. The earlier economy prevented inequalities of wealth from becoming so great as to become incompatible with equality of opportunity. The reverse is true of today's economy where personal incomes may range from less than $1,000 to over $500,000. This transformation of that earlier economy has been accompanied by an expanding service role of Government far beyond the limitations prescribed by 19th century America.

These facts raised the question if present-day America has discarded the essential culture of 19th century America. We found she has not. She is as much guided as 19th century America by the democratic, work, and enterprise belief systems. The difference lies in the relative importance she assigns to the demands of these belief systems.

1. *Policy Problems.* What has taken place is that as new conditions have thrown the action claims of 19th century beliefs into conflict with the claims of democratic and work beliefs, American people resolve the conflicts by a downward adjustment in the 19th century claims of enterprise beliefs. Four observations sustained this generalization. First, in opening up many different careers, the 20th century economy undermined the older high premium on capital accumulation as the exclusive test of devotion to work beliefs. This test has not been thrown away. But new conditions have led people to see there are many valid tests.

Second, the shift to the modern economy undermined the 19th century view that providing for one's own total security needs is an adequate test of minimum work ethic virtue. An individual's security in today's economy depends not only on his willingness to work and save; it also depends on the willingness of the business community to offer him an opportunity to work.

For this reason, individuals in today's economy may feel more committed than ever to earning high standing as proficient doers and yet victims of far greater insecurity than in the earlier economy. Faced with this fact, American people threw away neither their work beliefs nor their enterprise beliefs. Instead, they corrected the inadequacy of the older test by recognizing that responsibility for the security needs of the individual is a joint obligation of both society and the individual. This enabled them to meet the demands of all their beliefs with a new rule according to which people help each other meet their security needs through a collective saving procedure, known as the social security system.

Third, in creating enormous differences in personal incomes, the rise of the modern corporate economy generates serious conflict between (a) the 19th century enterprise belief demands for government that abstained from inequalitarian tax laws, and (b) work belief demands for a society that provided all its members with equality of opportunity for a productive life and work with fair returns.

Faced with this conflict, the Nation did not throw away either its enterprise beliefs or its work beliefs; it simply altered their relative importance so as to meet the demands of both with policies that placed a heavier tax burden on high incomes.

Finally, transforming the older economy of predominantly family business into corporate business generated conflict between (a) the enterprise belief in complete power to run businesses as they choose and (b) the democratic belief in the right of each to a voice in making the rules which all must observe.

Faced with this conflict, 20th century America threw away neither her enterprise beliefs nor democratic beliefs She simply altered the premium she previously set on the former to the point where she satisfied the demands of both beliefs with a collective bargaining procedure that obliges the representatives of labor and capital to formulate the work and pay rules with each other at the bargaining table. American people are as much committed as before to both entrepreneurial freedom and democratic freedom. Adoption of collective bargaining merely signified that they were not willing to buy the former at the expense of the latter.

Thus we found that the striking feature of the 20th century is the phenomenal capacity of American people for cultural growth—their power to meet the demands of their democratic, work, and enterprise belief systems with mutually satisfactory revisions of old rules of life and work under new conditions. Without this capacity, they would long since have wrecked themselves with crisis problems.

2. *Crisis Problems.* Even so, we found that present-day America is caught in three distinct crisis problems that feed on each other. Moreover, in her flight from an unrealistic 19th century optimism, she tends to trap herself in an equally unrealistic pessimism. The Negroes' rebellion against color discriminations is a

serious crisis in democratic beliefs. The revolt of the Radical Right against the expanding service role of Government reflects a serious crisis in enterprise beliefs. By apparently laying more and more people on the shelf through automation, for example, our economy is generating a crisis in work beliefs. In substance we found each of these crises to be as follows.

First is the Negro rebellion as a crisis in work beliefs. From the landing of the first boatload of slaves in 1619, both whites and Negroes have long related themselves under rules that rested on the belief that black skin proves inferior character. But in recent years, Negroes have alienated themselves from this belief by identifying themselves with the democratic belief in the equal dignity of all men. In this way, the Negro has acquired a moral conviction that turns him against a social order that condemns him to second class status; so much so that we live under the shadow of potential violence.

Yet we found that the common bonds between whites and Negroes are still substantial. For, while whites may hold the belief that color is proof of inferior status, their attachment to democratic beliefs is so strong that they recognize a rightness in the Negroes' grievances and feel an obligation to reach mutually satisfactory remedies. Knowing this, the Negro holds his rebellion within the bounds of passive resistance. These common bonds are a basis for real confidence in the ability of the two races to reconcile their differences. This confidence, however, is sobered by the fact that discriminatory practices have been capitalized in real estate values and other assets. Whites are thus under severe temptation to subordinate democratic freedom to entrepreneurial freedom. This increases the danger of violence.

We also found that the Radical Right reflects a growing crisis in enterprise beliefs. In substance the crisis is this: The people of the Radical Right are unable to follow the majority in their downward adjustments in 19th century limitations on the service role of Government. Thus, they seek to abolish the Federal income tax, and all foreign aid, abolish many domestic activities of Government, and stop the reapportionment of State legislatures. They have powerful weapons. By equating their minority beliefs with "true Americanism," they are able to use the hatred of Americans for alien "isms" in destroying their opponents.

Next, we discovered a crisis in work beliefs. We found our technologically dynamic economy is generating a crisis in work beliefs by apparently failing to provide increasing numbers of people with work opportunities. It does so by requiring an increasingly higher level of skills than many people now possess or may be able to acquire. This fact puts the belief or cultural foundations to the economy in a crisis. In virtue of their work beliefs, people feel obliged to prove their worth through the competence with which they perform a productive role in life; but in being laid on the shelf they become trapped by the conviction that they are devoid of the capacity for being of use to anyone. This tends to turn them against the social order that has disavowed its responsibility to provide all its members with opportunities for leading a useful life.

We found that the combined danger of these crises is greater than the mere arithmetical sum of their separate dangers. For there are not enough schools, jobs, and houses today to provide equal opportunities for Negroes and whites, even if there were no color barriers to opportunities at all. The pie that is supposed to be divided equally is at present too small. Making it bigger requires policies that would expand the rate of economic growth to the point of generating enough new employment opportunities for everyone to have a job who wants one. These measures would ease the crisis problems in both the democratic beliefs and the work beliefs, but they would intensify the crisis problem in enterprise beliefs. They would involve expanding the service role of Government much beyond the limitations now imposed by enterprise beliefs. Thus the Nation tends to stall on dead center for fear that, if it acts to relieve one crisis, it only worsens another. This in turn aggravates all the crisis problems.

Finally, we found that, in escaping the unrealistic optimism of the 19th century, 20th century America tends to trap herself in an equally unrealistic pessimism. For as C. P. Snow has pointed out, present-day literary intellectuals tend to turn the unrealistic optimism of the 19th century into the opposite belief that the more scientifically and technologically advanced the human race becomes, the more dehumanized and cruel is the world it generates. In this belief, the model of human nature is one in which the unlimited aspirations of the "I" component of the self are stymied by an actual self ("me") that feels devoid of capacities for achieving the significant life which his aspirations oblige it to achieve. Guided by this image of human nature, the responsibility of literary intellectuals is to use their artistic capacities in interpreting the self-resentments, hostilities, anguish, and despairs of personalities with infinite aspiration for greatness but hopelessly separated from the persons they feel obliged to be by what they regard as virtually zero capacities for achievement. Trapped in this sort of pessimism, the human animal deprives himself of motivations for grappling with his problems and responsibilities as well as he is able.

VI. FINAL COMMENT

In attempting this analysis of the "Cultural Crisis of Our Time," I have found myself engaged in the most formidable undertaking of my professional career, but also the most rewarding. While I am reasonably satisfied with the results at this point, the ground is so new that I look upon the present paper as fundamentally a progress report.

CHAPTER 2. VIEWS OF MAN AND SOCIETY IN THE AMERICAN TRADITION

Introduction

1. *Fostering the unique worth of the individual as the central purpose of a democratic culture:* The central purpose of a democratic civilization is commonly held to be the fostering of the unique worth (capacities and views) of each individual. Very closely related to this purpose is another: The powerful urge for endless improvement in customary views and practices, extending to every branch of knowledge or act and to any technique of living and making a living. In such a culture, literally no limit can be placed on the value of each individual to society as a whole, even those whom it may reject. For the only source of significant innovations in accepted opinion and practice is the exceptional (variant) ideas, sentiments, and observations of the individual.

Run over the familiar laws of science, art forms, political and religious beliefs of today. Do the same with the implements of work or recreation such as the electric light, the car, the reaper and the like. Usually their histories run back to a point where they had no other status or home than the "foolish" notions of some individuals that ran counter to the customary opinion and practice of his day. There is hardly a piece of machinery around the farm (e.g., the McCormick reaper) whose very name does not bear out this point. The same applies to every nook and corner of our environment: technological, intellectual, artistic, and religious.

More fully stated, then, the central purpose of a democratic culture is the fostering of the maximum growth of each personality, both (1) for its own sake, and (2) as an instrument of social advance—the continuous improvement of its established ways of thought and practice. Historically speaking, this affirmation by the whole society of the value (worth) of each of its members, as such an agent, is a really stupendous achievement. No other civilization has ever achieved a comparable ability to frankly acknowledge, in its basic law and day-to-day climate of opinion, that even its cherished truths and practices may be proved wrong and its errors remedied by individual observations and views which are out of line with accepted ways.

2. *Ideal freedom as power to refashion the world after one's own image:* Throughout this study runs the assumption that each person actually seeks to refashion the world, in part at least, after his own idea. This he would do if his power to act were not blocked by external restraints. Unfrustrated exercise of power to do as one chooses is thus the ideal status to which the human spirit aspires.

Except under complete conformity with the Divine Imperative (law of love) such complete freedom of power is, of course, impossible. For the envisioned state of political economy of no two individuals coincides at all

---

Edited version of an unpublished manuscript.

points. The will of each to do what he most wants is therefore checked by that of others. Accordingly, any actual social order (political, business, school, etc.) must of necessity at least partially reject each man's envisioned order. As a consequence, there is a vast extent to which the "I," the unique individual, can never be fully "at home" in the world. In great measure, the "kingdom" of each man's reason and conscience is truly "not of this world," because his power (freedom or opportunity) to translate it in full into actual fact is severely limited.

Nonetheless, he remains an agent of his "inner kingdom;" this he most approves and, in doing so, always finds himself somewhat out of line with accepted ways. What he most seeks is not to "adjust" himself to "things as they are," but to bring them more in line (at least at some points) with his own exceptional views and sentiments.

As a consequence, the group (cultural) striving for the fullest possible development of the unique capacities of each individual, for its own sake as well as means for improving accepted opinion and practice, coincides with his own desire for an opportunity (power, freedom) to revise the customary views in line with his own exceptional views. Only in this way can he be "himself" as well as an agent of the larger collective purpose of improving accustomed ways. The collective prizing (1) of the unique differences among individuals, and (2) zeal for improving present customs are thus complementary. Each leads to and reinforces the other. Both together (3) open the door to the power motif of each to make over, according to his own conception what is objectionable to him in the present order.

3. *Spirit of freedom as the desire for equal opportunity in three forms:* In these terms, all freedoms fall into three main types of opportunities. First is the opportunity to have a voice in the sovereign role—the process of laying down the rules (policies) which must be observed by the members of any social unit such as the family, school, club, church, place of business, and the state. Second is the opportunity of developing and using one's capacities in some social role (or roles) such as farming, medicine, teaching, and the like. Third is the opportunity to be a dissenter—a challenger of accepted opinion and practice at whatever point they may run contrary to one's own experience and outlook.

Persons not only want each of these opportunities, but also feel that any social unit treats its members unjustly if it gives to some a greater measure of such opportunities than it does to others. This means that the age-old struggle against oppression (injustice) is the same as the struggle against inequalities of opportunity in any or all of the three forms just stated. If thus interpreted, the principle of equal opportunity is a quite adequate tool for analyzing all the basic premises and values that make up our democratic tradition. These three forms of equal opportunity may be called the *equalitarian conditions of freedom.*

The main objective of this chapter is to examine the major premises on which rests each of the three equalitarian conditions of freedom. We will also examine the counter premises of the aristocratic (authoritorian) viewpoint which, in many guises, is the perrenial rival of the democratic view.

Opportunity for an Equal Voice in the Sovereign Role

1. *Necessity of conformity:* As previously stated, each person is the agent of an envisioned order of his own reason and conscience and no two persons are alike in all respects. What each ideally seeks is to translate this order into actual fact. Therefore, conformity to any rule imposed from without is irksome. Yet the necessity of a considerable degree of such conformity is inescapable, even in the "freest" of all conceivable societies. For no life is possible apart from one's membership in a social unit (or units) such as a family, school, business, state, and the like. And no social unit is possible without rules which all must obey. In great measure, therefore, the first law of life is order - obedience - and not freedom or power to do as one pleases.

2. *Necessity of conformity met through either unequal or equal sharing of sovereign role:* The power to lay down the rules which all must observe is called the sovereign role, as it can crush out all opposition. The fundamental differences in the "forms of society" depend on the way in which the opportunities for sharing this role are distributed. All such variations fall between two extremes: (1) Ideal dictatorship, where the whole power is lodged in a single person; and (2) ideal democracy where each person has an equal voice. Neither of these extremes has ever been fully achieved, or ever can be. Ideal dictatorship is as unattainable as ideal democracy. But that is unimportant. What is important is that moment by moment social *change* is always *tending* toward one or the other of these extremes. Men are always tending to have either a less equal or a more nearly equal opportunity to share in the sovereign role. They are never standing still in this respect. It is this tendency (not its ideal limits) that counts—where we are headed.

3. *Choice between more or less equal sharing of sovereign role as depending on the equality or inequality of men as judges of equity:* However, firm choice accelerates the rate of change in one or the other direction, as illustrated, for example, in the American and Russian Revolution, the Age of Jackson, the English Revolution of 1688 or the English Reform Bill of 1832.

But which direction constitutes the wisest choice? Everyone works out some sort of an answer to this question, as life does not forever permit him the luxury of an "open mind." The question involves an ethical issue of first magnitude.

The issue stems from the fact that any change in the rules which all must observe involves some change in the way in which goods and services, rights and duties, privileges and responsibilities shall be apportioned. As a consequence, every policy (sovereign decision) is a judgment of equity: what rule will best serve the interests of all concerned. Vesting each with an equal voice (either his own or that of his delegate) in the sovereign role reflects into the rules that are finally made the greatest variation of different individual viewpoints. As a consequence, this practice is quite in line with the democratic goal of making the maximum possible use of divergent views and sentiments in determining the rules which all must observe. But does this make sense? Does it not sacrifice qualitatively superior views to a low-grade common denominator of every Tom,

Dick, and Harry? Is the view of any ordinary individual on the equitability of a school-bond proposal, for example, on the same plane with that of a professional educator?

Whether the general interest is better served by the tendency toward a more equal or unequal sharing of the sovereign role thus turns on whether each man is the equal of any other as a judge of equity—fair play.

4. *Assumption that men are unequal as judges of equity as the basis of all aristocratic and dictatorial reasoning:* The cornerstone of authoritorian reasoning is the premise that "the few" are superior to "the many" in the capacity to judge what rules (policies) best serve the interests of all concerned. Therefore they are endowed "by nature and nature's God" with a moral right to do so. Those who hold this view contend that any action tending to give an equal voice to each in the sovereign role wrongs the superior individuals by denying them the role most suited to their abilities; and it wrongs the inferior by saddling them with responsibilities for which nature never intended them and for which no educational system can prepare them. It is, in fact, the most pernicious of all injustices, since it violates the most fundamental of all rules: the natural inequality of men as a judge of equity.

As a consequence, the ideal commonwealths, stemming from this aristocratic premise, have always been envisaged as coming to pass when some exceptionally superior class or individual gained a complete monopoly of the sovereign role. Plato is the classical example. Appalled by the democracy that condemned Socrates to the hemlock, he sketched with consummate art a social order that would give to each "his due"—a role in life most suitable to his capacities. Asked his opinion on its chances of adoption, he replied:

> Until philosophers are kings, or kings and princes of this world have the spirit and power of philosophy, and political greatness and wisdom meet in one, and those commoner natures who pursue either to the exclusion of the other are compelled to stand aside, cities will never have rest from their evils—no, nor the human race, as I believe—and then only will this our State have a possibility of life and behold the light of day.[1]

Unless this logic of inequality can be shown to be fallacious, one may "feel" that each should share equally in the ultimate power to formulate the policies which all must observe, but these may be mere feelings that cannot be supported by reason. Without the support of reason as well as "feelings of the heart," no creed of life can weather the storms.

5. *Necessity of choosing ends as showing the equality of men as a judge of equity:* A dictatorship of the elite would be entirely rational under either of two conditions. First, this would be the case if some specifiable aim, such as health, were prized above all else. Under this circumstance, the policy problems would simply be questions of which means could accomplish the accepted end with the least effort. Men are obviously unequal as judges of the most efficient ways of accomplishing the same purpose. Therefore, if health were prized above all else, the only intelligent form of society would be a dictatorship of physicians. And the same principle applies to any other end.

The fact is, however, that the rule (policy) making process is as much a matter of determining what *ends* shall be chosen, in the light of *given means* as it is of determining what *means* shall be chosen in the light of *given ends*. Life is an endless sequence of situations requiring decisions between incompatible ends—as when workmen cannot secure both health-care and adequate shelter for their families, when scholars cannot pursue their studies properly and at the same time make a living, and when farmers cannot have a "fair price" for their produce and also grow whatever they want in any amount they wish.

Second, even though policymaking is a process of selecting among alternative ends in the light of given means, an aristocracy of the elite would still be justifiable if there were a "law" by which the welfare consequences (satisfactions) of different policy (rule) choices could be compared (measured). The idea of the inequality of men as a judge of equity is inseparable from a "science" of welfare—the "Good" as the Greeks called it. Plato well recognized that his whole inequalitarian viewpoint would fall to the ground if there were no possibility of such a science. Unable to set forth its nature, his famous similies of the sun and of the line, and the allegory of the cave, are Hurculean efforts to leave the impression that a science of the Good is nonetheless actually possible.

Until very recently, the economist, upon discovering the law of diminishing marginal utility, felt he had made Plato's dream a reality. This law was believed to provide an objective standard for deciding what ways of distributing the nation's goods and services would yield the greatest total satisfaction for people as a whole. The law implies that the more one has of anything, say shoes, the less satisfaction he gets from additional units thereof. Assume that individuals have similar capacities for enjoying the "good things" of life. Then the satisfaction which a poor man can get from an additional dollar of income is greater than the discomfort which a rich man will feel from a dollar reduction in his larger income. Therefore, shifting a dollar from the rich to the poor adds to its want-satisfying power. Consequently,

> ... if we would maximize satisfaction from a given total social income (e.g., 300 billion dollars) the rational procedure is to equalize individual incomes.[2]

Were this true, the economist would be superior to everyone else as a judge of what policies are most equitable for all concerned.

On first sight the argument appears overwhelming. Who doesn't want everyone, including himself, to conform with "rational procedures?" Who would want policies deliberately aimed at reducing the want-satisfying power per dollar of national income?[3]

Yet, as Lionel Robins has pointed out, the argument is entirely specious.[4] For there is no means whatever by which even an expert can compare the magnitudes of the satisfactions (1) which a given action (e.g., high farm price supports) may produce in different persons, or (2) which alternative actions (e.g., going to a hospital or staying home in case of illness) may produce in the same person. Suppose the rich man says that an additional unit of income has greater want-satisfying power for him than it does for the poor man, whereas the poor man holds the opposite view. There can be no evidence that one is any more right or wrong than the other. If they disagree on which of them was the taller, they can settle the dispute by use of a yardstick. But there is no yardstick alongside which can be laid the satisfaction which a unit of income affords to

71

each. As a consequence, no one can be another's superior as a judge of whether a graduated income tax or a non-graduated poll tax is more equitable for all concerned. Therefore each deserves the opportunity for an equal voice in the sovereign process of determining which of these alternatives all must follow. The same principle applies to any other issue in which personal satisfactions and preferences are involved.

As between conflicting lines of conduct (ends), there is no way of judging which alternative is most equitable for all concerned except through balancing the want-satisfying results of each alternative against those of other alternatives which must be foregone if one is chosen. But no man can compare the magnitudes of the want-satisfying outcomes of such alternatives except as they register themselves in his own person. And there is no means by which anyone can show that his comparisons are superior to those of any other. Each may poke fun at the other. But that's all. None can show he is a better judge than others of which rule is most equitable for all concerned; nor, can anyone indicate which rule should be adopted. Here, the clodhopper, the technician, the philosopher, and the prophet all stand on an equal footing, and each deserves the opportunity for an equal voice in deciding what rules all must observe.

Men differ without limit with respect to knowledge of the ways and means of reaching any accepted end. The physician is superior to Smith on how to repair Smith's health. But, since the cost of doing so may involve sacrificing adequate food and shelter for one's family, each person is a better judge than the physician of whether his health should be repaired at the expense of something else. The economist is superior to others as a judge, for example, on how the adoption of a social security program of $100 per month for each person over 50 years old would affect the use of income for other services such as public roads, schools, and prisons, or change the demand for luxuries and necessities. But the reason and conscience of the economist is no better than that of the hillbilly on whether such a policy would add to or detract from the greatest happiness of all concerned. Nature creates no specialist in deciding what is most equitable.

6. *Equality of men as a judge of equity implies majority control but freedom to dissent:* A number of reasons require majority control of the rule making process and yet permit minority dissent. First, after a certain point, life demands an end of deliberation on policy issues. But, as hung juries and split court decisions abundantly show, even the same information on alternative proposals does not elicit the same judgments by all parties on what should be done. Consequently, no human life is possible without some measure of coercion—the necessity of conforming to rules which might run contrary to one's best judgment. There are but two alternatives—coercion of the majority by the minority or vice versa. The first obviously includes a greater degree of coercion. Yet this might be the most sensible choice, if the few were superior to the many as a judge of equity. However, the equality of men in this respect disposes of this consideration. There is no way of determining whether the minority or majority view is most equitable. All that is certain is that some action is necessary and that unanimity of agreement is impossible. Majority

control is therefore preferable to minority control because it can secure necessary action with the least amount of coercion. Either view may fall short of justice in terms of an impartial judge. There is no way of knowing. But it is certain that one is less coercive than the other.

For two reasons this equality of men as judges of equity, which calls for majority rule, also requires the right of free dissent and criticism so far as the public safely can allow. First, like majority rule, free dissent minimizes the coercion involved in enforcing uniform rules. For the amount of coercion which one feels in having to comply with distasteful policies is obviously less if he is not forced to also silence his tongue.

Second, the opportunity for a minority dissent, even of one, is required for the longrun improvement of today's majority decisions. One man's judgment on what is equitable may be as acceptable as any other's in the historic future. Today's majority decisions are often the acceptance of yesterday's minority view. Within the limits of the public safety, the voice of each should therefore be entitled to the same chance of gaining acceptance in the future, irrespective of whether it concurs in or dissents from today's majority.

It should be emphasized that, because of the equality of men as a judge of equity, counting votes is clearly not a valid method of determining the "rightness" or "wrongness" of any view. It is merely a way of meeting the necessity of establishing operating rules through backing up *some* policy views with a preponderance of coercive power. How the votes are counted has nothing to do with whether the majority or the minority view is actually the most equitable. But it has everything to do with the extent to which brute power is required to meet the overshadowing necessity of order. That the "voice of the people is the voice of God" is thus merely a form of idolatry, as alien to the spirit of freedom and science as to theology.

7. *The aggressive aspect of the desire of each to be his own master:* The first premise, then, on which rests the whole edifice of democratic civilization, is that men are equal judges of fair play while differing almost without limit in their skills and their knowledge of the means for reaching whatever ends their affections may set upon. On this foundation rest the deserts of each man to the opportunity for an equal sharing of the sovereign role.

This equality is further required as a necessary protection against the tendency of each to achieve his freedom through domination instead of mutual consent. Four conditions underlie this tendency: (1) An imperial quality of the desire to be a free man; (2) the impossibility of freedom apart from the instrumental relationship of man to man; (3) the existence of intelligence as the instrument of domination as well as of mutual consent; (4) an imbalance in the tendency to use oneself as a means of furthering needs and aims of others and the counter tendency to use others as a means to one's own.

Inherent in the urge of each to be his own master is an imperial quality. No life-role is more attractive to men than that in which one pictures himself as standing on his own feet, beholden to none, the sovereign of his own soul, the monarch of all he surveys. How far short each of us falls from his ideal status! How different is anyone's actual behavior from what it would be if he had the power to translate into actual fact his own envisioned kingdom instead of having to bow a thousand times a day to the stern necessities of actual circumstances.

Being animated with this imperial vision of absolute freedom is the glory of the human animal, whence spring his finest achievements. But the same animation is also the source of his tragedies. How many "cattle kings" and "nesters" of our early West "died with their boots on" rather than bow before some real or fancied aggression upon the "God-given right" of each to be his own master. To be sure, those that went to "Boot Hill" are commonly remembered as renegades, but that is mainly because they were "slow on the draw." The same principle applies to the Ozark-Appalachian feuds of the old days as well as to the mightier struggles in the name of "national honor." No deed more soils the escutcheon of any people than that of the U.S. Army in 1836, pursuant to a fraudulent treaty, driving like sheep some 18,000 peaceful Cherokees from their homes in the Smokies across 1,500 miles of wilderness to the Indian Territory, 5,000 of them dying like flies along the way; all to the end that the "free settler" might have more room. At all levels of life, in one form or another, men are striving for power over each other, not because they are thieves and robbers in the usual sense, but because each is driven by an irrepressible urge to extend the metes and bounds within which he alone is sovereign.

But the coercive use of force does not stem solely from the imperial nature of each man's desire to be his own master. This could cause no harm were it not for the instrumental relationship of man to man—the fact that the means to each man's purpose are ultimately other men's effort. No life, free or otherwise, is possible outside this relationship. As a consequence, the practical objective of the impulse of each to be his own master is that of establishing rules by which he can gain the services of other men without becoming subservient to anyone.

While this instrumental relationship of man to man is a necessary condition for aggression, it is not a sufficient condition. For each may function as a means to the other's needs under rules which render men either (1) equally free agents, or (2) some subservient to others. In the first case, the rules arise from the fact that they are equally desired from the standpoints of all concerned, whereas in the second case they arise from superior power.

Reason "cuts no ice" either way. It may function actually as an instrument of domination or mutual consent, being only one's ability to formulate common rules by reacting to his own role from the standpoint of himself and the role of others. In the cop and thief relationship, for example, each party governs his behavior toward the other by placing himself in the other's shoes. But each acts in this manner only as a means of subjugating the other to his own particular set of rules. No saint excelled the dictator in the ability to govern his behavior toward others by taking the attitude of the other. Behavior is equally "rational" in both cases. Only the ends are different. The saint acts as he does because he prizes that act which is equally desirable from the standpoint of himself in either the other's shoes or his own. The like is not true of the dictator. He does unto others as he expects them to do unto him, except that he does it first.

The final condition, then, for the aggressive nature of the desire of each to be his own master stems from two counter tendencies: (1) the inclination to use one's self as a means for furthering the needs and aims of others, and (2) the opposite inclination to use others as a mere means for satisfying his own desires.

If these tendencies were habitually of equal vivacity and force, there could be no aggression. Each individual then could not do otherwise than seek his own freedom under rules which he desired with equal force from the standpoint of both himself and others. Under this condition, each would fully achieve his desire for absolute freedom—doing exactly as he chooses without any external blocking. And no police or jails would be required. As David Hume so lucidly said:

> ... suppose, that ... the mind is so enlarged, and so replete with friendship and generosity, that every man ... feels no more concern for his own interest than for that of his fellows; it seems evident, that the use of justice would ... be suspended ... Why should I bind another, by a deed or promise, to do me any good office, when I know that he is already prompted, by the strongest inclination, to seek my happiness, and would, of himself, perform the desired service; except the hurt, he thereby receives, be greater than the benefit accruing to me? In which case, he knows, that, from my innate humanity and friendship, I should be the first to oppose myself to his imprudent generosity. Why raise land-marks between my neighbour's field and mine, when my heart has made no division between our interests; but shares all his joys and sorrows with the same force and vivacity as if originally my own? Every man, upon this supposition, being a second self to another, would trust all his interests to the discretion of every man; without jealousy, without partition, without distinction. And the whole human race would form only one family; where all would lie in common, and be used freely, without regard to property; but cautiously too, with as entire regard to the necessities of each individual, as if our own interests were most intimately concerned.[5]

As shown by the sacrificial deeds of all history, the spontaneous tendency to use one's self as a means to the needs and aims of others is often stronger than the counter tendency. But such cases are sporadic. As a rule the reverse is true, especially in group relationships. No one ever heard of labor or management affirming the other's needs and interest with the same vividness and force that it does its own. The same applies to other groups.

As a consequence, the desire of each to be the master of his own behavior is always tending to achieve its goal through domination instead of mutual consent and actually does so unless it is blocked by counter power. The strong do what they will and the weak suffer what they must.

8. *Equalization of power as a necessary condition of freedom:* However much a culture may be committed to the spirit of freedom, its chief problem is that of preventing this spirit from degenerating into some form of dictatorship. In some measure, this danger may be counteracted by exhortation—vividly portraying the spirit of fair play, mutual respect in spite of differences, live and let live. But chief reliance must be placed in external means—in procedures which increasingly equalize the final power of each to reject the policy (rule) proposals of any other. This does not, of course, remove the ultimate seat of the trouble. That each man is *potentially* a dictator is not wiped out by any mechanical equilibrium of power. Nor can one entirely purge himself of his

dictatorial tendencies. But others can and do check them in so far as each is provided an equal opportunity or power to block the proposal of any other. Under this condition, individuals (or groups) can agree to join in working out common rules which are at least acceptable from the standpoints of all concerned, even though they fall short of each man's view of what is best. No one can then feel that he is being forced to bow to the *superior* power of any other.

Complete equality of power is unattainable; neither ideal democracy nor ideal dictatorship is achievable in fact. What counts is the direction in which we are tending in our policy choices. Sanction of the equalitarian tendency ultimately rests on the fact that (1) it recognizes the equality of men as judges of equity, and (2) it is necessary as a protection of each against the other's inclination to realize his freedom through domination.

9. *Ideologies as smoke-screens of aggression:* In the celebrated words of David Hume, "reason is and ought to be a slave of the passions." This was implicit in the previous observation that intelligence may function with the same effectiveness in achieving one's freedom through either domination or mutual consent. As stated there, if one tended to affirm the needs and aims of others with the same vividness and force that he affirms his own, he would always function as the agent of an impartial equity. Were the "passions" of this nature, bias and coercion would be impossible.

As matters stand, however, the fundamental passion involved is not mutual love but aggression, since the tendency to use one's self as a means to other men's purposes is usually weaker than the opposite tendency. To be most efficient, this aggressive attitude must conceal itself, even from one's own eyes. The best concealment is to mask itself as a devoted agent of the interest of all concerned.

With the privileged classes the deception assumes the form of a "scientific" denial of the equality of each as a judge of equity, along with the correlative denial of the opportunity of each to the same voice (power) in the sovereign role. For example, nearly 2,400 years ago Aristotle, "The master of all them that know," declared that: "From the hour of their birth, some are marked out for subjection, others for rule ... The lower sort are by nature slaves, and it is better ... that they should be under the rule of a master. For he, ... who participates in the rational principle" (managerial ability) only enough to "apprehend" announced goals and lines of action but not to articulate them in the first place, "is a slave by nature."[6]

Aristotle's view might be excused because of its antiquity except that the same viewpoint in slightly different words is quite modern. For example, Darlington, an eminent English biologist, only recently laid down the proposition that the notion of equality is one of the three great illusions promoted by the great Semitic religions. Get rid of this illusion, and "the fundamental problem of human government ... can be treated by exact biological methods."[7]

This is, of course, a sheer deception. For, as previously shown, the only way in which anyone can reach a final judgment on the equity of alternative

76

policies is to weigh the prospective satisfactions of each alternative against the satisfactions of those alternatives which must be foregone. As a consequence, it is nonsense to assert that A is superior to B in knowing how these relative weights register themselves in B.

But exposure is never entirely successful in routing this deception. Trapped at one point, it simply remasks itself in a different dress from age to age.

Within the underprivileged classes, the coverup may be even more deceptive. For here the striving of each for his own freedom is not simply a struggle for a more equal voice in the sovereign role. It also includes the domineering animation of the "under-dog" to convert himself into a "top-dog" while masquerading as the maligned and suffering agent of equal opportunity for all and special privileges to none.

When thus concealed the aggressive attitude is much harder to unmask than when hiding behind the aristocratic ideology. The logical armor of equal opportunity is more puncture-proof because it is reinforced by man's conscience. For the tendency to affirm the needs of others may be assumed to be strong enough in all parties to at least endow them with a conscience. Persons do place themselves in the roles of others to the point of at least recognizing and having some sympathy for impartial justice. By and large, then, the conscience of all classes is somewhat on the side of the underprivileged.

It does not follow, however, that the conscience of the "oppressed" includes any greater love for an impartial justice (fair play) than does that of the oppressors. If this were true, a point would be reached in the under dog's struggle for "equality of power and privilege" at which he would cease his demands for additional power. But this seldom, if ever, happens. It is common knowledge, for example, that the most tyrannical landlord is often an ex-sharecropper and the most insufferable boss is often a "self-made man." While this principle usually holds for individuals, it applies almost without exception to group relationships. All history shows that the "lower classes" have always used the democratic ideal of an equal voice in the rule (policy) making process as a means of toppling their superiors from power, only to then turn around and oppose the extension of the same equality of those below. Again with great success, labor has raised itself to a position of immense power by declaring that it only seeks equal bargaining power with management. And, in doing this, labor has served the cause of justice. Yet the fact remains that there is little, if any, evidence that labor as a whole will ever reach a time when it will not use the ideal of "equal bargaining of power" as a justification for its desire for additional increments of power.

Every class thus tends to achieve its freedom through domination instead of mutual consent. Fidelity to the ideal of equal freedom for all is served by refraining from being "taken in" by any aristocratic or dictatorial line of reasoning, and it is also best served by being forever mindful of the poignant words of Marie Antoinette to the sea of under-privileged faces staring up at her from around the guillotine: "Liberty, liberty, how many crimes are committed in thy fair name." For the most pernicious error into which the devotees of the democratic ideal may fall is the belief that some particular class, by virtue of its peculiar experience, aptitudes or social station, is more the agent of the democratic ideal than any other.

Equal Opportunity to Perform Any Social Role

1. *Social roles as professional careers:* In their sovereign role, people (directly or through their representatives) lay down the rules which all must observe; but they make a living in their social roles. As participants in the sovereign role, they are citizens; but as agents of social roles they are farmers, masons, teachers, artists, entertainers, managers, physicians, lawyers, and the like. As citizens they are "generalists," passing judgment on what policies are most desirable for all. But in their social roles they are specialists, producing some particular good and service for men at large in exchange for a corresponding return of goods and services (income).

2. *Legal (conventional) equality and limited inequalities of income as the conditions of equal opportunities:* Being one's own master does not merely consist of the desire to perform a role of his choosing, but also in the power (opportunity) to do so. Such power requires two outside conditions which society may or may not make increasingly available to all alike.

The first might be called conventional equality of opportunity. This can be defined only negatively as not requiring for employments personal character- istics which add nothing to one's role performance and which cannot be altered by the individual. The color of a singer's skin, for example, adds nothing to the quality of his song; nor is there anything he can do to change his color. The entire system of "racial segregation" is a striking example of conventional inequality of opportunity. The second condition of equal opportunity is the limiting of extreme income inequalities.

Individual abilities are not a fixed but a changing datum, falling into three phases: (1) a long developmental period for bringing capacities to a point of actual usefulness, (2) an employable period for turning them into goods and services that further the aims of men at large, and (3) a retirement period after one's employable powers are expended. At every point income (goods and services) is necessary to the next step. Without it one is powerless; he is a slave and not a free man, whatever his legal status.

Obviously the Nation's stock of goods and services from its various employments may be so distributed that the share of some is far more than enough to meet the essential requirements of any useful role they may seek, while that of others falls far short of this point. Such distribution is incompatible with the idea that each should have an equal chance to live a life in line with his choice and capabilities. The pattern of income shares needed for this purpose cannot be stated with precision. Nor is the lack of such precision a stumbling block to improvement as long as the extremes are big enough to be perfectly obvious, which has always been the case. It is fantastic to assume, for example, that the prevailing pattern of income shares provides the sons of the Delta field hands and the sons of the rich with a similar chance to choose any career in keeping with their capabilities. The practical question is the extent to which equal opportunity is actually wanted.

3. *Equality of opportunity as incompatible with both equality of income and extreme income inequalities:* The acorn and the mustard seed have an equal chance to fulfill their life careers if each is provided with enough "goods and services" to enable it to be the kind of a plant it is capable of being. But their needs differ; therefore, correspondingly different quantities (as well as kinds) of goods are required to give each as good a change as the other to achieve its life potential. A sure way of giving them unequal opportunities would be to equalize their share of nutrients and other goods.

The same principle applies to persons. Individuals are similar but not identical. There are several million farmers in America but they do not follow this mode of life in an identical manner. All of them are one kind and yet each *as farmer* is unique, since no two are alike in their farming abilities, aptitudes, and interests. The same income will not provide them with an equally good chance of becoming the kind of farmer that each is most capable of being, and which gives him the most satisfaction.

In economic terms, equality of opportunity among individuals is an equivalence between the capacities of each individual and the income required for their fulfillment. But the quantity of income which satisfies this equation varies among individuals in line with the unique capacities of each. Both equalization of incomes and extreme inequalities of income are incompatible with the ideal of equal opportunity for all. In either case the income of goods and services to some is below what is actually required to enable them to follow the role of their choice and capabilities while that of others is above this point.

4. *Incompatibility between the ideal of equal opportunity and "free" market mechanism as an income distributor:* There is a profound incompatibility between this democratic ideal of equal opportunity and the "free" market mechanism as the sole distributor of the national income. For it is notorious that market transactions place no floor beneath which the income of anyone may not fall and no ceiling above which it may not rise.

In recognition of this incompatibility, the American people as a whole have increasingly resorted to political action as a means of providing individuals with more nearly equal opportunities by taking some income from those to whom the market gives much and reapportioning it among those to whom the market gives relatively little. A few examples of such action are: the homestead laws of the last century, establishment of publicly supported schools, regulation of public utilities, publicly supported research and extension services to farmers, price supports for farm products, the "school lunch" program, minimum wage laws, progressive income tax schedules, social security, unemployment insurance, employer liability insurance, and publicly supported health programs.

5. *Characterological basis of equality and inequality of opportunity to any social role:* Pigs and humans are alike filled with desires for want-satisfying goods. But that pig A and pig B should have the same chance at the feed-trough is presumably not an object which either regards as a "want-satisfying good". Each simply wants the whole trough. For the human animal, however, the *same*

chance of each at the same objects is one of his most prized goods. Why? Apparently because he has a self. A self is the kind of entity that places itself in different skins, as it were, and in some degree every self desires the same treatment from every other individual. Let anyone with a white skin, for example, imagine himself as in a black skin and then compare his chances of making his way in the world in each skin. He finds many doors of opportunity (such as the school or job he seeks), which are opened wide to him when he knocks in the white skin, are slammed on him when he knocks in the black skin. Yet, there may be exactly the same abilities, the same dreams and the same weaknesses in both skins. It is therefore inconceivable that he can desire that the same doors be opened to him in the one case but slammed on him in the other.

But the fact remains that any effort to reapportion the prevailing pattern of rights and privileges in line with a more equal opportunity for all meets with powerful resistance. And this opposition is seldom, if ever, the blind rage of a pig being forced from his trough. On the contrary, it abounds in the wholesome indignation of a righteous man being robbed of his just deserts. Inequality of opportunity thus appears to rest on characterological foundation as solid as the ideal of equal opportunity.

Evidently this foundation is a result of the disproportionate strengths of the tendencies (1) to use other men as a means to one's own purposes, and (2) to use one's self as a means to the aims and needs of others. There are situations, particularly in family life and friendships, in which the second of these is even stronger than the first. In such cases, there is never a conflict over how goods shall be distributed so that each shall have as good a chance as the other for realizing his personal goals. The spirit of the individual in this circumstance is to under-rate his own deserts and over-rate those of others.

In general, however, the first tendency is stronger than the second. There is no significant exception to this rule in group relationships. Therefore, however great the power and privilege of some may be, they usually feel that the value of their services to the public is less than their rewards; that they deserve more than they get and would be robbed if they got less. Therefore, any move toward a more equal distribution of income is opposed as an attempt to reward the undeserving by penalizing the meritorious. So potent is this bias that history offers no significant instance in which those of superior power and privilege have ever yielded before mere appeals to reason. They abdicate only before the threat of counter power.

6. *Ideological obstacles to a more equitable distribution of power and privilege:* This power struggle is but a surface indication of a more fundamental ideological struggle—competing views of what is fair and reasonable for all concerned. While superior power never yields to persuasion as such, it usually cannot retain its position unless it is able to "prove" that its privileges are justified by superior merit; otherwise its mass support slips to the opposition. Three such "proofs" have acted as important brakes on the trend toward more nearly equal opportunities.

a. Underprivileged unable to render same service as privileged even if given the same opportunity: In the first "proof" of this contention the fact is conveniently overlooked that capacities for performing especially useful or meritorous functions are themselves in great measure developed by the educational advantages which privilege buys and the opportunity for exercising authority which inheres in power. The superior abilities, arising from such superior opportunities, are then easily imputed to innate endowments. These endowments are then taken as *prima facie* evidence that the underprivileged "would not have the same capacity for rendering the same service if given the same opportunity." In this way reason is forced to "deny the oppressed classes every opportunity for the cultivation of innate capacities and then to accuse them of lacking what they have been denied the right to acquire."[8]

This particular defense of inequality of opportunity was used with powerful effect against the effort in 19th century England to establish State-supported schools. For example, when a bill for this purpose was introduced in Parliament in 1807, a Mr. Giddy, afterwards President of the Royal Society, objected as follows:

> However specious in theory the project might be of giving education to the laboring classes of the poor, it would be prejudical to their morals and happiness; it would teach them to despise the lot in life instead of making them good servants in agriculture and other laborious employment; instead of teaching them subordination it would render them fractious and refractory as was evident in the manufacturing countries; it would enable them to read seditious pamphlets, various books and publications against Christianity; it would render them insolent to their superiors and in a few years the legislature would find it necessary to direct the strong arm of power against them.[9]

John Randolph of Virginia was much more direct:

> Among the strange notions which have been broached since I have been in the political theatre, there is one which has lately seized the minds of men, that all things must be done for them by the Government, and that they are to do nothing for themselves ... A more pernicious notion cannot prevail. Look at that ragged fellow staggering from the whiskey shop, and see that slattern who has gone there to reclaim him? Where are their children? Running about ragged, idle, ignorant, fit candidates for the penitentiary. Why is all this so? Ask the man and he will tell you, "Oh, the Government has undertaken to educate our children for us."[10]

b. *Superior power and privilege as necessary to peace and order:* A second ideological road block against greater equality of opportunity is the general identification, by dominant groups, of peace and order with the particular social order of which they are currently the beneficiaries. Members of these groups appoint themselves as the apostles of peace and order while imputing "subversive" intentions to those seeking any change. This is an especially potent means of fostering otherwise unjustifiable inequalities of opportunity. For in every society there is a strong desire for harmony and the avoidance of strife. Those agitating for the elimination of specific inequities are thus placed at the normal disadvantage of imperiling the peace—"stirring up class against class." For example, concerning the pending Supreme Court decision on the constitutionality of the segregated school system, Governor Talmadge of

Georgia observed that it would be "a step toward national suicide." In the same vein, the *New York Tribune* is commenting on the defeat of Bryan in 1896 said,

> The wicked rattle-pated boy ... was only a puppet in the blood-imbrued hands of Altgeld, the anarchist, and Debs, the revolutionist, and other desperadoes of that stripe. But he was a willing pupil, Bryan was, willing and eager.[11]

History is replete with this tendency of the "privileged" to place the advancing classes under the opprobrium of anarchy and revolution.

c. *The creed of enterprise and equality of opportunity:* In some ways the historic creed of enterprise has been a powerful foe of inequality of opportunity, but its ally in other ways.

(1) *Opposed to conventional (legal) inequalities:* This creed has always stood like a rock against conventional inequalities. It insists that no individual shall be barred from any calling because of such personal traits as conditions of birth, color, or nationality over which he has no control and which contribute nothing to nor detract from the service of the role he seeks. The only question is: "Can he do the job?" If he can, he should have the same chance as anyone else, whatever his family tree, race, or color. In this respect, both the desire for freedom and the creed of enterprise demand that the door of opportunity be opened to all alike.

(2) *Modern version of creed of enterprise implies extreme income inequalities:* Yet there is a difference between the desire for freedom and the enterprise creed. For the creed rests on premises which largely overlook the truth that serviceable abilities are themselves the product of income so that actual equality of opportunity is impossible without severe political limitations on the extreme income inequalities which are otherwise generated by the "free" market process.

The premises are essentially these: All income is ultimately the product of individual effort. Each individual (or family) is entitled to the full product of his effort. But nature has fixed no point below which it does not permit individual abilities to fall, and no limit above which it does not permit them to rise. Therefore, simple justice requires a distribution system which imposes no manmade limitation on income inequalities. The "free" market meets these requirements. For after any exchange transaction, each party has the same amount of wealth (using the dollar as a measuring rod) as before; only the quality (form) of his possessions has changed. Moreover, this exchange process fixes no ceiling above which anyone's income may rise and no floor below which it may fall. "We advocate nothing," said Cobden, "but what is agreeable to the highest behests of Christianity—to buy in the cheapest markets and sell in the dearest." Therefore, so the argument goes, any state-made limitation of market income inequalities is coercive and unjust, as it is a use of police power to reward the undeserving by robbing the enterprising of their just deserts.

The literature of the last 300 years is replete with this line of reasoning. The following are typical. Said William Graham Sumner in 1884:

> ... God and Nature have ordained the chances and conditions of life on earth once and for all. The case cannot be reopened. We cannot get a revision of the ... rules of right living ... They consist in labor and self-denial repeated

over and over again in learning and doing . . . class distinctions simply result from the different degrees of success with which men have availed themselves of the chances which were presented to them . . . if there be liberty, some will profit by the chances eagerly and some will neglect them altogether. Therefore, the greater the chances the more unequal will be the fortunes of these two sorts of men. So it ought to be, in all justice and right reason. The yearning after equality is the offspring of envy and covetousness, and there is no possible plan for satisfying that yearning which can do aught else than rob A to give to B; consequently all such plans nourish some of the meanest vices of human nature, waste capital, and overthrow civilization.[12]

Though these vigorous words were penned 70 years ago, they were reaffirmed with equal vigor in the recent verdict on the central drift of modern times by The Economic Principles Planning Commission of the National Association of Manufacturers. The Commission said:

The government has adopted the role of "welfare state: and declared its will to attain the "four freedoms," "full employment," and other grandiose objectives. This it proposes to do largely by redistributing the wealth and the income of its people. By heavily progressive taxation it deprives its successful citizens of their product and gives it to the less successful; thus it penalizes industry, thrift, competence, and efficiency, and subsidizes the idle, spend-thrift, incompetent, and inefficient. By despoiling the thrift it dries up the source of capital, reduces investment and creation of jobs, slows down industrial progress, and prevents society from attaining its highest level of consumption.[13]

In addition to opposing political interference with market distributions of income on grounds of "despoiling the thrifty" of their deserts, this passage also implicitly opposes such interference by claiming it is a cause of unemployment. For "it dries up the source of capital, reduces investment and the creation of jobs."

The creed is also used in behalf of a substantial margin of unemployment. Probably no one has expressed this viewpoint with such candor as R. I. Nowell of the Equitable Life Insurance Society of the United States. Said he:

How about . . . full employment at high wages? . . . the leftist fringe insist that we must have full employment at high wages so as to maintain a high level of business activity, high purchasing power and high prices. I submit that full employment at high wages in a private enterprise economy is undesirable and self-destroying. Although some may term this position anti-social, I fully believe it is undesirable to have this brand of full employment if we are to continue our democracy in this country . . .

When jobs are so plentiful that one can quit a job today and get another as good or better tomorrow, there is an insidious loss of the desire to do good work . . . Our prevailing unemployment benefits have been pegged so high that much of the incentive to do satisfactory work and to find and keep private employment has for many people been destroyed . . . Our standards of destitution have become too high for the good of our people.[14]

In other words, according to this line of reasoning, we are forced to choose between democracy and a partial employment economy, on the one hand, and dictatorship and full employment, on the other hand, since having both full employment and democracy is impossible. For, according to this view, people will play no useful role in life unless forced to do so. Only two forms of coercion are available for this purpose: the spectre of starvation, inherent in a partial employment economy, and physical duress inherent in a police state. Hence, if we wish to have a democracy, we must have a substantial margin of unemployment so that the fear of starvation may be real enough to scare most people into doing a day's work for a day's pay. Conversely, if we choose to have a full employment economy, then we must replace democracy with dictatorship so that fear of the jail may replace starvation as a means of inducing everyone to do a day's work for a day's pay. Therefore, since we prize freedom above all else, we will take due care not to limit inequality of opportunity to a point where "our standards of destitution are too high for the good of our people."

(3) *Enterprise Creed as involving class differences in moral excellencies:* As expressed in the above passages, the enterprise creed reflects profound class distinctions with respect to certain moral excellencies. For the passages implicitly assert that all income ultimately arises from two characterological traits: (1) "industry"—the preference for work instead of leisure, and (2) "thrift"—the preference for spending less than one earns. Nature divides mankind into two broad classes. First are the relative "few" who seek, not wealth for its own sake, but the fulfillment of their creative powers through industry and thrift. Second, are the "many" who seek leisure instead of industry and spending instead of saving. What they most want is a life of unlimited consumption and exemption from useful effort.

As a consequence, says this theory, the "few" seek only to earn what they get and get what they earn. Accordingly, they are the kind in whom the tendency to use others as a means and the counter tendency to use themselves as a means to other life are of equal strength. The reverse is true of the "many." What they most want is not the income they deserve, but simply an income. By nature, they are aggressors, preferring a living through plunder if they have the power to do.

These are the underlying implications of each of the three passages cited above.

(4) *Older version of creed implies unequal sharing of the sovereign role:* In these explicit terms, the enterprise creed is as incompatible with the opportunity of each to the same voice in the sovereign role as it is with political limitation of extreme inequalities of incomes generated by the market process.

For the most part, this first incompatibility has not been emphasized since the Age of Jackson when the term "democracy" first became respectable. Since then no one can get a hearing if he is not a "believer" in the Jeffersonian gospel of the "people" as the best custodians of their liberties. The enterprise "line" since then has been to protect extreme inequalities from political limitation on the ground that such action can only lead to the defeat of the majority will by bureaucratic planners.

The Founding Fathers, however, had no confidence in the security of liberty under this approach. Believing that what the "many" most wanted was an income and exemption from useful effort, they clearly saw that majority control of the policymaking process could ultimately have no other objective than the plundering of the few by the many. The ideal limit of such aggression would be the equalization of all incomes. The reasoning of John Adams on this point is classic. He wrote:

> There is in every nation and people under heaven a large proportion of persons who take no rational and prudent precautions to preserve what they have, much less to acquire more. Indolence is the natural character to such a degree that nothing but the necessities of hunger, thirst, and other wants equally pressing can stimulate him to action. As a consequence, We may appeal to every page in history we have hitherto turned over, for proofs irrefragable that the people, when they have been unchecked, have been . . . unjust, tyrannical, brutal, barbarous, and cruel . . . Therefore, if each were provided the opportunity for an equal voice in the sovereign role the time would not be long before . . . pretexts (would) be invented by degrees to countenance the majority in dividing all property among them, or at least, sharing it equally with its present possessors. Debts would be abolished first; taxes laid heavy on the rich, and not at all on the other; and at last a downright equal division of every thing be demanded, and voted. . . . the idle, the vicious, and the intemperate, would rush into the utmost extravagance of debauchery, sell and spend all their share, and then demand a new division of those who purchased from them.[15]

But this identification of the objective of majority rule as the plunder of the few by the many (stopping only with the complete equalization of all incomes) is also a denial of the similar ability on the part of different individuals or classes to pass judgment on what rules are most equitable for all concerned, which is the cornerstone of the democratic edifice. For the equality of classes as a judge of equity can be maintained only: (1) if no class seeks to better itself at the expense of another class, or (2) if each class seeks to benefit itself at the expense of other classes in approximately the same degree. Under either of these circumstances, counting noses is not a method of determining the "rightness" or "wrongness" of any policy. It is solely a method of backing some viewpoint with enough force to meet the necessity for action. As a consequence, majority control is preferable to minority control, since it meets the necessity of conformity with less coercion.

But this reasoning is obviously incompatible with the idea that what the "have-nots" most want is to get power as a means of exploiting the "haves." In contrast the "haves" seek such power only as a means of enforcing justice— giving to each the equivalent of his contribution. Because of this difference in moral animations the latter are obviously superior to the former as a judge of what policies are most equitable. Deciding policy issues on the basis of a majority of noses, regardless of class, is the lesser part of wisdom because the equal freedom and justice to all depends on *whose* noses are counted.

For reasons already stated, modern exponents of the enterprise creed, such as those previously cited, side-step its clear political implications. The like was not true of the founding fathers. The words of John Adams are again typical:

> . . . men in general, in every society, who are wholly destitute of property, are also too little acquainted with public affairs to form a right judgment, and too dependent upon other men to have a will of their own . . . very few men who have no property, have any judgment of their own. They talk and vote as they are directed by some man of property, who has attached their minds to his interest . . .[16]

Therefore, liberty under rules which are most equitable for all is possible only through limiting the opportunity for a voice in the sovereign role to the relative few with high incomes. Hamilton's words are classic:

> All communities divide themselves into the few and the many. The first are the rich and the well born, the other the mass of the people . . . The people are turbulent and changing; they seldom judge or determine right.[17]

High income or property qualifications as a condition for franchise is, of course, the most direct means of precluding popular control of the governing process. Until late in the 19th century, this device was employed in England, where the middle class first used the concept of popular sovereignty in justifying their revolutionary ousting of the Stuarts and then refused to share such sovereignty with the lower class. But this deterrent to popular rule was wiped out in America at an early date by (1) the availability of cheap land, and (2) the fact that the Revolutionary zeal had greatly lowered the property requirements for voting in most of the colonies.[18]

The remarkable genius of the Founding Fathers lay in their capacity for devising a system of constitutional powers which they felt would prevent the capture of the Government by popular majorities despite the fact that the right to vote was widespread among all economic classes. Their organizing concept was called the principle of checks and balances—a principle which could be carried to the point of setting up a virtual dictatorship without placing the slightest restriction on the voting privilege. Hamilton possessed a keen grasp of this fact as shown in his use of the checks and balances doctrine to justify his idea that the President should hold office for life and have absolute veto power over all acts of Congress.

His colleagues rejected such extremes. But all used the principle of checks and balances to block popular control of the Government in three main ways. First, such control was thwarted by the fact that no two of the leading branches of the Government derive from the same source. The House of Representatives stems from the mass of the people. The Senate was elected by the legislatures of the States which almost uniformly had relatively high property qualifications for holding State offices. The President was to be chosen by electors selected by State Legislatures—an authority one degree removed from the voters at large. The judiciary was to be chosen by the President and the Senate, both removed from direct popular control and holding longer terms than the House.

Second, a sharp difference was made in the terms of the various branches of Government. The House of Representatives is chosen for 2 years; the Senators for 6 years, and the President for 4 years. The intention was to prevent majority opinion from capturing control of the whole Government at any particular election. Finally, majority opinion was subject to a further check in that measures agreed upon by either house can be rejected by the other, and those of the whole Congress in turn can be vetoed by the President.

Throughout this hierarchy of checks, the principle of popular sovereignty is never violated. For at no point is there a single power which is not ultimately derived from "the consent of the governed." The lower House is elected by a majority vote of the people. At the other extreme is the court whose Justices are appointed by the President who in turn is appointed by the electors who in turn are appointed by the State Legislatures who in turn are finally elected by the majority of the voters. Yet the Founding Fathers felt that majority control was so remote and indirect that the agents of Government would be free to act without fear of popular distempers. Their complacency rested, of course, on the fallacious assumption that such a system of checks and balances would preclude the rise of party Government.

(5) *The creed as converting a general trait of life into class distinctions:* As previously noted, a general trait of any individual or class is the fact that its tendency to use other men as a means to its own ends is substantially stronger than the opposite tendency. Consequently, each individual or class is something of a power hog, as he is always seeking more than his services deserve, and getting it if he has enough power to do so.

The imbalance of these tendencies as such is thus not confined to a particular class. It is common to any group: high income as well as low, labor as well as management, farmers as well as nonfarmers. There is truth in the proposition that the "have-nots" seek to "capture" the Government as a means of extracting more from the "haves" than their deserts. It cannot be said that they merely seek to limit unequal shares of the Nation's goods and services to a point where each has as good a chance as another to any role of his choice and capabilities. But the same is just as true of the "haves."

With respect to this aggressive attitude, mankind does not "divide between the few and the many . . . the rich and the well born and the great mass of the people." The contrary view simply imputed to a particular class—"the many"—an aggressive attitude which in fact is common to all. In this way the historic creed of enterprise may easily become an ideological smoke screen for exploitation of the "many" by the "few." It overlooks the fact that the more power (political or economic) any class captures the more it will increase its share of the Nation's goods and services. It would be startling for any class to say it deserves less than what it has power to get. This is as true of Hamilton's "rich and well born" as any other class.

As a consequence, at least two conditions are required for approximating a distribution of goods and services which is more in line with equal opportunity than the market process would otherwise provide. First, there must be a government with enough constitutional power to counteract the will of any class in the name of what it deems best for all concerned. Second, this power must be subject to capture by rival political parties in a successful contest for the majority consent. Only that party can capture the government which gravitates to policy commitments which are most nearly acceptable from the standpoints of all concerned.

(6) *The enterprise creed as indispensable aid in forming the Constitution:* The Founding Fathers overlooked this second political condition for approximating equality of opportunity; and understandably so, because they feel a situation in which even the first condition was absent. The Continental Congress was not a government but a debating society. It could contract debts but it had no power to collect revenues to pay them. It could declare war but

could not raise an army. It could not regulate interstate commerce though commerce and trade depended on such control. It could not determine a common currency though commerce was hamstrung without it. Power for these purposes was scattered among the State Legislatures which in turn had been captured by the "free-holders" and small shopkeepers.

Moreover, the "ideal of popular sovereignty" was about all the democratic ideal amounted to in those days. This idea had been a powerful weapon in striking down the "monarchical principle," to use Thomas Paine's expression. But it was virtually useless as a guide in replacing the "monarchy of George the Third" with some other form of central authority superior to any particular individual or class. The mere existence of such power is, of course, no assurance that it will be used for apportioning the Nation's goods and services to the end that the opportunity of any individual or class is as good as that of any other for carrying out its chosen role in life. But certainly any approximation of this end is impossible in the absence of such a power. Its creation required the inspiration of some other ideology than that of popular sovereignty. This inspiration was provided in great measure, by the creed of enterprise. Given the oppressive disorder that inevitably stems from the absence of a strong central authority, few ideologies can so inspire the creation of the requisite power for establishing order as the idea that mankind divided into (1) the industrious few, who seek only a government which will protect them in their right to the "full product of their hands," and (2) the indolent many who only seek political power to improve their ease and comfort by plundering the few. Without strong believers in such a creed, it is difficult to see how this Nation could have ever achieved a constitution which has been used with increasing effectiveness for realizing the ideal of equal opportunity in economic as well as political terms.

(7) *Creed of enterprise versus the spirit of enterprise:* Few, if any, animations have been more serviceable to this ideal than the *spirit* of enterprise, which differs from the *creed* of enterprise, just as the spirit of a religion may differ from its ritual.

The spirit of enterprise is an attitude which persons may assume toward their professional activity. In positive terms, it is the quest for personal excellence or achievement in one's chosen work, whatever his occupation or level of income. In negative terms, it is an aversion to performing a role that does not come up to one's capacities, even if his income were already enough to meet all his livelihood requirements. Certainly such an attitude involves some preference for industry instead of leisure.

Animated by this spirit, persons seek no hand-outs. These are distasteful as they signify professional impotence to a point beyond endurance. But as a means to a fairer chance of enabling themselves to realize their highest potential as worthwhile agents of common life, they often seek most energetically a larger share of the Nation's goods and services than is available to them as market remunerations for their services. They have increasingly demanded a government whose primary function is to "help people help themselves". Mainly, in response to this spirit, millions of dollars annually go into public education, into various farm programs, "TVA's," "subsidized" housing, medical care, and the like. All these have been opposed by the creed of enterprise but not the spirit of enterprise. The creed is obsolete; the spirit may prove eternal. The spirit requires a government that is constantly vigilant in limiting the market income inequalities to a point where each has as good an economic chance as any other to develop, and use to the fullest, his powers in any social role of his choice and capabilities.

Equal Opportunity to a Dissenter's Role

But even complete equality of opportunity to perform a social role would fall far short of the democratic goal: fostering the unique worth of each person, both for its own sake and as an instrument of social advance. Anyone may have interests which run counter to the customary. As every idea is an incitement to its adoption, one is always tending in some measure to remake the world in his own image. But mere equality of opportunity to any social role is quite compatible with a static society. It is conceivable, for example, that society might provide everyone with an equal chance to be a farmer or a poet and at the same time prohibit any change in the established farm practices or art forms. This is precisely the kind of social order at which Plato aimed in his *Republic*. He simply wanted to make sure that he got the "right" sort of customs set up at the start.

Such a static order, however "ideal," is felt as most oppressive in a democratic culture, whose central purpose is the utilization of the exceptional sentiments and views as means of improving the customary. Achievement of this purpose requires a dynamic order: an order in which authority is able (1) to maintain enough conformity to insure the public peace and safety, and (2) at the same time increasingly back up the propensity of the individual to deviate from accepted opinion and practice in line with his own best judgment.

All types of such behavior are here classified as the "dissenter's role." Expansion of the opportunity for all to participate in this role is a distinctive feature of modern society, and is considered under four main heads: (1) the dissenter as the growing point of social advance; (2) technological and ethical justifications of dissent; (3) conflict between the propensity for dissent and necessity of protecting the public safety; and (4) the salient traits of our individualistic culture.

1. *The dissenter as the growth factor in social advance:* At any moment established opinion and practice are changing only at a relatively few points, even in periods of violent revolutions. (Society would literally disintegrate were everything to change at once.) The starting point of innovation in any particular custom is the exceptional experience of some individual (or individuals). Such names as Ford, Edison, McCormick, Galileo, Darwin, Beethoven, St. Francis, and Luther are a sufficient reminder that there is scarcely a single object in our mental, emotional, and technological environment but which, in its beginning, had no other home or status than the "foolish notions" of "things as they are." For this reason conservatives are often defined as the worshipers of dead radicals. In great measure, the present order is but past orders modified in line with the thought of yesterday's dissenters. The future always belongs to the

dissenter, even though his present lot may be something of an outcast. This is true even after all due allowance is made for the fact that dissent is no guarantee to social immortality in any particular case.

a. *Negative and positive aspects of dissent:* There is both a negative and positive aspect of dissent. As an agent of exceptional views and sentiments, the dissenter is a "disturber of the peace;" so much so that there is a point at which any social order, however liberal and tolerant, must limit the freedom to dissent in the interest of public safety. Nevertheless, the purpose of dissent is not the destruction of social order as such, but rather a revision of accepted views and practice that will afford the dissenter the kind of social order which his conscience can approve.

b. *Dissent as a creative struggle within the individual and also between individual and society:* Each personality revolves about two foci, as it were–the typical and atypical aspects of experience. Any physicist, for example, is well versed in the views of his profession concerning the laws of falling bodies, and the like. On the other hand, he often observes phenomena which run counter to customary theories.

As a consequence, the process of dissent is no mere mechanical conflict between the individual on the one side and society on the other. It includes this, but it is also a creative struggle from within. As the agent of exceptional experience one stands in conflict with himself as the agent of typical sentiments and views. This tension, and the striving to resolve it, resides in him alone. The fact renders him a new beginning point of social advance. For it incites him to work out a new viewpoint (theory) which will account for both the experience of everyone and his own exceptional experiences.

c. *Research science as illustrating the creative process of dissent:* Research science provides the most developed form of this creative process. A researcher's problem is never that of giving a systematic exposition of the views which are shared by himself and his colleagues. On the contrary any problem, worthy of the game, always starts with some exceptional observation to an accepted "law," such as the identification of a case of sporadic disease at a time when personal contact was the accepted explanation (theory) of the spread of disease.

Such events that cannot be accounted for by presently accepted laws and theories have a unique logical status. They are robbed of any reality as an instance of a universal order, for one does not understand at the time how they can be fitted into an objective order. They lie between an old law (world), which they have demolished, and a new law which has not yet arisen. In this sense, they are subjective, not objective, since the only ground which can be assigned for their existence is simply their occurrence as a paragraph in the biography of the individual. Take, for example, Galileo's observation of the moons of Jupiter with his primitive telescope.

> For those who lived in a Ptolemaic cosmos these could have existence only as observations of individuals. As moons they had distinct meaning, circling Jupiter as our moon circles the earth, but being in contradiction with the Ptolemaic order they could depend for their existence only on the evidence of the senses, until a Copernican order could give them a local habitation and a

name. Then they were observed not as experiences of individuals but as instances of planetary order in a heliocentric system.[19]

Such events become *data* for other scientists because the individual can (and must) so describe the conditions, under which they occur to him, that if others attempt to pass off his testimony as make-believe, he forces them to become experiencers of the same facts in spite of themselves.

But subjective though they are (in the sense just defined), they constitute the "hard facts" of science; hard because they take place independently of any explanation of their cause or of the law which they follow; hard because they are unpredictable as you just stumble over them and bark your shins on them; hard because they are exceptional enough to break some law, some accepted idea. They are brute facts, at first unexplained and non-rational, unintelligible.[20]

In addition to being the data on which older laws and theories break, the exceptional experience is also the basis of the new hypothesis which replaces the old. It makes a "rebel" of the individual, transforming him from a mere agent, like others, of some prevailing sentiment and view into a challenger of it. This is true not only in research science but in all walks of life, even to little children. Research science is merely a highly developed, consciously controlled way in which one, in becoming a challenger of any accepted practice, may function more usefully to society than in any other capacity.

2. *Technological and ethical justifications of dissent:* Modern Western society has excelled all others in the extent to which it has approximated an equality of opportunity for dissent. What main types of reasons has it given in justifying the struggle for this opportunity? One is technological, meaning that the opportunity "pays off" by giving society an ever greater "control over its environment." But the more fundamental justification arises from the ethical nature of the policymaking process, and would hold even if dissent made no contribution to technological progress.

a. *Technological considerations:* The technological justification is most frequently expressed in connection with freedom of enquiry in scientific fields where it obviously leads to rapid change in the techniques of living and making a living. As Mead so vividly said:

> ... is an instrument by means of which mankind, the community, gets control over its environment... Science is something that enters into all the minutiae of life. We cannot brush our teeth without it. We cannot eat or drink without science coming in to tell us what should be eaten, what vitamins in the upper part of the alphabet ought to be used, how they can be obtained in the orange juice and the spinach that is on the menu. It tells us how to blow our noses and indicates with whom we may shake hands. There is hardly a point in life at which science does not tell something about the conduct that is an essential part of our living.[21]

As a consequence, Mead adds, the scientist is given "a freedom in his operation which is greater than that which anyone else in the community can demand." In fact his life is, in a way, independent of the community life. It goes on:

> ... in separate institutions, in universities that cloister themselves from the community, under separate foundations that demand that his work shall be entirely free so that the scientist may entertain whatever view he cares to hold, use whatever methods he has worked out ... He seems to stand outside the

community; and yet . . . his statements, the directions which he gives, enter the whole minutiae of social life.[22]

This is true. But it leaves the question: Would society back up individual departures from accepted views even if they did not "pay off" in terms of "material riches?"

b. *Relative unimportance of the technological justification:* These material fruits of dissent are spectacular, but they are not its primary justification. For among the most powerful affirmations of the freedom to deviate from the customary are cases in which there is not the remotest connection between dissent and any material advantage.

Recent trials of the Jehovah Witnesses are typical. To an extraordinary degree, the sentiments and views of this religious sect run counter to those of our society. They rest on a calculated date of the second coming of Christ and the battle of Armageddon and they include virulent denunciations of all other organized religions and churches, especially the Catholic Church, as works of Satan. They even forbid the oath of allegiance to the flag.

Adoption of their doctrines would involve profound changes in prevailing habits of life, but they would add nothing to the wealth of nations; in fact they might result in much impoverishment. Yet time and again American society, through its courts, has affirmed that the same freedom to dissent applies to the Witnesses as to the scientist. In a memorable opinion striking down a West Virginia statute requiring the oath of allegiance of school children, which the Witnesses refused to take, Justice Jackson said:

> The very purpose of a Bill of Rights was to withdraw certain subjects from the vicissitudes of political controversy, to place them beyond the reach of majorities and officials and to establish them as legal principles to be applied by the courts. One's right to life, liberty, and property, to free speech, a free press, freedom of worship and assembly . . . may not be submitted to vote; they depend on the outcome of no elections. . .
>
> If there is any fixed star in our constitutional constellation, it is that no official, high or petty, can prescribe what shall be orthodox in politics, nationalism, religion, or other matters of opinion or force citizens to confess by word or act their faith therein.[23]

c. *The ethical justification:* Justice Jackson's powerful words suggest that in our culture the dissenter's role is supported by strong ethical grounds instead of mere utilitarian considerations.

These grounds appear to lie in a threefold trait of the policymaking process: (1) a sharp contrast between questions of fact and questions of equity; (2) the need for enough conformity to maintain a social order; and (3) the equality of men as a judge of what is equitable in the light of given facts.

Questions of fact and of policy or equity differ in three main aspects. (1) Questions of fact take the form: Given such and such a series of events—like cases of contagious disease or the fluctuations of butter prices—what other series of events will explain the occurrence of the first series. Questions of policy take the form: In the light of given facts on a certain subject, such as the condition of the Nation's agriculture and its food and fiber needs, what rule of action is most equitable for all concerned, and therefore should be adopted? (2) In reaching decisions on what policies (rules) are most equitable in the light of given facts, men must fall back on their sense of fair play, whereas in answering questions of fact they can only fall back on special skills for establishing causal (uniform) connections between one series of events and another series which explains the behavior of the first. (3) Given the same procedures and conditions of investigation, men can and will reach the same conclusions on questions of fact. But the same facts are usually incapable of eliciting uniform judgments of equity, as is strikingly borne out by hung juries and split court decisions where the evidence is identical for all parties and where the spirit of impartiality is at its highest pitch. A substantial measure of coercion is thus inescapable.

Combining these features of the policymaking process with the equality of persons, as judges of equity, provides three ethical cornerstones for governmental procedures. (1) men deserve an opportunity for an equal voice in the sovereign process of laying down the rules which all must observe. (2) Majority control of this process is justified as a means of minimizing the degree of coercion required to maintain social order. However, (3) the assumed equality of men as judges of equity further requires that the opportunity for dissent by the minority, even of one, be "placed beyond the reach of majorities"—be "subject to no elections." For as previously stated, majority rule is not a way of determining whose particular policy (equity) views are erroneous and which are not. No such determination is possible, either by majority rule or by any other means. Later experience has often proved, even to the majority, that the dissenter was right. Therefore, maximum opportunity for the majority itself to later discover and correct its errors requires that it back up the free expression of the dissenting opinion even though it requires compliance in other respects.

3. *Conflict between the necessity of conscience to dissent and the necessity of protecting the public safety:* The Constitution boldly affirms the opportunity of each to dissent without interference whenever he so chooses. It reads:

> Congress shall make no law respecting an establishment of religion, or prohibiting the free exercise thereof; or abridging the freedom of speech, or of the press; or the right of the people peaceably to assemble, and to petition the government for a redress of grievances.

There is no suggestion here that, in case of conflict, the safety of the existing order takes precedence over the imperious demand of conscience for the kind of order which it can respect.

But suppose some individuals, for reasons of conscience actually oppose military drafts and war bond drives, or refuse to open their books to income tax inspectors, or insist upon polygamy as the proper form of marriage? Persons have insisted upon such exceptional practices time and again as being essential to the kind of a social order which they could approve. But the free expression of such a conscience has struck the general public as an intolerable threat to all social order, and therefore should be suppressed.

> This is natural and, in a certain sense, entirely justifiable. We have to have an order of society; and, if what is taking place shakes that order, we have no evidence that we will get another to take the place of the present one. We cannot afford to let that order go to pieces. We must have it as a basis of conduct.[24]

However much society may refrain from suppressing dissent, there still remains an area of conflict between (1) the necessity of protecting the safety (and "morals") of the present order against the dangers of dissent, and (2) the demand of individual reason and conscience for the *kind* of order it can approve. This conflict can never be completely resolved because of the inability of the same information or evidence to elicit uniform judgments of equity (policy).

The opinion of Jefferson, Lincoln, and of members of the Supreme Court are especially illustrative of this conflict.

a. *Jefferson:* Jefferson always talked and acted as if the right dissent were an absolute freedom to which the public safety was subordinate, though he never went so far as to lay down this proposition as a dogma for all time. He rested his position on four underlying ideas.

First, use of the unlimited right to criticize inflicts no physical injury on anyone, while the prevention of such injury is the only justifiable use of sovereign power.

> But our rulers can have authority over such natural rights only as we have submitted to him ... The rights of conscience we never submitted, we could not submit. We are answerable for them to our God. The legitimate powers of government extend to such acts only as are injurious to others. But it does no injury for my neighbour to say there are twenty gods, or no god. It neither picks my pocket nor breaks my leg.[25]

Second, in allowing an unlimited freedom to dissent, society provides itself with the maximum means (opportunity) for discovering and remedying its own errors.

> Reason and free enquiry are the only effectual agents against error. Give a loose to them, they will support true religion, by bringing every false one to their tribunal, to the test of their investigation. They are the natural enemies of error, and of error only. Had not the Roman government permitted free enquiry, Christianity could never have been introduced. Had not free enquiry been indulged at the era of the reformation, the corruptions of Christianity could not have been purged away ... Government is just as infallible too when it fixes systems in physics. Galileo was sent to the inquisition for affirming that the earth was a sphere... Reason and experiment have been indulged, and error has fled before them ... Truth can stand by itself.[26]

Third, because dissent is an efficient corrective of error, any State-imposed limitation upon it might seriously endanger the successful outcome of the young Republic's "great experiment" in whether "the people" were actually capable of self-government.

> No experiment can be more interesting than that we are now trying, which we trust will end in establishing the fact that man may be governed by reason and truth. Our first object should therefore be to leave open to him all the avenues of truth. The most effectual hitherto found is the freedom of the press. It is the first therefore to be shut up by those who fear the investigation of their actions.[27]

Finally, the "good sense of the people" will sufficiently counteract any threat to the safety of the present order arising from a fraudulent and abusive use of the unlimited freedom to dissent.

> The firmness with which the people have withstood the abuses from the press, the discernment they have manifested between truth and falsehood show that

they may safely be trusted to hear everything true and false and to form a correct judgment between them.[28]

The press lampooned Jefferson without let-up. This did not, of course, "break his leg" or "pick his purse," but it pained him more than if it had. In not limiting their opportunity to attack him, Jefferson laid great stress on the idea that he thereby voluntarily bore a heavy cross. To a friend he wrote:

> ... they (the Federalists) fill their newspapers with falsehoods, calumnies, and audacities...We are going through the experiment whether freedom of discussion, unaided by coercion, is not sufficient for the propagation and protection of truth, and for the maintenance of an administration pure and upright in its action and views. No one can fall, under this experiment, more than myself. Nero wished all the necks of Rome united in one, that he might sever tham at a blow. So our ex-federalists, wishing to have a single representative of all the objects of their hatred, honor me with that post, and exhibit against me such atrocities as no nation had ever before heard or endured. *I shall protect* them in the right of lying and calumniating.
> I have lent myself willingly as the subject of a great experiment, which was to prove that an administration, conducting itself with integrity and common understanding cannot be battered down, even by the falsehoods of a licentious press, and consequently still less by the press, as restrained within the legal and wholesome limits of the truth. This experiment was wanting for the world to demonstrate the falsehood that freedom of the press is incompatible with orderly government.[29]

In these passages, Jefferson clearly felt that he reflected great credit on his person in "willingly" subjecting himself to the discomforts of an "abusive" press as a means of assuring the successful issue of "the great experiment." In this he was right, as courageous acts are always a badge of good repute. But Jefferson's description of his deeds has a martyr-like connotation which is hardly justified. His description implies that he would have been acting entirely within his official prerogatives had he protected his person against the flails of a "free press" by restricting their otherwise unlimited right to dissent from his policies. If this implication is false, then his great discomfort at the hands of the press was simply a part of the cost of doing his clear and unmistakable duty. Conversely, if the implication were true, then his refusal to use his official power to limit dissent was indeed infused with a heroic quality, extending far above and beyond the line of duty.

Other presidents, especially Lincoln, have been lampooned as unmercifully as Jefferson by the "free press." They also have refrained from using their official power as a means of protecting the safety of their administration and personal comfort against the whips and scorpions of dissent. None, except Jefferson, have suggested that in so doing their deeds were anything more than the accepted cost which one must pay for the honor of being a public servant.

Jefferson's view of man and society did not take account of an irreducible area of conflict between the demand of the individual for the kind of a social order which he can approve, and the necessity of protecting the present order.

Fortunately, for the safety of his country, as well as his own psychic health, the events of his times did not put his idea of unlimited liberty of conscience to an acid test. No one has more extolled than he the ultimate in religious liberty, but what would he have done if faced with a religious sect whose conscience insisted upon polygamy? What would have been his attitude on the "wonderful correctness" of "the people" had they taken the same attitude toward him and his policies as the "lying and calumniating" press? It is easy to extoll the wisdom of the people when they are with you. Jefferson never had to show his colors under circumstances where he could not wrap about himself the halo of the people. Suppose his times had made it clear to him that dissenting voices were literally tearing to pieces the new Republic he loved. Would he still have resolved to "protect them in the right of lying and calumniating?" In the final showdown, would he have laid on the altar of unlimited liberty of *honest reason and conscience* to dissent, the very safety and existence of the present order which as a public agent, he was oath-bound to protect? Maybe not. His Embargo Acts and the Louisiana Purchase are evidence enough that, for all his talk about "experiment," he simply backed water instead of changing his mind whenever the experiment didn't conform to his "principles." In this he was a "moralist" of first order.

But whatever he might have done, the fact remains that his time spared him the excruciating ordeal of having to choose between preserving the existing order and protecting a dissenting conscience that demands the kind of an order it can respect.

b. *Lincoln:* Even in Jefferson's day such an ordeal was being hatched in the storm clouds of the South's "peculiar institution." It fell full blast on Lincoln only 35 years after Jefferson's death.

Lincoln was as sensitive as Jefferson to a moral order of personal reason and conscience, at variance with the status quo. But his times forced upon him the clear idea that one's conscience may be in sharp conflict with his official responsibility for preserving the existing order. He shared the inner conflict of a man who desired the replacement of a slave America with a free America, but who also saw that, as a public agent, he was powerless to lift a hand against slavery. At the same time, while prizing no less than Jefferson the unlimited freedom to dissent, he clearly saw that he must severely limit this freedom for the sake of preserving the nation he was oath-bound to protect.

This double conflict is illustrated in his debates with Douglas, in his view of the President's constitutional powers and responsibility, and in his interpretation of the freeing of the slaves as the act of the "Almighty" who "hath his own purposes" which were quite different from those of any participants in the War, North or South.

Douglas was completely indifferent to the rightness or wrongness of a slave order, persistently saying, "I do not care whether slavery be voted up or voted down." His only concern was that the white man of Kansas have a fair opportunity to vote on the matter; whichever way they voted would neither add nor subtract from his happiness. But Lincoln regarded this indifference to the moral quality of slavery as treason to the basic principle of the American Commonwealth. Said he:

> A house divided against itself cannot stand. I believe this government cannot endure permanently half slave and half free. I do not expect the Union to be dissolved - I do not expect the house to fall - but I do expect it will cease to be

divided. It will become all one thing, or all the other. Either the opponents of slavery will arrest the further spread of it, and place it where the public mind shall rest in the belief that it is in the course of ultimate extinction, or its advocates will push it forward till it shall have become alike lawful in all States, old as well as new, North as well as South.[30]

A little later at Cooper Institute in New York he said: "What do you think will content the South?" "Nothing," he answered, "but the acknowledgement that slavery is right. Holding as they do, that slavery is morally right and socially elevating, they cannot cease to demand a full national recognition of it, as a legal and social blessing. Nor can we justifiably withhold this on any ground save our conviction that slavery is wrong." That being so, there was no use, he said, "in grouping for some middle ground between right and wrong" or in "a policy of 'don't care' or a question about which all men do care."[31]

Soon afterwards he became President. But he did not regard this event as vesting him with any power whatsoever to impose upon men at large the kind of social order which his own reason and conscience demanded that all men ought to observe. Said he:

> If slavery is not wrong, nothing is wrong. I cannot remember when I did not so think and feel, and yet I have never understood that the presidency conferred upon me an unrestricted right to act officially upon this judgment and feeling. It was in the oath I took that I would, to the best of my ability, preserve, protect, and defend the Constitution of the United States. I could not take the office without taking the oath. Nor was it my view that I might take the oath to get power, in ordinary civil administration this oath even forbade me to practically indulge my primary abstract judgment on the moral question of slavery.... And I aver that, to this day, I have done no official act in mere deference to my abstract judgment and feeling on slavery.[32]

To be sure, Lincoln in the end used the power of his office to free the slaves, but not until it was crystal clear that this was an "indispensable necessity" to preserving the Union.

> When, early in the war, General Fremont attempted military emancipation, I forbade it, because I did not then think it an indispensable necessity. When, a little later, General Cameron, then Secretary of War, suggested the arming of the blacks, I objected because I did not yet think it an indispensable necessity.... When in March and May and July, 1862, I made earnest and successive appeals to the border States to favor compensated emancipation, I believed the indispensable necessity for military emancipation and arming the blacks would come unless averted by that measure. They declined the proposition, and I was in my best judgment, driven to the alternative of either surrendering the Union, and with it the Constitution, or of laying strong hand upon the colored element. I chose the latter.... More than a year of trial now shows no loss by it in our foreign relations, none in our home popular sentiment, none in our white military force - no loss by it anyhow or anywhere. On the contrary it shows a gain of quite a hundred and thirty thousand soldiers, seamen, and laborers.[33]

That the slaves were finally freed made a profound impression on Lincoln, as he could find no naturalistic explanation of this event. For he had acted merely as an instrument for saving the existing order—half-slave and half-free. Yet in pressing to this and with all his powers, the course of events terminated in a new order—without chains. As this was not the avowed goal of anyone, either North or South, how could its emergence be accounted for? Lincoln, a man who professed no faith, could find no explanation except the hand of God, guiding events to ends quite different from those of any man. His first expression of this viewpoint was in the letter to Hodges, cited above. Said he:

> I claim not to have controlled events, but confess plainly that events have controlled me. Now, at the end of three years of struggle, the nation's condition is not what either party, or any man, devised or expected. God alone can claim it. Whether it is tending seems plain. If God now wills the removal of a great wrong, and wills also that we of the North, as well as you of the South, shall pay fairly for our complicity in that wrong, impartial history will find therein new cause to attest and revere the justice and goodness of God.[34]

Nearly a year later in the Second Inaugural, the same sentiment was expressed in words of imperishable beauty.

While he felt that his public position gave him no power to translate into fact the free America which he desired, he was also the first American statesman to see clearly that the existing order cannot acknowledge that freedom to dissent is an absolute right, even though the individual's conscience may rebel against this necessity. For the exercise of such freedom, in the eyes of authority, may threaten the public safety; and when this happens, it must be suppressed to whatever point the authority deems necessary.

In line with this thought, Lincoln struggling with the turmoil of his times, placed more severe restrictions on the right to dissent than any other president, though the Supreme Court, a year after Appomattox, struck down the reasoning on which he based his restrictions. On September 24, 1862, he issued a proclamation, without statutory authorization, providing that during the "insurrection" all persons discouraging enlistment, resisting the draft, or guilty of any disloyal practice, were subject to martial law and liable to trial by court martial or military commission; and authorizing the suspension of habeas corpus in the arrest of such persons. Thousands were arrested without the opportunity for a hearing on the grounds of arrest and imprisoned without trial before ordinary courts. Newspapers in New York, Louisville, Baltimore, and Philadelphia were suppressed or suspended by military rules.

Lincoln justified these drastic actions on the ground that if he did not take them, freedom of conscience and expression would endanger the safety of the Nation. He said:

> The insurgents. . .and their sympathizers pervaded all departments of the government and nearly all communities of the people. From this material, under cover of 'liberty of speech', 'liberty of the press', and 'habeas corpus', they hoped to keep on foot amongst us an efficient corps of spies, informers, suppliers and aiders and abettors of their cause in a thousand ways. They knew that . . . the 'habeas corpus' might be suspended, but they also knew they had friends who would make a question as to who was to suspend it; meanwhile their spies and others might remain at large to help on their cause. Or if, as has happened, the Executive should suspend the writ without ruinious waste of time, instances of arresting innocent persons might occur . . . and then a clamor could be raised in regard to this, which might be at least of some service to the insurgent cause . . . Thoroughly imbued with a reverence for the guaranteed rights of individuals, I was slow to adopt the strong measures which by degrees I have been forced to regard as being within the exceptions of the Constitution and as indispensable to the public safety. Nothing is better

known to history than that the courts of justice are utterly incompetent to such cases. Civil courts are organized for trials of individuals, or, at most, a few individuals acting in concert - and this in quiet times, and on charge of crimes well defined in law. Even in times of peace bands of horse-thieves and robbers frequently grow too numerous and powerful for the ordinary courts of justice. But what comparison, in numbers, have such bands ever borne to the insurgent sympathizers even in many of the loyal States. Again, a jury too frequently has at least one member more ready to hang the panel than to hang the traitor. And yet, he who dissuades one man from volunteering, or induces one soldier to desert, weakens the Union cause as much as he who kills a Union soldier in battle. Yet this dissuasion or inducement may be so conducted as to be no defined crime of which the civil courts would take cognizance.[35]

In summary, the difference between Jefferson and Lincoln, concerning the bounds of the opportunity for expressing dissent, comes to this: Jefferson professed to see in individual dissent no threat to the safety of the present order, but a painful threat to his own personal ease and comfort; he implied that he had the power to restrict it if he so chose. He did not so choose because of the high value he placed on the absolute freedom of conscience and expression as a corrective of error and because of his confidence in the "good sense" of "the people" not to be misled by a "lying and calumniating press." In this way, he imputed to his own deeds a martyr-like quality as well as an absolute character to the privilege of dissent. In contrast, it never entered Lincoln's head that his office vested him with the slightest power to limit the privilege of dissent from his policies for the sake of his own peace of mind. However, his times placed upon him, as chief officer of the Union, the prime responsibility for preventing its dissolution. It was his considered judgment that freedom to dissent was limited by the safety needs of the existing order, and that the president was the proper authority to define where the freedom to criticize left off and where the need of public safety began.

c. *Attitudes of the Supreme Court:*   The Supreme Court was exceedingly slow in offering any guidance in drawing such a boundary. For 79 years after the ratification of the Constitution, it was silent on this subject.

The Court's interpretation of civil rights falls into two broad stages: (1) Placing the Bill of Rights beyond the reach of the Chief Executive and State Legislatures, and (2) laying down two tests—"the bad tendency test" and the "clear and present danger" test—on where the freedom to dissent must be subordinated to the needs of public safety.

(1) *Court displaces the Chief Executive and State Legislatures as guardian of dissent and public safety:*   The Court first entered the civil rights picture as a challenger of the executive's right to decide when freedom to dissent becomes incompatible with public safety. The Court's first action was to declare that Lincoln's restrictions of civil rights were unconstitutional, though not until a year after the Civil War was over. It never specifically denied that the opportunity to dissent was not limited by the public safety. But it sharply declared that no such "theory of necessity" justifies the executive in establishing this limit.

The occasion of this declaration (in 1866) was the case of one Milligan, a citizen of Indiana who was arrested by order of a military officer, confined to a military prison on charges of a conspiracy against the Government of the United States, inciting insurrection, etc. He had been engaged, according to the charge, in a plot to release rebel prisoners and unite them with a newly formed expedition against Federal forces. He was tried, convicted, and sentenced to death by a military commission. But the Court held that Milligan's trial by the commission was illegal on the ground that Congress had not authorized and had no power to authorize the trial even in wartime, of a civilian by court martial in loyal territory where the courts were in full and normal operation. Associate Justice Davis, speaking for the majority of the court, said:

> The Constitution of the United States is a law for rulers and the people, equally in war and in peace, and covers with the shield of its protection all classes of men, at all times, and under all circumstances. No doctrine, involving more pernicious consequences, was ever invented by the wit of men than that any of its provisions can be suspended during any of the great exigencies of government. Such a doctrine leads directly to anarchy or despotism, but the theory of necessity on which it is based is false; for the government, within the Constitution, has all the powers granted to it which are necessary to perserve its existance, as has been happily proved by the result of the great effort to throw off its just authority.[36]

For over 100 years the constitutional guarantee of the opportunity to dissent was quite narrow. For the first amendment merely prohibited Congress from passing laws abridging the freedom of religion, the press, or peaceful assembly and to petition the Government for a redress of grievances. The State legislatures could do what they pleased.

Very slowly the Court reached the position that State legislatures, as well as the chief executive, have no power to limit the freedom of dissent. Six main steps were involved in this nationalization of the Bill of Rights. (1) Before the Fourteenth Amendment there was no Federal constitutional restraint upon State interference with free speech and press, as the court had declared that the First Amendment did not apply to the States. (2) But did the Fourteenth Amendment include the liberties covered in the Bill of Rights? For over 60 years the Court held it did not. In 1900 (Maxwell vs. Dow U.S. 581) and again in 1908 (Twining vs. State of New Jersey, 211 U.S. 78) the Court declared that the Bill of Rights was not included in the list of privileges and immunities which the States were forbidden to abridge by the Fourteenth Amendment. (3) As late as 1922, it declared "neither the Fourteenth Amendment nor any other provision of the Constitution of the United States imposes upon the States any restriction about 'freedom of speech' " (Prudential Insurance Co. vs. Cheek, 259 U.S. 530). (4) But, even before this, some Justices were taking a contrary view. For example, in 1907, Mr. Justice Harlan, in a dissenting opinion said:

> I go further and hold that the privileges of free speech and a free press, belonging to every citizen of the United States, constitute an essential part of every man's liberty, and are protected against violation by that clause of the Fourteenth Amendment forbiding a State to deprive any person of his liberty without due process of law.[37]

Then in 1920, Mr. Justice Brandeis expressed essentially the same view (Gilbert vs. State of Minnesota, 254 U.S. 325). (5) By 1923 the Court began showing its conversion to this broadened conception of "liberty." In that year

Mr. Justice McReynolds, in an opinion holding invalid a statute forbidding the teaching of any language but English in a private school, defined "liberty," protected by due process clause, as follows:

> Without doubt, it denotes not merely freedom from bodily restraint but also the right of the individual to contract, to engage in any of the common occupations of life, to acquire useful knowledge, to marry, establish a home and bring up children, to worship God according to the dictates of his own conscience, and generally to enjoy those privileges long recognized at common law as essential to the orderly pursuit of happiness by free men.[38]

The climax of the conversion came in 1926. (6) One Mr. Gitlow was convicted of violating the New York Criminality Act of 1902 by circulating communist literature. He urged on the Court that the New York statute deprived him of liberty without due process of law by unreasonably restricting freedom of press. In a remarkable judicial turn-around the Court accepted Gitlow's contention, saying:

> For present purposes we may and do assume that freedom of speech and of the press—which are protected by the First Amendment from abridgment by Congress—are among the fundamental personal rights and "liberties" protected by the due process clause of the Fourteenth Amendment from impairment by the states. (Gitlow vs. People of New York, 268 U.S. 652)

By means of the Fourteenth Amendment the Court thus at long last put the whole Nation's backing behind the individual propensity to dissent from accepted opinion and practice by placing the Bill of Rights beyond the power of State legislature, as well as the executive and Congress, to abridge.

(2) *"Bad tendency" and "clear and present danger" doctrines as tests of compatibility of freedom to dissent and public safety:* By deciding in Gitlow's favor, the Court in no wise did away with the area of irreconcilable conflict between the public safety and the demands of individual conscience. Instead, it simply shifted from others to its own shoulders the burden of setting up some sort of criteria for handling this conflict. Where is the point above which the security of the present order can afford the luxury of dissent and below which it cannot? The Court has evolved two doctrines for dealing with this question. The first is called the "clear and present danger test"; and the other "the bad tendency test".

The "clear and present danger test" was first formulated in 1919 by Mr. Justice Holmes in Schenck vs. United States, 249 U.S. 47. This case arose in connection with the Espionage Act of 1917 which prohibited the willful making of statements intended to obstruct recruiting or enlistment, to interfere with the operation of the Military or Naval Forces; and it authorized the Postmaster General to refuse mailing privileges to any newspaper or person he believed to be using the mails to violate the Act. Schenck was charged with circulating pamphlets urging resistance to the draft. He claimed he was merely exercising his constitutionally protected freedom of the press. The Court applied to Schenck's pamphlets the test of whether their circulation created a "clear and present danger" of obstructing the draft. It found, in view of the facts, that they did. In formulating this test Mr. Justice Holmes said in part.

> We admit that in many places and in ordinary times the defendants in saying all that was said in the circular would have been within their constitutional

rights. But the character of every act depends upon the circumstances in which it is done. The most stringent protection of free speech would not protect a man in falsely shouting fire in a theatre and causing a panic . . . The question in every case is whether the words used are used in such circumstances and are of such a nature as to create a clear and present danger that they will bring about the substantive evils that Congress has a right to prevent. It is a question of proximity and degree. When a nation is at war many things that might be said in time of peace are such a hinderance to its effort that their utterance will not be endured so long as men fight and that no Court could regard them as protected by any constitutional right.[39]

The "bad tendency test" was formulated in 1925 by Justice Sanford (Gitlow vs. People of New York, 268 U.S. 652). This test arose in connection with statutes against "criminal syndication" which were passed by 21 States from 1902 to 1919. These statutes were evoked in the first instances by the growth of the Industrial Workers of the World, a labor group organized in 1905 in opposition to craft unionism and the conservative tactics of the American Federation of Labor. The I.W.W. proclaimed the "destruction of capitalism" as its ultimate aim, rejected collective bargaining, and advocated "direct action" through general strikes and sabotage as its chief means of contention. This movement waned after 1912. But laws against "criminal syndicalism" were given a new impetus by the post-war fears of social upheaval, occasioned by the Communist Revolution in Russia in 1917 and the organization of the Communist Party in the United States in 1919. The New York Criminal Anarchy Act of 1902 forbade persons by speech or publication to advocate the overthrow of organized government by violence. Gitlow circulated communistic literature which in lurid and fervent language, urged the workers of the country to engage in revolutionary mass action to bring about "a revolutionary dictatorship of the proletariat."

There was no evidence that the circulation of the literature had any effect. Obviously it created no "clear and present danger" of the overthrow of the Government. But the Court did not yield to Gitlow's plea that the statute was therefore an illegal suppression of his constitutionally protected freedom. On the contrary, it held his speeches and publications were illegal because they had a "tendency" to produce results dangerous to the public safety, even though they created no "clear and present danger" to the Government's overthrow. The State has a right to nip this tendency without waiting until its potentially dangerous results are on its door-step. Delivering the majority opinion of the Court Justice Sanford said:

That utterances inciting to the overthrow of organized government by unlawful means, present a sufficient danger of substantive evil to bring their punishment within the range of legislative discretion, is clear. Such utterances, by their very nature, involve danger to the public peace and to the security of the State. They threaten breaches of peace and ultimate revolution. And the immediate danger is none-the-less real and substantial, because the effect of a given utterance cannot be accurately foreseen. The State cannot reasonably be required to measure the danger from every such utterance in the nice balance of a jeweler's scale. A single revolutionary spark may kindle a fire that, smouldering for a time, may burst into a sweeping and destructive conflagration. It cannot be said that the State is acting arbitrarily or unreasonably when in the exercise of its judgment as to the measures necessary to protect the public peace and safety, it seeks to extinguish the spark without waiting until it has enkindled the flame or blazed into the conflagration. It cannot reasonably be required to defer the adoption of measures for its own peace and safety until the revolutionary utterances lead to actual disturbance of the public peace or imminent and immediate danger of its own destruction; but it may, in the exercise of its own judgment, suppress the threatened danger in its incipiency ... In other words, when the legislative body has determined generally, in the constitutional exercise of its discretion, that utterances of a certain kind involve such danger of substantive evil that they may be punished, the question whether any specific utterance coming within the prohibited class is likely, in and of itself, to bring about the substantive evil, is not open to consideration. . . .[40]

In sum, according to Justice Holmes, if no visible harm can come from a dissenter's inflamable talk, let him talk; whereas according to Justice Sanford, if his talk is inflamable, that is reason enough to stop it.

The "clear and present danger" test obviously established a much wider area for dissent than the "bad tendency test." Not since the Gitlow case, has the Court used the "bad tendency test"; but it has never been repudiated by the Court and is therefore available for future use.

(3) *The outcast dissenter as agent of social advance:* The opportunity to speak out and act in behalf of one's own views against established ways is one of the most prized treasures of Western society, and in the West especially, the gap has been narrowed between the security requirements of the existing order and the unrestrained expression of the imperious demand of dissenting reason and conscience. The Western world has been most ingenious in devising ways through which it is able to reject the dissenting view but keep the dissenter within the circle of good fellowship and tolerance.

But the fact remains that no society can ever provide a home within the law for all dissenters. Some must be cast out as a menace to order. In fear of chaos, the votaries of the existing order are impelled to silence the threatening dissenter. Yet dissent he must, be the consequences what they may. Take Henry David Thoreau, for example. In reference to his half-slave and half-free America he said:

How does it become a man to behave toward this American government today? I answer, that he cannot without disgrace be associated with it. I cannot for an instant recognize that political organization as *my* government which is the *slave's* government also.[41]

He practiced what he preached. He was jailed because of his refusal to pay taxes in protest against the fugitive slave law. Visiting him in jail, Emerson asked, "Why are you here, Thoreau?" Whereupon he replied, "Why are you not here, Emerson?"

Everyday folk, as well as historic figures, bear out the same point. Only recently, for example, the newspapers carried the story of a New England businessman, who in being locked up for refusing to let Government officials open his books to see if he was complying with the tax provisions of the Social Security Act, defiantly said he would rather be a jailed agent of our "constitutional freedoms" than the unjailed agent of their subversion.

Moreover, the most arresting feature of Anglo-Saxon culture is its realistic appreciation of this irreducible conflict. People of this culture do not stand idly by if dissenting voices present "a clear and present danger." Yet their best respects are reserved for their outcast dissenters, at least after the dust is settled. Those whom it most venerates in the long run are sometimes the ones it most crucifies in the short run.

The conflict between necessary order and the necessary demands of conscience for an order it can approve pervades their every breath and teaching. As short run realists they preach the subordination of the dissenter to the security of the current order. As long run realists, they council the conscience to stand its grounds though the heavens fall. The words of Theodore Parker are typical:

> If a statute is right, I will ask how I can best obey it. When it is wrong, I will ask how I can best disobey it—most effectually, with the least violence. When we make the priest the keeper of our creed, the State the master of our conscience, then it is all over with us.[42]

The appreciation of the rejected dissenter has several aspects. First, he commonly bears a heroic quality. Cast out from the present order, he stands alone and yet not alone. Within his inner forum there gathers a host of unseen witnesses whose voices are his voice and whose strength is his strength. In this way, he is able to "out-vote the world," as it were, and gain an inward power that is stronger than his chains.

Second, above all he is not a revolter against order as such. He is not seeking the right to be a promiscuous patron of the vices. Caught in such acts he is abashed as his opponents try to show that his dissent is mere hypocrisy. He is not, in short, a representative of anarchy and chaos, even though he is rejected for fear his views would actually have these results. Thoreau, for example, was not speaking as an agent of anarchy in saying that no man, without disgracing himself, could associate himself with the American government of his day. But he was speaking as the agent of a revised American order in which all men would be free instead of some free and the rest slaves. His view caused all manner of chaos before the issue was settled. The public safety indeed required his being jailed. Had the New England businessman, cited above, been allowed to flout the tax provisions of the Social Security Act, his actions would have caused chaos aplenty. He was not, however, speaking as the avowed agent of chaos but of a made-over "New Deal" order in which public officials were prevented from sticking their noses into the traditional privacy of an upstanding businessman.

Third, whether legal or illegal, all dissent has the same logical status or form. Its negative content is a disaffirmation of the present order, because of some objectionable element, whereas its positive element is the affirmation of the present order made over with its objectionable elements left out. Every dissenter is thus the harbinger of a new (revised) society.

Society, through its courts can and must at some point draw a line between dissenters who can protest within the law, because they are harmless, and those who can't because they would lay unclean hands on the palladium of the Republic. The first are blessed with the Bill of Rights; the second are stamped with the odium of a public menace. The only difference between them being that, in some cases, only the dissenting view is rejected while the dissenter himself is kept within the circle of good fellowship, whereas in the other cases he himself is rejected along with his peculiar ideas.

But the historic future often deals rudely with such legalistic fly-specking; the outcasts of one age sometimes become the patron saints of the next. This does not mean that every rejected dissenter will find a nitch for himself in some historic future. It may be that most of them are but flukes that sink forever in the debris of history. But the same is true of those whose dissent is covered by the Bill of Rights. Even the Bill of Rights, while actually phrased by George Mason, is but a late historic acceptance of a social order which in prior days had no habitat except the inner forum of outcast dissenters such as Roger Williams, the Quakers, and others—men who had to be fed to the wolves because of the threatening posture they offered to the social order of their day.

Therefore, the dissenter who is rejected for the sake of peace and order in the short run, may well be a far more creative agent of long run social advance than the tamer sort whose dissent is always within the law. The short run demands that we "judge," whereas the long run elicits the injunction, "Judge not lest ye also be judged."

(4) *Traits of our individualistic culture:* As previously stated individual life includes two foci, as it were. First are the typical or common aspects of experience. Second are the exceptional. As an agent of the first, each individual is a stabilizer of the status quo, a guardian of the tried and true, "a 100 percent American." As an agent of the second he is (or would be) an innovator, a potential danger or blessing; often regarded as a genius if he stands for a better mousetrap, but a crackpot if he advocates a better social order.

Both aspects of experience are essential to a dynamic social order. Were individuals agents of only exceptional observations and views, society would go to pieces; were they agents of only common views and sentiments, society would become static. The usual American is a strong combination of both. In no other nation do people have such a reputation as "lone wolf" individualists. Yet as Gunnar Myrdal has observed, America is the most culturally unified country on earth even though it is the most heterogeneous in point of racial stock and national origins.[43]

But however prized and important the typical aspects of experience, modern culture is highly individualistic because it places much greater emphasis on the atypical. This fact is borne out in the gearing of its skills to exploiting the exceptional; its "news" spirit; its reliance on ancient art-forms for expressing common sentiments deeply felt; its loss of a "sense of history;" its declining interest in "closed systems" (of nature and truth); and its "at homeness" in the evolutionary world-view.

a. *Skills geared to exploiting the exceptional:* Illustrative of the individualistic nature of modern culture is the fact that the ancient Greeks were far superior to us in the ability (skill) for expressing the typical experiences of the community but not in exploiting the atypical experience or view as the doorway to a "new world."

Take the field of biography, for example. In Plutarch's lives one has the biography of the Ancient world. But what he gives is essentially character types rather than individuals. That is, he presents his figures as typical heroes or typical villians. As Mead observed:

> They embody the altitudes and the views, the values, of the community to which they belonged. Or they stand out as striking criminals, people of the type of Alcibiades. But, on the other side, you have the person who is essentially of the hero character. These figures . . . represent the virtues and vices of the community. What we fail to find in these biographies as contrasted with modern biographies is just that which commonly goes under the caption of "local color". They do not try to record experiences just as they took place; there is no reference to the form of, say, the food the hero ate, nothing of particular interest in the matter of clothes, or his gold score, the elements which we bring in by way of making a person seem real to us . . . traits which belong to him alone and set him apart from anyone else.[44]

No modern criminal would be attracted by Plutarch's Alcibiades, who merely personifies the manners and attitudes which are typical of any crook. He would want the kind of biographical detail which showed how crooks differed from each other. Only the knowledge of such differences can help him in improving his own proficiency. He is not interested in any contemplative appreciation of the criminal-type, which Plutarch portrays with consummate skill.

Like the ancient artist, the ancient scientist also was most adept at breaking into simple components the general knowledge of the community on given subjects and systematically putting it together again in a highly logical order. One does not find in Aristotle's *Physics*, for example, a body of facts unfamiliar to everyday observations. The same is true of his *Biology* and other great works. The ancient scientist did not have the technique of "controlled observation and experiment." Therefore, he could not make the observation of exceptional events the basis of his "research" problems, nor bring the exceptional hypothesis to a decisive test. In modern science such observations constitute "data" independent of existing theory, and must be explained by a new theory before it can be accepted. Without the techniques of controlled observation and experiment, ancient science could not recognize the exceptional experiences which are had first by an individual, not the community, as its proper building blocks. As Mead says:

> Look through the literature of the ancient world, through such a really marvelous book as Aristotle's *Habits of Animals*, which sums up the biological knowledge of the ancient world. You will be struck by the fact that there is not a reference to a proper name, to an individual, as a basis for the accounts which are given of the animals with which Aristotle's treatise deals. He refers to a number of philosophers whose opinions he is combating; but when it comes to the statement of the character he is describing, he never once refers to any individuals as having made this observation or that. He does not rest the value of the thought he is presenting on the testimony of anybody.[45]

b. *The "news" spirit:* Without techniques for identifying and using the atypical as a basis of revising the common views, the ancient community was largely devoid of what we call "news"—that which deviates from the customary. Nor could they recognize the value of the uniqueness of the individual as a factor in social change. Whether in science, journalism, or art, modern skills are essentially ways of finding experiences which differ from the usual. Accordingly, we are more interested in "news" than in a more effective expression of the customary. We are not content with heroes that typify the common attitudes toward great odds. We want the biographer to tell just what took place in his hero's life so we can see how his experiences differ from our own. And we want to know his peculiar moods and reflections—even any of his food and dress habits if they run counter to the expected. These "little things" must be reproduced, as they are precisely the means which enable the community of readers to evoke within themselves the exceptional views and sentiments of the individual. In this way the modern artist not only "enriches" life, but is often an even more effective agent of social change than the scientist. Unless he succeeds in portraying how his characters differ from the usual run of folks, we feel that the writer has failed us.

The same principle applies to journalism, whether of the popular or scientific variety. Any newspaper would soon go broke if it reported primarily the customary (typical) experiences of individuals. There is relatively little interest in normal behavior and law-observing. So, the papers run to crime, divorces—"sensational stuff." But they are "sensational" for the same reason that the records of the positions of the stars about the rim of the sun were sensational when first reported. Any content of life is sensational and therefore has news value, which runs counter to the expected, whether in scientific journals or newspapers. In both cases, the reported happenings are "data" (sensational) because they cannot be explained as an instance of the normal or typical views and behavior. The difference in each case is simply the competence with which the conditions and nature of the data ("sensational" experiences) are reported.[46] As described and analyzed by the sensational press, the conditions and nature of exceptional experiences lead only to momentary excitements, while in the hands of the scientist the same data may lead to innovations in accustomed ways instead of mere thrills.

c. *Reliance on ancient art forms for expressing common sentiments deeply felt:* But the fact that attention is mainly on the exceptional, as the key to change in the customary, does not mean that modern people take lightly their common views and sentiments. On the contrary, many modern people feel deeply and would embody these views and sentiments in fitting symbols so as to prize them the more.

But their originality and their creative powers of expression in this respect are quite limited. Everyone shares, for example, common attitudes on industry and commerce—our staff of life. But look at the statues we put on Chamber of Commerce buildings. They fall flat because they fail to evoke the very attitudes they are intended to arouse. So, when the urge to express what is typical of us all is especially powerful, we usually fall back on ancient art forms.

For example, all share a deep affection for that solid integrity of character which keeps an iron grip on its conviction, however rough the going. Few, if any, have so personified this trait as George Washington. We long desired a fitting symbol of this fact. At last we succeeded; not through any art-form of our own, but with an ancient Egyptian obelisk—a slender 550-foot shaft of stone piercing the sky over the crowds ambling by in respectful memory of the "Father of his country."

Again all share a profound affection for the strong will that does justice, walks humbly, and is filled with compassion. Feeling that not since the prophets of old had anyone so embodied this spirit of life as Abraham Lincoln, the American people sought to express their feeling in a fitting symbol that it might shine a brighter candle to their feet. With consummate perfection, they finally did so in the Lincoln Memorial, often called "the shrine of the nation"—a lovely thing, past saying. But it is not a modern art-form. It is Greek through and through in every line and shadow—the kind of temple the old Athenians built on almost every hilltop to house their local deities. Except that we placed inside it our beloved national hero, inscribing the Gettysburg address on the wall to his left and the Second Inaugural to his right, there is nothing about it which bears the remotest connection with American life.

d. *Loss of a "sense of history"*: Loss of originality in articulating the common content of life and experience is not the only consequence of shifting attention from the traditional to exceptional views and sentiments. The same shift marks, in great measure, the loss of a "sense of history." The feeling that, "we don't know where we are going, but we are on the way,"[47] seemingly crowds out any vital interest in the past from whence we come.

This not only holds for the man in the street but for the scientist and artist as well. Giving lip service to the past as the best guide to the future, the fact is that the more scientific we become in a given subject the more of an ignoramus we become, by and large, of those on whose shoulders we stand. Seldom, for example, can one find a physics text that does not say that Galileo, by dropping large and small stones from the tower of Pisa proved that bodies of different weights fall at the same rates. This is sheer myth, of course, as the slightest reading of his eminent contributions will show.

This loss of a sense of history is even more strikingly illustrated by the disappearance of the epic—the art-form which narrates, in elevated style, the heroic events and achievements of a past whose spirit lives on in the present. Few epics are written any more, and, if written, they aren't read, by and large. Carl Sandburg's experience is typical. For years he had been haunted with the idea of writing the "American epic." During the struggle of the Great War he settled to the task, explaining why in a memorable passage.

> . . .we know when a nation goes down and never comes back. . .one condition may always be found. They forgot where they came from. They lost sight of what brought them along. . . .But the mockers came. And the deniers were heard. And vision and hope faded. . . .And men whose forefathers would go anythere, holding nothing impossible in the genius of man, joined the mockers and deniers. . . .I have reached the period of life when. . .past, present and future become one. I know it is more reality than illusion when I look back and see my grandson and his wife three hundred years ago in the town of Plymouth - and in the next moment I see him in a place named Valley Forge and she is at home with their child wondering when the war will end - and again I see him in that tornado of action called Gettsburg and amid the suffering afterward he find time to write her a letter.
>
> I see their faces the same in those days as now. From one spot of time to another the faces repeat. . . .

> In a very real sense there is no such thing as death of thought and energy. The will and vision that motivated people in Plymouth did not fade but moved on alive and written on faces at Valley Forge. It is still with us. . . .
>
> You may bury the bones of men and later dig them up to find they have moldered into a thin white ash that crumbles in your fingers. But their ideas won. Their visions came through. . . .How can we say they are sunk and buried. They live in the sense that their dream is on the faces of living men and women today. . .In a rather real sense, . . . they go on, their faces here now, their lessons worth our seeing. They ought not to be forgotten—the dead who held in their clenched hands that which became the heritage of us, the living.[48]

In the next 1000 pages, Sandburg uses the old world and the new as a great stage on which he unfolds with fine artistry the sweep of the American "vision and hope" through the centuries from Plymouth Rock to the recent war. But his books had few readers, not because of lack of time but of motivation. A people, whose field of vision is the novel and exceptional, as a gateway to change in established ways, can have little more than a casual interest in "where they came from"; however heroic the deeds of their fathers or splendidly their tale is told.

e. *Declining interest in "closed systems" (of nature or truth):* This rising interest in the exceptional aspect of individual life as the avenue to a different future is accompanied by a declining interest in "closed systems"—the idea that if we but knew all there was to know about the present state of the world, prevailing knowledge would be so complete that no exceptions to it could ever arise.

This idea of an immutable "real world," and hence invariable truth has left its mark deep and wide on the Western mind, beginning with the old Greeks. Over 2000 years later the same "faith" remained undimmed in the world-view of the great physicist Pierre Laplace. Said he:

> We ought then to regard the present state of the universe as the effect of its anterior state and as the cause of the one which is to follow. Given for one instant an intelligence which could comprehend all the forces by which nature is animated, and the respective situations of the beings who compose it—an intelligence sufficiently vast to submit these data to analysis—it would embrace in the same formula the movements of the greatest bodies in the universe and those of the lightest atom; for it, nothing would be uncertain and the future, as the past, would be present to its eyes.[49]

But it is clearly not self evident that the present is but (1) an unfolded past and (2) an enfolded future such that both the past and the future could be completely foreseen from complete knowledge of the present. Neither is this proposition supported by the slightest empirical evidence. From what tacit dogma, then, does it follow? Just this: *Effects are in and like their causes,* meaning that effects are qualitatively like their causes. Literally nothing can be included in later events (effects) which was not included in prior (causes).[50]

From this premise, and this alone, it follows that if we know all there is to know about the present, we could predict (know) with complete accuracy both everything that will ever happen and everything that has already happened. Nothing really new could ever happen under the sun. Change—evolution—is but the unfolding of what is already unfolded. Nature is thus a closed system (i.e., closed to the novel or exceptional); so likewise is any system of knowledge which reveals all there is to know about the *present*.

As just stated, however, there is no evidence that we could completely discern the past or future if we knew all there was to know about the present. Laplace tricked himself into feeling otherwise by his failure to see my distinction between logical connectives between propositions of our own making and causal relations between events with which we have nothing to do.

As a consequence, he inadvertently passed off as science the colorless dogma: *Effects are in and like their causes.* While Greek to the core, this dogma is not dead, even yet. For the modern scientist still affirms it when, in talking as a philosopher, he interprets the research process as being a tortoise-like approximation of a system of laws so complete that no exceptions to them can ever arise.

It may be observed, however, that such a world view, if actually realized, would destroy every central animation (value) of a democratic culture, including the research spirit itself. For there can be no place in such a world for social advance; and hence no place for a culture whose leading purpose is the fullest development of the unique capacities of each individual as a means to such advance. Nor could there be a place in it for controlled observation and experiments, laboratories or research scientists. For these have a role to play only where events may arise which cannot be foretold from any analysis of the present, however complete. In fact, there could be no place in such a world for the uniqueness of each personality since, if all future events are apprehended in the present, there is no possibility of an experience on the part of anyone which can deviate from accepted opinion and practice. Accordingly, any social order, centered in a Bill of Rights, would be sheer nonsense, as no occasion for dissent could ever arise. Moreover, everyone would be bored to death for the lack of "news," as there can be no news without the exceptional occurrence. Worse still, in such a world people would be without minds, since the "mind" is but a problem solving mechanism and the essence of any problem is a conflict between the customary and the exceptional experience and outlooks.

f. *Evolutionary world-view as "the home" of individualistic culture:* For such reasons, the spirit of modern individualism is increasingly ill at ease with the idea of nature as merely the unfolding of that which is already enfolded from the foundations of the world. It seeks a status in the universe which is no longer afforded by this classical interpretation of time and change. More congruent with the modern spirit is the evolutionary world-view that (1) genuine novelties do arise in nature, and, being qualitatively different from their prior states or causes, (2) they are unpredictable. No amount of analysis of the feudal economy, for example, can prevision the enterprise economy, nor can any insight in the quadruped world, however complete, foretell the rise of the bipeds. Not even if we knew all there is to know about the present could we foretell the "new heaven and the new earth" of tomorrow. (3) As they first arise, new facts or events are "irrational" in that they run counter to all prevailing views of what should happen. Being thus exceptional experience, (4) they constitute problems, the job of enquiry being to revise customary views and practices so as to explain them. (Always it is the law which is sacrificed; not the facts or novelties.)[51] In this way, (5) new pasts as well as new futures are always arising before the eyes. For the new theory constructs a different past to explain the occurrence of the novel events (new data) and predicts a different future from that foretold by older theories. Thus, for every generation a different Ceasar crosses the Rubicon and a new Jesus walks on Galilee.

In terms of this evolutionary view, the central value objectives of a democratic culture rest on more solid foundations than mere ignorance of all there is to know about any present state of nature. For even perfect (complete) knowledge would not give a system of truths to which nature will not evolve exceptions.

The door of nature is not closed to the advent of genuine novelties. The whole future is not enfolded in the present as is the oak in the acorn. It can be predicted only with probabilities, even to an intelligence who knew all there was to know about the present. Even with such intelligence on the part of everyone, exceptions would still arise in someone's experience, rendering him a dissenter and critic of accepted views and providing him the opportunity of advancing a more adequate account of nature.

The evolutionary world-view thus enables the modern individual, with his penchant for creative advance, to feel more "at home" in his universe. For it casts out the ideal of history as an approximation of a system of truth and practice which may not be rocked to its foundations by some dissenter. If our society is to be kept open so that its growth can continue, the individual as a dissenter must be taken into account; for it is the dissenter who often ensures social growth.

CHAPTER 3. ADDITIONAL ECONOMIC AND PHILOSOPHIC ASPECTS OF THE SPIRIT OF ENTERPRISE

In the early struggle with the theme of this chapter, I asked a number of friends what they conceived the spirit of enterprise to be, adding that I wished they would not "think it over" but simply give me the first thought that came to mind. Said one: "Enterprise is the fast buck—something for nothing if you are slick enough not to get caught." Another replied: "Enterprise is a rat race—get the other fellow before he gets you." Still another answered: "Enterprise is a profit-making economy as distinguished from socialism."

None of these characterizations is wholly false, as each puts a finger on some well-recognized feature of the workaday world of most of us. Yet, a moment's reflection shows all of them to be far from the essential truth. For enterprise is very much alive and respected in America as a mode of life and character that is prized above all others. No people, however, thus prize a manner of life whose dominant aspiration is for the fast buck, or to get the other fellow before he gets you. The same principle applies to profit making—the endless round of turning little piles into bigger ones. Even if the reverse were true, this mercenary definition of enterprise is too narrow. It says in effect that the peculiar attributes of character, embodying the spirit of enterprise, are a virtual monopoly of a particular occupational class—business. Most businessmen themselves would be the first to protest this. For we feel almost instinctively that the spirit of enterprise is universal, being equally at home in all employments—religion, teaching, medical, bricklaying, housecleaning, and the like, as well as business. It is thus false to identify enterprise as essentially a zeal for turning small sums into larger ones. On the contrary, its dynamics, we venture to say, is an aspiration for the achievement of some sort of character or a way of life and work which we genuinely respect and esteem above all others—an aspiration of such potency that, in great measure, it has lifted and carried America across the peaks and the valleys of her history.

But what sort of character is this? How may it be defined and the definition used in achieving a better understanding of "What makes America tick"? This is the first concern of this chapter.

I. The Meaning and Nature of Enterprise

Aspiration for Meriting Differential Status as the Dominant Striving of Men

Our point of departure in handling this question is the assumption that the dominant striving of the human spirit is the aspiration for meriting differential esteem (status or fellow acceptance) because of one's (individual or group) real or fancied superior capacities for deeds that are most prized by the larger community. It should be emphasized that the final object of this aspiration is

Selections from unpublished manuscript, "The Spirit of Enterprise as the Product of the Theologian and the New World."

not just the esteem or status. What is supremely desired is to be the sort of personality that deserves the higher esteem or status because of its superior capacities and deeds. The esteem—fellow acceptance—as such is an external good, like the contents of one's purse. One may stand high in the eyes of his fellows and yet be most depressed with himself because he is convinced that he does not deserve his exceptional status, feeling it would not be accorded him were it not for his family connections, or the smile of lady luck, or a fickle public that passes over others more worthy than he. Conversely, any individual, class or nation may deeply feel that the larger community withholds from them the higher status which their capacities and deeds, actual or potential, truly deserve. In such cases, they tend to become rebels, demanding a new order that will accord them the dignity they merit. For example, precisely this sense of injustice is the dynamics of both the American Negro's protest against every sort of racial discrimination and of the revolt of Asian and African people against "colonialism." This is not the kind of unrest that can be appeased with money. For the final concern of the status aspiration is not for economic goods but for being the sort of character whose capabilities and deeds increasingly merit the esteem of all observers, including oneself. Therefore, except as economic goods are effective symbols of this higher achievement, they are of little account.

Types of Tests for Relative Worthiness of Individuals for Social Ranks as Equivalent to Different Types of Cultures, Character and Ideals of Duty

Being common to all peoples, the aspiration for meriting differential status does not distinguish one culture, type of character, or sense of duty from another. However, under different conditions of living and making a living, this propensity for achievement works itself out in a variety of methods by which different communities test the worthiness of individuals for different degrees of public esteem otherwise known as rungs in the social ladder, ranks in the hierarchy of social employments, social roles, and the like. For example, the feudal culture, out of which the modern West evolved, was one in which the highest ranks were achieved by conquest. Under such warlike conditions of living and making a living the larger community, for the sake of its very survival, came to test the relative utility of its numbers by their capacities for exploit. Persons passing this test with flying colors were most honored; deemed most noble, and prized above all others as being most useful in meeting the community's felt need for plundering its neighbor, warding off aggression from without, and putting down insurrection from within. Those making only moderate marks by this test of public utility were relegated to the business employments, while the still less fit were placed in the ranks of manual workers, the dirtiest and hardest work being reserved for the ne'er-do-wells.

As the aspiration for achievement, under the conditions just mentioned, thus manifested itself collectively as a public demand that individuals demonstrate their worth through tests of exploit, so it manifested itself in solitary individuals as a striving for meriting differential status through superior prowess—all those qualities of character which make man a formidable animal.

Where the normal mode of living and making a living is peaceful industry, the public test of merit for differential status is workmanlike excellence in any occupation in which one is engaged. In such a culture, the type of character most prized is commonly called the self-made man as contrasted with the "Lord" of feudal times. As this shift in the test of merit for differential status amounted to a revolutionary change in the forms of culture and correlative character ideals, so it was also an equally revolutionary change in the indices of the heroic life—the noble and the good. For example, in line with the prowess test of merit, popular proofs of superior manhood consisted of styles of clothing, hair-do, and other trivia which showed at a glance that any individual was of no account if either he or his ancestors had ever had the slightest connection with either business or manual employments. During the Age of Jackson there was a high pitched revolt against all this. That was the era in which the self-made man ideal booted out the immaculate aristocrat as the supreme object of adoration. The American people rose up as in a righteous wrath and demanded that mudsill origins be used in place of broadcloth as the infallible proofs of whether or not a man deserved the highest place in the esteem and affections of his fellows. The worst thing you could then say about a man was that he was "born with a silver spoon in his mouth." Ever since, Hamilton's "rich and the well born" have felt themselves at a somewhat unfair advantage in the race of life.

As various public tests for meriting status differentiate the generic aspiration for such status into types of culture and correlative character ideals, so they likewise give rise to unique ideals of duty which individuals use in making either themselves or their community toe the line. For example, it is well recognized that the American farmer, in being moved by the aspiration for proving his good repute through superior industry, feels guilty of wasting his life and failing in his obligations to all those near him if he sits in the shade longer than is necessary to catch his breath when his fields need tending. Out of this peculiar sense of obligation, the farmer is said to drive himself from "sun to sun." But it is equally well recognized that, if he thus does his duty and then the larger community pays him little or nothing for his produce, there is no group more capable of rising up in righteous indignation and condemning his social order for not practicing what it preaches—its failure, that is, to reward with at least a decent living those who have diligently complied with its own work imperative. Farmers are often called economic illiterates but seldom are they ever thought of as delinquents in the moral mandates of enterprise.

In biology we think of the "life process" as becoming differentiated into various species in response to varying environmental conditions. In similar fashion we may think of varying social conditions of living and making a living as differentiating the propensity for achievement into many types of culture, character, and ideals of duty, depending on the way in which any given community measures (tests) the relative merits of its members for its various employments, esteem, privilege, wealth, and power.

The Spirit of Enterprise as a Peculiar Ideal of Duty

In line with this principle, the spirit of enterprise may be defined as the aspiration for meriting an ever higher sense of self respect, social and economic status through intensive development and use of one's workmanlike capabilities in any employment of his choice. In these terms, the spirit of enterprise is the feeling that one (individual or group) fails in his obligation to do the best he can by himself, his country and all men if he chooses the "easy ways" at the expense of his workmanlike excellence. Feeling that one has failed in measuring up to this enterprise ideal of duty commonly manifests itself as a sense of guilt for having frittered away one's time and talents, thereby bringing down upon himself the crushing judgment that his life is drawing to a close with nothing to show for itself except an accumulation of birthdays. In his autobiography, William Allen White has given a vivid account of how this sense of guilt assailed him upon his thirtieth birthday:

> In 1898 I attained the age of thirty. My name now appeared on the Gazette's masthead as W. A. White. I felt that there was something irrevocably sad in being thirty—middle age. I felt impatient at the futility of my life, that I had done so little and now it was about over. Willie White, the little boy who skipped a rock across the creek in a serpentine curve and died to become Will White, the youth who devoted himself to love and combat and music and became a slave to John B. Alden, the book publisher, and then passed away having begot Will A. White, the young printer, the reporter, the budding poet, the bridegroom—those three dead ancestors of mine seemed to be mocking me; seemed to be asking me; seemed to be asking me what I had done with the visions they had seen and given me, and what had become of the man they had brought forth. Those were haunting, disturbing questions. When I heard them coming suddenly into my consciousness in the still watches of the night, they prodded, wound up my energies, rehabilitated my ambitions and probably thwarted my vanity.[1]

That the spirit of enterprise thus involves a peculiar sense of duty is readily apparent in the everyday American judgment that of equally competent men in any field, the most deserving of esteem is he who, by his own diligence and industry, has lifted himself from the lowest point on the status ladder.

We venture the view that the cultural trait which most sets America apart is not its devotion to the democratic creed; other people equal, and may even excel us in this, as for example the Swiss, the Scandinavians, and the English. But here, more than anywhere else, at all social levels the aspiration for meriting differential rank takes the form of "trying to make something" of oneself through diligent use and development of his vocational capabilities. There is hardly a household in the land which does not fill its children with hope and assurance that a good future awaits them if only they develop their useful capacities to the full. To this end America prides herself on demanding, as no other country. "an equal chance" for all. In line with this observation, we shall argue in a later chapter that the American version of the democratic creed stems far more from this workmanlike form of the achievement aspiration than from the 18th century enlightenment doctrine of the perfectability of man. There is little place, as we shall see in the world view of enterprise, for this doctrine because a people with this outlook are of the almost instinctive persuasion that the propensity to "get something for nothing" is a deliquency of the human spirit which cannot be eradicated by a little more time, science, and education. It runs deeper than any environmental hooks can reach.

Awaiting the later development of the connections between the enterprise and democratic creed, it is sufficient to observe here that the dynamics of the American economy has always stemmed less directly from the abundance of our natural resources than from the fact that here as nowhere else the achievement aspiration is so effectively coupled with workmanlike modes of expression. To say that this outstanding cultural trait of America is the "effect" of her natural riches is like saying that a horse will drink if you take him to water, whereas we all know that he will do so only if he is thirsty. So, likewise the significance of the vast, virgin continent of an earlier day is not that it produced the spirit of enterprise, as the sun produces the tan, but that it answered in a magnificient way a prior thirst of our people for achieving the kind of personalities they most respected by refusing to choose the "easy ways" at the expense of their workmanlike excellence. The significance, then, of the American wilderness, as a character-forming force throughout three centuries of our national life, is not that it "created" the spirit of enterprise but that under its challenge, this spirit flowered into the American Dream. This theme will be amplified in a later section.

Economically speaking, the "easy ways," of course, are equivalent to "unnecessary" leisure and spending. No hard and fast line can be drawn between "necessary" and "unnecessary." Yet, each of us draws such a line whenever his sense of obligation to do his best by himself, his family, his country, or mankind is confronted with a choice of additional ease at the expense of his workmanlike excellence. No level of income, however high, ever completely exempts one from such choices.

The Spirit of Enterprise as Contrasted With Weber's "Spirit of Capitalism" and Veblen's "Instinct of Workmanship"

We should like to further explore the foregoing concept of enterprise by contrasting it with Max Weber's "spirit of capitalism," on the one hand, and Thorstein Veblen's "instinct of workmanship" on the other.

Weber defined the "spirit of capitalism" as an "obligation which the individual is supposed to feel and does feel toward the content of his professional activity, no matter in what it consists, in particular no matter whether it appears on the surface as the utilization of his personal powers, or only of his material possessions (as capital)." Weber adds significantly that this "peculiar idea . . . of one's duty in a calling, is what is most characteristic of the social ethic of capitalistic culture, and is in a sense the fundamental basis for it."[2]

In *form*, Weber's definition of the "spirit of capitalism" is quite similar to our concept of enterprise. In their larger contexts, however, the concepts differ in two fundamental respects. First, we view the enterprise sense of obligation as being only one of many ideals of duty which, under different cultural conditions, may arise from the aspiration for differential status that is common to all people alike. Nowhere does Weber appear to look upon his "spirit of capitalism" as a particular instance of this more generic aspiration for achievement. Therefore, as a tool of analysis, Weber's formulation and treatment of the "spirit of capitalism" has very limited usefulness for any purpose except dissecting the social and economic attitudes of the Puritan divines.

117

Second, Weber's great originality lay in perceiving that the modern sense of obligation to follow workmanlike ways, instead of the easy ones, does not stem from the slow accretions of technological advance and change in form of business organization but from older religious attitudes toward God's work. However, in this highly original insight, Weber, in our judgment, was overly preoccupied with the asceticism and the Calvinist doctrine of predestination. In this way he missed the essential purpose or spirit of the older religious sense of obligation to God's work, and which was carried over from the ministerial to other employments by the Protestant reformers. This is true because Weber did not recognize any essential difference between Oriental and Christian asceticisms. When applied to all occupations, both types lead to wealth accumulation, as each enjoins work instead of loafing and frugality instead of needless spending. Weber makes much of this point in his Economic History. It is well recognized, however, that Oriental asceticism was and is practiced for its own sake, which is not true of Christian asceticism. The latter is an extreme expression of the Divine Imperative which, in the present context, may be defined as the feeling that one is unfaithful in his duty as a workman in God's vineyard if he expends his energies in needless leisure and spending for the sake of his own comfort as long as the needs of any other are greater than his own.

In broad outline, the next section shows the historical connection between this Divine Imperative and the modern spirit of enterprise as a peculiar attitude which one may or may not assume toward his chosen work. In this way a warm kinship is recognized between the spirit of enterprise and the age-old religious traditions of the West—a bond which holds a high place in the affections of America long after the asceticism of the Middle Ages and the Calvinist Doctrine of Predestination have passed into the limbo of cultural antiques.

On first sight there is a striking similarity between the spirit of enterprise, as previously defined, and what Veblen called the "instinct of workmanship." He defined this as "a taste for effective work, and a distaste for futile effort...a sense of the merit of serviceability of efficiency and of the demerit of futility, waste or incapacity."[3] In another formulation, he said, "All men have this quasi-aesthetic sense of economic or industrial merit, and to this sense of economic merit futility and inefficiency are distasteful."[4]

In terms of either the spirit of enterprise or Veblen's instinct of workmanship, the ideal man would regard "waste" as any expenditure of human energies in leisurely and consummatory activities over and above that required to maintain one's workmanlike proficiency. Veblen would cringe at the suggestion of any similarity between his own outlook and that of the Puritan. The fact is, however, that no Puritan ever equaled his withering scorn of "conspicuous leisure and consumption." There was as little place in his value system as in that of any Puritan for any apparel more elegant than gingham or calico.

The sharp distinction between the "spirit of enterprise," as previously defined and Veblen's "instinct of workmanship" turns on what employments are regarded as "serviceable." Viewing the "instinct of workmanship" as man's "proclivity for turning the material means of life to account"[5] all occupations, according to Veblen, are essentially a waste of life which do not turn human energies and physical resources into material goods and services. Veblen's intent here is to oust the business and religious employments from the category of the useful, and therefore outside the pale of good repute. Business, in his workmanlike view of merit, is essentially predatory rather than serviceable. Said he:

> ... the businessman's activity ... is not to be classed ... as productive or industrial activity at all. Its objective point is an alteration in the distribution of wealth. His business is to sell and buy—sell in order to buy cheaper, buy in order to sell dearer. It may or may not, indirectly, and in a sense incidentally, result in enhanced production. The businessman may be equally successful in his enterprise, and he may be equally well remunerated, whether his activity does or does not enrich the community.[6]

Centered in the management of purchase and sales transactions with an eye to maximizing the net, and only incidentally in the process of production, business is essentially salesmanship, which in ideal terms is achieving an income through the capacity to "promise everything and deliver nothing." In these terms, secular business has much to learn from the clerics—the most accomplished salesman, according to Veblen, the world has ever produced. In a biting passage, he declared:

> The Propaganda of the Faith is quite the largest, oldest, most magnificant, most unabashed, and most lucrative enterprise in sales-publicity in all Christendom. . . .By contrast, the many secular adventures in salesmanship are no better than upstarts. . . . No pronouncements on rubber heels, soap powders, lipsticks, or yeast-cakes, not even Sapphira Buncombe's Vegetative Compound, are yet able to ignore material facts with the same magisterial detachment, and none has yet commanded the same unreasoning assent or acclamation. . . . Commercial sales-publicity of the secular sort evidently falls short, hitherto, in respect to the pitch and volume of make-believe which can be put over effectually and profitably. . . . It is of the nature of sale-publicity to promise much and deliver a minimum. . . Worked out to its ideal finish, as in the promises and performances of the publicity-agents of the Faith, it should be the good fortune of the perfect salesman in the secular field to promise everything and deliver nothing.[7]

In Veblen, we witness a singularly able man, who was deeply devoted to the ideal of achievement through workmanlike excellence in any useful employment of his choice, and who for this very reason found himself in bitter conflict with his enterprise civilization which was devoted to the same ideal. How is this to be explained? There are good reasons for supposing that, through living in the 19th and 20th centuries, he was in effect, if one may use the term, a small-scale reincarnation of the 17th century struggle between the Lutheran and Puritan outlooks on life—a fact he most effectively concealed with a debonair mask of agnosticism.

Veblen's parents were Norwegian immigrants to the Wisconsin frontier of the 1850's. They were Lutheran farmers and more than once the victims of sharp trading by Yankees in the small towns. Veblen had the highest esteem for his father, saying that his was one of the brightest minds he had ever known and that his first book, *The Theory of the Leisure Class*, was largely worked out on the farm under the stimulation of his father.

On numerous occasions, this writer has heard Norwegian students of economics say that this book is an excellent summary of the basic spirit and attitudes of Norwegian mores toward work and business. It is well recognized that the religious scaffolding of these mores is Lutheran to the core. It is also well recognized that the Lutheran tradition embodies two attitudes of fundamental economic importance. The first is the "work imperative"—the feeling that diligence and industry are the foremost marks of a Godly man. In abolishing monasticism, Luther eliminated a selected area for the practice of the higher righteousness, saying that the gospel could be exemplified in the midst of secular callings—except that he did not call them secular. As he had extended the office of priesthood to all believers, so he likewise extended the concept of a divine calling to all occupations.

The very expression "vocational guidance" comes directly from Luther. As God, Christ, the Virgin Mary, the Prince of the apostles and shepherds labored, so we all must labor in our callings. God has no hands or feet of his own. He must achieve his ends through human instruments—the lowlier the task the better. Luther never tired of defending those occupations which for one reason or another were disparaged, including the scholarly employments. Said he:

> Workers with brawn are prone to despise workers with brain, such as city secretaries and schoolteachers. The soldier boasts that it is hard work to ride in armor and endure heat, frost, dust and thirst. But I'd like to see a horseman who could sit the whole day and look at a book. It is no great trick to hang two legs over a horse. They say writing is just pushing a feather, but I notice that they hang swords on their hips and feathers in high honor on their hats. Writing occupies not just the fist of the foot while the rest of the body can be singing or jesting, but the whole man. As for schoolteaching, it is so strenuous that no one ought to be bound to it for more than ten year.[8]

In this high emphasis on the work imperative as the Godly way of life, the Lutheran and Puritan tradition speak with the same voice. In both cases, monastic "idleness" is a "stench." If Adam had never fallen, he would still have worked at tilling and hunting. Begging should be abolished.

But here the similarity stops. Luther resented business employments on the ground that their controlling objective is not the transformation of materials and physical forces into usable goods but the manipulation of purchase and sales transaction for the sake of making money, the making of goods being only a secondary consideration. In line with this ancient and medieval outlook, Luther drew a sharp, invidious distinction between occupations. Agriculture stood in highest esteem. Next were the handicraft occupations which, in the course of time, evolved into modern industry. Then came the occupational black sheep—traders and money lenders, which in the course of time evolved into the modern businessman. That Luther's scorn of these "nonproductive" employments was no less biting than that of Veblen is singularly exemplified in the cartoon that Luther placed on the title page of his tract on usury. In this cartoon a farmer is shown in the act of returning not only the goose which he had borrowed but also the eggs.

Thus, for all his penchant for sophisticated heathenism, Veblen was in fact the finest personification of the rock-bottom social and economic attitudes of orthodox Lutheranism that the world has ever produced. In view of his extreme pains to appear "scientific" at every step, it is ironic that, in his life-long preachment and elaboration of the "instinct of workmanship," Veblen is but a reincarnation in modern secular terms of the powerful social and economic attitudes of the famous 17th century clergyman—Martin Luther. As Luther was

120

able to use the esteem of a traditionalist civilization for the handicraftsman to hang the opprobrium of "under-the-table" performers on the businessmen of his day, so Veblen, by masking this same pre-capitalistic value judgment as the "instinct of workmanship," was able to similarly exploit the enormous prestige which present-day enterprise civilization bestows on his astute terminology. What Luther and Veblen alike most resented was a civilization in which the businessman has come into possession of the most precious of all treasures—the esteem and veneration which the indulgent multitude gives without price to those whom it looks upon as leading the kind of life that is most prized for its own sake. Luther resented it as being contrary to the will of God, and Veblen resented it as contrary to the "instinct of workmanship." Because of his approbation of work and disesteem of business, Luther could respect only a civilization that placed the craftsman in full control of the production process. So, likewise, Veblen for the same reason could respect only a world which lodged this control in technicians—engineers—which are merely Luther's handicraftsmen in modern dress.

> It is the part of technicians, between them, to know the country's available resources, in mechanical power and equipment; to know and to put into practice the joint stock of technological knowledge which is indispensable to industrial production; as well as to know and take care of the community's habitual need and use of consumable goods.[9]

Masking the traditional Lutheran work imperative as the "instincts of workmanship," Veblen resented the enterprise view and way of life because it invested the businessman with the right to "exercise a running veto power over the technicians and their productive industry."[10] At the same time, he saw quite clearly that there was little hope of ever doing away with the enterprise system, at least not in America. To do so, it would be necessary to exclude businessmen from all positions of trust. There, he saw, is the rub. For Americans, by and large, trust no other group but businessmen—the very group and the only group which Veblen regarded as completely unqualified for the social role they now play. So, after delivering his scathing indictments of the enterprise system on grounds of "scientific fact," he concluded: "There is nothing in the situation that should reasonably flutter the sensibilities of the Guardian or of that massive body of well-to-do citizens who make up the rank and file of absentee owners, just yet."[11]

Few, if any, men have been more deeply attached than Veblen to a life of achievement through workmanlike proficiency in some useful employment. This was the kind of life his fathers led. It was the kind that Veblen led and preached, as few have ever done. No enterpriser was ever more devoted than he to the work imperative. But he was the spiritual heir of the Lutheran tradition which, in its most creative epoch, had drawn a circle around the serviceable occupations that left the business employments outside the pale of good repute. In contrast, Veblen's America, by and large, was the cultural heir of the Puritan tradition which, in its most creative hour, achieved a more universal outlook—a world-view that embraced all occupations, including business, as equally worthy opportunities for earning the applause of conscience.

A tragic loneliness awaits any man who is caught in the head-on clash between his own deepest value judgments and those of his fellow countrymen concerning the type (way) of life that each most prizes. Thus denied the joys that arise from the sense of common bonds, his days are those of a stranger and across the threshold of the years he walks alone, a pathetic sojourner from another world, as it were, like the ghost of Hamlet's father. So, it was with Veblen. Born of immigrant parents on a Wisconsin farm in 1857, he was reared on a bleak frontier settlement by moderately enlightened parents among Norwegian refugees. As Dorfman explains, these Scandinavians, hardy and industrious, intent upon preserving the language and literature of their forefathers, were cut off from American society by an extreme form of cultural isolation. Thus, beginning with his cradle years, Veblen was an "outer." Leaving his rural and sectarian environment in 1874 to enter Carleton College at the age of 17, he began a long and torturous apprenticeship in academic maladjustment. Receiving his doctorate in philosophy at Yale in 1884 and a second doctorate in economics at Cornell in 1892 and attaining a far vaster erudition than even those two degrees suggest, it was not until he was 35 that he was even made a tutor. Not until he was 42 and then only after publishing his first book was he offered an instructorship at the University of Chicago.

Appearing at last in this great metropolitan center, he left behind him forever the country town, but not its impact upon his character. Imperfectly countrified, he could not be properly citified. His discomforts in both the rural and urban areas of his existence were now duplicated on the higher plane of his academic career, as he was never able to establish common ground with his colleagues and peers. This embittered him and filled his pen with sulphur. In the closing years of his life, he was so filled with weariness that he sought a traceless disappearance from the human scene. To this end he gave instructions that his body be burned and his ashes scattered to the four winds. Alienated throughout life from his fellows by his respect for a way of life they could not share, he did not wish in death to leave behind so much as a grave marker as evidence that he had ever lived.

Blessed with rare intellectual gifts, vast erudition, brilliant pernmanship, and kindled with a devotion from his Lutheran heritage to a workmanlike view of life that left out the business employments as an object of esteem, he was a peerless propagandist of an alien faith in a land of enterprise. As he always masked this clerical role with the appearance of a profound scientific undermining of the "ceremonial and magical beliefs" of enterprise, he tended to fill the business community, and more particularly its academic votaries, with apprehensions concerning the validity of its judgments as to the manner of life it most cherished. He could not batter down the walls of enterprise. These run too deeply to the Puritan tradition which, in contrast to the Lutheran, achieved those monumental innovations in social and economic attitudes that ushered in the modern world. But, like Socrates of ancient Athens, he was a most effective gadfly of the false pretensions of the "American system"—a self-deceiving pride which, if unpunctured, tends to corrode and corrupt any national ethos (creed of life) to a point of disrespect. In these terms, America may increasingly welcome the memory of this home-bred alien as one of her most illustrious sons.

In calling attention to the divergent views of business employments inherent in the Lutheran and Puritan traditions, we may note in passing that the latter is not to be narrowly identified with the handful that landed at Plymouth Rock in 1620. Broadly speaking, Puritanism includes all the descendants of the Protestant Revolt except Lutheranism on the one hand and Anglicanism on the other. It includes five main streams of American settlement. First were the New England Puritans whose descendants spread throughout New England, to New York, and to the Ohio Valley. Second was the great stream of Scotch-Irish immigrants of over 150,000 Presbyterians in the 18th century. They were descendants of the Presbyterian Scots who in the reign of James I had settled in Ulster on confiscated estates of rebellious nobles. Because of economic discriminations, religious persecutions, and land evictions, they took refuge in the New World. Entering the Middle Atlantic ports, this stream of Puritans flowed South along the Shenandoah Valley, turned West over the Alleghenies and traversed the present States of Kentucky and Tennessee and on down the Ohio Valley. Along this route a little earlier also flowed a third stream of Puritans. These were German immigrants, mainly from the Palatinate and Switzerland, and belonged to the reformed or Calvinistic branch of Protestantism. Beginning in 1709 and culminating in the middle of the century, this migration was the effect of war, invasion, persecution, and economic distress that had continued in Western Germany almost uninterruptedly since the outbreak of the Thirty Years' War.

A fourth stream of Puritans were the French Huguenots, coming to America after the Revocation of the Edict of Nantes in 1685 and settling in considerable numbers in South Carolina. A fifth stream were the Dutch of the Dutch Reformed Church who settled in New York and constituted an independent colony until 1664. Like the Huguenots they were good Calvinists. Other powerful sects included in the Puritan Calvinist branch of the Protestant Reform movement were the Baptists and the Methodists.

At the time of the Revolution, the population of the Thirteen Colonies was 2,500,000. The number of these who were in a broad sense adherents of Calvinistic or closely allied sects has been estimated as follows:

Congregationalists (mainly New England Puritans).	575,000
Presbyterians (mainly Scotch-Irish)	410,000
Dutch Reformed	75,000
German Reformed	50,000
Baptists	25,000
Total	1,135,000

The great Methodist expansion was just beginning. Catholics represented about 25,000 and Jews approximately 2,000. There were some Lutherans and also an indeterminate number with no religious creed.

Deducting these, the number of Anglicans could not have been more than 1,000,000. This figure, however, includes 533,000 Negroes, of which 476,000 were in the South and whose adherence to the creed of their masters was largely nominal. As compared with the Puritan sects the Anglicans were less zealous and their piety less central to their thinking and practice.

In view of these facts, it is safe to assume:

... that the influence of Puritanism ... contributed uniquely and profoundly to the making of the American mind when the American mind was in the making.[12]

The Spirit of Enterprise as Contrasted With the Economic
Man and Traditionalism

Before turning to a formal analysis of the casual connections between the older religious aspiration for superior achievement through devotion to God's work and the modern striving for differential status through intensive use of one's capabilities in any employment of his choice, we should like to explore the latter by contrasting it with the "economic man" on the one hand, and traditionalism on the other.

The polar opposite of the aspiration to merit differential esteem, through superior workmanlike achievements, is commonly recognized as the economic self—the self which above all else desires unlimited ease and luxury, and therefore resists any expenditure of useful effort except as a necessary evil—a means of avoiding the greater peril of being deprived of a livelihood altogether. Its kingdom of heaven is an income without work.

Going by different names in different epochs, this modern concept of the economic man is a familiar figure from the very dawn of Western thought. In Plato's *Republic*, for example, he is portrayed as the ideal tyrant—the one who affirms that, according to the "law of nature," what each of us would most like to have is an absolute monopoly of sovereign power because he could then use the capabilities and effort of the whole community solely as a means to his own purposes, utterly free of any sense of obligation to render any service in return. Throughout the ascendancy of the church the "economic man" is the theologian's "natural man." And it is well recognized that the modern labeling of this creature as the "economic man" is but a secularized version of the Biblical doctrine of "original sin." What is not so commonly recognized is that, in these terms, the enterprise tradition has always taken this doctrine seriously. That is, as previously stated, the enterprise outlook now, as always, is of the persuasion that the predatory attitudes, personified as the "economic man," are an inherent aspect of human nature, meaning that they cannot be wholly explained as the deposit of "bad institutions" nor can they ever be entirely eradicated by surrounding and conditioning men with a system of "good institutions." In this limited but important sense, the enterprise creed of life is not optimistic. Though the value judgments of the spirit of enterprise are diametrically opposed to those of the "economic man," respect of enterprise for the formidable staying powers of this animal is too great to ever permit an enterprise culture to take seriously the notion that men can ever lift themselves into the kingdom of heaven by their own bootstraps.

As the spirit of enterprise is thus the polar opposite of that of the "economic man," so likewise it stands in sharp opposition to the spirit of traditionalism.

As previously stated, the aspiration for meriting higher status through superior proficiency in some socially esteemed mode of behavior is common to all people. In this sense, there are no indolent people—no ne'er-do-wells. But the socially prized mode of behavior for proving one's merit to higher status varies from culture to culture. In the tight caste Hindu culture, for example, the status striving takes the form of proving one's merits to a higher status in the next life through superior proficiency in conforming with the rigorous requirements of his caste role in his present social order. An amazingly effective incentive to such conformity is the doctrine of reincarnation according to which one's status in the next life may range all the way from a heavenly being down to toads and vermin, depending on the proficiency with which one observes the prescriptions of his caste role in this life. Thus, as an inducement for the untouchable not to let his shadow fall across the path of a high caste, the brimstone of Dante's Inferno pales to insignificance in comparison with the idea that one's just deserts for violating his class responsibilities consist in being reborn as a centipede in his next life.

As the powerful aspiration for achieving an ever higher status for one's person, either in this life or the next, is thus the dynamics of the Hindu and enterprise culture alike, there is little point in the false pride, so typical of an enterprising people, that they are full of ambition for improving their lot whereas the same is not ture of many other peoples of the earth. It would be more in keeping with the facts for them to have the humility to inquire how they ever happened to fall into the "superstition" that, whatever one's income, the most appropriate means for proving his deserts to a higher status are the intensive development and use of his workmanlike capabilities. This is so rare a variant of the achievement aspiration that its existence almost staggers the imagination.

For the fact is that among most peoples the community approved mode of earning a higher status (self respect and public esteem) is other than proficiency in ordinary employments, particularly those involving manual labor and business activities. These symbolize demerit—waste of life, futility—incapacity for being the sort of personalities that are prized above others because of their (supposedly) superior capabilities. Such cultures are commonly said to be characterized by the spirit of traditionalism. Three traits place this spirit in sharp contrast with that of enterprise.

First, as a peculiar sense of duty, it is the feeling that one fails to do his best by himself, his family, class, country, or mankind if he persists in doing appreciably more work than is necessary to support his customary level of living. His felt duty is to work this much and then "take it easy," convinced that marked expenditure of his energies beyond this point stems from greed and miserliness and is therefore incompatible with his highest obligation.

Second, the spirit of traditionalism includes a very different concept of rationality from that of enterprise. Because the spirit of enterprise is an aspiration for achieving a higher status through greater industry, the enterpriser is most delighted with an offer of a larger volume of work at somewhat less pay per unit than a smaller volume because he would make a greater total income than otherwise. He would regard anyone a fool who would not do likewise. Yet, for the traditionalist, this whole attitude of the enterpriser is the epitome of irrationality—a fact delightfully expressed in Boudin's account of his conversation with an Indian in a South American village.

"I like your flute, I will buy it. How much does it cost?" "Five solas, senor."
"That seems like a lot to me; if I buy half a dozen, how much will you charge

me?" Of course, I expect to pay less for each flute, but the reply comes at once:

"That will be seven solas, senor."

Slightly puzzled, I continue the experiment. "What if I order a dozen?"

"In that case, it will be ten solas for each flute, senor."

"Look here! The more flutes I order, the more profit you will be getting, but instead of encouraging me to order more, you are discouraging me."

The Indian looks at me with an enigmatic and slightly mocking smile as if to say, "These white visitors are certainly strange people."

"But naturally, senor," he says, "to make one flute is fun; to make six would bore me; to make twelve would simply be unbearable." As Boudin there observes, "The Indian's attitude is dominated by his sense of the disutility of labor. His method of reasoning is perfectly rational, but his rationality is not mine."[13]

Third, it is widely recognized that traditionalist cultures are characterized by what an older generation of economists called the low productivity of high wages and vice versa. This means that if appreciably higher than customary wages are offered, workers will strongly tend to increase their leisure and decrease their working time to a point where their total earnings are sufficient to support their customary levels of living. Conversely, if lower than customary wages are offered, they do enough additional labor to keep their total earnings up to customary levels.

Impartial investigators have established the fact just stated. For example, in his study of Antigua, a sugarcane-producing island of the West Indies, Simon Rottenburg reports that the planters "lament their inability to find sufficient workers to take the cane crop off the fields within an optimum time period and the unwillingness of workers to perform certain tasks at all. Workers who do accept employment . . . refuse to work full work weeks but prefer to work relatively few days each week."[14]

Falacy of the Economic Explanation of Enterprise

While the high productivity of low wages in traditionist cultures is not to be denied, the usual employer's explanation of it is false. According to this explanation, workers have few wants but a strong desire for leisure; therefore if offered higher wages they will reduce their working time to a point where their earnings are approximately the same as before. An illustration of this theory is the report of the Economic Policy Committee of Jamaica, published in 1945. It has been paraphrased as follows:

Many workers [do] not want to work for wages regularly five or six days a week all the year round. . . ."They prefer to have a lower standard of living and more leisure; they are not educated to appreciate a higher standard of living, and would rather take life more easily than add to their material comforts."[15]

This statement reiterates the traditional opinion of the planter community, as exemplified in a report of 1891:

The number of people is, on the whole, quite sufficient for the sugar estates, but the difficulty is for the planter to obtain that regular labor upon which his operations depend. The labor difficulty was the cause of the abandonment of estates in the past years . . . All evidence shows that there is plenty of work and the wages for the Antiguan laborer, if he would, more largely than he does, take advantage of the opportunity."[16]

126

In short, according to this theory, more pay will not induce more work because the desire of workers for leisure is stronger than their desire for income over and above what is required by their customary level of living.

Upon investigation, however, Rottenburg discovered that the same workers who did less work in the cane field when offered higher than customary wages, were quite willing to do the opposite in the cane mills. He also found that sometimes a worker would refuse to perform some classes of work for wages, but do the same work without wages to assist a peasant neighbor in harvesting his crop.[17]

These exceptions to the employer theory showed that the effectiveness of higher incomes as incentives to additional industry depended on the reenforcement of some noneconomic incentive, which was present in cane-mill work but not in cane-field work. Further investigation showed that greater proficiency in cane-mill work was a means to higher status, but not in cane-field work. To work in the cane fields at any wage was "considered a disgrace," while work in the cane mills conferred dignity and good repute.

Evidently, whether or not higher income prospects are effective incentives to greater industry depends on whether one's community accepts such industry as the test of his merits to a higher status. As Rottenberg observes:

A man who has been brought up in a community . . . which attaches prestige to the possession of material goods will not begin to offer less labor until there is a large increase in the price for his service or until the price is very high. On the other hand, a man who lives in a society which values leisure and which attaches no social stigma to living at a close-to-subsistence level will begin to offer less labor when small increases occur and when the price is very low .... In these circumstances, movement between jobs and the number of hours worked or energy exerted at work may be more powerfully affected by the value system of the community than by the price of labor in different trades. Where this is ture, the expression of labor supply as a function solely of price gives the economist a dull analytical tool which obscures perception of the really significant relationships."[18]

The same point is borne out in our own American experience. Not so many years ago it was difficult to get people to do nursing at any price. The explanation was that it was considered disgraceful because it was dirty work. Gradually the public attitude changed so that this kind of dirty work symbolized society's esteem for meritorious industry. As this happened, relatively low rates of pay became sufficient incentives to induce people from all social strata into the nursing profession. The employment remained as dirty as ever, but the dirt was now of no consequence because it symbolized one's deserts to public esteem.

The reverse is true of other employments in some sections of the country. For example, in the late war, plantation operators in the Tidelands of North Carolina were having great difficulty getting their field work done. The trouble, as observed by this writer, was not the lack of workers to do the work. The explanation offered by the plantation operators was that wages had gone up to a point where the workers could maintain their customary mode of living on the income from four days of work per week instead of six; so they worked four and took it easy the other two. In line with this theory, the operators were certain that, if the "government would set up a regulation whereby the planters could charge the workers 40 cents instead of 20 cents a pound for fatback, they would get their farming done and thereby do their part in winning the war." There is no doubt but what the operators were correct, given the socially approved methods in the Tidelands for achieving status. For, in terms of those methods it mattered little how high their wages might be, cottonfield workers were accorded a very low status. Such work was therefore especially irksome and the higher the wages paid for it, the less of it the workers were willing to do. The same principle applies, of course, to employments among the Spanish-Americans of our Southwest.

CHAPTER 4. ORIGINS AND IMPLICATIONS OF
THE AMERICAN DREAM

The previous chapters focused on the connections of the enterprise ideal of duty with earlier monastic and Protestant attitudes toward God's work, on the one hand, and with the American Dream on the other. The present chapter focuses on the two central aspects of the Dream itself. More precisely we are concerned, first, with why American Romanticism was a tremendous reinforcement of the work imperative of the enterprise ethic, whereas the reverse is true of European romanticism. Second, we are concerned with the way in which the sense of world destiny, inherent in the Dream, has dominated the American approach to foreign problems from the birth of the Republic. This sense of destiny is commonly recognized as the messianic aspect of the Dream.

I. Romanticism: European vs. American

A. *Definition of romanticism:* Romanticism is here recognized as the propensity to unfold a dreamworld wherein the self achieves completion in thought and feeling of purposes and aspirations that are torn and frustrated by harsh realities.

B. *Value to the survival struggle:* In this way, the romatic impulse is of incalculable value to the "survival struggle," both individually and collectively. For, by repairing to their imaginative realms, people find renewal of vital energies that commonly enables them to withstand an otherwise unbearable heat and grind.

As a consequence, the harsher the actual circumstance of life, the richer and more lovely become the inward shrines. To a surprising degree only the "fat cats" are "realists;" not the lean and hungry "tabbies." It is commonly recognized that in no section of America is the romantic propensity so pronounced as among Southern people. Were this not the case it is difficult to imagine how they could have stood up under the destruction of their older slave culture, borne the ravages of invading armies, endured a decade of humiliation and wholesale swindling by Northern carpetbaggers, survived a poverty that forced them to mine their soil which in turn produced more proverty for over 75 years, and on top of all this withstood being virtually forgotton in Government policymaking and programming for the "general welfare" from the end of the Civil War until the New Deal. As these harsh, unfriendly realities are now passing, the Southerner's imaginative life is shifting from its older romantic skin into that of "hard-headed, practical realism," so called.

C. *Sociological conditions of European romanticism:* Nineteenth century Americans and Europeans are alike noted for their romanticism In both cases the dreamworld was a response to the hard fact of the actual circumstance. But the harsh realities of life differed in Europe and America, giving rise to correspondingly different dreamworlds and their effects on conduct.

Sections from unpublished manuscript, "The Romantic and Messianic Aspects of the American Dream."

Four types of sociological conditions underlay European romanticism: The failure of the French Revolution, the disillusionment of the Industrial Revolution, the suffocating Malthusian laws of population growth, and Ricardo's "Iron Law of Wages." These fell like a mailed fist on Europe's aspirations for a better world until it seemed as if the only alternative left to the human spirit was reconciling itself to its cage.

For Europe had "shot its bolt" in a heroic endeavor to bring to pass its bright new world. Feeling manacled with "monarchical institutions" and inspired by the Utopian "rights of man," she had made bold to strike her chains through the French Revolution, only to reap the Napoleonic dictatorship and, after its overthrow, the restoration of the "Old Regime," bag and baggage, under Talleyrand's Slogan of "legitimacy."

Again, feeling the pinch and grind of proverty and evisioning the horn of plenty in the birth of modern science, invention and the ever widening circle of the market, Europe had stood aside watching "free competition" ruthlessly clear away its older system of domestic industries and manorial agriculture as a pathway to technological advance, only to then find itself in the grip of an industrial order that even swept little children into mines for such long hours that they seldom saw daylight. In this way, the "promise" of the machine turned to dust. Said John Stuart Mill, "It is questionable if all the mechanical inventions yet made have lightened the day's toil of any human being."

Moved by this climate of despair to discover why Europe had been mocked in its Herculean effort to usher in the ought-to-be, Malthus concluded that Nature, whether physical, biological, or cultural, is not putty to be shaped into more humane kingdoms. It is what the theologian had always said it was: "A vale of tears." Therefore, wisdom lies in man's purging himself of the folly of his aspiration for social reforms. For the irrevocable law of population growth, according to Malthus, renders self defeating any effort to make life more livable. The additional mouths to feed, arising from what the good bishop called the urge for "domestic pleasures," will always exceed the ability of the additional hands (on the same amount of land) to feed the additional mouths. Suppose, for example, men reduce the killing rate of disease through improving their sanitation practices. Population growth will soon accelerate to the point of offsetting the reduced killing rate of disease with an increased killing rate of malnutrition. Therefore, do whatever they will, men will find that their reproductive inclination is always counter-balancing their effort to achieve a better living. These two propensities are ever tending to offset each other at the same old level of subsistence. This is the inviolate law of life.

From Malthus' view of the unremitting pressure of population on the food supply, Ricardo quickly deduced his "Iron law of wages," according to which income to the working man, on the average and in the long run, can never rise above mere subsistence, whatever policies the State may pursue. Suppose, for example, that the wage level were raised through State action above bare subsistence by as much as 10 percent. The better living standards thus made possible would incite a corresponding increase in the birth rate, thereby accelerating the killing rate of disease and malnutrition until population growth and increasing death rate again offset each other at the same per capita subsistence level as before.

Politicians were quick to catch the point. In the great corn law debate, for example, they thundered that labor could have no real interest in whichever way the question of protective tariff on farm products was decided. For if the tariffs were not repealed, "labor would eat black bread" and if they were repealed, "labor would still eat black bread."

Thus historic experience and "science" alike pointed to the same "realistic" fact: Man can attain the greatest possible measure of happiness only through reconciling himself to the "world as it is"—purging himself of the folly of his aspirations for a better lot. In this way, he will wipe out all his inner rebellion against the status quo; a rebellion which, because of its futility, is the fountain-head of all his anxieties.

But to renounce hope for an increasingly better lot and at the same time buckle down to a grim ordeal, day in and day out, requires a peculiar morale which apparently the voice of realism cannot inspire. For, without the renewal of vital energies that comes from the completion of human aspirations, in at least a dreamworld, men by and large are seemingly without the inner strength required by the survival struggle.

D. *European romanticism as escape from futility:* In two main ways, the romantic impulse came to the rescue of a despairing Europe. First, and probably most important, it resurrected before the inner eye the feudal past against which the European had revolted in the 18th century. But the past thus resurrected was now purged of all its old impurities in such a way as to afford the human spirit a consoling security that was denied by its present and seemingly all future social orders. In Tennyson's *Idyls of the King,* for example, the bloody intrigues, brutalities and rapine of the old feudal order are transformed into a shining realm wherein "every morning brought forth a noble chance and every chance brought forth a noble knight." Scott's writings, such as *Ivanhoe* and his "Lady of the Lake" are done in the same vein. Scott, a favorite author of his day, wrote when England was almost on point of civil war because of the stress and strain of the Industrial Revolution. Yet, in all his works, there is not the slightest trace of smoke stacks, of women sweltering in sweat shops for a pittance, and of children driving mules in deep mines. Instead there rises from his pen a feudal England, dotted with castle walls, cleansed of all squalor, grit, and grime and manned with Galahads that defend with their lives on the field of honor the good name of their chaste and charming ladies.

Second, the romantic imagination of the European found in nature as well as history an idyllic refuge from the realities. With bewitching poetic grace, this imagination breathed into the countryside those consoling attributes which prophetic genius had hitherto imputed only to the Creator—a fact best exemplified by the Lake Poets, particularly Wordsworth. As a youth, he was an ardent supporter of the French Revolution. Turning into a disillusioned liberal as its excesses became apparent, he finally reverted to an old style conservative. Barely escaping the Paris reign of terror with his life and seemingly having lost his fiancee in the holocaust, he repaired to a cottage in the beautiful English lake country with his sister, Dorothy, and friend Coleridge, supported by a small stipend from a well-heeled admirer of his promising abilities. Sensitive from childhood to quietness and beauty of the countryside, he now came to sense in nature "the anchor. . the nurse, the guide, and guardian" of all his "moral being," the like of which he had hitherto so vainly sought in "the dreary intercourse of daily life" with its "evil tongues, rash judgments" and "sneers of selfish men. For I have learned," said he:

> To look on nature, not as in the hour
> Of thoughtless youth; but hearing oftentimes
> The still, sad music of humanity,
> Nor harsh nor grating, though of ample power
> To chasten and subdue. And I have felt
> A presence that disturbs me with the joy
> Of elevated thoughts; a sense sublime
> Of something far more deeply interfused,
> Whose dwelling is the light of setting suns,
> And the round ocean and the living air,
> And the blue sky, and in the mind of men,—
> A motion and a spirit that impels
> All thinking things, all objects of all thought,
> And rolls through all things.

Anyone will forever treasure these eloquent lines who has felt the rapture of a storm or the blazing colors of the autumn hills. But the fact remains that, while this personification of Nature and the equally romantic resurrection of a beloved past soothes troubled souls, it induces a withdrawal instead of a greater thrust of energies into productive work. For nothing is more futile than the impulse to reinstitute the lure of by-gone days; and he cuts no brush who hears in every bush "the still, sad music of humanity" or "feels a presence" that "disturbs" him "with the joy of elevated thoughts."

E. *Sociological conditions of American Romanticism:* This is not the kind of romance that could guide the course of Empire through the Wilderness. The survival struggle in America was no less grim than in the Old World. An extraordinary morale was required to bear up under its grueling grind. Here a man not uncommonly had to bury his wife or child with his own hands and then turn to his plow to keep the wolf from the door. This was no place for a realist—one who sees only the "facts" devoid of all poetic embellishment. Without some capacity for romantic make-believe a man would go under. This the people of the Wilderness possessed in abundance.

But its expression and practical effect were quite different from that of the European, owing to corresponding differences in the underlying conditions of life. For within the spacious bounds of the New World, minds were emptied of frustrating memories of past defeats. More important, the Malthusian law of life did not apply. Since there was more land here than could be properly handled, however fast the population growth, the per capita outturn of all was increased by additional hands. The bigger the family, the more each could produce; therefore the better it could feed, clothe, shelter and otherwise mend itself. Thus, in the Wilderness, the biological urge for "domestic pleasures" was an aid and not a hinderance to the enterprise's striving for distinction through workmanlike excellence. The hardest fact about the Wilderness was that, however severe its privations and cruelties, it would yield like putty to whatever shapes and forms man might desire, if he but applied himself sufficiently.

132

F. *American Dream as both escape from and challenge to mastery of harsh realities:* In this setting, therefore, man's romantic imagination readily fashioned a dreamworld which provided not only a refuge from harsh realities without but also a new thrust of energy into productive work. For his dreamland was a poetic elaboration of the potentialities of his otherwise forbidding actual world—glittering promises which his hands could achieve if he but tried enough. As he saw the oak in the acorn, so likewise he saw farms in swamps and thickets, ports and cities in river-bends, paths of commerce along the wild-game trails, and even jewels in the grubby earth if he but dug and hoed enough. And, in his more sombre reflections, he saw in his not uncommonly early death from backbreaking toil the evidence of a better chance for his children and his children's children. In this way, the poetic powers of the earlier American at length invested the whole wide Wilderness, canopied under the vaulting heavens, not with Wordsworth's "still, sad music of humanity" but with the Creator's joyous Promise sought through ages past by the oppressed and downtrodden of all the earth, and to be achieved only at the cost of thrift and industry.

By virture of a romance, then, both the American and his cousins across the sea were able to tap sufficient vital energies to bear up under the grim severities of the early 19th century survival struggle. For reasons previously stated, the object of the European's romance was an idyllic past or a personified Nature. The consoling qualities of these dreamworlds yielded no kick-back of energy into the day's work. But they did take one's mind off the granite-like resistance of his actual world to his aspiration for a better life, thus preventing a sense of futility from sapping away his ox-like capacity for being driven to his daily grind with seemingly no prospect of reward except the same old level of subsistence, generation after generation. For contrary reasons, already noted, the American's Romance was with a dreamland of potentialities of his rough-handed actual world, and whose fulfillment awaited only his diligent industry. Retreating into this haven of his vision, he not only gained protection from the sleet and hail without but also a forward-thrust of practical drive that in an almost literal sense enabled him to mount up as with wings, to run and not be weary, to walk and not be faint. For within a century he had conquered his mighty Wilderness, a feat which even the Founding Fathers had thought would take a thousand years.

Thus the essential peculiarity of America lies not in the outward trappings of governmental forms and social structures but in the inward fact that here, as in no other land, the poetry of the human spirit became the handmaiden of enterprise. Here, as nowhere else, the song of life became a call to ceaseless effort—the conviction that today's dreamlands are the solid assurances of tomorrow's realities—that tomorrow men of industrious purpose will enjoy the triumph and peace of the Gods, having transcended their limitations through their own diligence and workmanlike capacities.

II. The Messianic Aspect of the Dream: The Sense of Destiny

But, however stirring may be this picture of men as the potential lords of nature, the fact remains that in a larger sense, it is but the periphery of the

American Dream. At its vital center is the far more potent vision of the Nation's destiny—the boundless affection and esteem that the coming ages would bestow upon this blessed land because America, so the vision ran, was chosen by a power greater than her own to be mankind's leader in achieving his age-old aspiration for a worldwide realm of law and justice, freedom and plenty.

A. *Typical expressions:* From the beginning, the National Dream included a strong sense of messianic purpose, clothed in vivid religious imagery. In landing at Plymouth Rock, William Bradford braced his little band with the reminder that "God hath made thee for a light unto the nations." Edward Johnson in 1650 spoke of New England as a place "where the Lord would create a new heaven and a new earth, new churches and a new commonwealth." A century later, President Stiles of Yale defined the Nation as "God's American Israel."[1]

The further the Nation pushed into the Wilderness, the stronger grew the conviction that America had been called of Heaven to create a new humanity. In this spirit, Jefferson proposed that the seal of the United States should bear the picture of "the children of Israel, led by a cloud by day and a pillar of fire by night." In his first Inaugural, Washington declared that, "the preservation of the sacred fire of liberty and the destiny of the republican model of government are justly considered, perhaps as deeply as finally staked on the experiment intrusted to the hands of the American people." Dr. Priestly in 1802 gave the strongest assurance that we were world trustees: "It is impossible not to be sensible that we are acting for all mankind."[2]

In his message to Congress in 1868, President Johnson expressed the messianic consciousness in highly popular terms:

> The conviction is rapidly gaining ground in the American mind that with increased facilities for inter-communication between all portions of the earth the principles of free government as embraced in our Constitution ... would prove of sufficient strength and breadth to comprehend within their sphere and influence the civilized nations of the world.[3]
>
> Beveridge of Indiana assured his countrymen that:
>
> God has not been preparing the English-speaking Teutonic people for a thousand years for nothing but vain and idle self-contemplation and self-admiration —And of all our race he has marked the American people as his chosen nation to finally lead in the regeneration of the world.[4]

This sense of messianic purpose did not pass with the frontier. It rings out in the 19th century doctrine of manifest destiny, in the Battle Hymn of the Republic, in the radical reconstructionists of the Civil War period, and above all in America's quest for worldwide law and justice, instead of favorable power alignments in her approach to foreign problems.

B. *The Dream as a sense of moral superiority:* The dominant note of this messianic aspect of the American Dream has long been the strong national sense of moral superiority in comparison with other cultural groups. This is especially evident in earlier invidious comparisons of America and other lands.

Thus, Timothy Dwight in 1794 advised his countrymen:
Look not to Europe, for examples just
Of order, manners, customs, doctrines, laws,
Of happiness, or virtue. Cast round
The eye of searching reason, and declare
What Europe proffers, but a patchwork sway,

The garment Gothic, worked to fritter's shreds,
And eked from every loom of following times.
Such as his sway, the system shows entire,
Of silly pomp, and meanness train'd t'adore;
Of wealth enormous, and enormous want;
Of lazy sinecures, and suffering toil;
Of grey-bread systems, the meterous dreams;
Of lordly churches, and dissention fierce,
Cites farcical, and phrenzied unbelief.
(Cf. Greenfield Hill, New York; 1794, p. 18.)

In the same vein, Jefferson proclaimed:

> If all the sovereigns of Europe, were to set themselves to work to emancipate the minds of their subjects from their present ignorance and prejudice, and that as jealously as they now attempt the contrary, a thousand years would not place them on the same high ground which our common people are now setting out. (Writings II, p. 249.)

Fifty years later DeTocqueville was reminded again and again of the same illusions of unique innocency:

> If I say to an American that the country he lives in is a fine one, "Ay," he replies, "there is not its equal in the world." If I applaud the freedom its inhabitants enjoy, he answers: "Freedom is a fine thing, but few nations are worthy of it." If I remark on the purity of morals that distinguishes the United States, "I can imagine" says he, "that a stranger, who has witnessed the corruption that prevails in other nations, would be astonished at the difference." At length I leave him to a contemplation of himself; but he returns to the charge and does not desist until he has got me to repeat all I had just been saying it is impossible to conceive of a more troublesome or more garrulous patriotism. . . . 5

This sense of moral superiority was no passing extravagence of a youthful country. Shortly after our entry into World War I, Wilson told his believing countrymen:

> There is not a single selfish element, so far as I can see in the cause we are fighting for. We are fighting for what we believe and wish to be the rights of mankind and for the future peace and security of the world.
>
> . . .
>
> We have gone in with no grievance of our own, because we have always said that we are the friends and servants of mankind. We look for no profit. We look for no advantage. America—is the only idealistic Nation in the world.6

This extraordinary statement cannot be explained as doubletalk, calculated to stir up war-morale. For Wilson justified it, as Hofstadter observes, "by going to the peace conference without a single distinctively nationalist demand to make, without a single claim for territory, indemnities, or spoils, with no more self-regarding national object than to restrain his allies, make a durable and just peace, and form a league that would secure such a peace for an incalculable future."7

C. *Secular and religious forms of messianic purpose:* The sense of messianic purpose may appear in secular as well as religious form. This statement is established by three observations. First, many American expressions of messianism are devoid of any specific reference to God. For the most part, this is true of Wilson's descriptions of America's world role. Second, all modern nationalistic aspirations of destiny are but different versions of the Biblical Kingdom of Heaven. From all the previous citations, this is obviously true of the American Dream. The same is even more evident of the Communistic Utopia wherein each of his own volition produces to the limit of his ability and receives according to his needs. Obviously, this is but a secular wording for the age-old Kingdom of God in which each is governed solely by the law of love—seeking the well being of every other with the same concern that one does his own.

Third, whether atheistic or "God-fearing," the striking characteristic of modern nationalisms is the profound sense on the part of each of being selected by a power greater than its own to play an auspicious role in bringing to pass a transmuted humanity in which each is moved by no impulse except a consuming passion for justice and happiness for all. Consider a typical expression of this Communist sense of destiny by its American missionary, William Z. Foster.

> Communism will inaugurate a new era for the human race. . . . will bring about the immediate or eventual solution of many great social problems. . .war, religious superstitions, prostitution, famine, pestilence, crime, poverty, alcoholism, unemployment, illiteracy race and national chauvinism, the suppression of woman and every form of slavery and exploitation of one class by another. . .
>
> For many generations the long list of utopians, the Platos, Mores, Fouriers, Owens, and Bellamys, have dreamed and planned ideal states of society. Their strong point was that they sensed mankind's capacity for a higher social life than the existing wild scramble. But their weak point ... was that they did not know what was the matter with society nor how to cure it . . .
>
> It has remained for the modern proletariat, under the brilliant leadership of Marx and Lenin, to find the revoluntionary way to the higher social order ... to work out a correct program and strategy of struggle ... to master generally the laws of social development ... and we may be sure that the revolution, in its upward course, will carry humanity to heights of happiness and achievement far beyond the dreams of even the most hopeful utopians.[8]

There is no difference between this sense of messianic purpose on the part of the modern communist and that of the French Revolutionaries as typified in Babeuf. Their purpose said he (quoting Babeuf), was to:

> ... make disappear all frontiers, fences, walls, locks on doors, all disputes, trials, all theft, murder, all crime; and Tribunals, prisons, gallows, torture, jealousy, instability, pride, deceit, duplicity; finally all vices. No more (and this, is no doubt, the most essential) of the ever gnawing tooth of the general restlessness, or the personal perpetual anxiety of every one of us, about our lot of to-morrow, next month, next year, in our old age, the fate of our children and their children ... Guarantee to every one of its members a state of stable felicity, the satisfaction of the needs of all, a sufficiency inalterable, independent of the ineptitude, immorality or ill-will of those in power.[9]

The distinction, then, between the religious and secular forms of messianic purpose turns on the nature of the Supreme Power which is viewed as selecting a given people as its instrument for bringing to pass the age-old prophetic dream of a worldwide realm of law and justice. In religious forms of messianism, this power is recognized as the Creator and Lord of Nature, whereas in the secular forms, Nature itself is substituted for the "One God." Thus, except for the "forgiveness of sins," the Communist imputes to the "dialectical laws of history" the same providential plan which Christians ascribe to the Almighty. From their sense of being on the side of history the Communists derived the same, if not greater, assurance of final triumph of the prophetic dream which Christians do from the sense of being on God's side. "We will bury you," said

Khrushchev recently to Western powers, because "history is on our side." In this he was only reaffirming a verse from the Communist Manifesto of 1848:

> Wage labor rests exclusively on competition among the laborers. The advance of industry, the involuntary promoter of which is the bourgeois, replaces the isolation of the laborers, due to competition, by the revolutionary combination, due to association. The development of modern industry therefore cuts from under its feet the very foundation on which the bourgeois produces and appropriates products. What the bourgeois, therefore, produces above all are its own grave diggers. Its fall and the victory of the proletariat are equally inevitable.

For the inevitability of this Communist world, Khrushchev added that: "If God existed, we would thank Him." In this he means he has no belief in a personal God that rewards righteousness, forgives sins, and punishes evil. But he is obviously dedicated to God in the sense of a kind of something-not-ourselves that will make the world behave the way we want it, to which he gives the name history.

From the vision of themselves as the chosen agents of this "false" God for at last fulfilling mankind's hunger for worldwide law and justice, the Soviets derive the same sense of undefeatable destiny that America derives from envisioning herself the chosen agent of the "true" God for achieving the same purpose. In this way, the Soviets may be a far more dangerous victim of idealistic deceptions than America has ever been. Little is to be gained, however, from the child's game of demonstrating one's own superior merits by contending that the faults of others are greater than its own. "Why beholdest thou the mote that is in thy brother's eye, but considerest not the beam that is in thine own eye?"

D. *Tension between human limitations and the infinitude of the aspiration for merited esteem (status) as the basis of messianic pretensions:* Any individual, class or nation is in great measure the prisoner of biases inherent in its particular way of life. Therefore, in equating its own sentiments and views with the Divine perspective concerning what ought and ought not be done for the good of the world, a people claim for their own world outlook a finality and universality which it cannot possibly have. By the same token, the virtures and capabilities of other peoples are correspondingly underrated and their faults magnified. The same applies, of course, to the sense of destiny on the part of all modern nationalistic dreams.

How is this extraordinary propensity for self-deception—moralistic pretensions—to be explained?

On this point the theologian appears to be closest to the truth. In substance, he holds that the deception arises as a means of escaping the tension between the limitations of the self and its aspirations for a pinnacle of distribution which can actually be merited only by the gods.

As Niebuhr observes, man is ceaselessly striving to enhance the prestige of his person without limit. To this end:

> He is not content with his truth. He seeks *the* truth. His restless mind seeks to comprehend the meaning of all cultures so that he may not be caught within the limitations of his own.

> Thus man builds towers of the spirit from which he may survey larger
> horizons than those of his class, race and nation. This is necessary human
> enterprise. Without it man could not come to his full estate.[10]

But the fact remains he is "a creature of time and place, whose perspectives and insights are invariably conditioned by his immediate circumstances."[11] Thus defeated in their aspirations for a status befitting the gods, men and nations are tempted to escape their limitations through a false pride—the subtle deception that one's person, class, race or nation is more capable, wiser, more deserving than it actually is and that others are correspondingly less wise and deserving. This, as Niebuhr observes:

> ... is at least one aspect of what Christian orthodoxy means by "original sin."
> It is not so much an inherited corruption as an inevitable taint upon the
> spirituality of a finite creature, always enslaved to time and place, never
> completely enslaved and always under the illusion that the measure of his
> emancipation is greater than it really is.[12]

The Battle Hymn of the Republic is a striking illustration of this propensity for achievement through self deception. In stirring music and majestic cadence, the hymn proclaims "God's truth is marching on." Actually it is only Yankee truth. The author projects into the South all the injustices leading to the Civil War, thereby imputing to the North an innocence and righteousness which mortals can never possess. The whole imagery of the hymn merely reflects the delusion that there can be no possibility of a difference between the North's truth and God's truth.

E. *The unlimited aspiration for merited esteem as liability and asset:* Reenforcing the aspiration for unlimited esteem is the aversion to being blamed. Men are thus pulled from in front by their love of the one and pushed from behind by their dread of the other. Short of a God-like perfection, there is no excellence which can fully protect a people from the horror of being held responsible for injustices that subject them to hostility and resentment. A chief concern of little children, adults and nations alike is to protect themselves against their dread. They cringe before it, seeking to flee it as a fox eludes the hounds. Shelter from blame and reproach is thus the most prized of all securities.

In face of this peril, a nation is confronted with two alternatives and its choice determines whether or not its aspiration for worldwide law and justice shall become a liability or an asset.

It may choose to protect itself against this peril through self deception which denies any share of the guilt for the injustices that set nations against each other. The most familiar and spontaneous type of such deceptions is commonly called a pretentious idealism. As already noted, this subterfuge involves the identification of national sentiments and views with a Divine perspective and hence the projection onto others of total blame for the injustices which set man against man. By this choice of a pretentious idealism, a people permit both their aspiration for distinction and their aversion to blame to become a powerful dynamic of world tensions and violence. This is true because, in over-rating their own virtues and downgrading those of others, their moralistic pretensions arouse the very resentments and hostilities which they seek to avoid.

138

As soon as events unmask the hypocricies of a pretentious idealism, a people may then seek to rehabilitate their self respect through an equally pretentious realism. This choice involves the affirmation of the sordid and ugly as being the final term of life. By the same token, devotion to ideal ends, especially anything that smacks of the American Dream, is dismissed as sentimental moonshine. The role of the hard-boiled realist, so-called, thus looms up as the high road to good repute, the role of the idealist being fit only for the soft heads—boobs and suckers. And any approach to foreign problems is an object of derision if it is moved by any sentiment except a coolly calculating egotism.

Such a pretentious realism set the tone of American life between the two World Wars. It proved as destructive to international order as a pretentious idealism. It did so by diverting the aspiration for unlimited esteem (and aversion to blame) from the service of worldwide justice to that of narrow egostistic concerns, thereby withering the national sense of responsibility for doing what it could have done in behalf of a more stable world order.

It is quite possible, however, for a people to choose a course of moral realism instead of destructive forms of self deception. This choice involves a recognition of the truism that America shares a common blame or guilt for the injustices that involve her in conflicts of fellow nations.

Part III.

Agricultural Policy Problems And The Family Farm

The initial chapter in this section, "The Place of American Agriculture in Mankind's Struggle Against Hunger," provides a broad historical setting for current American farm policy problems. In it, Brewster traced the continuing pressure of population of food supply, beginning with the famines of Biblical times in Egypt, and extending up to the current food crises in Asia. He showed how Americans have escaped the pressure of population on food supply, first because of the large unsettled expanses of the continent; and, in this century, by rapid farm technological advance. But in the process of exempting their Nation from the threat of famine, American farmers have set such an accelerated pace of technological advance that fewer and fewer farms are needed to supply an expanding flow of food and fiber. Consequently, the well-being of our rural people depends increasingly on a full-employment economy to absorb the out-flow of excess farm labor into nonfarm occupations.

Chapter 6, "Origin and Goals of Agricultural Policy and Programs," brings into focus the evolution of public policies and programs designed to aid farmers. Ever since colonial times, farmers have demanded public programs that would expand their productivity. Their early quest for free land was culminated in the Homestead Act of 1862. Subsequently, farmers sought additional public assistance through programs providing research, education, and credit, and the warding off of exploitation by business monopolies. But as farmers collectively increased their productivity, they began generating price-depressing surpluses. This situation constitutes the modern farm policy problem. Our high productive farm technology, in conjunction with limited markets, has created a clash between the desire of farmers to be assured of equal opportunity and income and the concept of freedom as involving no constraints on management of the farm business.

This conflict between two of our basic beliefs is the subject of Chapter 7, "Society Values and Goals in Respect to Agriculture." This chapter's description of America's policy-guiding creeds differs from Brewster's other treatments of the subject in one important way: He included here the creed of self integrity. This creed stresses the important role of the dissenter, whose exceptional sentiments and views are a source of new and better ways.

Chapter 8, "The Relevance of the Jeffersonian Dream Today," contains one of Brewester's most thorough discussions of the family farm. Tracing the development of the beliefs and values underlying the family farm from Medieval Europe through John Locke to the present, Brewster shows how the family farm, despite changes in its size and other outward appearances, has remained the predominant institution in American agriculture. The chapter includes a discussion of the possible technological innovations that could transform the sequential pattern of agricultural production into a simultaneous pattern.

Many people are confused over the function of the research social scientists. Immediately after World War II, physical scientists were complaining that social scientists had failed; clearly no one knew how to guarantee that nuclear energy would be used benefically rather than destructively. Outstanding physical scientists believed there should be a moratorium on research in their field until the social scientists "catch up with us."[1] In the back of their minds was the belief that the physical scientist should furnish knowledge of how to accomplish ends, but social scientists should tell us which ends we ought to strive for, which ends are morally justified.

Brewster maintained that it is the function of neither the social nor the physical scientists, *as scientists,* to tell the people what they ought to do. His definition of the role of the social science researcher is (1) to help locate and identify society's problems and (2) to show those involved in correcting these problems alternative ways of solving them, and the costs and benefits of accepting each of these alternatives. Thus, the work of the social science researcher bears directly on the problems of policy formation and decision-making.

Chapter 9, "Role of the Researcher in the Formation of Public Policy," contains Brewster's most thorough treatment of the researcher's function in the formation of public policy. In it he draws a basic distinction between the ethically neutral task of men as researchers and the ethical role of people in their capacities as citizens, legislators and policymakers. Having made this distinction, he points out a number of agricultural policy problems that merit the attention of research economists, and suggests ways in which the mathematical economic models could be improved to provide knowledge that is indispensable to public policymakers.

The chapter, "Philosophy: Principles of Reasoning Especially Applicable to Science," was developed from notes Brewster used for discussions with Dr. Harry C. Trelogan's seminar in the U.S. Department of Agriculture Graduate School, entitled "Research Methods in the Social Sciences." In these lectures Brewster examined the genesis and nature of modern research. He discussed deductive and inductive reasoning in the context of a dynamic concept of science. He showed that the scientific method includes a considerable amount of art or genius in addition to the inductive and deductive thought processes.

---

[1] See especially, *Physical Science and Human Values,* ed. E. P. Wigner, Princeton, Princeton University Press, 1947.

CHAPTER 5. THE PLACE OF AMERICAN AGRICULTURE IN MANKIND'S STRUGGLE AGAINST HUNGER

In a few broad strokes, let us place American agriculture in the perspective of mankind's long struggle against hunger.

A good beginning point is one of the earliest Biblical stories—the story of Joseph, the lad sold into Egyptian slavery who eventually became the king's first minister and achieved distinction through his foresight of famines ahead and his establishment of national policies that protected Egypt and her neighbors against their devastations.

We come now at least 1500 years closer to the present. In the year 476 A.D., we see St. Augustine, one of the shining geniuses of all time, standing on the shores of Alexandria watching the fall of his beloved Rome to the invading Goths from the North. What the great bishop did not see was that these barbarian hordes had been set in motion some hundreds of years earlier by nomadic tribes of Central Asia who, in quest of new food supplies, began their westward trek across the Urals, the steppes of Russia, and the plains of Poland, thus generating the vast population upheavals that eventually overran the frontiers of the Roman Empire.

Now, swing on down through the years to 19th century Europe. The first half of this century was a period of profound disillusionment and despair. Moved by her 18th century optimism, Europe had put forth her mightiest effort in trying to bring to pass her bright new world through a complete and violent removal of monarchical institutions in favor of domocratic ones resting on the axiom of natural equity.[1] But instead of achieving success, she brought down on her head the holocaust of the French Revolution with its aftermath of Napoleonic dictatorship and imperialism, and after that the restoration of the "old regime" under Talleyrand's slogan of "legitimacy" and Metternich's reactionary leadership of the Congress of Vienna and for more than 30 years thereafter. So total was the failure of the revolution that Europe sought escape from her frustrations through romantic return to the security and order of the very feudal past against which she rebelled so heroically at the outset of the revolution.[2]

Disillusionment was as bitter in the economic as in the political sphere. Convinced that the new sciences and technological advance would bring to pass the horn of plenty, England stood aside watching "free competition" ruthlessly clearing away her older system of domestic industries and manorial agriculture. She then found herself in the grip of a monster, as it were, which swept women into sweat shops and little children into deep mines as mule drivers for such long hours that they seldom saw daylight. In this way, the "promises" of the machine

---

Reprinted by permission of New England Agricultural Economics Council. Pages 3-15 of "Agriculture in an Increasingly Urban Society," paper presented to the Council at Durham, N.H., June 28, 1961.

turned to dust, prompting John Stuart Mill to declare: "It is questionable if all the mechanical inventions yet made have lightened the toil of any human being."

Even earlier, this climate of despair moved a young clergyman, Thomas Malthus, to ask *why* men are defeated time and again even in their most gigantic efforts to bring to earth their dreams and visions of a better life. In effect, his answer was that for all time hunger is a killer that no power on earth can conquer. He put his law this way: Population increases in geometric ratio/: 2-4-8-16-32, etc. Food supply increases in arithmetic ratio: 2-4-6-8-10, etc. Malnutrition, starvation, disease, pestilence, and wars kill off the population until its numbers come into balance with the food supply at bare subsistence levels.

No crueler law of life was ever formulated than that educed by this kindly minister of God. His was a big and powerful idea. In all intellectual history, few ideas have left a mark so wide and deep on man's concept of human destiny as the Malthusian Law of unrelenting pressure of population on food supply. This law was an important guide to Darwin in developing his survival-of-the-fittest theory of evolution. It also led Ricardo to his Iron Law of Wages, which opened the floodgates of laissez faire capitalism. For under this law, nothing could be done through political action to improve the lot of workers. For example, in the great Corn Law debates of the 1830's, an English lord declared that labor could have no possible interest in the issue. For if Parliament repealed the protective tariffs on farm products, "labor would eat black bread, and if it didn't repeal them, labor would still eat black bread." Within this dismal framework of ideas, Marx developed his theoretical foundations of modern communism as the new plan of world salvation.[3]

In very great measure, present-day America is the product of the operation of the Malthusian law of life throughout 19th century Europe. From 1750 to about 1910, the population of Europe expanded from approximately 140 million to almost 400 million. This startling change generated catastrophic pressure of population on food supply. Hunger gnawed increasingly, even in good years. And when crops failed, millions of peasants learned that poverty is a dog whose teeth sink deep. Handlin etches their plight in these vivid words:

> "The struggle for existence grew fiercer "–In awe the peasant saw his fields barren, yielding nothing to sell, nothing to eat. He looked up and saw the emptiness of his neighbor's lands, of the whole village. In all the country round his startled eyes fell on desolation. . . . The empty weeks went by, marked by the burial of the first victims. . ., a heartsick weariness settled down over the stricken cottages . . . .The endless tolling of the sexton's bell, the narrowing family circle were shaping an edge of resolution. . . . "made clear that his only choice was to emigrate or to die". . . . The empty road was pointing out its form. . . . He would leave now, escape. . . . never see the sight of home again. He would become a stranger on the way, pack on back, lead wife and children toward some other destiny.[4]

In this way, the Malthusian law of life generated one of the greatest migrations in history. Within a century, it uprooted well over 35 million peasants from their ancestral homes of 1,000 years and drove them to the shores of the new world: more than 6 million from the German Empire; 2 million from

Norway and Sweden; 5 million from Italy; more than 11 million from eastern and southeastern Europe; 4.5 million from Ireland; and more than 4 million from the British Isles.[5]

These people came seeking farms but very few ever reached the land.[6] All but a fraction were trapped in the cities. Day-to-day existence was close to the bone. But their physical hardships were as nothing compared with their heart-rendering alienation from human bonds. This took three forms:

(1) They sought standing in the esteem and affection of native Americans. This they were denied. Biases of old American stock forced them into slums and ghettos and menial jobs; they became stockyard workers, janitors, street sweepers, peddlers, mine diggers, pick and shovel gangs, and, in general, took all the burdensome jobs of commerce.[7] Their strange speech, thick accents, peculiarities of dress, odd habits of life—these were the badges that set them apart and walled them out.

(2) Thus cut off from human ties in the new world, their hunger to belong welled up in imagination as an aching loneliness for renewed ties with the old world—a yearning which Handlin has captured with rare effect in the following summary of salutations in their letters to those they left behind:

> ...to my dearest...to every him and her who filled the days of the old life and whom I will never see again....To the aged parents who bred and nurtured me, who took trouble over, shed tears for me and now have none to comfort them;...to my comrades of the fields; to all the kin who joined in festivals; to the whole visible communion, the oneness, of the village that I have forfeited by emigration; to each I send my greetings.[8]

By thus reaching backward, they hoped that somehow they might belong in the homeland. Even the birds that fly away from their native places hasten to return. How, then, can ever a man feel really happy condemned to live away from where he was born? But so it was.

(3) Thus cut off from human ties in both the old world and the new, parents sought healing for their aloneness through drawing closer to their children, toward whom they felt guilty because of not meeting their obligations. These highly destructive anxieties of aloneness and guilt move them to say "let us sacrifice and live only for the children. If there is any hope in this world, it is not for us but for them."

But they were even denied the closer bonds they thus sought with their own flesh and blood. For, as Handlin points out:

> With bewilderment the immigrants learned that to be willing to sacrifice was not enough, that their children must be also willing to accept the sacrifice; and of that there could be no confidence. The initial dissimilarities of experience widened with time as youngsters ventured out from the home and subjected themselves to influences foreign to their elders. The life of school and the life of the street completed the separation between the generations.[9]

In thus increasingly tearing them apart from human ties, the Malthusian law of life weighted down their years with killing anguish to the very end.

Happily, this bleak picture is not the final note. In the lives of their grandchildren, their dreams came to flower. In them, the strange ways of their peasant ancestors were replaced by American ways, so that during the social upheavals of the 1930's and 1940's, the third generation of immigrants broke the yoke of prejudice that chained their fathers to menial jobs. And they also broke out of the slums and ghettos into spreading suburbias[10] where they found the bit of ground, the spread of grass, and the patch of sunlight so precious to their fathers who were trapped in the nooks and crannies of our metropolitan centers.

Thus the bulldozers that now push our urban world farther and farther into rural America are in great measure but the latest forward thrust of those mighty migrations of 35 million peasants from a hungry Europe in the 1800's. There is then a startling connecting between our mushrooming suburbias today and the grim, cruel operation of the Malthusian law of life throughout the countryside of 19th century Europe.

So we like to think that from happier isles those victims of this law may look down in gratitude that its terrors have been left behind by their grandchildren in our far-flung suburbias where refrigerators and deep freezes are filled with the abundance from American farms, and where their many other wants are ministered unto by the industrial America, which stands as a monument of the suffering, toil, and anguish of their peasant grandfathers.

But within only a small part of earth have men succeeded in freeing themselves from the Malthusian law of life. Most people of the world are still caught in its claws. In 1942 and 1943, more than a million persons starved to death in India. China is now suffering from famine, as was true to Central Africa this last winter. In the so-called underdeveloped countries, there is no denying the Malthusian law that new mouths multiply faster than the food supply until they balance at bare subsistence levels. For example, when the Aswan dam in Egypt is finished, it will bring in several million acres of new land, greatly expanding present total food output. But reports are that the population is accelerating so rapidly that by the time the dam is finished, the pressure of population on the food supply will be as great as it now is, and living levels will be no higher. There is apprehension that this may prove true also of the large reclamation projects underway in India and Pakistan.

Nonetheless, there is growing confidence that we can break the curse of the Malthusian law so that no person on the face of earth need ever go to bed hungry. In this spirit, President Kennedy has emphasized "our desire to cooperate in every feasible way in the global attack on hunger and malnutrition."[11] In similar vein, Vice President Johnson recently declared that the need of the hour is "a bold creation of new institutions which will permit a continuing attack upon world poverty,"[12] and that "we must dedicate ourselves to proving to the poor of the world that freedom offers the surest path out of poverty," adding: "For one or the other—either freedom or poverty—must end. The two cannot live together. One or the other must conquer."[13]

The basis of this new confidence and resolution stems in no small measure from phenomenal achievements of American agriculture. Let us consider four of these achievements.

(1) Its productivity is the wonder of the world. Other nations have far more farmworkers and land, but we produce a greater share of the world's

output of food and fiber than any other nation, as shown by these figures:[14]

	Population (millions)	World farm production (percent)	Farm production per capita (dollars)
U.S.A.	174	15.8	152
Soviet Union	209	9.9	79
Mainland China	645	15.6	40

(2) Through his extraordinary productivity, the American farmworker enables us to have a bigger industrial labor force than the Soviet Union, even though our total labor force is much smaller, as indicated by the following figures:[15]

Labor force	USSR (mil.)	USA (mil.)
Total civilian	106.4	69.4
Nonfarm	58.1	62.0
Farm	48.3	7.4

In accomplishing this feat, each American farmworker on the average supports 26 persons with ample foods and fibers as compared with only 7 persons in 1910.[16] If it were not for this prodigious gain in their productivity, it would take 27 million farmworkers instead of the present 7.4 million, to meet domestic food needs and exports at 1959 levels. Roughly speaking, only about half as much of the factory worker's time is required to get approximately the same amount of food in 1958 as in 1929.[17]

(3) It is not in industry but in agriculture that we are witnessing the fastest technological advance. With about the same total quantity of resources, agriculture produced about 1½ times as much food and fiber in 1959 as in 1940.[18] Throughout the 1947-57 period, gain in output per man in farming averaged 6.2 percent per year, as compared with 3.7 percent in manufacture and only 2.3 percent in all nonfarm industries.[19]

(4) Finally, America has always been exempt from the Malthusian law of life. Here, our distress has never arisen from the pressure of population on food supply but from pressure of the food supply on population. Prior to this century, we reversed the Malthusian law by means of the virgin continent, and in this century, we reversed it through rapid farm technological advance.

Throughout the 19th century, our population, like that of Europe, was expanding much faster than farmworker productivity. But we beat the Malthusian law by generating new farms out of the frontier at an appreciably faster rate than population growth generated new market outlets. In a measure, the new markets were provided by the great population increase that was associated with the rise of the Industrial Revolution in Europe.[20]

Malthus recognized that the enormous virgin lands of America exempted her from his general law, but he held that this exemption would last only as long as the frontier held out. The closing of the frontier near the beginning of this century aroused fear that the Malthusian law would soon take over and we would become an increasingly poor and hungry people. This fear in turn induced a great drive to further the agricultural sciences. Thus the first 15 years of this century marked Knapp's invention of the so-called "demonstration method," which was first implemented mainly through local Farm Bureaus and then put to work in a big way with the establishment of the Federal Extension Service in 1914.

But the fear of the Malthusian law proved short lived here. Since the 1920's, technological advance in our agriculture has generated productive capacity and output of food and fiber at an appreciably faster rate than domestic population growth has generated additional market outlets. Throughout the 1950's, the average gain in our population was 1.7 percent per year and the average gain in our farm output was 2.4 percent.[2][1] So rapid has been the rate of farm technological advance that farm output averaged about 8.7 percent more than consumption needs from 1952 to 1957, the latest year for which data are available.[2][2]

This fact is loaded with peril for the farm sector of our society. For a 4- to 5-percent increase in the aggregate supply of food may result in as much as a 20-percent decline in farm prices.[2][3] Without some remedial action, this relationship is enough to break the back of agriculture.

When placed in the world perspective of mankind's long struggle against hunger, this peril is profoundly relevant to the larger concern of our urban society and the whole free world as well, for at least two reasons.

(1) Our very large excess farm productive capacity is rightly a source of growing confidence that by transferring our farm know-how to other lands, we can help men upset the Malthusian law of life all over the world. As shown in the operation of Public Law 480, it affords us an excellent means of furthering economic growth in underdeveloped countries. The job is difficult, but there is little doubt that it can be done on increasing scale.

(2) All sectors of our society realize that a full employment economy[2][4] is essential to the security of our world position. What is not so well recognized is the extreme dependence of agriculture's well being on a full employment economy, as there is a close relationship between national employment levels and outmigration of workers from American farms. Therefore, if given a full employment economy, we could expect manpower in the form of excess farms to shift into higher paying nonfarm employments. But when the economy is operating at less than full employment, agriculture is highly subject to excess workers, productive land, and farm capital. As Hendrix has shown, this is true for at least three reasons: (1) the relative ease of entry into farming; (2) the relative disadvantage of farmworkers in competing with nonfarmworkers for limited job opportunities in distant towns and cities; and (3) the rapidly declining farm labor force because of technological advance alongside large natural increases in the farm population.[2][5]

For these reasons, slackening growth rates of the national economy throughout the 1950's damned up excess labor into more farm units than were needed to meet food and fiber demands at reasonable prices. In part, this backup of excess farmworkers merely took the form of low-production farms, which are usually associated with rural poverty, not with the pressure of food supply on food demands. But it also took the form of excess productive farms which greatly increased this pressure, thereby intensifying the cost-price squeeze for agriculture as a whole.

This squeeze in turn functions as a powerful generator of continuously greater excess farm productive capacity. For, when trapped in this squeeze, the individual farmer is faced with the necessity of offsetting his loss of income from lower prices by reducing his cost per unit of output and expanding his production. To do this, he must strain every effort to adopt cost-reducing and output-increasing technologies, which usually increases his capital investment.[26] As all farmers are forced to meet their cost-price squeeze in this way, the continually generate still greater excess capacity and even greater price- and income-depressing surpluses. Thus the farmer is caught in a bind that forces him to run ever faster in order to keep standing still.

The present distress of our highly productive rural society thus points up two facts of profound concern to our increasingly urban world. (1) It spotlights the need for a far greater national effort to utilize our large excess farm productive capacity in helping vast regions of the globe in their desperate struggle to break the yoke of the Malthusian law of life, as we have so thoroughly broken it here. (2) With equal clarity, it spotlights the fact that the well being of agriculture and the security of our world position are wrapped up in the same critical need for vigorous policies to bring to pass a full employment economy—an economy that will give America the opportunity she deserves to get her highest potential on the move and thus meet her full obligation to do the best she can by herself, her posterity, and her friends throughout the world.

This national and world perspective of our exceedingly productive agriculture tends to beget within our increasingly urban mind the larger measure of patience and sympathetic understanding that is needed in dealing effectively with our long-standing farm problem.

CHAPTER 6. ORIGIN AND GOALS OF AGRICULTURAL POLICY AND PROGRAMS

Farmers, individually and cooperatively, have struggled with their problems for many decades in the hope of achieving a better life for themselves and their families. In recent years, this struggle has centered on problems of supply, demand, and price of farm products. When production outran demand, farmers called for Government action to provide relief from an economic situation that they could not correct individually. But Government action often includes control and regulation. To some, this implies infringement on the traditional freedoms of the American way. Basically, what is the role of Government in agricultural affairs? And how is this role reconciled with our fundamental beliefs? Let us examine more closely the origins of agricultural policy and our thinking on the goals of agricultural policy.

The Struggle for Equality

From the formation of the Republic until about 1860, the great struggle of farm people was to persuade society, through Government, to adopt land policies that would enable the working farmer with little or no cash to have access to land which he and his family could convert into a productive farm with their own labor and management. Early land policies were distinguished by extreme inequality of opportunities for acquisition of public land. The smallest unit offered for sale by the Land Act of 1796 was 640 acres. The minimum price was $2.00 an acre and the total price had to be paid within a year. As most frontiersmen had little money, such policies gave moneyed men a virtual monopoly on opportunities to acquire public lands, which they commonly turned into speculative gains through resale in small tracts to farm families. From the beginning of the Republic and continuing through many administrations, the dominant problem of rural people was to achieve equitable policies for disposal of public land. This struggle reached a climax in the Homestead Act of 1862, which offered a quarter-section of land to anyone willing to spend 5 years of work to transform it into a farm. Larger acreages and a shorter period of time were later established by other acts of Congress.

Even before the issue of public land was resolved, farmers began to realize that equal opportunity to acquire public land was not enough to enable them to fulfill their aspirations for a better life through superior industry. They found that they also needed technical knowledge of ways to make their work more productive. To this end, over the next half-century (roughly from 1860 to 1914), they sought to establish and strengthen agricultural research and educational institutions. The Government responded through the Morrill Act of 1862, which established the Department of Agriculture and the present system

Selections from "Origin and Goals of Agricultural Policy and Programs," Brewster's contribution to *Farm Production Trends, Prospects, and Programs*, U.S. Dept. Agr., Agr. Inform. Bul. 239, May 1961.

of land-grant colleges, the Hatch Act of 1887, which established the modern system of agricultural experiment stations, and the Smith-Lever Act of 1914, which established the agricultural extension service.

In addition to research and education, farmers also found themselves in need of capital loans on longer terms, a need that private lending institutions were not meeting adequately. In due course, this need was met by the establishment of the Federal Land Bank, and later the organization of the Farm Credit Administration which included real estate credit, production credit, and credit for farm cooperatives. The Farmers Home Administration and the Rural Electrification Administration were added in the 1930's.

Achievement of a procedure to acquire public land, agricultural research and education, and credit institutions helped farmers achieve equality of opportunities to produce. But the opportunity to produce and the opportunity to enjoy a fair return for what is produced are quite different. Generally, since the Civil War, except for war periods, farmers have felt themselves to be more the victims of institutions that withheld opportunities for a fair return than of institutions that failed to give equality of production opportunities.

Two grievances aroused the farmer movements of the late 19th century: Government fiscal policy and the rise of the monopolistic power in business, especially in the fields of transportation, storage, and warehousing. After the Civil War, the Government pursued tight money policies which tended to restore the purchasing power of the dollar to prewar levels. As farmers, by and large, were in debt, such policies forced them to repay the dollars they borrowed with dollars that represented substantially more farm products. To remedy this inequality, they sought Government fiscal policies that would balance the purchasing power of dollars borrowed and those repaid. But hope of reaching their objective collapsed with the rout of Populism in the presidential election of 1896.

The second objective of the farmer movements was to achieve protection from exploitation by business monopolies. Farmers sought the help of Government in counteracting the economic power of railroads, grain exchanges, elevators, warehouses, and other types of business that exercised monopoly powers. In seeking this objective, they were joined by other groups. Their struggle met with some success with the passage of the Interstate Commerce Act of 1887 and the Sherman Anti-Trust Act of 1890.

The larger fact, however, is that by the close of the 19th century, rapid technological advance had a vastly different impact on the premachine economy of predominantly family units of production in agriculture than it had on industry. Technical advance in agriculture was chiefly within family units. In contrast, technical advance in industry quickly replaced family units or firms with much larger firms, which had the economic power to maintain a high degree of price stability.[1] In this way, the opposite impacts of technical advance on the premachine economy presented to the farmer a new obstacle in his quest for equality of income opportunities.

An equally formidable obstacle was found in the highly inelastic nature of both demand and supply of farm products. Thus, farmers can be increasingly efficient and productive and yet suffer chronic low incomes, even though the

152

general economy is prosperous. Farmers can become the long-term victims of a squeeze that drains off to the rest of society the major benefits of their rapid advance in cost-reducing and output-increasing technologies. To ward off this eventuality has been a major objective of farmers and farm leaders since the 1920's. They have sought Government measures that will enable them to balance their output with consumer demand for food and fiber at reasonable prices.

One aspect of this struggle was a preoccupation with farmer's cooperatives. Interest in cooperatives reached its peak in the late 1920's. Many thought that through cooperatives farmers could solve their own economic problems by bringing modern business practices to bear on agricultural purchasing and selling. Through the Capper-Volstead Act of 1922, farmers did achieve for cooperatives exemption from some of the restrictions of the antitrust laws. Many cooperatives organized during this period were successful. But by and large, the chief economic problem of the major commodities did not yield to the cooperative approach.

Farmers still sought more direct ways of achieving equality of income opportunities. As a part of the effort, a parity formula was worked out in the 1920's to indicate the prices that would give farm products generally the same per unit purchasing power in terms of goods and services used in both production and farm family living as prevailed in the base period 1910-14. That period had been relatively stable both in technology and in the relation of farm prices to cost.

Throughout the 1920's, many farmers and farm leaders believed that equality of income opportunities for agriculture could be achieved by extending to agriculture the principle of a protective tariff. They reasoned that this could be accomplished by segregating total farm output into two portions—the first representing domestic needs, the second representing exports. For the first portion, farmers were to receive the world price plus the difference between the world price and the parity price. For the second portion, they were to receive only the world price.

This concept of a tariff for agriculture might have worked before World War I, when we were in debt chiefly to European countries and our interest and principal payments provided them with dollars to purchase large quantities of foods and fibers that we produced in excess of domestic needs. This was not the case, however, after World War I, when we shifted from a debtor to a creditor Nation. As this shift became evident in the late twenties and early thirties, the struggle for equality of income for farmers shifted from the protective tariff principle to direct control of output.

Farm Price and Production Programs

A variety of farm price and production programs were put into effect in the 1930's. Many of these programs have continued to the present. In summary, they include: (1) Acreage allotments and marketing quotas with price supports on such crops as cotton, tobacco, wheat, peanuts, and rice; (2) incentive payments to encourage shifts in land use and conservation practices; (3) marketing agreements and orders that enable producers of a specific commodity or in a given geographic area, such as the New York milkshed, to fix prices for different uses of a product and to regulate the volume of products that can be marketed; (4) provision for direct purchases of perishables; and (5) disposal of surpluses through export programs and through programs to expand domestic consumption. The latter type of program includes direct distribution to welfare clients and public school lunches. More recently, similar distribution has been made to friendly foreign countries through private agencies such as CARE and by other means. Provision is made also for selling to friendly foreign countries surpluses to be used for economic development projects in these countries. Finally, there are provisions for using our surpluses to barter with foreign countries for strategic materials, and for finding new uses of farm products through utilization-research programs, both at home and abroad.

Constitutional Basis of Farm Programs

Like much legislation dealing with industry, labor, and social security, the statutes that underlie farm price and production programs greatly expanded the role of Government in economic affairs during the 1930's. In this way, the programs collided with the enterprise belief (according to which economic and social progress lies in a sharp separation of society into (1) a large economic sphere without collective restraints on individual action and (2) a small political sphere of popularly controlled Government, which leaves the economic realm to the competitive rivalry of private interests).

This conflict came to a showdown in the courts for two reasons. The Tenth Amendment of the Constitution provides that powers not delegated to the United States by the Constitution, nor prohibited by it to the States, are reserved to the States, or to the people. This means that however equitable an act of Congress may be, the Supreme Court may declare it null and void unless, in its view, the act is an expression of one or more of the powers specifically delegated to the Congress. The question, then, was whether or not the Congress had the power to put the Federal Government into the economic affairs of agriculture.

The second reason had to do with the interpretation of the delegated powers. Some provisions of the Constitution are sufficiently specific to enable reasonable men to agree readily on their meaning. This is true, for example, of the provision that "The Congress shall assemble at least once in every year." But it does not hold true for such provisions as: "The Congress shall have power: To lay and collect taxes . . . to provide for the . . . general welfare;" "To regulate commerce . . . among the several States;" and no State shall "deprive any person of life, liberty or property without due process of law." Terms like "due process of law," "general welfare," and "commerce among the States" mean different things to different people at different times.

The Supreme Court of 1936 struck down the Agricultural Adjustment Act of 1933. This act called for farmers to reduce their acreages in six basic commodities in return for benefit payments to be derived from taxes levied on the processing of the commodities for consumption. On January 6, 1936, in the case of U.S. vs. Butler, Justice Roberts delivered the majority opinion of the court, declaring that the processing tax provisions of the act were not a legitimate use of Federal taxing power, as they were levied to finance a system of regulating power. It was held that the Congress had no power to regulate in this way; therefore, it could not tax to do so.

Congress acted quickly to change the approach to farm problems in order to bridge the gap in the economic machinery of the New Deal created by the decision in the Butler case. On February 29, 1936, the Soil Conservation and Domestic Allotment Act was passed to continue the gains in production control and farm income achieved under the 1933 legislation. The 1936 act provided, among other things, for direct incentive payments to farmers to reduce acreage of basic crops and to undertake conservation practices. It also provided for a system of local and State committees to administer programs within the legislative and administrative framework. The Agricultural Adjustment Act of 1938 strengthened and added to these provisions.

Three provisions of these acts are especially critical with respect to their constitutional base. These are (1) making cash payments from the Federal Treasury to farmers for conservation practices; (2) extending loans to farmers on surplus crops which are to be stored under Government seal; and (3) assigning acreage allotments and using marketing quotas whenever two-thirds of the producers of a given commodity have voted for them. The first two provisions rested their constitutional justification on the power of the Congress to tax and spend for the general welfare. The third provision, like those of the Agricultural Marketing Act of 1937, rested on the power of the Congress to regulate Interstate Commerce.

These provisions have been tested in many court cases. There seems to be no longer any question about the constitutionality of farm legislation, at least of the types now in effect. However, in considering future farm laws, constitutional powers and limitations must be recognized.

Presupposition of Farm Programs

The attempts made to achieve equality of income opportunities for agriculture involve collective restraints on individual action that are incompatible with enterprise beliefs and, therefore, distasteful, except as a short-term means of warding off severe declines in farm income. Thus, in the 1930's and 1940's, farmers and farm leaders thought that an expanding economy with high levels of employment would eventually take all the foods and fibers that farmers could produce at parity price levels.

Because of low purchasing power by most people in the 1930's, average per capita consumption of food was low. Under this circumstance, farmers and farm spokesmen justified the farm programs in the short run as measures necessary to counteract the Great Depression. They justified them as long-run measures only on the basis of the "ever normal granary" principle. This meant, for example, that if a series of good years resulted in bumper wheat crops, depressed incomes of wheat farmers could be prevented by wheat acreage allotments and by storing surplus wheat for use in lean years. In this way, wheat prices would be stabilized at equitable levels and the consumer would have an abundance of wheat at reasonable prices in lean as well as in bumper years. With normal weather and good economic conditions, the programs would become inoperative. They would come into play only as protection against short-term emergencies.

This justification of the farm programs as long-run measures tended to be confirmed by the experience of the 1940's when, because of the large demands generated by World War II, the programs became inoperative as market prices for all farm products rose above support levels. Upon the close of the war, the programs were retained on the old idea that they were necessary as a means of protecting farm prices against downswings of the business cycle, but then became largely inoperative in the upswing. Thus in the 1940's, as in the depression 1930's, people believed that, if given continuous high levels of employment, the price-support programs could be laid on the shelf and kept there except when needed as protection against temporary emergencies.

The Crisis of Abundance

The experience of the 1950's casts serious doubt upon the validity of this thesis. The lesson of the 1950's is clear. For a long time to come, even the currently high levels of employment and rapid growth of the national economy may be accompanied by a large excess farm production capacity and price-depressing surpluses. Agriculture is caught in a long-run squeeze.

In this way the very technical advance long called for by the belief of farm people in superior industry as a proper way of meriting an ever higher social and economic position in life now throws into serious conflict their deep-seated work ethic and enterprise beliefs. For, in generating price-depressing surpluses year after year, technical advance tends to prevent them from sharing equitably in the benefits of their increasingly superior industry.

Here is the conflict. Farmers tend to want a program that will balance farm production with demand at fair prices. Such a program would help them share equitably with society in the cost-reducing benefits of increasingly superior industry and technology. But the price for such a program includes collective restraints on farmers to run their businesses as they please.

Resolution of this deep-seated conflict of key beliefs and values, indigenous to American agriculture is a foremost problem to be resolved in farm policy deliberations of the 1960's.

CHAPTER 7. SOCIETY VALUES AND GOALS IN RESPECT TO AGRICULTURE

The central farm problem of our generation is excess productive capacity in agriculture which is reflected in price-depressing surpluses and the relatively low-income position of agriculture. There are other farm problems, but most of them are rooted in this one. Therefore, it constitutes the orientation of this paper.

The theme of this conference, "Goals and Values of Agriculture," is most appropriate. For the heart of any serious social problem is a conflict of deep-seated value judgments concerning the kinds of people and forms of social organization that are most prized.[1] In such conflicts, choice of goals is inhibited by uncertainty as to what alternatives are possible and which ones are most desirable. Determinate goals arise as component judgments of traditional value systems become identified and reweighted in light of appraised alternatives to present ways of living and of making a living.

In line with this concept of goal formation, four premises provide the framework for handling the subject of this paper. (1) Our large excess farm capacity is the product of our Machine Age. (2) This age, including modern scientific agriculture, is in great measure the outgrowth of America's premachine creeds of life that were so weighted as to be harmonized wonderfully well in our premachine economy of predominately family production units in both agriculture and industry. (3) The very technical advance generated by these creeds now throws them into conflict at many points, thereby creating serious policy problems in all major sectors of our society. (4) Technical advance has proceeded rapidly in both agriculture and industry since the Age of Jackson. But the impact of such advance on the premachine institutions differs radically in each case. For up to now at least, the shift to machine methods remains quite compatible with family production units in agriculture, whereas in industry the same shift has long since transmuted the older system of family units into modern corporate firms requiring perhaps hundreds of thousands of workers, disciplined and guided by a vast hierachy of bosses, supervisors, and managers.

Through these opposite impacts, should we not expect technological advance in agriculture and industry to have induced the farm and nonfarm sectors of society to give substantially different weights to the component beliefs of America's premachine creeds? If so, what is the nature of the cultural gap thus generated? More importantly, new forms of economic organization have arisen in the nonfarm sectors in response to technical advance in industry. Could these have introduced impediments to resource movements that are the basic cause of agriculture's large excess capacity? In this indirect way, may not technical advance in industry be generating the same conflicts among America's premachine creeds within the farm sector of society that it has long since

Reprinted by permission from *Goals and Values in Agricultural Policy* assembled by the Iowa State University Center for Agricultural and Economic Adjustment, ©1961 by the Iowa State University Press, Ames, Iowa. Editorial changes have been made.

generated within the nonfarm sector? If so, may this not eventually induce farm people to reweigh these beliefs in a fashion similar to that long since found desirable by the nonfarm population?

Analysis of these issues leads to the conclusion that whether or not society knows what weights to give its older creeds so as to achieve desirable goals for agriculture is now indeterminate. For there is no concensus on whether the impediments to the rate of outflow of resources needed to remove excess farm capacity lie in characteristics peculiar to farm people themselves or in nonfarm market imperfections generated by technical advance in industry. This means that both the value aspects and the organizational aspects of the farm problem are like the sides of the same coin; each can be known or resolved only in light of the way in which the other is understood and resolved.

In developing the grounds for this conclusion we need to consider two preliminary questions: (1) What are the key value judgments that have been the chief guides to policy formation in America since early times? (2) What is the model of social organization that traditionally has been prized as the vehicle of their fulfillment? Although we have considered these questions to some extent elsewhere, they are indispensable here.

Value Judgments as Expressions of the Status Principle

This paper is not concerned with values in general. Unless values are tied down to specific judgments of what is valuable and why, talk of values is pretty much up in the air. Our interests center in a few strategic judgments of value that have functioned as chief guides to policy formation in American life since early times.

Before identifying these judgments we should note that running through them all is the status principle which gives each of them tremendous strength and driving power.

As a possession, status is the standing—the dignity, the approbation and esteem—that each human being covets for himself in the eyes of all observers, including his own. As a dominant drive of action, status is the aspiration of men for an ever higher standing and the fear of falling to a lower one. Although the status aspiration includes many traits that are of analytical importance,[2] the most relevant here is the fact that its vital center is a love of merit and an aversion of demerit. This sense of merit and demerit is the experience of self-acceptance or self-rejection that arises from the conviction that one demonstrates or fails to demonstrate an equivalence between his capacities for achievement and the level of approbation and esteem he covets.

This means that the status striving cannot be equated with the mere thirst for popularity. To be sure, this is an important aspect of the status drive. As William James observed. "No more fiendish punishment could be devised . . . than that one should be turned loose in society and remain absolutely unnoticed by all the members thereof. If no one turned round when we entered, answered when we spoke, or minded what we did . . . a kind of rage of impotent despair would ere long well up within us, from which the cruelest bodily tortures would be a relief . . ."[3] This, however, is only half the truth. An equally fiendish punishment is the feeling that one is so barren of meritorious capacities that he is unable to deserve the esteem of anyone. We are often popular with others but unacceptable to ourselves. Any attempt to equate status striving with thirst for popularity alone thus falls to the ground.

Thus including a sense of merit and demerit, the status aspiration can be gratified neither by social esteem alone nor by self-esteem alone. The complete objective is twofold: To be the kind of person who deserves self-approbation, and also to belong to a social order that recognizes one's deserts. Every individual or group makes commitments of mind and conscience concerning which alternative ways of living and making a living are the proper ones for this purpose. These commitments are the value judgments that are a people's chief guides to policy formation, and in this way, they shape their destiny.

America's Policy-Guiding Creeds

Early in American life, this status aspiration unfolded into at least four groups of value judgments that are relevant to our problem. These groups are called the work ethic, the democratic creed, the enterprise creed and the creed of self integrity.[4]

The Work Ethic

The work ethic centers in four component judgments.

(1) The first is called the work-imperative. Negatively expressed, this imperative is the judgment that one fails to deserve the esteem of self, family, country, and even all men if he places love of backward or "easy" ways above love of excellence in any useful employment of his choice. Positively expressed, it is the judgment that the proper way to fulfill the status striving is to be a person who merits his own high esteem because of proficiency in his chosen field and therefore deserves a social order that prizes him for the same reason. With the so-called materialistic income incentive thus encompassed in the sense of merit, the drive that leads the farmer to adopt new cost-reducing and output-increasing technologies is obviously not merely a love of money but the aversion of mind and conscience to ways of life that deserve disesteem.

(2) The work-imperative includes the judgment that of many possible character types, the Self-Made-Man Ideal is the one most worthy of respect and emulation. For this imperative precludes any tie-up of status deserts with such personal traits as race or family pedigree, which add nothing to one's proficiency in a given employment. In all considerations of merited advance, what counts are such things as initiative, diligence, and technical competence, which release one's potential into creative endeavor.

(3) Third, at an early stage in American lore, the work ethic came to include the optimistic judgment that, in their creative potential, men and nations

alike possess ample means of closing the gap between their present circumstances and their aspirations. According to this faith, human capacities are sufficient to improve the lost of the common man without limit. To believe less puts a ceiling on the American Dream and belittles the promise of American life. Thus the work-ethic is a wellspring of hope and confidence in a brighter future for all.

(4) Finally, in its judgment that proficiency in any employment of one's choice is the proper test of status deserts, the work-imperative obviously includes a unique concept of justice. This concept is expressed in the judgment that society owes to each man (a) the equivalent of his contributions and (b) also equal access to the necessary means of developing his creative potential to the fullest extent possible. The first of these is called commutative justice; the second is the justice of equal opportunity, sometimes called distributive justice.*

There is no "natural" harmony between these. Meeting the first debt requires that society place no limit on inequalities of income that are out of line with equivalence of individual capabilities and contributions. At the same time, individual capabilities are themselves largely the function of goods and services that are within society's power to extend or withhold. Consequently, distributive justice may require severe limitations on income in equalities that many regard as incompatible with commutative justice—equivalence between productive contributions and remunerations.

The Democratic Creed

The second key set of society values that has been in effect since early times are the two central judgments of the democratic creed: (a) All men are of equal worth and dignity, and (b) none, however wise or good, is good or wise enough to have dictatorial power over any other. These judgments include a positive concept of freedom which is expressed in the saying that all deserve an equal voice (or power) in shaping the rules which are deemed necessary for the sake of the general welfare. Thus, the democratic meaning of freedom has never been the mere absence of collective restraints on individual action. It has always meant that men are free from arbitrary power when the views of each have the same weight as those of any other in shaping the common rules that all must follow for the sake of the common good.

The Enterprise Creed

A third creed, indigenous to premachine America, is called the enterprise creed. Its component values are expressed in four important judgments. (1) The individual (or his immediate family) is and ought to be responsible for his own economic security throughout life. Therefore, (2) a primary function of government is to prevent the imprudent from pressing either government or business into sharing the burden of their economic security.

---

*Editor's Note: In Brewster's later writings, notably chapter 1 of this volume, he used a different definition of the term "justice of equal opportunity." In the later definition, both commutative and distributive justice are caught up in the term justice of equal opportunity.

By equating the burden of economic security wholly with individual responsibility, this pair of judgments renders work ethic beliefs the handmaiden of laissez faire attitudes. For it follows from this equation that if the individual winds up saddled with the hardships of insecurity, this is merely evidence of a misspent life—habitual distaste for the work-imperative whose just deserts are privation. Thus government sins if it seeks to liberate him from his hardships by either direction or indirection. A typical expression of this habit of thought runs as follows:

> The government has adopted the role of the "welfare state" and declared its will to attain the "four freedoms," "full employment;" and other grandiose objectives. This it proposes to do largely by redistributing the wealth and the income of the people. By heavily progressive taxation it deprives its successful citizens of their product and gives it to the less successful; thus it penalizes industry, thrift, competence, and efficiency, and subsidizes the idle, spendthrift, incompetent and inefficient. By despoiling the thrifty it dries up the source of capital, reduces investment and creation of jobs, slows down industrial progress, and prevents society from attaining its highest level of consumption.[5]

The second pair of key judgments in the enterprise creed are these: (3) Proprietors or their legal representatives deserve exclusive right to prescribe the rules under which their production units shall operate; therefore (4) a prime function of government is to prevent anyone, including the government itself, from encroaching upon the managerial power of proprietors to run their businesses as they please.

In contrast to the democratic creed, this pair of judgments includes a negative sense of freedom. To be free means to be left alone to run production units as one pleases, unmolested by collective constraints on the managerial power of proprietors. There is scarcely a greater source of mischief than this confusion of the negative meaning of freedom with the positive sense of freedom implicit in the democratic creed. This confusion drags virtually the whole American heritage under the skirts of the enterprise creed. In this way, this creed has been used over and over in efforts to block almost every piece of social legislation ever passed on the ground that it threatened our democratic way of life. A typical expression of this habit of thought runs thus:

> It does not follow that because our difficulties are stupendous or because there are some souls timorous enough to doubt the validity and effectiveness of our ideals and our system, that we must turn to a State-controlled or State-directed economic system in order to cure our troubles. That is not liberalism; it is tyranny.[6]

Thus by confusing the sense of negative freedom implicit in enterprise beliefs with the sense of positive freedom implicit in democratic beliefs, and by equating the burden of economic security wholly with individual responsibility our enterprise creed obviously makes democratic government the handmaiden of laissez faire sentiments and views; otherwise, it ceases to be democratic. Thus the creed tends to render us:

> ... singularly unable to do well those things that cannot be done for profit and which depend upon the initiative ... of the community working through the state. Thus we are hamstrung

Thus we are hamstrung with the half conscious assumption—

> that those things which can only be done effectively by the community are in some way on a lower level than those which are effectively done for profit by individuals and private groups.[7]

In generating this assumption, our enterprise creed is essentially the core of "the great American inhibition" that many analysts hold:

> ... prevents us from ever doing enough toward ... making medical care available to all families without bankrupting them, toward even such an obvious thing as the development of a reasonably efficient and well integrated system of transportation.[8]

The Creed of Self-Integrity

A final set of key values in our premachine heritage comprise the ethic of self-integrity. This ethic relates to the status deserts of dissenters. Its central judgment is that in case of conflict, both the individual and his group (or groups) are responsible for seeking a new mode of thought and practice that will unify the hitherto conflicting views of each. In line with this judgment, (1) the community prizes its dissenting members as its agents for achieving new knowledge and practices that will enrich the life of all, and (2) the dissenter in turn feels a strong obligation to identify himself with his own exceptional sentiments and views. In this spirit, both the individual and his group (or groups) take each other's role in order to find a way of composing their differences.

This ethic of self-integrity is best exemplified in research experience. Such experience involves a conflict—a tension—between the exceptional observations and thoughts of the individual thinker and some theory or concept believed true by his professional group. The very core of any genuine scientific problem is the fact that the individual has unique observations that cannot be explained as instances of a law (or laws) which others hold to be true. Thus he has an outlook on the universe which belongs to him alone—an outlook that runs counter to that of his community, say, with respect to how a certain disease spreads from person to person.[9] In all such conflicts, both the individual and his group (or groups), if committed to the ethic of self-integrity, share the common judgment that the highest responsibility of the individual is to follow the dictates of his own exceptional insights to the last ditch as a means of either being proved wrong or of discovering and presenting his community with solutions for its problems—with new truth, new art forms, new songs, and new ways of relieving pain, and achieving happiness in all walks of life.[10] This judgment binds them together with bonds of mutual respect despite their differences. This ethic bears good fruit. There is hardly an implement of modern life, a piece of art, or a law of science whose history does not run back to where it once had no other home than the strange idea of some dissenter.

The Model of Social Organization Traditionally Viewed as Fulfilling Our Premachine Creeds

The component judgment of the work ethic, the democratic creed, the enterprise creed, and the creed of self-integrity—these are the deep-seated society values that have functioned as chief guides to hard decisionmaking since early times in America. They are rural to the bone; yet they do not stop at the farm fence; they inhabit the mind and conscience of all America. No temples are built to them; nor are they put in shrines; neither are they chiseled in stone: theirs is a finer abode—millions of firesides throughout the length and breadth of the land.

But the fact remains that there is no natural harmony among these value systems. Except for the democratic creed and the ethic of self-integrity, the component judgments of any one creed cannot be derived from those of the other creeds. In fact, they are shot through with incompatibilities. This is true of the democratic creed and the work ethic, for example. Men do not possess any specific meritorious capacity in equal degree; hence there is a sharp clash between the democratic creed that all deserve status of equal dignity and worth and the work ethic belief that they should be accorded differential status in line with their productive contributions, economic or otherwise. Again, a people may feel deeply committed to the work ethic judgments and yet completely reject those of the enterprise creed. Apparently, this is the case among the Soviets.[11] People may be so committed to the work ethic and so averse to the enterprise creed that they feel that for practical purposes the democratic creed should be laid on the shelf; at least, for the time being.

Because of these and other implicit incompatibilities, America's dominant creeds of life present us with difficult problems in social organization. The difficulty is rooted in two main facts. First, the human mind is incapable of blueprinting any conceivable social order that can rub out the implicit conflicts of these creeds. With great rigor and originality, reason can construct many alternative social orders—ideal systems of associated life. But these alternatives simply represent competing ways of living and of making a living. None can wipe out the implicit incompatibilities cited. This means that any given set of social rules or customs is possible only by virtue of a unique set of relative weights that we give our divergent creeds of life. Each change in these weights calls for a corresponding change in our ordering rules of life, and in turn change in our ordering rules is possible only if we give correspondingly different weights to the components of our creedal heritage. This means that the value aspect and the organizational aspect of any social (policy) problem are joined like Siamese twins. Neither can be resolved except as the other is resolved. Each side involves a knowledge problem. In organizational terms, this problem is a question of what alternative to customary rules can be spelled out and its results quantified. In value terms, the problem is a question of what new weightings of competing creeds would be required by the alternatives to our customary ways.

This brings up the second difficulty: No amount of rigor in any conceptual system of rules and no amount of completeness in quantitative measurements can determine what uniform weights to give our competing judgments of what is desirable and why. For each individual or group is its own unique weighting mechanism. Thus theory and measurement can never specify what change in customary rules constitute the appropriate solution to any social problem. This is not the office of theory and measurement; their office is simply that of a tool to be used in analyzing the conditions that are generating present conflicts, and in quantifying the outcomes of alternatives that people might choose, giving new

163

weights to their competing values in doing so. Because their office is thus instrumental, the ideal models of scientific theory and measurement are not to be equated with so-called *normative* systems of life and social organization. Such systems always rest on value biases which unless recognized lurk behind the mask of scientific objectivity.

Yet despite their implicit incompatibilities, the fact remains that in the premachine era, America's competing creeds of life were bound together with a unique system of weights in a new model of social organization that is commonly recognized as constituting one of the most unified belief systems in history.[12] This model is called the Lockean model. It takes its name from John Locke who, in his *Treatise of Civil Government,* first held that the good world lies in a sharp division of society into a big natural order, subject to no collective restraints on individual action, and a tiny political sphere of popularly controlled government that keeps its hand off what Locke called the "State of Nature," which Adam Smith baptized in the new name of "natural liberty," and which is today called the "free market." This model obviously gives very heavy weights to the value judgments of the enterprise creed, a fact never more accurately expressed than by Jefferson in his famous maxim: "That government is best which governs least." Cogent reasons for these heavy weights lie in the historic events that entered the shaping of this model and the sinking of its roots deeply into American life and character. As modern social structures are a series of adjustments of this model and its uniquely weighted value judgments, attention on its salient features and the great events that shaped it provides pertinent data on why we think and divide as we do on present issues, the current farm problem being only one of many.

However, as these are treated elsewhere,[13] we pass over them here except for the observation that in no country have actual social structures so approximated the Lockean model as those of premachine America. This is true because in that era both the farm and nonfarm segments of our society were characterized by systems of predominantly family production units, which is actually the kind of economic organization presupposed by the Lockean premises.

Divergent Impact of Technical Advance in Agriculture on Premachine Economy of Predominately Family Production Units

With these observations in mind, we note the widely held view that the various beliefs and values of people are largely a function of the social structures in which they live. In line with this assumption should we not expect the influence of technical advance on the relatively heavy weights given the enterprise creed in the past to differ for agriculture and industry? For its impacts on premachine institutions in each case are as opposite as the poles. Family production units are as characteristic of present-day mechanized agriculture as in the premachine era, whereas in industry family production units have long since passed into the realm of memory.

The reason lies in a fundamental difference in the nature of the "Industrial Revolution" in agriculture and in industry. This fact is evident from the vantage point of earlier times when farming and manufacturing were alike in respect to the sequence in which operations were carried on in productive units. Normally in both instances, they were done sequentially, one after another; usually by the same individual or family. Shift to machine methods quickly wiped out this age-old similarity. For, with minor exceptions of certain specialized poultry and livestock operations,[14] the shift to machine agriculture leaves relatively undisturbed the sequential pattern of operations that has prevailed in farming since the domestication of plants and animals. In contrast, the same shift in industry transmutes this sequence into the modern simultaneous pattern of operations that is characteristic of the factory system. Thus in agriculture, the "Industrial Revolution" is merely a spectacular change in the gadgets with which operations are performed, whereas in industry it is a further revolution in the premachine order or sequence in which men use their implements.[15]

This second aspect of technical change is the one that demolished the older order, as it multiplies the number of concurrent operations far beyond the number of workers in a family. Thus from the standpoint of sheer physical necessity, such advance has long since replaced the premachine system of family units with immensely larger ones, often requiring thousands of workers with different concurrent tasks that must be coordinated and guided by layer upon layer of supervisors and managers.

In contrast, technological advance in agriculture is mainly a spectacular change in the gadgets with which operations are performed. For this reason, machine methods and power, by and large, are as compatible as hand techniques with either family or larger-than-family units of production. Their compatibility with family units lies in the fact that, by and large, farm operations remain as widely separated by time intervals after mechanization as before; hence the number of things that can be done at the same time in farming is as close as ever to the number of workers in an ordinary family. But machine methods are equally compatible with larger-than-family units, as they introduce no new obstacle to expanding farm size beyond the capacity of an ordinary family to do the work in any *particular* operation. Such expansion simply involves multiplying the units of technology that are already on well-organized family farms, as in general nothing about larger-than-family units of production in agriculture is technologically unique. This means that now, as in the premachine era, virtually all economies of scale are realized well within the size limits of family farms. Greater returns to management but not appreciably lower cost per unit of output may be realized from larger-than-family farms.

As the acreage of land available for farming is now approximately fixed and as machine methods increase the area of land one can cover per unit of time, marked growth of machine farming involves a sharp reduction in the total number of family farms and farmworkers such as is now occurring.

Technological advance in agriculture thus has the singular distinction of being mechanically progressive but socially conservative. It creates no new occupational class of people whose new ways of living and of making a living force them to reweigh America's premachine creeds of life in light of their new needs of livelihood and sense of status deserts. Farm people may be experiencing painful conflicts among their older creeds, but the point here is that the generator of such conflicts lies outside their own rapid technological advance.

Reweighting Creeds in Response to Organizational Needs of Technical Advance in Industry

The reverse is true among nonfarm people, however, because of thorough-going incompatibility of technological advance in industry with premachine institutions. The organizational aspect of this conflict has found at least partial resolution in the rise of modern organizations of business and labor; and the value aspect of the conflict has led to a sharp downward reweighting of the enterprise creed. This reweighting has increasingly liberated democratic government from its former linkage to laissez faire attitudes, thus enabling it to become increasingly the handmaiden of work ethic concepts of equity. These observations bear out this point.

(1) In separating the managerial and labor roles of family production units into wide-flung bargaining classes, technological advance in industry quickly generated a conflict between the older enterprise beliefs (that to proprietors or their legal agents belongs the exclusive right to run their business as they please), and the democratic creed (that each deserves an equal voice in shaping the rules which all must observe for the sake of their collective welfare). For as the older identity of firms and households was destroyed it became evident to the new laboring classes that the freedom they most prized was liberation from the former complete power of management over plant operations. To achieve this freedom, the so-called liberals sought a government that (a) would recognize that the power to shape the working rules of industry is in fact a joint power of all parties involved and (b) therefore a prime function of government is to protect the joint exercise of this power under legalized collective bargaining procedures.

The conservative classes, who still held to the weights given the enterprise creed in the premachine era, remained convinced that the world would fall apart if the positive meaning of freedom implicit in the democratic creed were made the organizing principle of industrial as well as political spheres of national life. As they were dedicated to the older laissez faire sentiments and views, their aim was to carry over into the Machine Age the older Lockean vision of the good world as one in which the chief end of government is to prevent anyone, including government itself, from interfering with the prerogatives of proprietors to run their businesses under whatever rules they see fit to prescribe. This was their summum bonum. To achieve it was the very essence of freedom.

Thus the very liberations deemed most precious by the so-called liberals were viewed as sure roads to serfdom by the so-called conservatives. This means that unless we pinpoint the specific maladies from which specific individuals or groups seek liberation, there is scarcely a whiff of wind between the teeth so devoid of meaning as the word "freedom." One man's freedom is the other man's tyranny, just as one man's orthodoxy is the other man's heresy. These conflicting views of freedom take the form of a power struggle wherein each participant seeks to persuade the public to reweigh its traditional values so as to make legitimate its own particular version of a free life by imposing corresponding restraints on its rivals. With the various collective bargaining acts since the 1930's, the so-called liberals succeeded in pursuading society to give considerably more weight to the positive meaning of freedom in our democratic creed at the expense of its negative meaning in our enterprise creed.

(2) Similarly the shift to machine industry threw our enterprise creed and work ethic into sharp conflict with respect to the proper locus of responsibility for the individual's economic security. In separating firms from households, this shift split into separate classes the ownerships of labor services and the implements of work. Under this condition, the individual may possess even greater devotion to the work-imperative than before and yet have less economic security than ever, because his security now depends upon the way in which the management classes and not himself invest and use his savings. Under this circumstance, the so-called liberals were quick to see the fallacy of the enterprise creed's concept equating insecurity with the just deserts of one's habitual distaste for the work-imperative. Hence the new freedom they most prized was liberation from the injustices of this error. To achieve it, they sought a revised social order in which government, corporate management, and the individual would shoulder their fair share of collective responsibility for the latter's economic security.

Remaining dedicated to the premachine weighting of the enterprise creed, conservatives opposed any such social order, saying that it would lessen the self-reliance and industry of the rank and file. Not until the 1930's did the Nation abandon their persuasion; thereupon, it was found that public observance of collective responsibility for individual security was in fact a spur to greater productive effort and not a deterrent.[16]

(3) Still again, technological advance in industry brought to a head the potential conflict between the work ethic concepts of commutative and distributive justice. For, in splitting apart firms and households, it removed the older limitation on size of firms to the point at which families could supply most of their labor and management. In this way, it led to such great income inequalities that they were increasingly adjudged by so-called liberals as incompatible with the work ethic judgment that society owes to each an equal opportunity to the minimum income needed to develop and use this productive potential to the fullest extent possible. Thus the freedom the liberals most prized was liberation from the injustice of this inequality of opportunity. To achieve it, they sought a remodeled society in which a chief end of government is to establish and maintain greater equality of opportunity by taxing the rich more heavily so as to make more services available to all alike.

In contrast, by remaining dedicated to the premachine weights of our central creeds, conservative classes by and large were honestly convinced that the liberal proposals so violated our work ethic concept of commutative justice that they would dry up the incentive to productive effort[17] by subsidizing "the idle, the spendthrift, incompetent, and inefficient;" by despoiling the thrifty; by slowing down new job-creating investments and thus preventing "society from attaining its highest level of consumption."[18] The rise of progressive income taxes is only one of many evidences that the work ethic concepts of commutative and distributive justice have been substantially reweighted in line with liberal sentiment.

The foregoing types of drastic downward adjustments in the weights formerly given to the enterprise creed have enabled modern industrial America to achieve new freedoms from all sorts of oppressions by placing collective restraints on individual action. Through cultural influence, technological advance in industry has done much to liberate democratic government from its older linkage to laissez faire attitudes, thereby enabling free men to use collective power increasingly as the servant of the equity mandates of the work ethic.

Is Technological Advance in Industry Inducing Value Problems in Agricultural Society Similar to Those it Has Induced in Nonfarm Society?

The question now arises as to whether technological advance in industry is inducing value problems in our agricultural society similar to those it has long since induced in our nonfarm society. The issue turns on the answer finally given to two opposite theories concerning the essential cause of agriculture's large excess capacity. According to one theory, the cause lies in the characteristics peculiar to farm people. This explanation may be called the endodermal theory of the farm problem. The other theory holds that the cause is the fact that new market structures arising from technical advance in industry impede the amount of out-migration of farm people that is needed to rid agriculture of its burdensome excess capacity. This explanation may be called the environmental theory of the farm problem.

Our concern here is not to prove which theory is false and which is true, but to show that their value implications are as opposite as night and day. To do this, we need to sketch the salient features of each theory.

The reasoning of the endodermal theory proceeds from the premise that the labor market behaves approximately in line with the competitive model. This means that if farm people themselves are responsive to their employment opportunities, then as surely as hens lay eggs and cows have calves, farm people with relatively low incomes, if given ample time, will shift into higher paying nonfarm employments until there is reached the combination of land, labor, and capital under which comparable rates of return are realized from all similar resource uses in all sectors of the economy. However, during two decades of so-called economy, outfarm migration has not been anything like enough to do this; the lack is so great that agreement is general that the earnings gap between farm and nonfarmworkers of comparable labor capacities is wider than can be explained by all factors consistent with perfectly functioning markets. Underemployment in agriculture is getting worse, not better.[19] This means that there are serious impediments to the rate of outfarm migration needed to rid agriculture of its large excess capacity.

Where do these impediments reside? According to the endodermal theory, they lodge in either of two characteristics of farm people, or in both. One is their atypical values: they prize such experiences as country life, hunting, fishing, loafing, and being self-bossed more highly than they do society's work ethic sense of obligation to improve their social and economic status by pulling up stakes and moving to higher paying employments assumed to be available elsewhere. The other impediment is alleged to be their lack of knowledge concerning their employment opportunities.

Assuming the correctness of this theory, the value aspect of the farm problem is clearly not a knowledge problem of what new weights we need to give our older creeds; it is merely a question of stirring up sufficient unction to enable us to observe the policy prescriptions of the competitive model. Assuming that society acted in strict consistency with its creedal heritage, this unction would take either of two forms, depending on whether the cause of excessive manpower in agriculture were held to arise from their atypical values of farm people or from lack of knowledge of their best employment opportunities.

(1) If emphasis is given to atypical values, it would take the form of pronouncements that society's creed of self-integrity obliged it to respect farm people's judgment that a life of low income, combined with being one's own boss and the like, is more worthy of esteem and emulation than a life that seeks ever higher economic position by hopping from lower to higher paying employments like a bird from limb to limb. To be sure, our society places high premium on superior proficiency in economic rather than noneconomic employments. However, owing to the heavy weight long given the creed of self-integrity, ours is also a society that feels a still higher obligation to respect honest dissent from its own predominantly commercialized version of the work ethic. This respect bids it honor the atypical values of farm people instead of bothering them with programs designed to stir up right motivations in them and reform their character so as thereby to rid agriculture of its large excess capacity. Thus to the extent that the large excess capacity of agriculture results from atypical values of farm people, it poses no public policy problem except in great national emergencies when atypical values must be sacrificed for the sake of national existence.

(2) The story differs, however, if main emphasis is given the view that the underemployment of farm people is due to their lack of knowledge of higher paying employment opportunities, assumed to be available to them in the nonfarm economy. Under this circumstance, the unction needed for removing agriculture's excess capacity would take the form of pronouncements that the weight which society has long given its work ethic sense of distributive justice

obliges it to equalize the educational opportunities of farm people. Such programs might well proceed on three fronts: (1) A widespread information service in rural areas concerning nonfarm employment opportunities; (2) an expanded labor recruitment service for such opportunities; and (3) grants of public funds.

But this blissful absence of hard-fisted value problems loses validity if the environmental theory of the excess capacity of agriculture is accepted.[20] To develop this point, we need to note that this environmental theory falls into two main parts. In the first part, the logic proceeds from the fact that the assumption that lack of knowledge of labor sellers about their employment opportunities is the cause of their underemployment is incompatible with the assumption that the nonfarm market behaves in approximate conformity with the competitive model with respect to labor. For perfectly competitive conditions for profits and survival would necessarily force nonfarm employers into competitive bidding and labor recruitment to the point at which they equate marginal costs and returns for this activity, as for their other activities. In this way, they would extend to farm people as well as to others the knowledge of higher paying nonfarm opportunities. But this is precisely what they do not do normally. This means that we cannot say in one breath that the labor market behaves in conformity with the competitive model and in the next breath that the cause of underemployment is the lack of knowledge of sellers of labor services concerning their employment opportunities. Such ignorance is compatible only with imperfect markets, not with the competitive model.

But why is agriculture saddled with a disproportionate share of the Nation's total underemployment? Why isn't underemployment spread proportionately among all sectors of the economy?

The second part of the environmental theory explains this in terms of three characteristics of the farm economy. (1) Agriculture is the only major industry that conforms to the competitive model in both freedom of entry and flexibility of labor earnings. Restrictions are seldom placed on entry of qualified wage workers into farming. Although much capital is needed to enter agriculture as an operator of a highly productive farm, relatively little is needed to become an operator of a low-producing farm.

(2) With respect to age, physical condition, education, ethnic and geographic origins, and other factors, employers are enabled to screen workers over and above actual job requirements. These screening practices yield a large job-seeking advantage to nonfarmworkers. For example, a relatively larger percentage of underemployed farmworkers are above the age limit and below the educational and physical standards used by many nonfarm employers to screen job seekers beyond economically significant job requirements. Again, when new jobs open, farm people are more likely to be left out because of their greater distance from the new job openings which makes it harder for them to be on the spot when the openings occur.

(3) Finally, more than any other occupational group, agriculture is characterized by a combination of rapidly declining labor needs and a natural labor increase that greatly exceeds the replacement needs created by deaths and retirements.

170

With these characteristics and with limited food and fiber outlets, a perfectly competitive agriculture is joined to a larger nonfarm economy that is normally characterized by less than full employment and by imperfect labor markets that are generated by technological advance in industry. Only under these conditions can its own rapid technological advance continually generate excess farm capacity, which is reflected in the fact that from 1949 to 1956 total farm output averaged 8 percent more than consumption needs.[21]

If this environmental explanation of agriculture's excess capacity is correct, it follows that market imperfections generated by technological advance in industry are inducing the value conflicts in the farm sector of the society like those they have long since induced in the nonfarm sector. Three observations bear out this point.

(1) Through its nonfarm market imperfections, society violates its own work ethic sense of both commutative and distributive justice with respect to agriculture. For in permitting these imperfections to impede an otherwise sufficient outflow of resources from agriculture, it puts farmers in a cost-price squeeze that so siphons off the benefits of their improved industry that they are the lowest paid of any major occupational group. Thus society violates its own work ethic sense of commutative justice with respect to farm people.

Again viewed in a time perspective, this underemployment of farm people lessens both their capacities and their incentives to invest in improving both their capital and their personal capacities. Thus in addition to being saddled with most of the economy's underemployment, farm people have been less able than nonfarm people to build up their productive potential. In this way, society's nonfarm market imperfections violate its work ethic sense of distributive justice with respect to farm people by withholding from them an equal opportunity to the minimum of goods and services necessary for developing their capacities to the fullest extent possible.

(2) If the only consequences of nonfarm market imperfections were the mere violations of society's deep-seated work ethic concepts of commutative and distributive justice with respect to farm people, then unction could stir up remedial action almost automatically because everybody is for justice until faced with the question of whether it may not cost too much in terms of other values, such as the privilege to run one's business as one pleases. This is precisely the question that is raised if the cause of agriculture's excess capacity is the resistance of nonfarm market imperfections to enough outflow of farm resources to resolve the farm problem. Under this circumstance, remedy might be found through a national policy of comprehensive supply controls to limit aggregate farm output to aggregate demand at stable prices. In principle, farmers tend to want such a program to protect them against a market that denies them an equitable share of the benefits of their technological advance. But they also resist it in the belief that it is wrong to deny proprietors the right to run their businesses as they please.

At issue is not a question of the democratic freedom of each to have an equal voice in laying down the rules which all must observe for the sake of the general welfare; the issue is the kind of malady from which the farmer most

171

seeks liberation. Does he most prize a democratic order that restrains him from farming as he pleases in order to free him from being deprived of an equitable share of the benefits of his increasingly superior industry? Or does he most want a democratic order that subjects him to this injustice but leaves undisturbed his proprietary power to farm as he pleases? Either choice is consistent with our democratic creed. Thus, society's value problem with respect to agriculture is strictly a clash between its deep-seated love of commutative and distributive justice inherent in our work ethic, and the equally deep-seated love of the sense of negative freedom inherent in our enterprise creed.

(3) As of now, society does not know what weights it should assign to its older creeds in order to provide workable goals for agriculture. It has only conflicting values. In line with the negative freedom implicit in its enterprise creed, it wants a world that places no collective constraints on the customary privilege of farmers to grow whatever and however much they please. In line with its work ethic sense of justice, it also wants a world that returns to farmers an equitable share of the benefits of their cost-reducing and output-increasing technologies. Because of these competing ends, society has no knowledge of what alternative to present marketing and production structures might fulfill its work ethic concepts of justice through a minimum of collective constraints on the farmers to run their business as they please. Neither does it have any clear idea of the extent to which it might want to achieve a greater fulfillment of its work ethic sense of equity at the cost of foregoing some prized negative freedom of enterprisers to direct their businesses as they please. Thus, in this instance, America has no clear knowledge of what it most wants; neither the kind of people, the kinds of actions nor the forms of social organization it most prizes and aspires to achieve.[22]

Such conflicting values are the very heart of the knowledge problem that is the center of policymaking, or the process of goal formation. For this reason, any serious social problem is ethical to the core; therefore, as Dewey aptly observed, "anything that obscures the fundamentally moral nature of the social problem is harmful" as it "weakens personal responsibility for judgment and for action'" and thus "helps create the attitudes that welcome and support the totalitarian state."[23]

(4) By throwing its older work ethic and enterprise creed into serious conflict with respect to our large excess farm capacity, nonfarm market imperfections thus generate a knowledge problem of determining both the most appropriate ends or goals of agriculture and also the most appropriate means of their achievement. "Ends" and "means" are thus equally indeterminate. For the *means* to any entertained goal are the other goals we would forego if we chose it. Through repeatedly taking one as tentatively chosen (given) and weighing it against the other, we finally reach a decision on appropriate ends and appropriate means simultaneously.

In the example under discussion, society's knowledge problem is that of reaching a decision as to how much less weight to give its enterprise creed than formerly so as to achieve greater fulfillment of its work ethic concepts of commutative and distributive justice by returning to agriculture a more equitable share in the benefits of its cost-reducing and output-increasing technologies. Conceivably, the latter may be accomplished through many alternative types of collective actions, all in line with the positive sense (meaning) of freedom implicit in our democratic creed. But how much will each alternative add to agriculture's share in the benefits of its cost-reducing and output-increasing methods, and how much more restraint will each alternative place on the older privilege of farmers to farm as they please? Without comparative knowledge of both types of consequences of each alternative, society does not have the data it needs in deciding which alternative is a desirable end. All it has to go on are rival judgments of value that cause dissension among people.

Conclusions

The foregoing analysis leads to three conclusions. (1) The first concerns the role of economic theory and measurement in the resolution of value problems, which we take to be the heart of all serious social problems. Clearly, society sorely needs a way of nailing down both the qualitative and quantitative results of alternatives that is wholly indifferent to the value biases of all individuals or groups. Economic theory is well suited to this need. For, at every step, it reasons from that premise that men seek to act in ways that will maximize their satisfactions irrespective of differences in particular value judgments that determine whether certain experiences are satisfactions or dissatisfactions for given individuals. Based on this premise, economic analysis is oriented to variations in the mere quantities of satisfactions, which in great measure are weighted and reflected in the relative prices that people are willing to pay for goods and services. It is not concerned with the value judgments that underlie these price-weighted quantities of satisfactions.

If, for example, the city of Las Vegas suddenly shifted from a gambling oasis to a resort for ministers, the change in the value judgments thus wrought would greatly increase the want-satisfying power of religious literature relative to slot machines in that area. But this fact would have no effect on the formulas involved in predicting the new price of such literature and slot machines; and in manipulating these formulas, it would be immaterial to the economist as an *analyst*, whether the way of life most prized by the people of Las Vegas were that of saints or gamblers.[24]

Because of this ethical neutrality, economic theory and measurement are admirable instruments for finding out the cost-price consequences that society would be likely to experience in using alternative ways of ridding agriculture of its burdensome excess capacity. Working in this way, economists can provide society with data it sorely needs in resolving its knowledge problem concerning which of many alternatives to present market structures will be most likely to fulfill its work ethic concepts of commutative and distributive justice for agriculture with the fewest possible constraints on the negative freedom that is implicit in our enterprise creed.

(2) But perhaps all this is premature. It is surely premature if it is presumed that we already know that the nonfarm market system behaves in approximate conformity with the competitive model. Under this circumstance, society's only value problem with respect to agriculture is that of enough unction to induce farmers and others to follow the policy prescriptions of the competitive model of economic theory. If the endodermal explanation of agriculture's large excess capacity should prove to be correct, we should expect the passing years to mark a sharply widening cultural gap between the farm and nonfarm sectors of society with respect to the relative weights that each gives to America's dominant creeds for the sake of making life as free and just as possible under modern conditions.

(3) Thus our final conclusion is that until consensus is achieved concerning the causes of agriculture's large excess capacity, both society in general and farmers in particular can have no clear knowledge of either the value aspect or the organizational aspect of the farm problem because, as explained, neither aspect can exist apart from the other. Until we can clarify what are the causes of the farm problem, we have no way of knowing, so far as I can see, what are the value conflicts that we must face up to in dealing with it. To come to decisive grips with the causes of agriculture's excess capacity is a tough job of analysis. But short of this, nothing definitive can be said on society's values with respect to workable goals for agriculture.

CHAPTER 8. THE RELEVANCE OF THE JEFFERSONIAN DREAM TODAY

It is timely to take a current look at Griswold's "Farming and Democracy." In this way we may gain improved understanding and appreciation of long-standing and deeply motivating beliefs in our rural traditions, and their role as policy directives from Colonial times up to now.

As Griswold observed, Jefferson's devotion to the family farm stemmed from his belief in a "causal relationship between family farming and the political system of democracy."[1] A prime concern of Griswold was with the validity of this belief. He devoted two chapters to disproving it. We shall not belabor this issue further; a more fruitful question is why such a belief became so much a part of our folklore in the first place.

As we interpret him, Griswold's concern with the supposed causal relationship between farming and democracy grew out of his observation that the New Deal "revived the Jeffersonian Ideal and made the family farm an explicit goal of policy."[2] He might have added that this revival, like revivals in general, did not include a definition of what was being revived; in this way it generated one of the greatest definitional blizzards of all time. Why this was unavoidable will become apparent as the discussion proceeds.

I take the Jeffersonian Dream to mean Jefferson's affection for and desire to establish and preserve an agriculture of freeholders—full-owner operators, debt free, unrestricted by any contractual obligations to anyone—all in all, pretty much the monarchs of all they survey.

The freehold concept of the family farm was an unusually effective policy directive throughout most of the settlement era. Then the worm turned. An appreciable transformation of freeholders into debtors and tenants was noticeable by 1880. Since that date the relevance of the Jeffersonian Ideal to present problems has continued to decline in the sense that it has failed to generate the kinds of policies and programs required to maintain a high approximation of a freeholder agriculture.

But we know that a predominantly family farm agriculture has not disappeared; that the fostering of this institution remains an important objective of farm policy. In my judgment this will be the case for many years because the family farm is not on the way out, although some dangers confront it now as in the past. Naturally in taking this position I have in mind a definition—a concept—of the family farm which is my gauge for what facts are relevant and what facts are not relevant to the issue.

As used here, a family farm is an agricultural business in which the operating family does most of the work and is a *manager* of ongoing operations of the business as well as a *risk-taker* in the outcome (financial returns) of the business venture. In this definition, *operatorship is equated with varying degrees of managerial power and with risk-taking involving management and production inputs, including labor.* As used here managerial power is equated with the operator's prerogatives to negotiate contracts and to make decisions concerning the combination of resources.

Reprinted by permission from *Land Use Policy and Problems in the United States,* edited by H. W. Ottoson; University of Nebraska Press, 1963. Minor changes have been made.

This definition applies to the Jeffersonian freeholder and the modern family farmer alike. In both cases, most of the farm work is done by the operating family who is a risk-taking manager in the outcome of the business. However in the usual case they differ substantially in their degree of risk-taking managerial power. The Jeffersonian freehold was a very high approximation of the self-sufficient firm. By this we mean a firm from which the will and interest of all conceivable participants in the business, except those of the operator, are totally excluded. In the self-sufficient firm, the operator alone is the sole risk-taker in the outcome of production activities he is guiding and coordinating. Thus the managerial power of the Jeffersonian Freeholder was absolute, as he was totally independent of all commitments to outside parties concerning the way he used the resources of the firm and the kind of products it produced. In his managerial decisions, he never had to take account of the will or interest of another living soul. The Ages had always equated managers of self-sufficient firms as lords—the monarchs of all they survey.

But in industry, this self-sufficient firm disappeared as a representative institution with the close of the handicraft era, and agriculture has been making departures from it since about 1870. And each step in its progressive extinction has aroused new anxieties concerning the future of the family farm.

Family farms are those on which operating families are risk-taking managers and do most of the work. I maintain that such farms are not losing their relative position in American agriculture. I regard these as family farms. But usually the managerial power of their operators is not absolute; it is limited in varying degrees by contractual commitments of the operators with outside participants in the farm business, such as the landlord, the banker, the contractor seeking products of specified qualities, and even the government. Committing certain of their services to the operators, these outsiders seek legally binding commitments of the operator to follow certain lines of behavior as means of protecting them against loss of their stakes in the operators business. The operator enters into these commitments because he believes the services of the outsiders will enable him to achieve a more profitable business than otherwise. Whether or not this proves to be the case turns on his abilities to guide and coordinate the operations of his business to a successful issue. No one would assume that a modern road builder is not an independent operator simply because he agrees to produce a product that meets the specifications of his customers who send out inspectors to see if he is complying with the specifications he agreed to meet. We do not make this assumption because his contract specifications do not destroy the fact that he remains in some degree a risk-taking manager in the outcome of a business. The same principle applies to farming.

It may be that much of the confusion over what is meant by the family farm stems from the lack of a clear image of the operator's degree of risk-taking managerial power under the contractual foundations of modern farming. We know it lies somewhere between two extremes. It lies to the left of that absolute lordship which belonged to the self-sufficient firm that excludes all participants in the business except the operator, as did the Jeffersonian freeholder. It also lies to the right of the "directed worker" with whom the farm operator is sometimes equated in literature on "vertical integration." In line with this fact, I equate farm operators with managers and risk-takers in the outcome of their business undertakings, and then equate a family farm with a business in which the operating family does most of the farm work. By a larger than family farm, I mean any agricultural business whose total labor requirement is such that the usual farm operating family cannot supply most of it.

One further definitional matter. In this paper we commonly use the term "proficient family farm." By this we mean a family business in agriculture with sufficient resources and productivity to yield enough income to meet expenses for (a) family living; (b) farm expenses including depreciation, maintenance of the livestock herd, equipment, and land and buildings, and interest on borrowed capital; (c) enough capital growth for new farm investments required to keep in step with technological advance and rising levels of living. Farms without this level of resources and productivity are inadequate farms, and they are either disappearing or being supplemented by income from nonfarm sources, usually off-farm employment.

Proficient family farms may come into being through the reorganization of inadequate units or because hitherto larger than family farms fall into the category of family farms as a result of substituting capital for labor to the point where the operating family is able to do most of the farm work.

In using these concepts, I do not mean that they are *the* true ones—their status in this respect will turn on how useful they may prove to be as guides in measuring and interpreting the kinds and directions of changes now occurring among the business units of American agriculture. I expect to modify the concepts I am here using whenever further research investigations warrant it.

In these terms, we will have a family farm agriculture as long as most of our farm production is done by business units in which operating families are risk-taking managers who do most of the work. In keeping with his times, Jefferson thought of the family farm in terms of the restricted freeholder meaning of the term. However, I believe it is in keeping with his larger spirit to expand his Dream to include contractual as well as highly self-sufficient firms like the freehold. In Jefferson's time, there was no conflict between an agriculture of proficient family farms and the need of opportunities for farm people. There is a severe conflict today as only around 1 million such farms are all that would be needed to supply all the foods and fibers which society wants at reasonable prices.

With these preliminary remarks in mind, this paper centers in five major themes.

(1) Since Colonial times, two distinct personal and policy-guiding beliefs have been indigenous to the farm and nonfarm sectors of our society. First is a deeply moving commitment to proficient work as the hallmark of praiseworthy character; the second is an equally firm belief in the natural or moral right of men to acquire all the property they can from the earnings of their work. The first of these commitments stemmed from the revolutionary interpretation of the ethical significance of proficient work by the religious reformers of the late

16th and 17th centuries, and was a complete reversal of Ancient and Medieval attitudes toward economic work. In line with this new sense of obligation, people soon found themselves producing beyond the limit required to support their customary needs. But in doing so, they ran into head-on conflict with the age-old belief that the natural or moral right of men to acquire property, as a fair reward for work, is limited to the amount required to produce their customary needs. John Locke, the greatest of the Natural Rights philosophers, resolved this conflict by demonstrating that the older belief was true only in very primitive, savage societies in which a money economy was totally absent.

(2) From early Colonial times, American settlers carried the radical belief in proficient work, as the badge of superior merit, alongside the equally radical Lockean belief in the natural or moral right of individuals to acquire as much property as they can from the earnings of their work. These directives have been stable motivations throughout both the settlement and post settlement phases of our history.

Throughout the era of cheap land and relatively inexpensive farm technologies, these directives were a powerful generator of the Freeholder Ideal to which the name of Jefferson is attached. For, if land is free or very cheap, obviously farm families can achieve a greater reward for their proficient work as debt-free, full-owner operators, than as renters, or as owners with varying degrees of credit obligations. This is not necessarily the case, however, if land is increasingly scarce and capital requirements of proficient farms are growing larger. As these conditions came to pass with the close of the settlement era, the same directives called for departures from the freeholds to contractual relationships with creditors, landlords and others as means of achieving proficient farms. This separation between the farmer's actual status of limited managerial power and his hitherto absolute power was made sufferable by the new idea of an "agricultural ladder" that enabled farm people to envision their departures from the Freeholder Ideal as actual stepping stones to its fulfillment.

(3) Working hand in hand with the foregoing directives to a Freeholder agriculture in the settlement era, was the belief inherited from feudal times that tenantry and wage status are a badge of inferior character. More specifically farmers demanded freeholds as the best means of enabling them to earn as much as they could as a fair reward for working as proficiently as they could, and they also demanded freeholds as the best possible means of escaping the ancient onus of tenantry and wage status as a badge of inferior character. But this "marriage of convenience" began cracking up with the disappearance of cheap land and the increasing capital requirements of proficient farms. For these conditions generated increasing conflict between the ancient devotion to the Freeholder Ideal with the more modern devotions to proficient work as a badge of personal excellence and to acquisition of as much earnings and property as one can get as fair reward for his proficiency. In this conflict, the age-old devotion to a freehold agriculture, as a citadel of superior virtue, proved an increasingly weak competitor.

(4) In developing the foregoing themes, emphasis is placed on the economic or materialistic implications of the ethical directive to proficient work

178

at the expense of its larger humanitarian or idealistic implications. To correct this imbalance, we shall point out that the operation of this directive in American life not only has led the whole Nation along remarkable paths of material progress, but has also enkindled a "practical idealism" which has long distinguished our people, and has infused the higher reaches of the spirit with the promise of the American Dream of what lies in store for men devoted to proficient use of their creative power. Furthermore, our historic commitment to proficient work, as tangible evidence of personal excellencies, includes commitments to distributive as well as commutative justice, both of which the plain man calls the "justice of equal opportunity." If we fail to counterbalance the economic import of our historic commitment to proficient work with its equally idealistic import, then with our own voice we convict ourselves of the common but false charge that America is the most materialistic civilization on earth. We shall seek to avoid this error.

(5) Our fifth theme concerns the current status and prospects of the family farm, considered as a business in which the operating (management and risk-taking) family does most of the work of the business they operate.

Salient Features of the Medieval Landlord Civilization Out of Which Our Farm and Nonfarm Society Emerged

Of all our major economic institutions, the family farm alone has a lifespan which connects our atomic age with the ancient and medieval landlord civilization out of which America and modern Europe emerged. To know and understand the belief forming role of the family farm in the life of the Nation is to be wiser men concerning our whole American civilization, especially since our fathers were mostly family farmers throughout our 200-year settlement era when our national character and institutions were in their most formative period.

In keeping with this fact, Griswold found it necessary to step back into the older landlord civilization out of which our rural society and modern Europe emerged in order to find the proper point of departure in understanding the Freehold Ideal. We need to follow the same procedure, especially since in our judgment, there is more in this Ideal than is disclosed in Griswold's analysis. There is no other way of determining which of the deeply motivating beliefs, underlying this Ideal, were carryovers from the older landlord civilization of Europe, and which ones were profoundly revolutionary breaks with this older order. To make this clear, six strategic features of this older culture need to be identified. In substance, they are as follows:

(1) Commonly called feudalism but more accurately known as a traditionalism, this precapitalistic landlord civilization was distinguished by a system of master-servant beliefs and correlative institutions that distinctly segregated the managerial and labor roles of life into separate classes, called lords and serfs. The nobility were viewed as essentially personifications of divine-like managerial wisdom and power to know and administer an impartial justice for all classes.

179

Those saddled with the work of the world were viewed as so lacking in managerial intelligence and other virtues that they were essentially personifications of turbulent passions and labor capacities, fit only for producing subsistence for the whole community.

(2) This master-servant hierarchy both nurtured and rested on the equation of proprietorship with the spirit of self-mastery and other virtues, and on the correlative equation of tenantry and wage status with subservience, turbulent passions, and mental and moral incompetence.

(3) This older culture necessarily included a Self-Sufficiency Ideal of Freedom. For within the master-servant relationship, the free man can be envisioned only as the one who has absolute command over all the personal services and other resources required to meet his needs. To the feudal lords, for example, it was self-contradictory to say in one breath that one is a free man and in the next breath say that his living depends on market exchange between producers and consumers.

(4) This older hierarchy of superiors and inferiors both generated and rested on the belief that exemption from economic employments is prima facie evidence that one possesses the praise-deserving qualities of mind and character, and that dependence on such employments proves that one is so deficient in meritorious capacities that he deserves only the lower stations, even servility.

(5) This aversion to economic work as a badge of disrepute went hand in hand with the further belief that capital accumulation should be limited to the amount of goods and services required to support the customary needs of people in their various social roles or life stations. Acquiring property in excess of these limits was equated with greed and miserliness. Thus, this older culture would have been shocked by James Madison's axiom, widely shared by the founding fathers, that the chief object of good government was the protection of men in their "different and unequal faculties of acquiring property."[3]

(6) Finally, this older landed hierarchy of superiors and inferiors was the outward institutional expression of the belief that natural inequality is the proper guide to use in relating man to man with reciprocal rights and duties in all spheres of life. In line with this belief, the good society was viewed as one which invests the individual with only those rights and duties which mark him as an instance of a particular class. In one man it lodges the rights and duties of all serfs; in another the rights and duties of all artisans; in another the rights and duties of all landlords, and so on. In this way, the common sense of this older civilization tossed aside as nonsense the democratic belief that all men have a common nature in virtue of which they deserve an equal status that entitles each to the same bundle of rights and duties, whatever his particular social (class) roles may be.

Proprietorship as a Badge of Good Repute and Tenantry as a Badge of Servility

The striving for personal significance is apparently so universal that we assume men the world over share a profound *aversion* to being identified with status symbols which their age and civilization deem sure proof of servile attitudes and other vices. From Plymouth Rock and Jamestown on, the driving power of this tremendous urge for personal significance was a potent generator of the dream of an agrarian America of freeholders long before it was named the Jeffersonian Dream. For, in permitting the hitherto separate roles of lords and serfs to be recombined within the same skin, the 2 billion acres of virgin continent gave working people the chance to escape the age-old equation of tenantry and wage status with servility through becoming freeholders, and in this way to identify themselves with the dignity—the esteem and proud sense of independence—which the Ages had always posited in the lords of the land. The emerging agriculture of family farms along the moving frontier of the New World thus generated within everyday people an envisioned realm of equal dignity and worth, which all America soon enshrined within her national self-image much before Jefferson's day. Jefferson did not invent the Jeffersonian Ideal; he merely identified his name with an Ideal which freeholders themselves already had embedded in their very bones.

By enabling plain people to view themselves as equally lords of the land, our earlier expanding agriculture of freeholders generated the aspiration for democracy long before even the brightest minds of the Age were able to liberate themselves from the inherited equation of proprietorship with civic virtue, and nonproprietorship with civic vices. Two observations illustrate this fact. The founding fathers were still so guided by the carryover of this ancient equation that they were unable to envision the possibility of a democratic society in terms of a predominately wage and salaried population. At the Constitutional Convention, James Madison expressed this state of mind in these blunt words:

> In future times a great majority of the people will not only be without landed, [sic] but any other sort of, property. These will either combine under the influence of their common situation; in which case, the rights of property and the public liberty, will not be secure in their hands: or which is more probable, they will become the tools of opulence and ambition, in which case there will be equal danger on another side. [4]

In similar vein, Daniel Webster declared:

> A republican form of government rests not more on political constitutions, than on those laws which regulate the descent and transmission of property. Governments, like ours could not have been maintained, where property was holden according to the principles of the feudal system; nor on the other hand, could the feudal constitution possibly exist with us. Our New England ancestors brought hitherto no great capitals from Europe. They left behind them the whole feudal policy of the other continent. They came to a new country. There were, as yet, no lands yielding rent, and no tenants rendering service. The whole soil was unreclaimed from barbarism. They were themselves nearly on a general level in respect to property. Their situation demanded a parcelling out and division of the lands, and it may be fairly said, that this necessary act *fixed the* future frame and form of their government. The character of their political institutions was determined by fundamental laws respecting property. [5]

As our earlier expanding agriculture of freeholders was the prime generator of an increasingly strong demand for political democracy, so this political objective in turn generated powerful demands for public land policies that would strengthen democratic government through enabling people with little or no capital except their labor to become freeholders. This strategy was expressed with uncommon clarity and eloquence by Thomas Hart Benton in the great land policy debates of the 1840's:

> Tenantry is unfavorable to freedom. It lays the foundation for separate orders in society, annihilates the love of country, and weakens the spirit of independence. The farming tenant has, in fact, no country, no hearth, no domestic altar, no household god. The freeholder, on the contrary, is the natural supporter of a free government; and it should be the policy of republics to multiply their freeholders, as it is the policy of monarchies to multiply tenants. We are a republic, and we wish to continue so: then multiply the class of freeholders; pass the public lands cheaply and easily into the hands of the people; sell, for a reasonable price, to those who are able to pay; and give, without price, to those who are not. I say give, without price, to those who are not able to pay; and that which is so given, I consider as sold for the best of prices; for a price above gold and silver; a price which cannot be carried away by delinquent officers, nor lost in failing banks, nor stolen by thieves, nor squandered by an improvident and extravagant administration. It brings a price above rubies—a race of virtuous and independent laborers, the true supporters of their country, and the stock from which its best defenders must be drawn.[6]

While this reasoning enabled early America to turn her inherited equation of proprietorship and civic virtues to the service of democratic ends, it did so at the high cost of an invidious distinction between proprietors and nonproprietors with respect to moral excellencies. The longevity of this distinction is astonishing. For example, in an address not many years ago the head of one of our more conservative trade associations spoke as follows:

> Today the greatest threat to democratic institutions. . .and ultimately to freedom itself, lies in our big cities. They are populated for the most part with the mass of man, devoid of intelligence, and devoid of civic responsibility. . . .He will vote for anyone who offers him something for nothing, whether it be subway fares for half-price or public housing at one-third price. . .Our one hope of survival as a free country is that rural and semi-rural areas will dominate most of the state legislatures through their representative and still dominate the House of Representatives at Washington.[7]

Jefferson's Contribution to the Freeholder Ideal

Jefferson is distinguished by his sharp differentiation of all proprietors with respect to civic virtues. He did so with a neat logic which sets up a causal relationship between freeholders and democracy. Here is the logic. (1) "Corruption of morals. . .is the mark set on those, who. . .depend for it on the casualties and caprice of customers. Dependence begets subservience and venality, suffocates the germ of virtue and prepares fit tools for the designs of ambition."[8] Holding precisely the same belief, the feudal lord would have declared that Jefferson took these words right out of his mouth. In both cases, the conclusion follows from a Self-Sufficiency Ideal of Freedom which is actually incompatible with market dependence.

182

(2) Owing to its relative noncommerciality in Jefferson's time, farming enabled people to produce most of their own subsistence and in this way liberated them from dependence on "the caprice of customers" for a living; thus generating a proud spirit of personal independence which brooks no outside interference with the sense of self-mastery. Thus, the really significant output of family farming is not food and fiber, but the brick and mortar of democratic society. In Jefferson's words:

> Those who labour in the earth are the chosen people of God. . .whose breasts he has made his peculiar deposit for substantial and genuine virtue. It is the focus in which he keeps alive that sacred fire, which otherwise might escape from the face of the earth.[9]

(3) From the premise that farming and nonfarm employments produce opposite types of character, Jefferson deduced his third premise of political science. Here it is: The possibility of a democratic society diminishes directly with the increase of the ratio of nonfarmers to farmers. He expressed this deduction in these words:

> . . .generally speaking the proportion which the aggregate of the other classes of citizens bears in any state to that of its husbandmen, is the proportion of its unsound to its healthy parts, and is a good enough barometer whereby to measure its degree of corruption . . . . The mobs of the great cities add just so much to the support of pure government, as sores do to the strength of the human body.[10]

Throughout this reasoning, Jefferson, as Griswold observed, claimed a virtual monopoly of "good morals for farmers."[11] So completely different is the spirit of his disquisitions on farmers and nonfarmers from the spirit of the Declaration that it is difficult to realize that they were both composed by the same man. Lincoln, a farm boy and as matchless a politician as Jefferson, referred to the Declaration as containing "the true axioms of democracy." But in speaking to a large gathering of farmers at the Wisconsin State Agricultural Society at its annual fair on September 30, 1859, he referred to the equation of farmers with superior excellencies as a device for flattering farmers. Said he:

> I presume I am not expected to employ the time assigned me in the mere flattery of farmers as a class. My opinion of them is that, in proportion to their numbers, they are neither better nor worse than any other people. In the nature of things they are more numerous than any other class; and I believe there really are more attempts at flattering them than any other, the reason for which I cannot perceive, unless it be that they can cast more votes than any other.

There is no question but that Jefferson served the already indigenous devotion of rural America to an agriculture of freeholders with singular distinction. But other than creating an ingenious device for flattering farmers, no useful purpose is served through imputing to them a virtual monopoly of good morals. Yet, there is no mystery concerning the survival power of this myth. For any group is most happy to be singled out and assured by high authority that they are "The chosen people of God" in "whose breasts he. . .keeps alive the sacred fire, which otherwise might escape from the face of the earth."[12] It would be less than human to expect farmers to stand up and deny it, and its oratorical potential is obviously too great to be overlooked by alert politicians and others seeking the good graces of the countryside.

Revolutionary Interpretation of the Ethical
Significance of Proficient Work

Attention is now directed to the fact that the carryover of the ancient aversion to tenantry and wage status as the badge of inferior character was by no means the only directive to a freeholder agriculture throughout the settlement era. Equally potent directives were a revolutionary interpretation of the ethical significance of proficient work, which stemmed from the 16th and 17th century religious reformers, and a correspondingly revolutionary interpretation of the natural or moral right to acquire property, which stems from John Locke, the greatest of the Natural Rights philosophers.

The revolutionary interpretations of the ethical significance of proficient work, as sure evidence of highest personal worth, came into Western society in substantially the following manner.[13] In their break away from the Mother Church, the religious reformers of the 16th and 17th centuries had to face up to the question of what occupation is most truly appropriate for the upright man. According to the traditional view, such employment was boxed up in the monasteries where every moment of the 24-hour day was organized into a systematic series of routines that were known as the Holy Callings. As long as the reformers left this view unchallenged, it was impossible for them to complete their break away from the Mother Church. They completed the break by taking the position that all employments, whether composing sermons, painting pictures, making mousetraps, or growing corn, are equally appropriate ways of showing that one possesses qualities of mind and character that deserve his own highest respect and esteem and the respect and esteem of others as well.

The following are typical illustrations of this revolutionary belief. Richard Steele an exceptionally able minister, put it this way:

> God doth call every man and woman...to serve him in some peculiar employment in this world, both for their own and the common good....The great Governour of the world hath appointed to every man his proper post and province, and...he will be at a great loss, if he does not keep his own vineyard and mind his own business....[Therefore] Be wholly taken up in diligent business of your lawful calling, when you are not exercised in the more immediate service of God.[14]

Again he clothes the same belief in these poetic lines:

> How is it that ye stand all the day idle? ...Your trade is your proper province... Your own vineyard you should keep....Your fancies, your understandings, your memories...are all to be laid out therein.[15]

As a guide to the use of time, Cotton Mather expressed the same belief in these words:

> There should be...some *Settled Business,* wherein a Christian should for the most part spend the most of his Time; and this, that he may Glorify God, by doing of *Good* for *others,* and getting of *Good* for *himself.*[16]

And Baxter, with his usual lucidity, emphasized the same point in more detail:

> Keep up a high esteem of time and be every day more careful that you lose none of your time, than you are that you lose none of your gold and silver. And if vain recreation, dressings, feasting, idle talk, unprofitable company, or

sleep be nay of them temptations to rob you of any of your time, accordingly heighten your watchfulness.[17]

Under the guidance of this new belief, the profound need of achieving proofs of personal significance required ceaseless action, and an end to "taking it easy." In the words of Baxter:

> It is for action that God maintaineth us and our activities; work is the moral as well as the natural end of power....It is action that God is most served and honoured by...the public welfare or the good of the many is to be valued above our own.[18]

This expanding concept of God's work to include all occupations released an avalanche of productive aspirations that literally reshaped the world. Vast energies that hitherto found release in building great cathedrals now found new expressions of the heavenward urge in sailing the seven seas, turning deserts into gardens, conquering pests and disease, breeding scrub stock into find herds, transforming hovels into firesides of good cheer, and building new social worlds, new churches, new schools, new governments—new ways of living and of making a living in all spheres of human endeavor. These were the new songs of salvation.

No amount of riches ever exempts one from the responsibility for further expression of his powers in productive employment—a fact which the able Baxter put this way:[19]

> If God shew you a way in which you may lawfully get more than in another way (without wrong to your soul, or to any other), if you refuse this, and choose the less gainful way...you refuse to be God's steward,...you may labour to be rich for God, though not for the flesh and sin.

Then he continues:

> Will not riches excuse one from labouring in a calling: No: but rather bind them to it the more; for he that hath Most wages from God, should do him most work. Though they have no outward want to urge them, they have as great a necessity of obeying God, and doing good to others, as any other men have that are poor.

In thus placing proficient work in any employment within the category of tangible evidence of character which most deserves emulation and esteem, this new breed of minister was obliterating the sharp and clear line which the Ages had hitherto drawn between secular and religious employments. No one has ever expressed this new attitude toward the ethical significance of work more truly than did Hiram Goff, a simple shoemaker, in a conversation with his minister, John Jessig. To strike up pleasant chatter Goff remarked:

> I believe in honest work. Work is the law of nature and the secret of human happiness.

His minister replied:

> I am glad to see a man who can use the humblest vocation to the glory of God as you are doing.

This made the shoemaker's hair stand on end. Said he:

> There ain't no such thing in this wide world, pastor, as a humble vocation. Listen, you are a minister by the grace of God...I am a shoemaker by the grace of God. You'll carry up to the judgment seat a fair sample of the sermons you preach, and I'll carry up a fair sample of the shoes I've been making. If your sermons are your best, and my shoes are my best, He'll say John and Hiram, you have used your talents about equally well. It's just as necessary for people to have good shoes as it is good sermons.[20]

No greater incentive to proficiency is conceivable than this identification of the services of any employment with sure evidences (proofs) of character which most deserves emulation, respect, and esteem for its own sake. For, whether it takes a religious or a secular form, this belief diverts the insatiable striving for evidence of personal worth from the "easy ways" into a ceaseless striving for being proficient, even far beyond one's actual abilities. Any amount of earnings one can ever generate from his work will always fall short of the amount he needs for the sake of showing he has all the initiative, genius, imagination, knowledge of right policy, and other virtues which entitle him to as much approbation and esteem as he would like to deserve and enjoy. Thus no achieved level of proficiency, however high, can ever release him from the felt obligation to strive for a still higher level. If he succeeds in making two blades of grass grow where only one had grown before, his thirst for a still finer image of himself then obliges him to find a way of making three blades grow where only two had grown before.

This deeply motivating belief not only directs people in their working activities, but also in their leisure employments—activities done without pay such as vacations, club activities, and the like. As many writers have pointed out, we work as hard to generate evidence of personal worth through use of our "vacation time" as we do of our "work time."[21] Energized by this directive, people seldom find any rest and would be bored if they did; always they are on the move and never are so taut as when everything gets quiet and there is nothing to do except sit. In a passage previously cited, the great minister Baxter declared, "It is action that God is most served and honored by." By and large, American people, both farmers and nonfarmers, have long since tended to lose the older feeling that the proper purpose of proficient action, whether in "leisure" or "work" time, is to serve and honor God, but this has scarcely weakened their devotion to proficient action as the best way to serve and honor themselves and others.

Conflict Between Proficient Work and the Precapitalistic Concept of Right to Acquire Property

Attention is now directed to the fact that the revolutionary commitment to proficient work, as a badge of character deserving highest emulation and esteem for its own sake, threw people into head-on conflict with the precapitalist (traditionalist) concept of the right to acquire property.

There were two aspects of this older concept. The first was that a man had a natural or moral right to "the full product of his hands." This belief was tied into the further belief that one's natural or moral right to acquire property is limited to what he can work with his own labor and use the products from. The justifying ground for this limitation was the belief that if one acquired more property than needed for this purpose, he deprived others of that land and other property which they needed for making a living.

Both aspects of this concept harmonize wonderfully well as long as people

186

limit their work to the amount required to support their customary needs. But they were thrown into sharp conflict with each other as soon as people took to themselves the judgment that proficient work is sure evidence of character that most deserve respect and esteem for its own sake. For under the guidance of this belief, the striving to justify the highest possible valuations of one's personal worth becomes a motivation to work as much as one is able and to receive the full product of his hands as the just reward of his proficient work.

In line with this directive, people found themselves producing in excess of their customary needs. To put this excess product of their work to proficient use, they exchanged it for money, which they invested in additional land, shops, stores, and the like. In this way, they expanded their possessions much beyond the amount they could work with their own labor, and also beyond what they needed for their own subsistence. This subjected them to the charge of depriving others of their natural and moral right to as much property as they needed for making a living.

Here was a conflict of ethical beliefs that was the very heart of the serious policy problem of 17th century England. Government was on the spot. If it took the position that men could not acquire more property than they could work themselves and use the products from, it would thereby deny the individual his natural or moral right to the full product of his work whenever he was proficient enough to produce more than he needed for his own living. This didn't make sense. On the other hand, if government protected the individual in his natural right to the equivalent of his productive contributions whenever he produced more than he could use, then the government enabled some men to acquire more property than they needed for a living through depriving others of their right to acquire as much property as they needed. This alternative made as little sense as the first.

These conflicting meanings of the older concept of property generated the fundamental policy question of what is the primary responsibility of government to the governed, anyway. This kind of "value problem" can easily lead to civil war.

John Locke to the Rescue

The answer which John Locke worked out for this question was no less a revolutionary departure from the past than was the religious reformers' identification of proficient work with sure evidence of character deserving of emulation and esteem. For, in using widely accepted presuppositions, Locke demonstrated that the traditionalist concept of the moral right to acquire property held true only within exceedingly primitive societies where a money economy was totally absent. But whenever men consent to treat money as the exchange equivalent of all other forms of property, their nature-given right to acquire property, as fair reward for proficient work, expands to the limit of their abilities to contribute an equivalent amount of goods and services to society. This revolutionary concept worked hand in hand with the equally revolutionary belief in proficient work as the sure evidence of supremely praiseworthy character.[22]

Presuppositions

Locke derived his radical theory of property from the following widely held presuppositions concerning the prepolitical societies, which he called the "state of nature:"

Postulate I: In negative terms, the state of nature is characterized by a total lack of central political authority. This means three things. First it lacks:

> an established, settled, known law, received and allowed by common consent to be the standard of right and wrong, and the common measure to decide all controversies between them.[23]

Again it lacks:

> . . .a known and indifferent judge, with authority to determine all differences according to the established law.[24]

Finally it lacks:

> a central "power to back and support the sentence when right, and to give it due execution."[25]

Expressed positively, the state of nature is characterized by men who are "equally kings," each being:

> . . .absolute lord of his own person and possessions, equal to the greatest and subject to nobody. . .without a common superior on earth with authority to judge between them.[26]

Postulate II: In the state of nature (prepolitical society) men are directed by reason to observe the "law of nature." This rational or moral directive

> . . .teaches all mankind who will but consult it, that being all equal and independent, no one ought to harm another in his life, health, liberty, or possession; for men being all the workmanship of an omnipotent and infinitely wise Maker. . .are His property. . .sharing all in one community of Nature, there cannot be supposed any such subordination among us that may authorize us to destroy one another. . .Everyone as he is bound to preserve himself. . .so, by the like reason when his own preservation comes not in competition, ought as much as he can, to preserve the rest of mankind, and not. . .take away or impair the life, or what tends to be the preservation of the life, liberty, health, limb, or goods of another.[27]

Not only is each man obligated to observe this law of nature but also to use force if necessary in requiring others to observe it.

> . . .that all men may be restrained from invading other's rights, and from doing hurt to one another, and the law of nature be observed, which willeth the peace and preservation of mankind, the execution of the law of nature is in that state put into every man's hands, whereby everyone has a right to punish the transgressors of that law to such a degree as may hinder its violation. For the law of nature would. . .be in vain if there were nobody that in the state of nature had a power to execute that law, and thereby preserve the innocent and restrain offenders; and if anyone in the state of nature may punish another for any evil he has done, everyone may do so. For in that state of perfect equality, where naturally there is no superiority or jurisdiction of one over another, what any may do in the prosecution of that law, everyone must have a right to do.[28]

Postulate III: Transcending "the law of nature," in case of conflict, men in the state of nature are directed by the law of "self-preservation."

...the first and strongest desire God planted in men, and wrought into the very principles of their nature, is that of self-preservation.[29]

Rightful concern and responsibility for self thus takes precedence over concern and responsibility for others, in case of conflict. This means that nature endows men with absolute rights but only relative duties, as duties stand on the same footing as rights only when their observance requires no sacrifice of one's own right to life and pursuit of happiness.[30]

Postulate IV: By the very act of birth, nature and not civil society confers on all men a rightful ownership claim to their labor or productive capacities:

...every man has a property in his own "person." This nobody has any right to but himself. The "labor" of his body and the "work" of his hands. . .are properly his.[31]

Postulate V: Earliest societies were characterized by an absence of money as well as a central political authority. Locke describes this condition as:

...the first ages of the world, when men were more in danger to be lost, by wandering from their company, in the then vast wilderness of the earth than to be straitened for want of room to plant in.[32]

Though characterized by abundance of natural resources—potential plenty—this sparsely settled, highly undeveloped, primitive society is actually a state of "penury" in terms of usable goods:[33] "Nature and the earth affords only the almost worthless materials as in themselves:" such as acorns, berries, leaves, or skins. Existence is thus close to the bone; and no one can secure more than the bare necessities for self-preservation.

From these postulates Locke deduces his theory of property.

The Right to Only Limited Property in a Pre-money Economy

In the first part of his theory, Locke demonstrates that within a pre-money economy, the "law of self-preservation" invests each man with a natural or moral right to acquire as much property as he needs for making a living, and that the "law of nature" (reason) denies him the right to acquire more. For if he did, he would be depriving others of their right to enough resources to support their survival needs.

Locke felt obliged to demonstrate this concept of limited right because traditional reflections on the "beginning ages" of the world had long raised doubt as to whether there can be any justification of the so called right to private appropriation of natural resources. This doubt had its roots in the Biblical dictate that the earth and its fruits were originally given to mankind in common.[34] As Locke says:

...this being supposed, it seems to some a very great difficulty how anyone should ever come to have a property in anything.

Then he continues:

But I shall endeavor to show how men come to have a property in several parts of that which God gave to mankind in common, and that without any express compact of all the commoners.

His proofs are as follows: (a)

...every man has a "property" in his own "person". . .Whatsoever, then. . .he hath mixed his labor with, and joined it to something that is his own, [he] thereby makes it his property. . .it hath by this labor something annexed to it that excludes the common right of other men. For this "labor" being the unquestionable property of the laborer, no man but he can have a right to what that is once joined to, at least where there is enough, as good in the common for others.[35]

Locke then applies this labor method of rightful appropriation to the "parts of nature which God gave to mankind in common."

The first part are the perishables such as acorns, berries, wild fruit, and wild game. When and why do such "fruits of the earth" become the rightful and exclusive possession of anyone? He answers:

'Tis plain, if the first gathering made them not his nothing could. That labor put a distinction between them and the common. That added something to them more than nature. . .had done, and so they became his private right. . .And taking this or that part does not depend on the express consent of all the commoners. . .The labor that was mine removing them out of that common state they were in, hath fixed my property in them.[36]

(b) Locke next shows that the same principle applies to precious metals and wild lands.[37] For if men did not have some means of appropriating to their private uses that which "God gave mankind in common," they would soon perish. The only fair way of doing so is through their own work; otherwise one would have to get his subsistence by robbery.

(c) Locke next shows that within a pre-money economy, the amount of property one may rightfully acquire, is limited to the amount required to support his necessary needs.

First, a man may appropriate only as much as leaves "enough and as good" for others.[38] This limitation is imposed by the similar right of others to have enough resources to support their survival needs.

Second, with respect to perishables, one's right to appropriate is limited to the amount he can use before it spoils. If he picks more wild berries than he can use before they spoil, he wastes what others need for their subsistence.

Third, in a pre-money economy, the right to appropriate land is limited to what one can use with his own labor by the fact that any larger amount is worthless. In Locke's words:

As much land as a man tills, plants, improves, and cultivates, and can use the products of, so much is his property. He by his labor does, as it were enclose it from the common. Nor will it invalidate his right to say everybody has equal title to it, and therefore he cannot appropriate, he cannot enclose without the consent of all his fellow-commoners, all mankind. God, when he gave the world in common to all mankind, commanded man also to labor, and the penury of his condition required it of him. . .He that, in obedience to this command of God, subdued, tilled, and sowed any part of it, thereby annexed to it something that was his property, which another had no title to, nor could without injury take from him.[39]

Enlarging one's possession beyond this point is a sheer waste of effort.

For supposing an island, separate from all possible commerce with the rest of the world. . .what reason could anyone have there to enlarge his possessions beyond the use of his family, and a plentiful supply to its consumption, either in what their own industry produced, or they could barter for like perishable, useful commodities with others. . .What would a man value ten thousand or a hundred thousand acres of excellent land. . .where he had no hopes of commerce with other parts of the world, to draw money to him by the sale of the product? It would not be worth the enclosing, and we should see him give up again to the wild common of nature whatever was more than would supply the conveniences of life, to be had there for him and his family.[40]

Introduction of Money Removes Older Limitation on Right to Acquire Property

Having shown why the right to acquire property in a pre-money economy is limited to the amount each needs to support his survival requirements, Locke next shows that this limitation ceases to hold true as quickly as a money economy emerges. The major steps in his reasoning are as follows:

(a) Prior to consent to the introduction of money, "labor gave a right to property,"[41] but not afterwards. For in the process of introducing money, men agreed to divide among themselves all the hitherto unappropriated lands and other resources, thus wiping out the earlier natural right to acquire property from what "God gave all in common" by merely mixing his labor with raw resources.

> . . .in some parts of the world (where the increase of people and stock, with the use of money, had made land scarce, and so of some value), the several communities settled the bounds of their distinct territories, and by laws, within themselves, regulated the properties of the private men of their society, and so by compact and agreement, settled the property which labor and industry began. And. . .either expressly or tacitly disowning all claim and right to the land in the other's possession, have by common consent, given up their pretenses to their natural common right. . .and so have, by positive agreement, settled a property amongst themselves in distinct parts of the world.[42]

Wherever this agreement to use money has not been made, much of nature's resources remain unappropriated and in a state of waste:

> . . .there are still great tracts of ground to be found, which the inhabitants thereof, not having joined with the rest of mankind in the consent of the use of their common money, lie waste. . .and so still lie in common; though this can scarcely happen amongst that part of mankind that have consented to the use of money.[43]

(b) Again, according to Locke, the consent to the introduction of money included consent to unequal possessions:

> . . .since gold and silver. . .has its value only from the consent of men. . .it is plain that the consent of men have agreed to a disproportionate and unequal possession of the earth. . .I mean out of the bounds of society and compact; for in governments the laws regulate it; they, having by consent found out and agreed in a way how a man may rightfully and without injury, possess more than he himself can make use of by receiving gold and silver, which may continue long in a man's possession, without decaying for the over-plus, and agreeing those metals should have a value.[44]

(c) Again, in Locke's view, consent to the introduction of money included consent to the wage relationship, based on the contract of individuals involved:

> . . .a free man makes himself a servant to another by selling him for a certain time the service he undertakes to do in exchange for wages he is to receive; and though this commonly puts him into the family of his master, and under the ordinary discipline thereof, yet it gives the master but a temporary power over him, and no greater than that is contained in the contract between them.[45]

(d) Again, in consenting to treat money as the exchange equivalent of all other properties, men intended that money was not merely a medium of exchange, but capital in that it rightfully earns its owner interest just as land earns rent. Its earning power stems from mutual agreements among those having unequal possessions.

> . . .by compact [money] transfers that profit, that was the reward of one man's labor, into another man's pocket. That which occasions this, is the unequal distribution of money; which inequality has the same effect too upon land, that it has upon money. . .For the unequal distributions of land, (you having more than you can, or will measure and another less) brings you a tenant to the land. . .the same unequal distribution of money (I having more than I can, or will employ, and another less) brings me a tenant for my money. . .[46]

Locke Turns the Tables on the Traditionalists

In this reasoning, Locke neatly turned the tables on the precapitalistic concept of appropriation according to which the individual had a natural or moral right to the full product of his labor, but a right which was limited to only as much property as was necessary for his customary needs. The advent of money removed this restriction for two reasons.

First, it removed all limits on the amount of possessions individuals may seek to acquire. For, if one can acquire more land than he can work himself, others will pay him rent for the privilege of using it, or he can exchange it for money and then loan out the money for interest, or invest it in a business and reap a profit from it. Thus as Locke said:

> Find out something that hath the use and value of money amongst his neighbors, and you shall see the same man will begin presently to enlarge his possessions.[47]

Second, in addition to thus releasing each man's desires to expand his possessions without limit, money provided society with the means of returning the individual the full equivalent of all he could possibly produce, however much this might exceed the amount required to support his customary needs. Therefore, if for any reason the individual was motivated to produce more goods and services than required to support his customary wants, then the ancient justice of receiving "the full product of his labor" gave him a natural and moral right to more money than required for his customary needs. Since the difference between his total product and his subsistence needs (savings) was his to use as he pleased, he had a perfect right to exchange it for more property than he could work with his own labor. Thus, the more proficiently each man works, the more he gets riches for himself in return for equivalent riches he gives to society—a fact which Locke pointed out through a comparison of the pre-money economy of the Indian tribes with that of his native England. The former, said he:

> . . .are rich in land and poor in all the comforts of life. . .for want of improving it by labor, [they] have not one hundredth part of the conveniences we enjoy; and a king of a large and fruitful territory there feeds, lodges, and is clad worse than a day laborer in England.[48]

Locke's Theory of Property As Reenforcement of the Radical Ethical Interpretation of Work

In thus using the traditionalist's own presuppositions as a means of proving that the natural right to the full product (or money equivalent) of one's labor also included the right to acquire more property than required to support one's customary needs, Locke rescued the religious reformers from devastating attack. For, while ministers might use the Scriptures in supporting their radical belief that men fail in their moral responsibility if they choose the less gainful way when "God shows them more gainful ways," they were intellectually defenseless against the charge that they were actually teaching people to enrich themselves through exploiting their brothers. Locke relieved them from this embarrassment by showing how it follows from the money linkage of commodities with each other that society is most enriched when each man receives the full product (or money equivalent) of his labor even though he may acquire more property than he can work with his own labor.

Commitments to Proficient Work and Right to Acquire Unlimited Property as Dominant Directives of Settlers

The older landlord civilization could provide no home for radicals who were committed to the beliefs (1) that proficient work is the true mark of upright men, and (2) that there is no justifiable limit on the amount of property which any individual has a natural or moral right to acquire from the earnings of his work, except the limit of his abilities to produce goods and services for society. These presuppositions pointed to a new destiny and were a different faith from that which the older landlord civilization had trusted and guided its feet by for a thousand years. So, the new radicals had no choice except to tear up this older order or get out. They did both. American settlers stemmed mainly from those who got out.[49]

Attention is now directed to five main ways in which their heritage of radical commitments led them to revolutionary departures from ways of life and social organization generated by older traditionalist beliefs, some of which they also shared.

(1) In line with their directive to proficient work, settlers demanded a freeholder agriculture. For within their virgin continent of cheap land, a system of debt-free, full-owner operated businesses gave each individual a better chance to earn and accumulate more property from proficient work than could any other system. Settlers also demanded a freehold agriculture because full-owner operatorship enabled them to escape the onus of "subservience and venality" which the Ages had imputed to tenants and wage workers.

This traditionalist motivation reenforced the proficiency directive for a freeholder agriculture, but it was not the dominant factor. For, the desire for freeholder status as means of escaping the onus of tenantry could be met by public land policies which limited farm sizes to what the usual family could handle with its own labor and management, except perhaps for relatively short seasonal labor peaks. But such policies were incompatible with the Lockean belief that each man's natural or moral right to a fair reward for his industry is violated by any State-made limit on the amount of possessions he may acquire.

To be sure, in their long struggle for equitable land policies, settlers did limit their *request* for land from the Government to the amount a man and his family could handle with their own labor. But this limited request did not arise from any belief that this was all the land one had a moral right to acquire; it stemmed from the fact that under any alternative policy, settlers were fleeced by absentee speculators. If, for example, the Government sold only large tracts, it gave monied men a monopoly of first opportunities to acquire title to public land, which they could turn to a speculative profit by resale in small tracts to settlers. As a protection against such exploitation, settlers demanded policies whereby the Government would give the man with little or no capital, except his labor, the first opportunity to acquire at least as much public land as he and his family could work themselves, but would place no limit on any additional amount which one might acquire through his own initiative and industry. In this spirit, the settlers, like John Locke, were a highly capitalistic minded people.

·Griswold argues that Locke's concept of natural right to only limited property was "confirmation, if not inspiration for his [Jefferson's] ideal community of small land holders."[50] This may be correct. But it is appropriate to add that Locke's whole aim was to show that this traditionalist concept of right to only limited possessions applied only to pre-money societies and not to money economies like those of the settler. Under such conditions, the heart of Locke's theory is that each man has a natural and moral right to acquire as much property as his initiative and industry will enable him to acquire, however much his possessions may exceed the amount he can work with his own labor. In this belief, Locke never had more kindred disciples than the settlers themselves.

(2) With respect to improving prevailing ways of living and making a living, the settlers' directive to proficient work comes into clear dominance over traditionalist biases in favor of old methods handed down from father to son. To be sure, there are many instances of their resistance to change. A classic example is the often cited hesitation of pioneering prairie farmers to use the steel plow for fear it would "pizin the land." In reasoning from such cases, and their number is legion, the impression is sometimes given that settlers were fundamentally "tradition bound," and that present-day agriculture resulted from the fact that scientific and technological leadership of the land grant colleges and commercial pressures of modern industry simply *engulfed* our older rural society with a tidal wave of proficiency beliefs and values which were never indigenous to farm people.

This puts the cart before the horse. It overlooks the fact that long before the rise of agronomists and agricultural engineers, the settlers, by and large, were well known for their belief that one fails in his duty to earn the respect and esteem of himself and others unless he is on the alert for improved ways of removing drudgery and relieving want and privation from his own household, his country, and even the whole world. From earliest times, this belief bore good fruit. For however much the settlers may have been slow to change their ways, the fact remains that innovators were their heroes. In emulating such heroes, they become "tinkerers" long before the rise of agricultural specialists. Out of their tinkering, prior to the 1860's, came most of the basic machines and implements which entered into the mechanization of agriculture during the late

19th century. Widespread agricultural fairs centered around their interest in improved farming. It is thus no accident that the so-called "captains of industry" who guided the building of Industrial America from the Civil War on to around 1900, were mostly migrants from family farms of premachine America.[51] Viewed in this light, our Machine Age, including modern scientific agriculture, is the cumulative expression of the prior commitment of farm and nonfarm people alike to increasingly proficient endeavor as the hallmark of praiseworthy character, and not the other way around.

To be sure, the spectacular advance of the last 100 years in either industry or agriculture would be inconceivable without the cooperation of scientists and technological leaders with businessmen and farmers alike. But it does not follow that they were a sufficient condition. From the very beginning, they couldn't have gotten their foot in the door, as it were, except for the fact that farmers and businessmen were already seeking ways of working more proficiently. Both yesterday and today, biases of farmers for the old ways have often impeded a faster rate of progress than was actually achieved. But we know of no reason for supposing that such biases have been more pronounced among farmers than nonfarmers, especially so in view of the fact that for a century the gain in output per worker has been nearly as rapid in agriculture as in industry, and in the last decade it has been appreciably faster.

(3) The dominance of the proficiency directive among settlers is especially evident with respect to what is commonly called "quietism" and "activism." *Quietism* is the technical term used in denoting such traditionalist commitments as the belief that work is the badge of inferior worth, and that no sensible person will do no more of it than is necessary to support his customary needs so as to have ample time for good fishing, picnics, festivals, wholesome leafing, delightful companionship of coon dogs, and the like. *Activism* is the technical term used in characterizing people in whom the proficiency directive is so urgent as to be a well-nigh insatiable need for ceaseless action as means of earning favorable valuations of their worth.[52]

In these terms, it is questionable if any people were ever so completely energized by the proficiency directive as American farmers and others of the settlement era. Historians picture this fact in many ways. For example, in their account of America from 1820 to 1850, Morrison and Commager observed that this period:

> ...was America's busy age...Each Northern community was an ant hill, intensely active within, and constantly exchanging ants with other hills. Every man worked...the few who wished to idle, and could afford idleness, fled from the approbrium of 'loafing' to Europe where they swelled the chorus of complaints against democratic institutions...The Northern American had not learned how to employ leisure; his pleasure came from doing things.[53]

Such zeal for industry is far in excess of that which we would expect of a people cherishing ancient ways and whose summum bonum was a freehold big enough to support their customary needs and provide escape from the ancient onus of tenantry as a badge of subservience. This traditionalist motivation characterized French peasants who finally succeeded in achieving their Free-holder Ideal through the French Revolution. But for this very reason they differed from the American settlers as night from day. DeTocqueville pointed out this fact in a memorable passage:

> In certain remote corners of the Old World. . . . The inhabitants, for the most part, are extremely ignorant and poor; they take no part in the business of their country and are frequently oppressed by the government, yet their countenances are generally placid and their spirits light.
>
> In America I saw the freest and most enlightened men placed in the happiest circumstances which the world affords; it seemed to me as if a cloud habitually hung upon their brow, and I thought them serious and almost sad, even in their pleasures.
>
> The chief reason for this contrast is, that the former do not think of the ills they endure, while the latter are forever brooding over advantages they do not possess. It is strange to see with what feverish ardor the Americans pursue their own welfare; and to watch the vague dread that constantly torments them, lest they should not have chosen the shortest path which may lead to it.
>
> A native of the United States clings to the world's goods as if he were certain never to die; and he is so hasty in grasping at all within his reach, that one would suppose he was constantly afraid of not living long enough to enjoy them. . . . A man builds a house in which to spend his old age, and he sells it before the roof is on; he plants a garden and lets it just as the trees are coming into bearing; he brings a field into tillage, and leaves other men to gather the crops; he embraces a profession, and gives it up; he settles in a place, which he soon afterwards leaves to carry his changeable longings elsewhere. If his private affairs leave him any leisure, he instantly plunges into the vortex of politics; and if, at the end of the year of unremitting labor, he finds he has a few days' vacation, his eager curiosity whirls him over the vast extent of the United States, and he will travel fifteen hundred miles in a few days, to shake off his happiness. Death. at length overtakes him, but it is before he is weary of his bootless chase of that complete felicity which forever escapes him.
>
> At first sight, there is something surprising in this strange unrest of so many happy men, restless in the midst of abundance. The spectacle is, however, as old as the world; the novelty is, to see the whole people furnish an exemplification of it.[54]

Thus energized by an insatiable hunger for proficient action, it is questionable if the settlers' thirst for innovations was any less intense than that of modern farmers. The safe conclusion appears to be that the settlers' quest for novelty could not be gratified nearly as rapidly as that of modern farmers since they had no vast system of research institutions and agricultural specialists to feed them an ever hastening stream of new farm know-how. But this handicap does not obscure the fact that from earliest time until now the driving power of the typical farmer's proficiency image of worthwhile life so keeps him on the move that what he most dreads is the arrival of the day when he must retire and "take it easy."

(4) The same belief in the ethical significance of work, which thus energized settlers with a boundless activism, also generated a peculiar brand of practical idealism which has always distinguished our people. In virtue of this belief, the settlers were seeking a work bench on which to prove themselves. This they found in a virgin continent of potential plenty. But this realm of potential plenty was a hard world, especially so for a people with little or no capital except their bare hands. But however severe the privations and cruelties of the new continent, it would nonetheless turn into marvelous shapes and forms under the touch of patient industry; and soon there emerged the inspiring vision of a

196

whole wide wilderness transforming into farms, homes, and thriving cities in response to diligence and creative toil. As men saw the oak in the acorn, so they envisioned farms in swamps and thickets, ports and thriving cities on river bends, paths of commerce along the wild-game trails. In this way the poetry of the spirit joined the sinews of the hand with the stuff that dreams are made of. Thus was born the American Dream as the felt assurance of nature and Providence alike that, in the capacities for superior industry, men have ample means to bring their actual circumstances increasingly in line with their aspirations. As Santayana observed, the typical American is "an idealist working on matter."[55] This fact accounts for his skittishness toward either visionary idealism or crass materialism, and of no one is this more true than the usual farmer. Few things so get on his nerves as the preaching of "ideals" that are without tangible promise of such materialistic outcomes as conquering disease or unlocking the secrets of photosynthesis. Thus, his "idealism" and his "materialism" are like the sides of a coin. The one is inconceivable without the other, although neither is identical with the other. Accordingly, if one calls him a materialist, he scowls. Call him an idealist, and he wonders if you think he is soft headed. But call him a practical idealist, and he dilates with good feeling. Add that he is a self-made man, and he bursts with pride. His "practical idealism" is thus only another name for his work ethic faith that, in their capacities for proficient industry, men have ample means for bringing their actual conditions increasingly in line with their dreams or visions through an ever greater mastery of nature, both human and physical.

(5) Finally, the same directive for proficient work which generated the settlers' demand for a freeholder agriculture, his thirst for innovations, his ceaseless activism and practical idealism, also included unique concepts of equity. For the belief that the key responsibility of the individual to himself and society is to earn high standing through increasing competence in any useful employment of his choice obviously includes the further belief that society owes three reciprocal debts to individuals. These debts are the obligations to (a) provide all its members with opportunity or access to the means (e.g. public schools) necessary for developing his potential to the fullest extent possible, (b) offer opportunities for productive roles in keeping with his abilities, and (c) give each a fair return for his contributions. Thus the directive to proficient work places society under duties to the individual which are no less binding than those which it places on the individual to himself and society. Accordingly, it is as impossible for the individual not to resent the unfairness of a society which fails to do its best to discharge all of these debts to the individual and at the same time expects him to earn good repute through proficient work, as it is for society not to resent the unfairness of the individual who seeks a living and a favorable valuation of himself, but is unwilling to earn these goods through superior industry.

These three concepts of equity are all caught up in what is commonly called "the justice of equal opportunity." The first two debts are called distributive justice, and the third is called "commutative justice." That is, distributive justice includes the belief that society owes to each (a) access to the means necessary for developing his potential as fully as possible and also (b) the opportunity for a productive role in keeping with his abilities. Commutative justice includes the belief that society is obliged to return each a fair reward for his contributions.

There is no "natural harmony" between these beliefs. Individual capabilities are themselves largely the function of goods and services that are within society's power to extend or withhold. Therefore, distributive justice may require severe limitations on income inequalities that many might regard as incompatible with the right of each to a fair return for his contributions.

It is interesting to observe that the settlers rejected the medieval method of resolving this conflict; yet, thanks to the abundance of cheap land, the resolution they actually achieved closely approximated the one called for by the medieval theory of natural right to only limited possessions. As previously stated, the heart of this theory is the belief that each man has a natural or moral right to the "full product of his labor" but that his right to acquire property is limited to the amount which he can work with his own labor in supporting his customary needs. Obviously this limitation precludes the possibility of inequalities of income ever becoming so great as to throw the just demand for equal opportunities for personal development and creative roles into conflict with the equally just demand for each to receive the equivalent of his contribution.

But the settlers held this limitation would rob the industrious of their just deserts. They did so because of their Lockean belief that, if the individual produces more than he needs for a living, he has a natural and moral right to exchange the surplus for money, which he may invest in additional property that yields additional money, which he has a right to invest in still more income-producing property. There is no conceivable limit on the income inequalities which this process may generate. For there is no assignable limit to the diverse and unequal capacities of men for proficient industry and wise investment.

But, as Madison ably stated, this means that protection of "different and unequal faculties of acquiring property" is the first object of government,[56] however great may be the income inequalities which are generated by their unequal capabilities. But no government can be totally committed to this objective and also totally committed to (1) providing all its citizens with access to the means necessary for developing their potential as fully as possible, and (2) offering them opportunities for productive roles in keeping with their abilities.

This contradiction was resolved in early America by the abundance of land. For with relatively inexpensive farm technologies and enough "dirt cheap" land available for everyone, no one would work another man's land because he could earn more by acquiring title to a farm big enough to fully utilize his own labor. Thus, the abundance of land held income inequalities within very narrow limits, and in this way prevented any conflict that would have otherwise arisen between the competitive requirements of commutative and distributive justice.[57]

But today the conflict is serious, made so by high-priced land, highly productive farm technologies, limited outlets for farm products, and a national economy with 5 to 6 million unemployed. Under these conditions, price-depressing surpluses siphon off to the rest of society a disproportionate share of the cost-reducing benefits of the farmer's increasingly superior industry. Thus commutative justice is disturbed. Seeking to rectify this inequity through programs designed to cut back production to the level at which total supply balances total demand at reasonable prices, improves incomes for agriculture as a whole. However, such programs may worsen the inequality of opportunity to productive roles and fair incomes among the relatively few families who are on proficient farms and the great bulk who are on inadequate farms. Seeking to rectify this inequity through credit programs designed to accelerate growth in the total number of proficient farms generates additional price-depressing surpluses, thus worsening the lack of fair returns to farmers as a whole. Seeking to get out of all these boxes through programs designed to move surplus workers out of agriculture expands the national pool of unemployed. This further infringes on the natural and moral right of all citizens to productive and fairly rewarding roles in keeping with their abilities.

Thus, all our genius and wit are far less effective than was the abundance of cheap land of the settlement era in limiting income inequalities to the point of harmonizing the otherwise seriously conflicting demands of distributive and commutative justice.

The Widening Gap Between the Freeholder Ideal and Proficient Practice

As previously explained, the Freeholder Ideal was an agriculture of businesses in which the will and interest of all participants are totally excluded except those of the operating families who do most if not all the work of their businesses. In such self-sufficient firms, the managerial and risk-taking role of the operator is that of absolute lord and master over all conceivable operations of his business. Divested of all commitments to any outsider, such as creditor, landlord, Government, or others, the freeholder was truly the monarch of all he surveyed.

Furthermore, until the late 19th century, the actual status of farm families and their Ideal status as freeholders were identical. The Actual and the Ideal were not hooked together by an "agricultural ladder" in which a would-be freeholder started out as a farm hand, worked a few years until he saved enough from his wages to buy a line of equipment, then became a tenant until he could save enough to buy a farm with the help of creditors, then worked and saved a few more years until he could pay off all his creditors and then live out the evening of his life in the proud feeling that he was absolute lord and master of all that lay within his fence lines. Farmers of the settlement era would have regarded this separation of the Ideal from the Actual (Theory and Practice) as a monstrosity. For their Ideal was an agriculture in which the young man began the race of life as a freeholder—a debt-free, full-owner operator, and the ladder of his dreams extended from that point on up.

Thus the concept of the "agricultural ladder" is wholly the product of the post settlement era and stemmed from the need for assurances that continual departures from dying Ideals are in fact merely stepping stones to their fulfillment. Four observations bear out this point.

(1) As cheap land gave out and farm technologies became increasingly expensive, the amount of land and other resources required for proficient farming quickly exceeded the amount which the usual farm family could acquire with its own limited assets. In line with this fact, increasing numbers of farmers and family operators departed from their freeholder status by seeking the help of creditors who would supplement their limited resources with real estate as well as capital loans on reasonable terms. Both public and private lenders responded to this invitation. But the price of their doing so was a debt contract that limited the farmer's absolute managerial power over his own equity until creditor liens were satisfied. In this way, a wedge was driven between his actual status and his Ideal status as a freeholder. But sufferance of the gap was made easy by the faith that, within a few years of diligent industry and thrift, debtor operators would accumulate enough savings to pay off their creditors and wind up their later years as the absolute sovereigns of a Jeffersonian freehold.

Two innovations in practices of farm lenders in recent years indicates that the essential function of agriculture credit today is to enable operators to acquire operating control over proficient farms through perpetual credit. First this fact is implicit in the establishment of 40-year real estate loans. For the lifetime of such loans substantially exceeds the productive lifespan of the usual farmer. Second, the same fact is implicit in the use of loan renewals and lengthening the lifespan of chattel loans. It is also implicit in a small increase in incorporated family farms.

(2) As increasing numbers of family farmers sought the help of creditors in purchasing farms, so they likewise sought the help of landlords who would supplement their working capital by lending them the use of their land and buildings. Landlords responded but the price of their response was a rental contract that limited the operator's absolute managerial power. For example, to protect his contribution to the operator's business, the landowner might require commitments of the operator to follow a specified rotation system, and make no alterations in fixed improvements without the landowner's approval. In this way, a second wedge was driven between the actual status of increasing numbers of family farmers and their Ideal status as freeholders. But again the sufferance of this gap was made easy by the faith that within a few years of diligent industry and thrift the usual tenant operator would eventually save enough to achieve a debt-free, full-ownership status.

(3) Since the 1930's, farmers have sought Government assistance in helping them to balance their output to total demand at fair prices. Government has responded with price-support guarantees. But the cost of this response has been production contracts which again limit the hitherto absolute managerial power of the farmer to produce whatever amounts of commodities he chooses. In this way, a third wedge has been driven between the farmer's actual managerial status and his Ideal status as a freeholder.

(4) In recent years, merchandisers of a very limited number of foods like poultry, table eggs, and certain fruits and vegetables began by-passing wholesalers and warehouses and going to first processors in the marketing chain with contracts which specified the prices which they would pay for specified volumes, delivery dates, and quality characteristics of given products. First processors in turn translated their contracts into corresponding production contracts with farmers—the first producers. Thus, in addition to creditors, landlords, and the Government, contractors, including feed dealers, have entered into the farmer's business with contractual arrangements that further limit the historic Ideal of himself as the absolute master of a self-sufficient firm. Today, the farmer is only a relative master of a contractual firm.

It is often said that "the family farm as we have known it is on the way out." Right. But this has been true for nearly 100 years. It first became true when the family operator allowed creditors, especially real estate creditors, to be participants in his business, thus limiting his absolute managerial power with contractual commitments to comply with specified rules which his creditors deem necessary for the protection of their interest in the farmer's business. Again the family farm, "as we have known it," disappeared when the operator consented to the land-owner becoming a participant in his business, limiting his absolute managerial power with commitments whereby the landowner could send out the sheriff if he didn't live up to this agreement.

Still again, the family farm "as we have known it" disappeared when family operators by the millions sought for their Government to become a participant in their business by guaranteeing them price floors in exchange for commitments which limited the farmers' hitherto absolute power to produce any amount of whatever products he pleased. Finally in some sectors of agriculture the family farm "as we have known it" has disappeared because the operator has allowed contractors to become participants in his firm through contracts which specify both the price and the product he may produce. In return the farmer limits his absolute power to produce as he pleases with commitments to comply with certain specified practices which will meet the specifications of the contract.

In following their 3-century directive to be proficient farmers, actual family operators over the last 100 years have steadily shifted their operations from self-sufficient firms to contractual firms. I see no possibility of turning the clock back. If this be true, the Jeffersonian Dream in the strict sense of the word is dead.

But is it realistic to be this strict?

Prospect

For an agriculture in which operating families do most of the work and have varying degrees of risk-taking and managerial power is very much alive and on the go. Otherwise an increasing proportion of total farm work would be accounted for by hired labor, and also an increasing proportion of total farm output would be accounted for by larger than family farms, that is, farms using more hired labor than can be supplied by an ordinary farm family, which is approximately 1.5 man-years. Unless both of these changes were definitely underway, an agriculture of predominantly family farms could not be going down the drain. They do not appear to be underway.

Actually the proportion of farm work done by hired workers declined rapidly but both declined at about the same rate, although the rate decline in hired work was somewhat faster.[58] Again, family-operated farms accounted for over 74 percent of total farm marketings in 1954 as compared with nearly 67 percent in 1949.[59] Preliminary indications are that approximately the same relationships obtained for the 1954-59 period as for the 1949-54 period. (The figures cited were unaffected by changes in farm wage rates or prices received by farmers.)

But the fact that the family farm is not going down the drain does not mean that the road ahead is clear of danger. My chief apprehension stems from two areas; one pertains to the nature of future farm technologies, the other to the increasing capital requirements of proficient farms.

In the visible future, will scientists and engineers develop farm technologies that make possible the widespread introduction of the factory process into food and fiber production, as was done in industrial production at the beginning of the Industrial Revolution?

Before the rise of the machine process, agriculture and industry were characterized by a sequential pattern of operations in which the various production steps were separated by time intervals, so that the same individual could perform one production step after another until the final product was the embodiment of his own planning and effort. The shift from hand to machine methods quickly wiped out this premachine similarity of agriculture and industry. But the shift to machine production in farming, by and large, does not transform the age-old sequential pattern of operations into a simultaneous pattern. If it did, plowing, cultivating, and harvesting would need to be done concurrently. But nature does not permit this; she separates these operations by very wide time intervals.

Were this not the case, the shift to machine farming would quickly multiply the number of things that must be done at the same time far beyond the number of workers in any family. In this way, it would destroy the premachine institution of family farms (or businesses) and replace them with factories. For a factory is simply a production organization in which the many steps involved in making a product, such as an automobile, are divided into different places along a production line and done concurrently with the input-output rate of each operation controlled by the flow rate of materials between operations. No family could possibly operate a factory. The number of things that need to be done concurrently is far greater than the number of workers in many, many families.

In some agricultural processes, nature separates production steps by very short intervals. This is true of the timespans between animal feedings, for example, and milking cows. Approximation of the factory process in farming has

202

been achieved to some extent in these situations. In such instances, the family farm becomes a physical impossibility for the same reason that a family factory is unthinkable in industry. In the main, however, the "Industrial Revolution" in agriculture is mainly a spectacular change in the implements with which operations are performed, whereas in industry it is a further revolution in the sequence of productive operations.

The age-old sequential pattern of operation is the physical basis of the family production unit, in either industry or agriculture. It is long since gone in industry. Can it be expected to continue indefinitely in agriculture? There is reason to suspect it will not. The family farm would go out like a light, if the secrets of photosynthesis were unlocked, as it seems they surely will be. It is said we are now closer to this achievement than we were to the atomic bomb in 1905 when Einstein opened up the possibility of it with his famous formula for the equivalence of matter and energy.

Even much before this event, scientists and engineers may go far in wiping out the physical possibility of the family farm through discovering profitable ways of separating the production of crops and livestock on the same farm throughout the Corn Belt and elsewhere. Should this happen, there probably would not be much left of family farming. From a physical standpoint, livestock feeding can now be organized into an approximate factory process. Although my foresight is very limited, the day may not be far off when specialists will bring forth profitable farm technologies that will wipe out the wide time intervals between the many operations on given farm products.

In addition many fear the family farm is on the verge of being wiped out by its expanding investment requirement. It is not uncommon for proficient farms to represent real investments from $75,000 to over $200,000, and non-real estate investments of an additional $35,000 to $75,000.

How can individual families with assets of this magnitude pass them on intact to the next generation? The ready answer is that the farm real estate owners may combine into relatively large corporations, convert their assets into stock shares and then protect the value of their assets and assure reasonable dividends by appointing boards of directors who will hire professional farm managers to see that farming is carried on in a proficient manner. By withholding rental privileges, and offering stock shares in exchange for renters' investments in working capital, the corporation would be able to induce family farmers now on a rental basis to become shareholders in the corporation. At their option they might remain on the same farms as before, but as wage or salaried workers of the corporation under the direction of professional managers.

This may happen, but there is an obstacle that may prevent it from happening very soon. As I see it, the obstacle is this. The relationship between prices received and prices paid by farmers has seldom been sufficiently favorable to make possible a return to labor comparable to that of workers of similar capacities in nonfarm employment. If agriculture had to compete with industry for workers in the same general labor market, then to take over in great numbers in any given area, large farming corporations would have to pay workers as much as they can earn in other employment, else they would choose industrial employment. Furthermore, from early times up to now really large agricultural businesses have become the dominant institution in American agriculture only in those regions, such as the far West and the plantation areas of the South, where peculiar institutional arrangements have enabled agriculture to secure large supplies of relatively cheap labor outside the general labor market and in this way escape the necessity of competing with industry for labor services. No similar institutions prevail throughout all the major regions in which family farming has long been the dominant business unit of American agriculture, and as I see it there is little possibility of such institutional developments in these areas. Therefore, my guess is that investment requirements of proficient farms will fail to proceed to the point of wiping out a predominantly family farm agriculture in the visible future.

Expanding investment requirements may become incompatible with the family farm without leading to big stock-share corporations. The trend in farm mechanization is in the steady direction of larger capacity machinery and equipment which decreases labor per unit of output. Fuel, oil, and other machine costs might be cut appreciably by larger business which enables operators to purchase supplies in wholesale, rather than retail, lots. Savings might also be achieved in farm marketing costs. Such factors suggest that we may be reaching a point where increasing numbers of operators, by expanding their business to 4- or 5-man farms may be able to achieve enough savings in costs to compete with industry for labor. This eventuality might or might not involve large stock-share corporations, but in either case it would wipe out the family farm. The main obstacle to this development, as I see it, is high risk on large investments which stems from uncertainty of farm prices and incomes. I do not expect these obstacles to be overcome in the near future, but I may be mistaken.

Conclusions

The foregoing analysis leads to five main conclusions:

(1) Considered as a business in which the operating family is a risk-taking manager of an undertaking in which it does most of the work, the family farm is no less a dominant institution of American agriculture now than it was in Jefferson's day. The difference lies in the fact that the typical family farm of his day was a highly self-sufficient firm in which the will of the operator was absolute; his power to run his business as he pleased was not limited by outside participants, such as his creditor, his landlord, his government, or buyers of his products, or his suppliers, such as the feed dealer. Furthermore, in Jefferson's day of cheap land and low capital requirements per farm, there was a high correlation between this concept of a self-sufficient firm, in which the operator's will was absolute, and the requirements of a proficient farm—that is, a farm with sufficient resources and productivity to utilize a "full line of equipment" and generate ʹat least enough income to meet expenses for operating costs, fixed charges, family living expenses, and enough capital growth for new investments

to keep in step with technological advance and rising levels of living. Under modern conditions, this older concept of the self-sufficient firm has long ceased to coincide with the requirements of a proficient farm. In the actual life of farm people, requirements of proficient farming have taken precedence over values which may attach to their image of themselves as absolute masters of their businesses. As a result, the typical family farm of today is a contractual firm in which the operator's managerial power and risk-taking are limited in varying degrees by his commitment to follow certain rules under which others are willing to extend him services that enable him to operate a more proficient farm than he could otherwise do.

(2) In Jefferson's time no one did more than he to advance the cause of scientific agriculture. From this fact, we may infer that he sought above all else an agriculture of proficient family farms. Such an agriculture is not possible today except as the usual family seeks and secures the help of other owners of production and marketing services. In light of this fact, we may infer that Jefferson would expand his agricultural Ideal to include contractual firms in which families consent to limit their otherwise absolute managerial power with commitments under which others are willing to extend them production and marketing services they need for becoming operators of proficient farms.

(3) In these terms, the traditional Ideal of a predominantly family agriculture of proficient farms remains as relevant to present-day policy considerations as in the settlement era. In that era, implementation of the Ideal merely called for equitable land policies that gave families with little or no capital except their labor first opportunities to acquire fee-simple ownership to enough public lands for a proficient farm. Today the lines of implementation are quite different. At least four deserve mention.

Achievement of an agriculture of proficient family farms calls for continual improvement in agricultural credit policies and programs to enable competent operators of inadequate farms to expand their resources and productivity to farms of sufficient size to effectively utilize a full line of equipment. As this is done, we approximate an agriculture of farms which are able to produce foods and fibers for society at minimum cost per unit of output. Limited available data on the economies of farm size indicate that, under conditions of reasonable prices for farm products, such an agriculture will enable operating families to have earnings for their labor and management which are comparable to earnings of people of similar capacities in nonfarm employments. The data also indicate that in most types of farming, farms which are larger than proficient family farms would not be able to produce foods and fibers at less cost per unit of output, although they would return greater profits to management because of their larger volume of output.

Again, achievement of the traditional agricultural Ideal of proficient family farms calls for continual effort to establish and maintain equitable contracts between tenants and landlords; between operators and contractors seeking products of specified grades and quality; and between Government and farmers seeking ways to bring total farm output in line with total demand at reasonable prices. Third, in connection with new land developments, such as large reclamation projects, implementation of the family farm Ideal calls for policies that keep the door of opportunity open to families seeking to become established as operators of proficient farms. Finally, implementation of the Ideal calls for continual scrutiny of tax laws to see that these do not take unfair advantage of proficient family farm operators.

(4) But the striving to achieve this Jeffersonian agriculture of proficient family farms runs into conflict with another historic Ideal of ample opportunities for farm people for productive work in return for which they earn decent incomes and the high standing they seek in their own eyes and in the eyes of others. When land was so abundant as to be "dirt cheap" there was room enough in agriculture for every family to have a proficient farm that wanted one.

Today, this is far from true. In 1959, there were over 2.4 million commercial farms. Depending on what assumptions are used, one may reach somewhat different estimates of the number of proficient family farms that would be needed to provide society with all the foods and fibers it wants at reasonable prices. But, all the "educated guesses" I know of indicate that about 1 million proficient farms would be enough to do this job.

Achieving an agriculture of proficient family farms comes at a very high price when the cost of it is the uprooting of well over half the present commercial farm population. It will not do to say they will shift into higher paying nonfarm employments. This alternative is limited by a lack of over 5 million opportunities for the needs of the national labor force. It also is severely limited by the fact that farm families commonly lack the training and skills required to take advantage of nonfarm opportunities and also by the fact that anyone's occupational mobility is definitely circumscribed, once he has trained and geared himself for a particular career such as farming, mining, or teaching and research.

Above all, the clash between the drive for proficiency and the need of opportunities for farm families is not basically a knock-down-drag-out struggle between an agriculture of family farms and an agriculture of larger farms. For, as previously explained, in terms of the proportion of total farm work and total farm output accounted for by farms on which operating families do most of the farm work, family farming is not losing out. This means that the drive for achieving the historic agricultural Ideal of proficient family farms is in fundamental conflict with the equally historic Ideal of providing ample opportunities for farm people; and this conflict cannot be resolved by "programs to save the family farm."

(5) This does not mean surrender of the family farm Ideal, but it does mean that policies and programs to achieve it must be incorporated within the larger objective of finding opportunities for farm people who are otherwise sacrificed by an overwrought dedication to the agricultural Ideal of proficient family farms. The overriding concern of Jefferson was with policies that would provide abundant opportunities for people; and his interest in an agriculture of proficient family farms was incidental to his larger concern with the need of people for opportunities.

If this be a correct estimate of the man, the first requisite of Jeffersonian principles bids us turn attention more directly to ways of expanding educational opportunities for rural areas and of creating more new nonfarm employment opportunities in both rural and urban sectors of the Nation. Only as we move toward this objective of more abundant opportunities for all people do we open a realistic road to more rapid achievement of an agriculture of proficient family farms for all who remain in farming. That, as I understand it, is the true relevance of the Jeffersonian Dream today.

CHAPTER 9. ROLE OF THE RESEARCHER IN THE FORMATION OF PUBLIC POLICY

All of you well know I am not an econometrician. This means that I will not involve myself in the mathematical structure of the models themselves. Had you desired this type of critic, I am sure you would have selected someone else for the spot I am now in.

This assignment gave me the profitable opportunity to do six things, which I have wanted to do for a long time. These were the chance to (1) read and assimilate empirical studies done in recent years on interregional competition in agriculture; (2) classify the various current transportation and interregional competition models with respect to their central objective and basic assumptions, the implications of their solutions, and their major findings; (3) identify important types of farm policy problems for which needed information can be achieved only through research studies on interregional competition in agriculture; (4) evaluate interregional competition models as an aid in resolving policy problems; (5) reach, I hope, some well-grounded judgments concerning the direction of further developments of models for interregional competition; and (6) finally, receive the benefit of the fine papers and the discussion of this workshop.

In all of these stages of preparation, my curiosity was guided by a key question: To what extent, if any, is the economics profession making progress toward building interregional competition theory into predictive knowledge? For example, how much of a specific production service would flow from this area to that if such and such were the rules concerning price supports or acreage allotments on cotton or feed grains?

At the close of World War II, the data needed for achieving such knowledge were virtually nil; neither were the mathematics and computer technologies adequate for handling the data. Workers simply had to start from scratch. And when you do that, you must begin by selecting very simple problem situations in which the number of variables you have to measure are the fewest possible. Then you move on to successively more complex problems until enough variables are handled that citizens, educators, lawmakers, and administrators feel that the analysis provides them with indispensable guides to understanding the policy questions, regardless of the degree of probability you can attach to your conclusions.

When this stage has been reached, public policymakers will feel they are shortchanging themselves unless they seek you out and take serious account of your findings in reaching their decisions on what rules people should follow for the sake of improving their welfare. When we succeed in carrying interregional

---

This chapter is a shortened version of a paper that was presented as "Review and Critique of Workshop in Interregional Competition," at the Annual Southern Farm Management Research Meeting, March 1964. The omitted portions of the original paper deal with the mathematical formulation attributed to Madden—not an essential part of Brewster's presentation. Other editorial changes have been made.

competition models to the point where our findings are thus prized as indispensable aids by public decisionmakers, our discipline will be valued as a predictive science; at least as I use the term.

When that day arrives, I wonder if anyone will be talking about "normative economics" on the one hand, and "positive economics" on the other? My wonderment stems from two main sources. (1) In preparation for my present assignment, my review of the various interregional competition studies made since World War II, as well as the various able papers presented at this workshop, all led me to the conclusion that the profession has made remarkable headway in developing interregional competition theory in the direction of predictive science in the sense just defined. (2) Yet, I found many knowledgeable people, particularly those having to provide policymakers with useful information, quite impatient with all the studies under consideration. Their impatience did not stem from failure to grasp the limitations of data and simplifying assumptions which the authors of all the interregional studies carefully pointed out. Instead, their impatience stemmed from an irritation with studies that proclaimed to give solutions to "normative problems"—solutions that in effect say

> if society's values are such and such, then the interregional resource shifts of the magnitudes indicated in this study are the ones policymakers should strive for.

What policymakers are seeking is not this, but information on the kinds of outcome that will occur if they choose alternative A as compared with those they may expect if they choose alternative B.

Interregional competition studies do not as yet provide such information. In my judgment, they do not do so because we have not yet succeeded in measuring enough economic variables to make predictive statements concerning outcomes of various policy alternative 5 to 10 years hence. But many critics feel the reason is that the profession is busying itself with "normative" problems instead of "real" problems.

The point is that the semantics of "normative problems and solutions" generates a very serious roadblock to appreciation of the real progress the profession is making in building interregional competition theory into a predictive science. With the hope that eventually a semantics may be developed that can more successfully reflect this progress, I would like to attempt an appraisal of the direction of research on interregional competition in agriculture as an aid in resolving important farm policy problems. I will attempt to do this through four main steps: (1) Sketch the essential difference between policy problems and research problems and their inderdependence; (2) identify some important farm policy issues that are continually on our doorstep; (3) evaluate current transportation and spatial equilibrium models as an aid in the resolving of these problems; (4) make some suggestions as to the direction of needed future research.

Policy Problems and Research Problems: Their Essential Difference and Interdependence

Policy problems are struggles of people to reach hard decisions concerning what ought and ought not to be done on specific issues. To decide what rules all should be obliged to follow, and to execute such decisions is the responsibility of men as citizens, as legislators, and as administrators of public and private agencies. Life permits no evasion by any citizen of these responsibilities.

Decisions on what rules people are obliged to observe range all they way from daughter's questionable boy friends to what ought and ought not be done in Vietnam. No amount of ignorance absolves us from making these decisions. For example, the parent has to make a decision on a daughter's questionable boy friend, however imperfect or perfect the parent's knowledge of the results of the decision may be. And, decisions on whether or not we should have price supports *will* be made, as will decisions on how far to go in Vietnam, however imperfect or perfect our prediction of the outcome of whatever choice is made.

In terms of my limited understanding, men in their role *as* scientists (whether physical or social) do not address themselves to questions of what ought to be done—with questions of what actions are most equitable from the standpoint of all concerned.

As scientists—*as* analysts—*as* technicians—men are concerned only with what will happen if such and such is done; not with whether such and such ought to be done. For example, recently I had two questions put to me: Are negotiable quotas desirable for farm commodities such as cotton and wheat? If so, should they be used to foster optimum size farms? In my role as a citizen, I have certain opinions on these questions. However, in my role as an analyst, I could only give information on what the effects would be if quotas were made negotiable; but as an analyst I could not judge the desirability of these effects, the ends that would be achieved by certain Government program.

Again, I am presently involved in research determination of the economies of farm size—how per unit cost and total profit vary with size of business when all other variables are held constant. As a researcher, if I understand the meaning of the term, I *am not* (and must not be) concerned over whether we should have an agriculture of optimum size farms, or less than optimum size farms, or larger than optimum size farms. *As* researcher, what I *am* concerned about, and have a professional obligation to be concerned about, are answers to such predictive questions as: How will a farmer's unit cost and profits be affected *if* he achieves a certain size? What will be the effects on farm employment opportunities and on general economic development of a region *if* agriculture is organized into increasingly efficient and profitable size units? In short, as a researcher I no more pass judgments on whether farmers *ought* to alter their farm sizes than on whether they *ought* to shoot squirrels. As a researcher, I am concerned with effective means of attaining ends, but not with choosing the ends to be attained.

This does not mean I am neutral on *ought-questions* (policy) as a person; it means only a small part of me is a researcher, a parent, and the like; and that I shouldn't get my various personality roles confused with one another.

211

Two general types of research are generally recognized: pure and applied. In pure research, the scientist is liberated by society from the necessity of justifying his quest for new knowledge on the basis of whether it may have practical uses. In applied research the reverse is true.[1]

Our culture supports the scientist in pure research endeavors out of the faith that in the long run he will turn up theoretical findings that will eventually have practical applications through applied research. This means that our culture is one in which pure research and applied research are prized for exactly the same reasons—namely, their practical usefulness in achieving an increasingly predictable and manageable world.

'Twas not so among the ancient Greeks. Their *sumun bonum* was a life of contemplation, rather than a life that continually expanded man's control over his environment. Our culture is one that gives the *"vis vita"* boys—the devotees to new knowledge for its own sake—a place in life because in the long run they prove to be very useful from a practical standpoint.

I am loath to think what tiny research budgets we would have were it not for the plain man's faith in the long run practical utility of the pure research scientist.

Solutions to research problems are a much needed aid to resolution of policy problems. For, in being confronted with ought-questions, people do not know what new conditions are throwing their hitherto harmonious values into conflict—say their desire for adequate medical care and their desire for no collective restraints on the power (freedom) of physicians and patients to deal with each other on whatever terms they choose. Neither do they know what alternatives to present actions might be possible. And they have little or no knowledge of what would happen if they did such and such, instead of what they are now doing.

People take a scientific approach to their policy conflicts in so far as they recognize that such conflicts are clashes between the relative merits and demerits of competing values or goals, and not struggles between total good and total evil, such as total freedom vs. serfdom or total free enterprise vs. socialism. To the extent and only to the extent that rivals over what-ought-to-be-the-rules share this sense of doubt concerning the validity of their divergent policy veiws, they bring into their policymaking deliberations a vitual role for the research scientists—people with specialized skills for finding answers to if-then questions.

In this role, the researcher's job is fourfold: (1) To identify past and current conditions which are generating serious conflicts among people over what rules all should be obliged to follow on specific issues; (2) to help in constructing alternative actions for consideration; (3) to quantify the measurable outcomes of each alternative; and (4) to call attention to hitherto unnoticed measurables as well as unquantifiable variables that deserve consideration. Thus, the *research process lies inside the large policymaking process.* The latter is the ethical job of people in their capacities as citizens, representatives, and administrators of finding workable answers to what rules rivals should be obliged to follow on specific issues.

Another component of the researcher's role is sometimes said to be the construction of policy alternatives for consideration. Researchers can be quite useful in this phase of policy formation. For they sometimes understand the relationships among the yardsticks better than nonresearchers, owing to their intensive training and experience in dealing with these yardsticks. However, this construction of alternatives is a distinct job for which both technicians and nontechnicians may be qualified participants; hence it should not be confused with the third of the above components of the researcher's role—the job which he alone has the specialized compentence to perform.

But it is important to recognize that both conceptually and factually the researcher's job is not to provide *solutions* to policy questions. He couldn't, even if he were omniscient. For more is required in resolving conflicts over what rules should and must be observed than can ever be reached by even a completely predictive science on what outcomes may be expected *if* such and such alternatives are chosen. For decisions on what rules are most equitable (or feasible) turn on (1) the relative weights (degrees of desirability or importance) people give to the predicted outcomes of various alternatives, and (2) the fact that each individual is his own unique weighing mechanism. Like Justices of the Supreme Court, the rest of us often reach opposite policy conclusions from exactly the same evidence.

In the face of this fact, we should take note of the hankering after such instruments as psychic microscopes by means of which the scientist could prowl around inside people's skulls, nat onto the relative weights which individuals eventually attach to the outcomes of various action alternatives; stick numerical values of these weights into our general utility equations; then shovel the whole wad into a computer; press the button; and then read off the tape scientifically determined answers to policy problems—universally valid answers to what rules *rational* men should be obliged to observe in any controversial situation.

In this way, imaginary gadgets like psychic microscopes continually feed and keep alive the image of a completely deterministic universe wherein scientific imagination reduces all ought-questions to if-then questions. But the reduction, even in concept, is a chimera. Here is why.

In any actual perplexity over what the rules ought to be, say about daughter's questionable boy friend, the very essence of the perplexity is a sense of conflicting desires which empty the individual of any settled notion of which alternative he most wants. Thus the very nature of ought-perplexities is one in which the individual (or group) doesn't know what he wants; he is baffled, confused, with no clear idea of what his responsibility is or ought to be, because for the time being he is without any relative weights to assign to competing alternatives. Therefore, the scientist would not find the relative weights he is looking for, even if he had the psychic microscope that enabled him to probe inside people's skulls in their hour of policy doubts.

As an aid to helping themselves reach their own individualistic decisions on policy questions, people prize the researcher for his specialized capacities to provide them with information on the kinds and quantities of outcomes which each wants to take account of before deciding among competing alternatives. But, as previously explained, each person is his own weighting mechanism. Giving different weights to the same evidence, people reach different conclusions concerning what rules all should be obliged to observe. Therefore in policy conflicts, even the most perfectly predictive science conceivable can never do more than (1) point out the conditions that are now throwing into conflict hitherto harmonious rules of life and work; (2) suggest alternatives to present rules; and (3) forecast their outcomes. In short, solutions to scientific inquiries—answers to if-then questions—are never more than mere data which people want to take account of in their larger inquiries concerning what rules all should be obliged to observe.

Note three important implications. First, with respect to his response to any ought (policy) question, each person possesses a freedom—a self-directing capacity—to assign different weights to the same evidence. No amount of scientific answers to if-then questions can ever invade this freedom. Were this not the case, there would be no conceptual reason why the computer could not grind out the *right* answers to any policy problem such as the civil rights issue, the farm surplus problem, and so on.

Second, solutions to research (if-then) questions and policy (ought) questions are as different as night and day. Conflicting views over the speed of light, for example, are never resolved by a power struggle over which view shall prevail. The reverse is true of policy sentiments and views. Decisions on what should be done with respect to such matters as Medicare, for example, must be made. Yet, seldom if ever can unanimous agreement be reached on what the rules should be—not even if the outcomes of all alternatives could be perfectly predicted. For as we have seen, people give different weights to the same foreseen outcomes. This means that no "solution" to any policy problem is ever possible in the scientific sense of the word.

Third, in a democratic society, solutions to policy problems are simply some sort of majority consensus concerning what alternatives on specific issues are most desirable and workable. But no one in his right mind ever assumes that a majority consensus is ever a universally valid answer as to what rules will actually give each his due, and therefore all should be obliged to observe. Short of Divinity itself no such validity is possible. From the standpoint of any truly unbiased observer, the minority consensus, even of one, may be right and the majority wrong. There simply is no scientific way of determining which is what.

Acceptability of majority consensus rests on no scientific grounds whatsoever. It rests on two nonscientific grounds. First, in the absence of all collective restraints on the freedom of each to do as he sees fit, men turn on each other like wolves. Such behavior is generally felt to be the worst of all evils, including a Hitler tyranny. The second ground is the widespread belief that rule by some sort of majority consensus involves a lesser degree of a coercive power than rule by minority consensus.

As scientists, men are unfettered by any need for specifying norms, as reflected in such statements as: "If the norms of society are the norms of this model, namely; profit maximization, then society can achieve the indicated improvements." In such statements the scientist is burdening himself with unnecessary psychological lumber. This lumber is the feeling that *as* technician he is obliged to select research criteria that are morally acceptable to society. If the reader rejects the premise that profit maximization is the norm, the only desired end, then he tends to reject the results of the research. However, the researcher can choose his words in such a way as to avoid this "surreptitious morality." He can say, for instance: "The tendency of entrepreneurs to maximize profits is a force which is, if not counteracted by other forces, will bring about the following conditions." Such a statement is devoid of normative judgments, and it keeps the researcher's eye on the ball, which is answering *if-then* questions. In this way, his whole energies are unblocked and unfettered by concerns with *ought* questions.

In their responsibility as deciders of what ought to be done, people in the absence of research findings have little to guide them except the fervor of up-in-the-air doctrines that are full of heat but no light. Conversely, fruitful selection of research problems is exceedingly dependent on the researcher's sensitivity and knowledgeability of rival views over what rules all should be expected to observe. For, unless guided by this sensitivity and knowledgeability of specific issues, questions selected for research tend to be a "sterile" type whose solutions shed little light on what outcomes people can expect *if* they do such and such. In this way, the research process fails to do as much as it might in meeting the need of people in their policymaking capacity for achieving an increasingly predictable and manageable world.

Farm Policy Issues Continually on Our Doorstep

In keeping with this fact, the following groups of farm policy problems are listed for discussion purposes. The list is not exhaustive. But it does include a sampling of issues which are likely to be with us for considerable time to come.

Some do not call for interregional research types of studies, but many do. In these remarks, main emphasis will be on those that do. But these are put into context with other policy issues so as to help keep interregional research needs in perspective with other research needs.

Need for Projecting Changes in Agriculture: In virtually all questions over what rules should be followed, people in their policymaking capacity are continually calling for information on how the numbers, sizes, and other characteristics of farms are changing over time - how will they look in a year, or in several years. For the Nation as a whole, by region, and by type and size of farm, how do present numbers compare with numbers which may be expected under proposed policy alternatives, including *laissez faire?*

There is thus a research need for projecting these changes in such a way as to provide wanted information on the future of the "family farm" by types of farm and by region.

How to Administer Present Programs: A second area of policy concerns centers around how best to administer present programs. For example, what should the location price differentials be for supported commodities? Transportation models have been developed and are being used for this type of analysis. Weaknesses in this model, including assumptions of fixed supply and demand quantities, have led to the use of more general spatial equilibrium analysis.

Again, how should the benefits of price support and export subsidy be allocated among producing regions? (This question is implicit in the immediately preceding one.) Spatial equilibrium analysis is necessary here to provide the effects of any system of supply control, price support, and subsidy rules on benefits accuring to producers in specific regions.

Again, what are the projected effects of present and proposed price support (and other) programs on interregional production patterns? Starting with analysis of the *laissez faire* situation (above), additional constraints can be built into the model so as to reflect alternative controls and subsidies. Solutions obtained give insights into probable effects of these proposed alternatives on equilibrium conditions of agriculture.

Again, what should the level of the price supports be, at present and over time? And how long should they be continued? Still, again, what should be regulated (e.g., futures trading, etc.)? How?

Finally, administrators and others are commonly called on for recommendations on institutional constraints placed on agriculture from the outside, such as ICC freight rates. Agricultural scientists are continually asked what changes, if any, are feasible. Interregional competition studies could be an important aid to this area of policy concern.

New or Revised Controls or Subsidies to Improve the Level of Income or Reduce Income Variability: In this sphere of policy concerns, decisionmakers are continually confronted with questions of what controls and/or subsidies are desirable, by commodity and region, and over time. Again, at least at the national level, policymakers are continually confronted with questions concerning what programs, if any, are needed to protect the family farm. Does it need protection, and if so, should it be? Should "larger corporation" farming and vertical integration be regulated?

Rural Development: In recent years, much policy concern gathers round what is called Rural Area Development. But there is considerable bafflement as to what workable economic meaning can be attached to rural economic areas in today's fast changing social structures. Professor Fox has made a distinct contribution to needed conceptualization of "functional economic areas." But researchers have hardly scratched the surface in developing quantitative delineation and analysis of such areas. This very much needs to be done as means of providing guidelines for rural areas development policies and programs.

Foreign Agriculture: Finally, a growing and vital area of farm policy concern centers in questions pertaining to foreign agriculture. For example, what advice should be given to underdeveloped economies in terms of land and credit reform, as well as aid to backward agricultural societies? Again, what are the market potentials abroad at present and in terms of projected levels of economic growth? And what is our competitive position in world trade?

Evaluation of Interregional Competition Models As Aids to Resolving Policy Issues[2]

The point is that increasing knowledgeability and sensitivity of researchers to such areas of agricultural policy concerns as these are indispensable to formulating increasingly fruitful and predictive types of research problems and projects.

The Need for Predictive Research Has Always Been With Us: Questions have always come up requiring predictive answers. Even during World War I, we had to make estimates. Computers weren't available then. They wouldn't have done us any good anyhow: Models had not been developed; even the theories were inadequate, and few or no data were available.

During and After World War II, We Had Some Improvements in the Predictive Arts: Theories and analytic models were improved (transportation model and linear programming came in during the 40's). Computer science developed and machines became available. In the early 50's linear programming (L.P.) was applied to agriculture. This work was pioneered by Danzig, Waugh, Heady, and others. Skilled economists began developing area models as additional uses were recognized and as the theories were expanded. Transportation models were developed and applied early to certain problems for which they were relevant.

Use of L.P. Models to Predict or Project Structural Economic Changes in Agriculture as Part of an Adjustment Toward General Equilibrium: Heady and Egbert made early applications to the grain-producing industry. This work was severly limited in its usefulness as an aid to policy formation. This weakness was recognized by the authors. Lack of data and computing facilities dictated their approach. The study *did* qualify, however, as good pure research, in that it was a vanguard for further developments in models of this kind.

Subsequent models have been more refined. These improvements were possible through (a) improvements in data availability, (b) computer capacity, and (c) advances in theory and methodology of interregional competition analysis.

At present, our biggest constraint is lack of data. Very large, fast computers are now available, though at very high costs. Computer capacity is much less an effective constraint now than previously. Lack of computing funds is often a more relevant criterion for limiting the scope of analytic models. Lack of data further limits the refinement of our models. This is why: Currently, lack of data and high computer costs force us to aggregate, lumping together nonidentical firms, production processes, resource supplies, and demand units.

But even with these weaknesses, results have begun to reach the "applied" stage. They can be of some practical use in answering policy questions. And they do make possible improved qualitative judgments on what could and should not be done.

217

Some Suggestions As To The Direction of Future Development In Our Models

Improving the predictive power of our analytic models is a much needed aid to policy evaluation. Achieving this improvement involves providing answers to two broad kinds of questions: What will be the *end result* of the adjustments toward equilibrium, and what will be the nature of the *adjustment process?*

More fully stated the first question is, what would be the essential nature of our agriculture in the future, after complete adjustment to equilibrium under each alternative policy proposal? The question of "what point in the future" is especially important here. The point must not be too *far* in the future. For too many things are unpredictable in the very long run, such as technology, resource base, demand, and the like. Therefore, "long-run" solutions to "long-run" questions have very limited usefulness. On the other hand, the planning horizon must not be too *short*. For too many things are fixed in the very short run. By the time results are available, they are outdated.

We need to shoot for an infermediate time period, say 5 to 10 years hence. Within such an intermediate period, we need studies that consider (a) all currently recognized concrete proposals as well as (b) those presently in effect, and (c) additional proposals developed by researchers and others. And the studies need to be carried on to a point where predictive judgments could be made on how agriculture would look than at the end of this intermediate period, under each policy alternative in terms of (a) regional patterns of production of various crops and classes of livestock, and (b) distribution of sizes and types of farms in each region and nationally.

Second, to be useful for policymaking needs, the studies should be designed to illuminate the nature of the process of adjustment toward equilibrium under the proposed and existing policy alternatives. How long it will take to reach equilibrium? Which segments will "arrive" first? Which segments will offer the most resistance? What will be the nature and extent of the growing pains accompanying the adjustment under each alternative? What may be done to ease these growing pains? What are the means of prolonging the adjustment period, and what are the accompanying costs and benefits? Finally, what are the means of speeding up and making less painful the adjustments, and what are the accompanying costs and benefits?

Concluding Remarks

For reasons stated previously, my feeling is that our profession has every reason for just pride in the progress that has been made in our science. Starting from scratch at the close of World War I, it has moved far down the road in the development of increasingly accurate lines of predictive research.

In view of this past achievement, I am confident that within the next decade, our predictive research will fully arrive. Then, when asked the question, "If acreage allotments on cotton are changed by so much, what will be the consequences over the next 3 to 5 years?" We will be able to give answers, and they will be a whale of a lot better than horseback estimates.

CHAPTER 10. PHILOSOPHY: PRINCIPLES OF REASONING ESPECIALLY APPLICABLE TO SCIENCE

The branch of philosophy that deals with rules of valid reasoning is called logic. There are two divisions of logic: deductive and inductive. While I cannot go deeply into the details of either, I can indicate the essential nature of each and how they both fit into the research activity. I hope to do this in a way that shows how the usual account of the nature of deductive and inductive reasoning falls far short of the actual research process. That is, I hope to show that no adequate formal account of problem-solving behavior is possible. The "scientific method" involves a great deal of "art," "genious," "sense," which cannot be caught up in any logical formula of inquiry. At every step, the *results* of inquiry must fall into rigorous logical form. But the *process* of discovery includes a great deal of doing for which there is no logical formula.

A few observations on the nature of science provide a useful point of departure in developing our theme. The endeavor we call scientific is the striving to explain occurrences as instances of uniform rules, called generalizations or concepts. Thus Newton sought to explain the orbits of the planets and heavenly bodies as instances of gravitational attraction of mass particles. Since Pasteur, we have sought to explain communicable diseases as instances of micro-organisms preying on a host. Malthus sought to explain the many defects of man's striving to escape poverty as instances of the tendency of population to increase geometrically and the food supply to increase arithmetically. Adam Smith sought to explain expansions of national wealth as instances of competitive rivalry forcing self-seeking individuals to run their businesses in ways that will yield them the greatest profit. Keynes sought to explain levels of national employment as instances of the way in which national income is divided into expenditures for capital goods (investment) and for consumption goods.

Static and Dynamic Views of the Nature of Science

In the static view of science, research is equated with striving to find out the structure of the universe—how it works—what reality really is. The terminal goal of science is thus the achievement of a set of interconnected principles, laws, and theories that fully explain the universe of particular happenings—a system of generalizations so complete that no exceptions to them will ever occur. Were this ideal ever reached, the laboratories could then be closed and mankind could take up other tasks. Men would then have liberated themselves from the laborious search for new generalizations. They would be as the Divinity, experiencing the pure joy of beholding all truth in a single conspectus of thought. This is the *vis vita*—the life of contemplation (as opposed to the life

---

Developed from an outline used in discussions in September 1964 with Dr. Harry C. Trelogan's seminar in the U.S. Department of Agriculture Graduate School, entitled "Research Methods in the Social Sciences."

of work or action) which the ancient Greeks held to be the highest of all goods, and whose achievement is the chief end of man.

This static view of the research quest for explanatory generalizations is an expression of common sense attitudes toward employments. According to these attitudes, men share an aversion to processes that have no terminal goal, feeling they involve a futility and waste of life. We want to get the bridge built, the mine dug, the book finished, the crop gathered into barns. If the job were envisioned as endless we would, according to this theory, feel defeated before we started, and never begin. So likewise, in scientific employment, common sense seeks the optimistic feeling that at some point in all the generations to come, we can get the job done—find a system of interconnected generalizations which once and for all explains the universe of individual happenings as instances of invariant rules.

But research findings in physics in recent years tend to upset the static view of research employments. For example, since the days of Decartes and Newton, there have been two rival theories concerning the nature of light—the wave theory and the corpuscular theory. Forty years ago, no one assumed that light could be both corpuscular and undulatory; that would be absurd. And physicists were sure that one day an experiment would be devised that would prove which of the rival theories is correct. But this view is now down the drain. As the distinguished chemist James B. Conant observes:

> The conceptual scheme which accommodates all the known optical phe-
> nomena satisfactorily (and has done so for several decades) is one in which a
> corpuscular picture fits one set of experiments, a wave theory certain others;
> *no experiment can be envisioned that will answer a question which was once
> thought of prime significance*, namely, *is light really corpuscular or undulatory
> in nature?*[1]

In line with such findings, Conant rejects the common sense—static—view of scientific employment. He offers a dynamic view, which he defines thus:

> Science is an interconnected series of concepts and conceptual schemes that
> have developed as a result of experimentation and observation and are fruitful
> of further experimentation and observations.[2]

In this dynamic view, research employments have no terminal goal. For all eternity, the job of finding explanatory rules is never done—the bridge never finished. The possibility of *vis vita*—the contemplative life—is a chimera. For the validity of new generalizations and the significance of every new empirical finding is measured by it as a guide to further generalizations and experiments. From the standpoint of the common sense, this dynamic view equates research activity with:

> ...a form of madness...[a] frantic chase of concepts and conceptual
> schemes where validity depends only on their breeding new experiments which
> in turn generate new ideas and so on, *ad infinitum*.[3]

Despite their radical difference, the static and dynamic concepts of the research process have a common factor. Both are a quest for cumulative knowledge, and in this quest, any specific inquiry is provoked (begins) by observations that are exceptions to prevailing generalizations. Ideally, the research process terminates in more inclusive generalizations that explain all the happenings accounted for by previously accepted laws and theories, plus an indefinitely wider range of happenings that were exceptions to the prior set of generalizations.

A simple example is the older "contact" theory of communicable diseases versus the modern "germ" theory. The exceptional observation was that of patients who, without previous contact with other patients, had the same disease symptoms. Medical scientists searched for a new and more inclusive generalization that would explain the exception. The same principle applies to all other instances of research science, such as the geocentric versus the heliocentric theory of the solar system, or the mercentilist versus Adam Smith's explanations of economic growth.

The cumulative nature of scientific activity sharply differentiates it from noncumulative areas of inquiry.[4] To illustrate, men of letters commonly make propositions concerning right and wrong actions, the beautiful and ugly. They seek wisdom—valid generalizations—no less than the natural or social scientist. But the search for truth in these areas seemingly is not cumulative. Thus, if Archimedes visited a high school physics class today, he would feel terribly behind the times. But if Socrates attended an ethics seminar of Walter Lippman's, Bertrand Russell's, and John Dewey's, he would feel depressed over the fact that after 2,400 years of human progress, the wisest heads could tell no more about the nature of justice than he already knew, which he said was little or nothing. He could show that justice was not what other people said it was, but could make little headway in demonstrating what it really was.

Unlike areas of cumulative knowledge, the quest for valid generalizations in noncumulative knowledge deals with propositions which are not falsifiable. For example, there is no way that a devoted aristocrat like Calhoun or Aristotle could disprove to a devoted democrat like Jefferson or Lincoln the premises of the democratic creed—that men are of equal dignity and worth; that none, however wise or good is good or wise enough to be invested with arbitrary power over any other; that therefore each is entitled to be a participant in deciding on the rules which all should observe. Research science is thus restricted to a narrow band of life in which falsifiable generalizations are possible.

Saying that scientific activity generates cumulative knowledge does not mean it is more important than or superior to noncumulative areas of inquiry. Indeed, in some cases, it might be less important. This possibility led Conant to say:

> A dictator wishing to mold the thoughts and actions of a literate people might be able . . . to leave the scientists . . . alone, but he must win over to his side or destroy the philosophers, the writers, and the artists.[5]

There is a widespread belief that scientific disciplines are superior to nonscientific ones as incubators of a spirit of impartial and accurate analysis of facts. This is questionable. Conant voices the doubt in these words:

> To claim that the study of science is the best education for young men who aspire to become impartial analysts of human affairs is to put forward a very dubious educational hypothesis at best. Indeed, those who contend that the habits of thought and point of view of the scientist as scientist can be transferred with advantage to other human activities have hard work documenting their proposition.[6]

Neither are scientific disciplines more important as vehicles of deductive and inductive modes of reasoning. If one doubts this, he could easily settle it by reading a work such as Plato's *Republic*. No document excels its brilliant grasp of formal reasoning, and appeal to empirical observations, yet the whole book is about the nature of justice.

But our concern is with the role of deductive and inductive reasoning in specific research inquiry—activities that (a) are continually provoked by inadequacies of prevailing generalizations; and (b) terminate in new, more inclusive generalizations that explain the new, but exceptional observations.

Nature of Deductive Reasoning

Deductive reasoning is inferring conclusions from prior propositions called premises. In such reasoning, the only test of valid deductions is the law of contradiction. In other words, the conclusions cannot be denied or affirmed without similarly denying or affirming the premises. For example:

> All A is B.
> All B is C.
> Therefore all A is C.

This is a valid deduction; the conclusion cannot be denied once the premises are granted. To take another example:

> All A is B.
> Some B is C.
> Therefore some A is C.

This deduction is invalid because the minor (second) premise does not provide a necessary connection between the major premise and the conclusion. Again:

> If a conservative party is elected, tariffs will remain high.
> Tariffs remain high.
> Therefore, a conservative party has been elected.

Here once more the deduction is invalid. Election of a conservative party may turn on a condition other than tariffs remaining high. Therefore, the premises are not necessary evidence of the conclusion.

Deductive logic or reasoning is concerned only with *formal truth*—the relationships between propositions which yield necessary conclusions from given premises. But necessary connections between propositions may not yield true statements about empirical happenings in the real world; likewise, empirically false statements used as premises may yield true statements about matters of fact. Consider this example:

> Sparta was a democracy.
> No democracy has any kings.
> Therefore, Sparta had no kings.

Both premises are false; but the conclusion is logically valid just the same.

We must constantly be on our guard to avoid the common error of supposing that in scientific reasoning we proceed only from premises that are true. The scientist is constantly confronted with alternative hypotheses, no more

222

than one of which can be true; he generally throws out as false the ones which imply conclusions contrary to observable facts.

The idea that false premises must imply false conclusions is also a widespread impression, and a serious error. Consider:

All Mexicans are citizens of the United States, and all Virginians are Mexicans. Therefore, all Virginians are citizens of the United States.

The conclusion is true, but the premises are false. Nevertheless, the deduction is logically valid since it is impossible to deny the consequent if the antecedent is affirmed. Empirically, however, it is an unsound argument.

Finally, true premises do not necessarily yield true conclusions. Consider:

Perfect beings can live together without law.

Men are not perfect.

Therefore, men cannot live together without law.

In this case, the premises are not sufficient evidence for the conclusion. The major premise does not predicate ability to live without law to perfect beings only.

Strictly deductive sciences, like formal logic and mathematics, are not concerned with whether or not real happenings conform to their generalizations. For example, whether real space is euclidian or noneuclidian does not affect the method by which either a euclidian or noneuclidian geometry is constructed. Deductive generalizations lay down general conditions to which particulars must conform if there are any instances of the generalizations. But they do not imply or demand the existence of any occurrences conforming to them. Geometry, for instance, does not say there are such things as empirical points or lines, but rather that if there are points, then a straight line is the shortest distance between any two of them, inasmuch as we have stipulated the logical relationship between them. For example, if there are unicorns, then each of them has only one horn.

In contrast to strictly deductive sciences, the natural and social sciences begin and end with the actual world. Thus, natural and deductive sciences demand generalizations which express invariant connections among given kinds of empirical happenings. Consequently, research methods cannot be wholly deductive, though deduction often plays an important role in the discovery of such generalizations. At what point in inquiry does deductive logic enter and what part does it play in furthering inquiry? This question leads into a consideration of deductive logic as an element of research activity.

Deductive Reasoning as an Element of Research Activity

Deductive reasoning comes at a rather late stage in the research process. The starting point in research is an experienced conflict between exceptional observations and accepted generalizations. The ability to perceive that a given experienced happening cannot be explained by prevailing theories is not a common talent among men, including highly trained professional people. Masters of the theory often are unhappy because they can't get their teeth into any vital problem. They are unable to sense happenings that are at variance with received beliefs and, consequently, they cannot raise significant questions. They seek superiors who will give them problems to which they can apply their "skills." Thus the research process includes far more than can be boxed up in any formalized body of rules concerning the nature of the scientific method or the laws of logic. For no amount of knowledge about the rules of valid reasoning can give us any rule enabling one to ask significant questions. The goal of inquiry is a solution of the conflict between exceptional data and prevailing views. The solution is an invariant relationship between specific facts such as the flooding of the Nile and other apparently unrelated facts (such as the rainfall in Central Africa) so that one may be predicted from the other. But how do we go about finding such connections?

A persistent belief is that researchers simply go out "looking" for all the facts. This belief dominates Karl Pearson's famous book, *The Grammar of Science*. The summary of the first chapter reads thus:

> The scientific method is marked by . . . careful and accurate classification of facts and observation of their correlation and sequence . . . . [7]

Concerning this belief, Conant says:

> I dissent entirely . . . . It seems to me, indeed, that one who had little or no direct experience with scientific investigations might be completely misled as to the nature and methods of science by studying this famous book.[8]

Conant is right. A simple search for classifiable facts is futile. One could observe the rise and retreat of the Nile to the end of time without finding the explanation for this phenomenon—an invariant relation between the inundations and the rainfall in Central Africa. The main question is not what are the facts, but what are the relevant facts, and which facts are causally related?

Hypotheses come into inquiry as guides—pointers—to relevant facts. Once an investigator feels he has hold of a real problem, he does not first seek the facts; he seeks suggested explanations or solutions of the difficulty which is generating his inquiry. When formulated in propositions, these suggestions are called hypotheses. They are felt to express "relevant" connections of facts. Whether or not they actually do this depends on subsequent inquiry. Here again is the fact that the scientific method cannot be fully caught up in logical formulae. A hypothesis may be believed to be relevant, and then shown to be a blind alley by later inquiry. Conversely, some facts are often believed irrelevant which subsequent investigations show to be relevant. Thus, no rule can be given for "hitting upon" relevant hypotheses. The English logician De Morgan observed:

> A hypothesis must have been started, not by rule, but by that sagacity of which no description can be given, precisely because the very owners of it do not act under laws perceptible to themselves. The inventor of hypotheses, if pressed to explain his method, must answer as did Zerah Colburn (a Vermont calculating boy of the early nineteen-hundreds) when asked for his mode of instantaneous calculation. When the poor boy had been bothered for some time in this manner, he cried out in a huff, "God put it into my head, and I can't put it into yours."[9]

We can only say that the function of hypotheses is to direct our search for order among facts. But a hypotheses can do this only as its implications are made explicit. This is the role of deductive logic in furthering research inquiry. Insofar as it shows the implications of hypotheses, deductive reasoning leads to the rejection of explanations which imply happenings contrary to known facts; and in this way, it leads to experimental testing of logically satisfactory hypotheses. Two examples will help to make this point clear.

First, let us take a closer look at the phenomenon of the Nile's periodic flooding. In his travels, Herodotus asked the reason for the periodic flooding of the Nile. He was searching for a general rule—an invariant connection between the Nile floods and facts of a different kind. One theory was that the Etesian (northwest) winds blowing from the Mediterranean cause the rise in the river by preventing the Nile water from running off to sea. Herodotus refuted this theory by discovering that it implied consequences contrary to known facts. Here is his reasoning: If the blowing of the Etesian winds produced inundations, other rivers should behave as the Nile does. But other rivers do not overflow the banks when the wind blows in from the sea—the blowing of the Etesian winds is not invariably followed by inundations. In his own words:

> ... if the Etesian winds produce the effect, other rivers which flow in a direction opposite to those winds ought to present the same phenomena as the Nile, and the more so, as they are smaller streams, and have a weaker current. But these rivers, of which there are many both in Syria and Libya, are unlike the Nile in this respect.

Our second example concerns Galileo's account of the velocity of falling objects. Galileo considered two hypotheses: The first hypothesis held that accelerating velocity was a function of distance of fall. Galileo argued that this generalization implied a body travels instantaneously through a certain portion of its path. Believing this was physically impossible, he rejected it on deductive grounds alone. His reasoning ran thus:

> If the velocities are in proportion to the spaces traversed, or to be traversed, then these spaces are traversed in equal intervals of time; if, therefore, the velocity with which the falling body traverses a space of eight feet were double that with which it covered the first four feet (just as the one distance is double the other) then the time-intervals required for these passages would be equal. But for one and the same body to fall eight feet and four feet in the same time is possible only in the case of instantaneous (discontinuous) motion; but observation shows us that the motion of a falling body occupies time, and less of it in covering a distance of four feet than of eight feet; therefore it is not true that its velocity increases in proportion to the space.[10]

Galileo next considered the hypothesis that change in the velocity of any freely falling body during an interval of time is proportional to that interval. Or, $v = at$, where v represents final velocity, a the speed acquired in one second, and t the number of seconds that the body has fallen. In other words, the acceleration is constant. In Galileo's words:

> ... we may picture to our mind a motion as uniformly accelerated when, during any equal intervals of time whatever, equal increments of speed are given to it.[11]

But this definition could not be tested directly. Consequently, he made an experimental assumption that:

> The speeds acquired by one and the same body moving down planes of different inclinations are equal when the heights of the planes are equal.[12]

For example, he says:

> . . . my reason tells me at once that a heavy and perfectly round ball
> descending along lines CA, CD, and CB would reach the terminal points A, D,
> B, with equal speeds . . . provided the planes are hard and smooth, offering no
> resistances.[13]

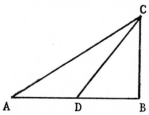

Then, from his acceleration hypothesis Galileo deduced numerous implications which were capable of direct verification. For example, from the hypothesis $v = at$, he derived the proposition that the distance traversed by freely falling bodies are proportional to the square of the time of their fall. Or, $s = \frac{1}{2}at^2$. Then follows an experiment that divides one epoch from another.

> A piece of wooden moulding or scantling, about 12 cubits long, half a
> cubit wide, and three fingerbreadths thick, was taken; on its edge was cut a
> channel a little more than one finger in breadth; having made this groove very
> straight, smooth, and polished, and having lined it with parchment, also as
> smooth and polished as possible, we rolled along it a hard, smooth, and very
> round bronze ball.
>
> Having placed this board in a sloping position, by lifting one end some
> one or two cubits above the other, we rolled the ball, as I was just saying,
> along the channel, noting, in a manner presently to be described, the time
> required to make the descent. We repeated this experiment more than once in
> order to measure the time with an accuracy such that the deviation between
> two observations never exceeded one-tenth of a pulse beat. Having performed
> this operation and having assured ourselves of its reliability, we now rolled the
> ball only one-quarter the length of the channel; and having measured the time
> of its descent, we found it precisely one-half of the former. Next we tried
> other distances, comparing the time for the whole length with that for the
> half, or with that for two-thirds, or three-fourths, or indeed for any fraction;
> in such experiments, repeated a full hundred times, we always found that the
> spaces traversed were to each other as the squares of the times, and this was
> true for all inclinations, of the plane, i.e., of the channel, along which we
> rolled the ball. We also observed that the times of descent, for various
> inclinations of the plane, bore to one another precisely that ratio which, as we
> shall see later, the author had predicted and demonstrated for them.
>
> For the measurement of time, we employed a large vessel of water
> placed in an elevated position; to the bottom of this vessel was soldered a pipe
> of small diameter giving a thin jet of water which we collected in a small glass
> during the time of each descent, whether for the whole length of the channel
> or for a part of its length; the water thus collected was weighed, after each
> descent, on a very accurate balance; the differences and ratios of these weights
> gave us the differences and ratios of the times, and this with such accuracy
> that although the operation was repeated many, many times, there was no
> appreciable discrepancy in the results.[14]

To fulfill its role as a means of reaching new generalizations, any hypothesis needs to have certain formal properties. It must be formulated in such a manner that through deduction, predictions can be made from it; otherwise it fails to make possible reaching a decision on whether or not it may solve the problem under consideration. Two aspects of this requirement deserve mention. Often the most valuable hypothesis cannot be directly verified. For example, Galileo's acceleration hypothesis could not be established by direct observation. Therefore, to be of use it had to be stated so its various implications could be clearly traced, and the directly variable ones subjected to experimental confirmation.

In this connection it should also be noted that the constituent terms of the hypothesis must denote a determinate experimental procedure; otherwise, it will not yield variable generalizations. For example, take the statement, "The universe is shrinking in such a way that all lengths contract in the same ratio." This may be true but no observable happening can be predicted from it. Hence it is unverifiable and unfalsifiable. It is empirically meaningless. Again, many hold the hypothesis that the belief in a Providence is a stronger force working for righteousness than concern for one's fellow man. This proposition has no verifiable consequences unless one can assign an experimental procedure for measuring the relative strength of the forces involved. Still again, for many years, a prevailing opinion of economic theory was the principle of diminishing marginal utility. According to this hypothesis, the want-satisfying power of a dollar varies with the number of dollars one possesses. Thus, a dollar would enable a poor man to achieve a greater quantity of satisfactions than a rich man. Hence, the more nearly a nation divided its total income equally among its members, the greater would be the total quantity of satisfactions from any given national output of goods and services. Then Professor Robins pointed out that there is no conceivable way of determining whether the quantity of satisfactions a rich man gets from a dollar is greater than, equal to, or less than the quantity a poor man gets. There is no unit of satisfaction similar, say, to a unit of length. Thus, he made it clear that the principle of diminishing marginal utility is valid for one person, but does not permit interpersonal comparisons.

A second requirement is that a hypothesis provides a solution to the problem which generated the inquiry. Nonetheless false hypotheses are not always useless. For a false hypothesis may lead attention to unsuspected facts or relations between facts. The Babylonians had many false notions about magical qualities of the number seven. But they were led to look for and find the rarely seen planet Mercury by their belief that the heavenly bodies visible to the naked eye, which move among the fixed stars, had to be seven in number. As De Morgan remarked: "Wrong hypotheses, rightly worked, have produced more useful results than unguided observation."[1][5]

Third, to lead to more inclusive and verifiable generalizations, a hypothesis must be capable of being refuted; that is, a verifiable hypothesis must be falsifiable. Many popular generalizations fail to meet this requirement. The proposition "All men are mortal" cannot be refuted, since no matter how aged a man might be he is still conceivably susceptible to mortality. But restate the hypothesis and say, "All men die before they are 200 years old." In this form, finding a 201-year-old man would refute the statement. Consider the proposition, "Whatever happens is the work of Providence or the unconscious self." This theory does not enable us to state which kind of happening could refute it. Consequently, it is useless as a working hypothesis.

Genesis of Modern Research Science: 17th Century Fusion of Workman's Art of Experimentation with Scholar's Deductive Reasoning from Speculative Ideas

Neither deductive reasoning from given premises nor experimental testing of deductions distinguishes scientific from common sense inquiry. Like the scientist, the ordinary workman throws his problem into an "if-then" form; he draws the implications of his hypothesis; and then tests his deductions by empirical observations of whether his predictions transpire or not. For example, confronted with a stalled car, the mechanic asks, "What's the matter?" He might surmise the cause is dirt in the gasline. He puts his hunch into a hypothesis: "If the line is blown out, the engine will start." Then he checks his reasoning with an experiment—blowing out the line and trying to start the engine.

In many statements about scientific inquiry, deductive reasoning and experimental testing are held to be the only essential attributes of research activity. If this were true, then everyone could say he has been a scientist all his life. What are the differential traits of scientific and common sense inquiry?

Scientific inquiry includes a conceptual (theoretical) component which is absent from common sense inquiry, and the latter includes practical objectives which are often absent from the former. The theoretical component of scientific research is speculative ideas concerning the essence of things as revealed in their definitions and necessary (conceptual) connections. As Aristotle observed, "A definition is a phrase signifying a thing's essence."[16] By essence he meant a set of fundamental attributes without which no concrete thing can be the type of thing it is. Thus the essence of a circle is a plane figure, every point of which is equidistant from a fixed point. This set of attributes tells us what a circle is; all the "peculiarities" of a circle necessarily follow from it.

The definition or essence of a thing is its *genus* plus its *differentia*. *Genus* is the part of the essence or definition that is common to different kinds of things. Thus "plane figure" is not only the *genus* trait of a circle, but also of a triangle, ellipse, hyperbola, and so on. These figures differ in kind, but they all belong to the same *genus*. The *differentia* is that part of the essence (definition) of a thing which distinguishes its species from other species of the same *genus*. Thus the *differentia* of a circle is "having all its points equidistant from a fixed point"; the differentia of a struggle is "being bounded by three straight lines." As Aristotle first made clear: "The basic premises of demonstrations are definitions."[17] And it is with such demonstrations and their empirical verification, that the research investigator is concerned. The purpose of the scientific experimenter is to test a prediction which is made as a deduction from a conceptual scheme. Thus, he tests a theory of the causal relationship between things or happenings. Not only is his purpose to test such deductions, but the deductions themselves are what give rise to his experiment in the first place.

228

The theoretical component of research science is mainly absent from a farmer's deductions, for example. The workman's objective is not the testing of a deduction from a conceptual scheme; instead his aim is to test an idea of how to reach some practical goal such as getting the car started, the radio to work, a mad bull in a pen. The difficulty that generates common sense inquiry is a blockage of effort to reach a practical goal—not exceptional observations to deductions from broad, general ideas concerning the nature of things as revealed in their definitions and logical connections.

Deductive reasoning from conceptual schemes and the art of experimentation both antedate the rise of research (experimental) science. The former was invented and practiced by intellectuals of ancient Greece. The latter was practiced by workmen from time immemorial. But the two arts were long practiced by different classes who paid little attention to each other. Artisans rarely if ever bothered about testing deductions from theories. The logical thought process of drawing deductions from conceptual schemes was the province of intellectual classes who rarely paid attention to empirical findings.

Through trial and error experiments with ways of meeting practical needs, workmen often discovered happenings that were contrary to the scholars' deductions from conceptual schemes. This led to no scientific advance, as the two arts were separated into class employments and hence had no effect on each other. For example, an important conceptual scheme of ancient Greek and Medieval scholars was a "full universe." In this concept, empty space was impossible; hence the expression, "Nature abhors a vacuum." From this concept followed important deductions. To get water to run out of a hole at the bottom of a barrel. A hole must be made at the top so as to let air in from the outside, thus making room for the water to run out at the bottom. Similarly, a suction pump will raise liquids to an indefinite height; otherwise, a vacuum would be created—something that was unthinkable. But from ancient Roman times, miners knew that a suction pump would not lift water over 32 feet. To get water out of deep mines, they built pumps in tandem, each lifting the water about 32 feet. For over 1,000 years, the intellectual classes seemingly knew nothing of this experimental finding. Galileo says his attention was called to it by some artisans.

By the 17th century we find investigators bringing into being modern research science by combining deductive reasoning from general ideas, invented by the Greeks, with experimental testing of practical ideas, first practiced by artisans. In some way, not recorded, Torcelli in 1644 had gotten hold of the general concept of "a sea of air" which exerts pressure on all objects in it, just as the water exerts pressure on all bodies below the surface of the ocean. From this concept, he reasoned that if air pressure sustains a column of water 34 feet high, it will sustain a liquid (mercury) 14 times heavier only 1/14 as high— approximately 30 inches. Then he became an artisan as it were, testing how his ideas worked—seeing if they would lead to new empirical findings. He took a glass tube about a half inch in diameter and 3 feet long, sealed it off at one end, filled it with mercury, placed his forefinger over the open end, inverted tube, submerged the open end in an open vessel, and removed his finger. He found that he had created a vacuum, for the mercury dropped, leaving a really empty space in the upper end of the tube. Thus he had invented the first barometer. Air pressure balanced a 30-inch column of mercury, as he predicted.

In a like manner, Galileo, in reasoning from his concept of uniform acceleration, was behaving like an ancient Greek intellectual. But in rolling balls down inclined planes, as means of testing his deductions, he was behaving like an artisan.

Modern research science was thus born about three centuries ago through the union of age-old empirical procedures of workmen with deductive reasoning from general ideas, first invented by the intellectuals of ancient Greece.

Inductive Reasoning

Having considered deductive reasoning and its role in leading inquiry to new generalizations, we now turn to inductive reasoning. What is it? What sets it apart from deduction? Very different answers have been given to this question, and the dust is not yet settled.

Historically, deductive and inductive reasoning have been viewed as antithetical modes of inference. In this historical view, *deductive logic* is concerned with rules that enable us to infer particular conclusions from universal premises; while *inductive logic* is concerned with rules (conditions) that enable us to infer universal conclusions from particular premises. Otherwise expressed, the real nature of induction is the process of reasoning from some observed cases to a universal conclusion regarding all similar cases, some of which are unobserved. The problem is to find logical justification for the inference from some to all, rather than from all to some.

The first part of this historical view defining deduction is clearly false. No conclusion of a deductive inference can be a particular, unless at least one of the premises is particular.

But is there a unique type of inference which proceeds from particular premises to universal propositions? In their book, *Logic and the Scientific Method,* Cohen and Nagel said, "No." From Aristotle on, the test case has been called an *intuitive* induction. Intuitive induction consists of examining several cases of qualitative wholes and perceiving a general rule in them. To take an example, imagine Boyle studying behavior of a gas at a constant temperature. He may have written numerical measures of its volume at different temperatures in parallel columns, as follows:

Pressure	Volume	PV=C
1	12	12
2	6	12
3	4	12
4	3	12

Examining these particular observations may have enabled him to "see" in them an instance of a universal law—*viz,* that the product of pressure and volume is constant if temperature is constant. Such perceptions or intuitions of common patterns in particular cases represent a state in getting our knowledge. As Eaton has observed:

> This actual world consists of a multitude of particulars continually passing into one another in the process of becoming. These particulars exhibit conjunctions of characters and relations, which present themselves again and again. The seasons return; the offspring reproduces the form of the parent; the moon alters its phases and the tide rises and retreats along the shore. Everywhere the particulars of the actual world suggest generalizations and these generalizations are subsequent to, and dependent on, the particulars.[18]

But is *perception* of formal patterns in particular instances a unique type of inference? Cohen and Nagel say, "No." They base their denial on these grounds: An actual logical inference is analyzable into a premise and a conclusion. But "seeing" a universal in particular cases is not analyzable into premises and conclusions. Therefore:

> ... intuitive induction ... cannot be called an *inference* by any stretch of the term. It is not a type of argument analyzable into a premise and a conclusion. It is a perception of relations and not subject to any rules of validity, and represents the gropings and tentative guessings of a mind aiming at knowledge. Intuitive induction is therefore not antithetical to deduction, because it is not a type of inference at all .... *There can be no logic or method of intuitive induction.*[19]

What then is the difference between deduction and induction? The Cohen and Nagel answer turns on kinds of evidence involved in establishing inferred generalizations. *Deduction,* they say, is not concerned with the empirical truth or falsity of its premises, but only with formal conditions under which conclusions necessarily follow from premises. *Induction* is concerned with the method by which the empirical truth of the premises is established. Cohen and Nagel put it thus:

> The proper contrast is not between deductive and inductive inference, but between inferences that are necessary and inferences that are probable. For the evidence for universal propositions which deal with matters of fact can never be more than probable.[20]

In their view, inductive logic is thus another name for probability and statistical procedures.

Deductive and Inductive Reasoning as an Inadequate
Account of the Scientific Method

Now we will sum up, and see what's wrong with this as an account of the scientific method. The heart of research inquiry, as we have said, arises from a conflict between exceptional observations and prevailing generalizations, and terminates with new generalizations that explain the exceptional experiences as instances of a rule, which in turn can explain all the observations accounted for by older theories. In this process deduction is the process of deriving necessary conclusions from given premises; and induction is another name for probability, statistical, and experimental procedures used in establishing the probability that new generalizations which are observed to be true in some cases, will be true for all possible cases.

Thus conceived, both types of reasoning come into the search for new generalizations at a very late stage—almost the tail end. According to Cohen and Nagel's account, deductive logic does not enter this search until *after* hypotheses emerge. For its role is that of developing the necessary implications of given hypothetical solutions to a felt problem. Then the job of these implications is to guide the search for relevant facts. Thus, deductive logic is an indispensable element of research behavior; without it, the quest for new generalizations gets nowhere. Researchers should not go out, as Francis Bacon and Pearson advised, just looking for (classifying) all the facts as means of finding new truth (generalization). For if we do, we get nothing but "descriptions" that mean little or nothing.

But hypotheses come into any specific research activity at a relatively late stage. The hard thinking is over with by the time we get a sensible hypothesis, and what is left is the fun of seeing how it pans out. We do not, however, experience a conflict between exceptional observations and prevailing generalization and then suddenly jump to new generalizations that may resolve the conflict. Between these stages of inquiry there is a wide gap, a gap filled with much mental and emotional struggle, a gap which the individual may never succeed in closing. When equated with procedures for testing the probability of generalizations, inductive logic comes into the research process at an even later stage than deductive reasoning.

Thus the modern account of deductive and inductive inference fails to give any inkling of the most important and difficult phase of scientific inquiry. This is the initial stage. What do we do—what mental and overt operations must we execute—to transform a puzzling, confused situation into knowns and those that are unknown but which we want to find out? Until this is done, we have no researchable questions, and until we have such questions we have no problem. When we get the knowns identified and the unknowns isolated, they evoke hypotheses and guide the search for relevant facts. An enormous amount of analysis is required to "find" a problem and get it into a form that will induce a hypothesis. Northrop used Galileo's study of projectiles as an example for developing this point.[21] For illustrative materials, Dewey used the formation of the dew and the identification of malaria as a kind of parasitic disease.[22]

I would like to use my own experience with the problem of the impact of technological advance on premachine economy of family businesses in industry and agriculture. The problem stemmed from a growing skepticism concerning a widely held generalization on this matter. The generalization was this:

> Mechanization in industry quickly wipes out older systems of family production units, replacing them with factory units.
> Family production units remain the dominant type of farm business.
> Therefore, the continued existence of family business in farming proves the technological backwardness of agriculture.

My background experience led to felt exceptions to this statement. For instance, during the past 100 years the mechanical aids to farming have multiplied beyond belief, and during this same period the increase in America's agricultural output has made our country's farming system one of the wonders of the modern world. Neither of these facts indicates technological backwardness. Nevertheless, prevailing theories—about farming or anything else—are not overthrown by exceptional observations, but only by better theories, the heart of which run to fundamental definitions.

Several definitional problems were present in my research on the factory process in agriculture and industry. What is the essence of a factory? What is a family business, either in industry or agriculture? Once these questions were answered, research could proceed.

The popular impression is that rapid rates of farm technological advance are inconsistent with an agriculture made up predominantly of family farms. This is a hypothesis that can be tested with the help of inductive logic, since certain predictions follow from it. If it is true, one would expect the proportion of larger-than-family farms to be on the increase. One would expect that the proportion of hired labor is increasing while that of family labor is decreasing. One would expect to find that in the upper size groups the proportion of larger-than-family farms is increasing faster than family farms. And one would also expect to find that the farm marketings accounted for by the larger-than-family farms are on the increase.

Define the family farm any way you like, but you will find that the predictions of the popular hypothesis are false.

My problem was to find a new theory that would explain the compatibility of technological progress and family-size units of farm production. I would call the operation I used in doing this inductive logic. I grew up with medieval farming techniques; later I had experience with machines, and I farmed with both. I found the same techniques on family farms and on larger-than-family farms. I have also worked in factories and in industry where family units of production are unthinkable. What is it about machine production that makes it compatible with family units in farming but incompatible in industry?

In farming, nature separates operations with very wide time intervals, so that the number of operations that can be done at the same time is as close to the number of persons in a family after mechanization as before. When you substitute the machine for the horse, or the cornpicker for the husking peg, you do not change one iota the time intervals that separate operations on a farm. You plant corn in the spring. In the fall you harvest it.

The converse is true in industry. For example, to substitute machines for making a shirt or a pair of shoes is to transform a sequential pattern of operations into a simultaneous one. Doing everything at once quickly multiplies the number of workers needed far beyond the number of workers in an ordinary family.

In looking at individual cases, I simply "saw" in them what appeared to be a general rule. This perception is induction, as Aristotle defined it, and I agree with Aristotle. I looked at specific cases before my very eyes and they induced in my mind that concept of a new relationship that seemed to explain my observations as instances of a general rule.

As a last step, this hypothesis, like the popular theory I hoped to replace, had to be tested. Its implications had to be deductively developed and verified. It had to meet the crucial test of explaining not only the specific problems with which I was concerned, but all the occurrences accounted for by older theories as well.

Conclusions

In the Cohen and Nagel view of deductive and inductive logic, the early and most difficult stages of the research quest for new generalizations fall between the slats, meaning they are devoid of deductive and inductive inferences alike. I think this is a mistake. The hard part of research is the initial phase—(a) discovering a conflict between prevailing theory and exceptional experiences and (b) getting ideas of suggested solutions. Deductive development of well stated hypotheses and testing their probable truth comes in very late stages of our search. What goes on in the earlier stages? Is it not characterized by making and checking inferences from some to all cases, and then deducing implications of general concepts? It seems absurd to say no. Yet this is what we are forced to say if we equate induction with probability and statistical procedures. If this is all that induction means, why not drop the term? It adds nothing to the meaning of probability and statistical procedures. Besides, these statistical procedures are as deductive in nature as geometry or calculus.

Cohen and Nagel's whole case rests on the idea that inductions like "seeing" general relationships in particular cases is not an inference at all. All inferences, they hold, are analyzable into two components—premises and conclusions. But "seeing" Boyle's law, or the nature of a factory, in a few cases cannot be broken down into such components.

The Cohen and Nagel argument rests on an arbitrary assertion that all reasoning must have the properties of deductive inferences—passage of mind from premises to conclusions. Thus, by definition, "seeing" or "inducing" a general rule in a few cases is not a type of reasoning at all. I find no grounds for arbitrarily equating all inferences with deductive inference, and then equating the word "induction" with probability and statistical procedures. The hard fact is that we do get premises on which we perform deductive operations, and we get them through seeing formal patterns in particular cases. Why not call this inductive inference? In this view, every step of problem-solving activity includes (1) making deductions from given premises that (2) lead to new observations, which in turn (3) induce "seeing" new premises, and so on until the problem is resolved or we realize we can't solve it.

Yet, even if this view be correct, there is much in the research quest for new generalization that cannot be reduced to systematic rules of right reasoning. No rule can be given that will lead one to perceive conflicts between prevailing generalizations and exceptional observations. But without such perceptions, there can be no scientific problems, as I understand the term. Again, no rule can be given that will lead one to induce from or "see" in his experiences new hypotheses that may lead to the resolution of his problems. In this important sense, research includes far more than mere logic, whether deductive or inductive. It includes insight, genius, groping, pondering—"sense" which can't be boxed up in any formalized procedures. The logic we can teach; the art we cannot. The results of what we have done at any stage must fall into logical form. But the full process of discovery—creativity—is not equivalent to the logical structures that are discovered.

Part IV

Economic Development
and Cultural Change

Many economists have attempted to discover the essential nature of the economic growth process. But usually they have limited their analysis to such economic variables as investment, consumption, income, and the marginal propensity to save, with emphasis on the probable effects of new production and marketing technologies.

Brewster's broad training in philosophy, sociology, and history enabled him to bring a fresh perspective to the study of economic development. He recognized three interlocking components of economic development. The first is *technological*—the creation and putting to widespread use of increasingly productive hardware, along with the knowledge and related skills necessary for carrying on an increasingly successful conquest of nature. His second component of development is *structural* or *organizational*—the regrouping of people under new institutional and organizational rules that enable them to generate and put to widespread use increasingly productive technologies. The third component is *cultural*, involving an important part of society's heritage of convictions. Brewster believed a clear understanding of the organizational and cultural aspects of a country is essential as a starting point for international policy formation when we attempt to transplant our technologies into their society.

Always a student of the American culture, Brewster sought a clearer understanding of the social problems accompanying economic development and urbanization. Now that a decreasing number of American farmers are serving an increasing number of nonfarmers, the thinning out of farmers is generating some serious social and economic problems in rural areas. In Chapter 10, "What Kind of Social and Economic Order Do We Want in the Plains?" Brewster discusses the underlying causes and the inevitable effects of change; and he suggests some possible solutions to the problems created by change. He shows that the public and private service institutions in the Plains would become more effective and efficient if they were restructured to conform with functional economic areas. He points out, however, the value conflict involved in the painful choice between historic forms of rural organizational and proficiency concepts of persons and society.

Brewster developed his last and most complete discussion of the structural or organizational components of economic development in "Traditional Social Structures as Barriers to Change," presented here as Chapter 11. In developing this chapter, Brewster was strongly influenced by a manuscript by Marion J. Levy, later published as the book: *Modernization and the Structure of Societies: A Setting for International Affairs* (2 vol., Princeton: Princeton

University Press, 1966). In this paper, Brewster focuses on the question, "Why are people in economically backward societies so reluctant to concert their individual behaviors into increasingly broader network of large-scale specialized units of collective action which are necessary for the development and widespread use of modernizing technologies?"

In developing an answer to this question, he provides valuable new insight into the process of economic and cultural growth.

CHAPTER 11. WHAT KIND OF SOCIAL AND ECONOMIC ORDER DO WE WANT IN THE PLAINS?

In reviewing the literature on the Great Plains, one is struck by an anxiety concerning the future. This same anxiety has increasingly pervaded virtually all rural America since World War II. It is the fear that rapid rates of technical advance have generated an irreconcilable conflict between two intensely valued objects in American life. One is proficiency concepts of personality and society which American people have long used as guides to increasingly satisfactory life. The other valued object is a historic image of rural America. This image includes two major components—a farm component and a community component. The farm component is a predominant system of family farms; the community component is a system of small towns and related institutions such as the district school, the village church, and local governments. Devotion to this historic system of rural organizations has often been called "rural fundamentalism."

Incidently, I find no substantive difference between rural and urban America, except density of population per square mile. But this is enough . . . . Relative to other occupations, farming requires an enormous amount of space per job. For example, my present job requires about 100 square feet. But when I was on a farm in Colorado with my father, my job required 640 acres—nearly 28 million square feet.

In dollar and cent terms, the conflict in the Plains between the proficiency drives for organizational change and the urge to hold onto historic patterns of rural organizations, runs like this: (1) Devotion to proficiency concepts leads to laborsaving technologies which continually increase job space per worker. But total work space is virtually constant; therefore, (2) by increasing job space per worker, the proficiency drives lead to fewer and fewer people per square mile in the Plains where population has always been sparse because of semi-aridity. (3) This in turn leads to increasing per capita cost of public and social services, provided the carryover of 19th century systems of rural organizations like schools, churches, and local governments, are not restructured into fewer but more proficient units.[1]

This restructuring is manifesting itself as a movement of people from farms and small towns to larger population centers. Can it be headed off short of three things: (1) The continuing shift of people from small towns into larger population centers; (2) the reorganization of social and public service institutions into fewer but more proficient size units; (3) and very substantial shifting of farm residences to towns or along strategic highways from whence farmers and ranchers commute to work after the fashion of people in suburbia? Certainly such a broad-gauge restructuring of 19th century rural organizations is a promising way of offsetting the mounting social and public service costs per capita now resulting from the population thin-out in much of the Plains under the impact of technological advance.

Reprinted by permission of the Great Plains Agricultural Council. Paper presented to the Council, Santa Fe, N.M., June 1964.

But is this solution worth the sacrifice? No, if a higher premium is placed on historic forms of rural organization than on proficiency concepts of persons and society; otherwise, yes. People differ in the relative importance they attach to these valued objects. For this reason they may differ sharply concerning what should be done about reorganizing local schools, churches, and government units into larger ones. Such differences call for reappraisal of old beliefs so as to reach a new consensus on new organizational rules of life and work. This is not easy; it is painful to reduce the premium on ways called for by one set of attitudes in favor of ways called for by another set. To get out of such binds, it often helps to clarify the nature of the conflicting beliefs concerning what should be done.

With this fact in mind, we need to spell out more fully the proficiency concepts of personality and society which are deeply ingrained in American character. And we also need to sketch briefly the way in which these proficiency concepts guided the formation of the very historic system of rural organizations which are today in such sharp conflict with the proficiency directives. In this way, we can place our topic in the broad perspectives of history and national character it deserves.

Proficiency Concepts of Personality and Society as Dominant Directives of Rural America Since Early Times

Three observations bring into focus the proficiency concepts of personality and society. (1) They are rooted in the feeling (belief) that increasing excellence in all employments is the proper way of earning ever higher standing of one's respect and esteem and the respect and esteem of others as well. In this belief, what counts is not *what* one does, but *how well* he performs his social role in the community, whether it be growing wheat, building bridges, writing songs, or making mousetraps. No socially approved employment is any "higher" or any "lower" than any other as a chance for achievement. If one's specific employment contributes to the welfare of his community, what matters is not whether his occupation is painting pictures or making cheese but whether he fails to use his employment as an opportunity for developing his own potential as fully as possible.

(2) This drive for increasing proficiency in all employments clearly includes commitment to the innovator type of personality as the one most deserving of emulation, respect, and esteem. For such personalities are most characterized by high level need and capacity for identifying themselves with long range purposes in the confidence that with their own initiative, insight, and creative industry, they can turn risky situations into favorable outcomes, and in this way lift themselves from even the lowest to the highest stations.

Such people possess the creativity that is necessary for carrying forward economic and cultural progress without assignable limit. For there is hardly an implement of modern life, a piece of art, or a law of science which does not run back to where it once had no other home than the strange idea of some innovating personality—a constructive dissenter who checked and disciplined his

240

exceptional views against prevailing ones until he succeeded in developing his own to a point where others eventually accepted them as superior to their own.

America, as a whole, and especially rural America, has always placed a high premium on innovational personalities. In glancing at the heroes of our folklore, it is astonishing to see how frequently the brightest stars are those who have found new ways of turning into fortunes such lowly matters as making chewing tobacco, or butchering hogs, and then turned the fortunes into endowments of great universities, hospitals, churches, and other feats of philanthropy.

(3) This high premium on productive personality evidently includes a concept of proficient society. For it makes no sense to hold that being increasingly proficient is the individual's central responsibility to himself and his society without further holding that the central responsibility of society is to meet three debts to individuals. These debts are the obligations to (a) provide all its members with opportunity or access to the means (e.g. public schools) necessary for developing their potential to the fullest extent possible, (b) offer opportunities for productive roles in keeping with their abilities, and (c) give each a fair return for his contributions. A greater generator of anxiety over the meaninglessness of life is scarcely conceivable than a system of social organizations (institutions) which fills individuals with a high-level need of earning self-respect as proficient personalities and then withholds from them opportunities (a) for developing their potential as fully as possible, (b) for productive roles in keeping with their capacities, and for (c) rewards in keeping with their contributions. Were this not the case, the national conscience would not be disturbed by the fact that the unemployment level of the total economy has hovered around 5.5 to 6 percent of the labor force for several years and no assured let-up is in sight.

Carryover of 19th Century System of Rural Organizations as High Approximation of Proficiency Standards Under Limited Capabilities of Horse-Drawn Technologies

Acting under these broadly guiding proficiency concepts of personality and society, earlier America translated her dreams and visions into the very historic system of rural institutions which is today in such sharp conflict with continued allegiance to these same historic proficiency guides to life and work. This was a prodigious achievement, extending from the time of Jamestown and Plymouth Rock on to the close of the Settlement Era around 1920. During this 300-year period, there spread out over the face of the continent approximately 6 million farms, representing about 30 million people, and 15,000 farm-based towns representing about 18 million people. These towns ranged in size from a few hundred to 10,000 people. But 87 percent of them had less than 2,500 persons.

Including one-fifth of the continental United States, the Plains proper was the last of America's many physical frontiers. During the 50-year period from 1870 to 1920, there spread over the 8 Plains States and the Plains portion of

241

Texas and New Mexico, a rural society of over 800,000 farms representing approximately 4 million people, and a rural town population of nearly 2 million.

This historic order was laid out within the capabilities of horse-drawn technologies. Farm sizes were geared to the acreages which families could handle with a set of horse-drawn machines and equipment. Similarly, the sizes of banks, grocery stores, clothing stores, schools, and churches were determined against the background of travel by wagon over poor roads. Farm families did a large part of their shopping in small villages of less than 1,000 people separated from each other by 4 to 8 miles so that people could get to town and back in a few hours travel by carriages over dirt roads. In the main, counties were laid out in sizes that would enable people on the far sides to reach the seat towns in a day's travel with a horse and buggy.

Against the background of horse-drawn technologies, this system of rural organizations was a high approximation of proficiency standards. For example, given the horse and wagon, a rural society that provides a district system of one-room schools does as good a job as can be done of providing youth the educational opportunities for developing their capabilities as fully as possible. And the same principle applies to local churches, small town business establishments, and local governments.

New Proficiency Standards

But the technological foundations of this 19th century system of rural organizations have been buried so deeply an archaeologist can't find them. Today's motorized and computerized technologies have greatly enlarged the minimum efficient size units of all types of organization, whether farms, industries, stores, medical centers, schools, churches, or local governments. Present-day rural America is tending in the direction of these new minimuns. Consider a few.[2]

(1) In the era of horse-drawn technologies, an efficient size store was a general store, run by a family operator, servicing approximately 100 families or 500 people. Today, the *supermarket* is the basic unit of consumer goods retailing. And a minimum efficient size supermarket requires a population base of 5,000 to 7,000 persons.[3] Preferring more efficient size business establishments, which present-day technologies make possible, more and more farm people are driving on by the little towns where they used to stop.

(2) Take schools as another example. Dr. Conant has suggested that a graduating class of at least 100 pupils is an absolute must for a minimum-quality high school. Like a minimum-size supermarket, this calls for a population base of 6,000 to 7,000 persons, as only 1.6 percent of the population falls in the 17-year age group.

(3) Again, the American Library Association suggests an expenditure of $2.35 per capita. At this figure a population base of 5,000 persons is required to provide services of a librarian, a building, and money for new books and periodicals.

(4) Again, how large a population base is required to enable owner-operators of various types of business establishments to earn only $7,000 for their labor and management? Economists at Kansas State University have estimated as follows: nearly 1,400 people for a clothing store, about 2,700 for a men's clothing store, and 6,700 for a hardware store.

(5) It is commonly held that a church needs as many as 600 members to have an adequate budget for a good building, a pastor's salary of $5,000, a youth program, a home and foreign missions program, and theological scholarships. As about 60 percent of the population are church members, this means that a population base of 1,000 persons is required to support a single vital and adequate self-supporting church. As people are widely distributed among various denominations, it appears that a population base of 3,000 to 5,000 people is required for a system of self-supporting vital churches.

(6) Most towns on the Plains are under 1,000 people. But the minimum sizes of proficient businesses, schools, medical centers, and the like under present-day technologies call for towns from 2 to 3 times this large. This is about the extent to which farm people are tending to expand their farms. For example, during my high school days in Western Kansas in the 1920's, a family could handle from 320 to 640 acres in dryland wheat farming with a minimum complement of horse-drawn equipment and some extra help at harvesttime. With today's motorized equipment, the same labor force can handle roughly 2 to 3 times this much land. And, as we shall see, this is the direction in which farm sizes are tending in the Plains.

Redesigning Great Plains Society to the Capabilities of New Technologies

If rural people of 19th century America had possessed today's technologies they surely would have laid out an economy of fewer but larger farms, fewer and larger towns, fewer business functions in villages of a few hundred persons, and fewer but larger units of public administration. What are their descendants doing?

The answer is substantially threefold: (1) They are rapidly restructuring the farm and town component of their older society into fewer but more proficient size units. (2) In so doing, they are reducing population density per square mile and increasing per capita costs of public services. (3) However, they are not as yet doing much to offset this through restructuring their inherited system of local government, or through altering the historic identity of farms as places where people both work and live.

A. *Redesigning the farm component of 19th century rural society.* Throughout the United States, the farm component of rural society divides into a rapidly expanding sector, on the one hand, and a rapidly contracting sector on the other. The Plains are an outstanding example of this fact. Here this dividing line is now approximately 1,000 acres compared with 500 acres in former years. During the 1939-59 period, there was a 37-percent increase of farms with 1,000 or more acres, and a 40-percent decrease of all farms (table 1).

Should these trends continue another two decades, the farm component of the Great Plains economy would include only about 45 percent as many farms as in 1959–285,000 instead of 521,000. As there appears to be little reason to doubt the general magnitude and direction of this trend, it is safe to say that people of the Plains have hardly more than begun their drive to recombine land and resources into fewer but larger farm businesses.

B. *Remapping the town component of the Great Plains economy.* And the same principle applies to the town component of their inherited economy. Consider the high points of two investigations.

(1) In his study of rural organizations in North Dakota, Voelker reached three important conclusions concerning trends in town sizes. First, that State has 15 cities and villages of 2,500 or more persons; and their future is bright. In Voelker's words:

> Considerable industrial and commercial development had taken place in most of these 15 cities in recent years. There is no evidence to suggest that any of them has reached its full potential.[4]

Table 1.–Change in number of farms by specified acreage groups in the
Great Plains proper for specified years

Size in acreage	Number of farms				
	1939	1944	1949	1954	1959
Under 100 acres	187,226	167,876	142,643	118,062	82,707
100 to 179 acres. . . .	192,508	149,827	127,488	102,715	78,031
180 to 259 acres. . . .	84,419	80,011	77,569	67,426	53,485
260 to 499 acres. . . .	177,154	169,484	160,497	150,177	132,150
500 to 999 acres. . . .	91,661	94,323	95,366	96,553	95,761
1,000 and over	57,788	66,406	69,753	74,673	79,268
Total	790,756	727,927	673,316	609,606	521,402
	Percent of 1939				
Under 100 acres	100	90	76	63	44
100 to 179 acres. . . .	100	78	66	53	41
180 to 259 acres. . . .	100	95	92	80	63
260 to 499 acres. . . .	100	96	91	85	75
500 to 999 acres. . . .	100	103	104	105	104
1,000 and over	100	115	121	129	137
Total	100	92	85	77	66

Source: United States Census of Agriculture.

Second, of North Dakota's 537 nonurban villages, only 50 to 55 (less than 10 percent of the total) are emerging as primary farm service centers. Ranging from 1,000 to 2,500 people, these 50 to 55 towns:

> ... are and will continue to be, the most important shipping and marketing centers for farmers in all parts of the State except in areas adjacent to urban centers ... Most of them have made substantial population gains since 1940, apparently at the expense of the smaller surrounding villages.[5]

Third, but the future is not bright for the remaining 487 (or 90 percent) of North Dakota's towns and cities of less than 1,000 people. Population increase was projected for only 23 of them, 57 were expected to about hold their own, and the remaining 407 were expected to decline. The report used these words:

> By the close of the settlement in North Dakota—about 1915—many cities and villages had been laid out than were needed, even for the horse-and-wagon farm economy ... The advent of the automobile, and tractor, the improvement of roads and highways, and the trends toward larger farms have made even more of these villages unnecessary. A few have passed into oblivion, their remains being a crumbling formation in some farmer's field, or a grain elevator at a lonely railroad siding. Many other villages have declined to a point where they no longer have much significance as trading centers. Others are still actively competing for the farmer's business, their main hope of survival ... At stake are the business investments, homes, and life savings of thousands of people.[6]

(2) Important investigations of the town component of rural society in the Great Plains are underway in Kansas and Nebraska. Drawing on these investigations, Nesmith has made three important generalizations.

First, towns with less than 1,000 people, and often those with 1,000 to 2,500 persons, are too small to meet rural people's sense of minimum proficiency standards. For:

> The more successful farmers, with increased disposable incomes, were more likely to shop away from their hometown. Thus the town merchants had a steadily declining number of potential customers; the remaining customers were less and less likely to be satisfied with the limited selection of the small town.
> ... When asked to indicate the adequacy of facilities provided by small towns, most of the residents and rural customers described them as inadequate....[7]

Second, in this way small towns are being replaced by fewer, larger ones at even a faster rate than the change in total population suggests. For:

> A glance at the population figures for a number of towns may lead one to believe they are holding their own. Many exhibit stable populations. Some even seem to be growing.
> But the figures on age distribution and population trends in the surrounding rural areas make it clear that the apparent growth is merely a temporary adjustment that foretells accelerated declines. The population pyramids become rectangular and (in some instances) inverted triangles, as the young people leave and the production of native stock slowly grinds to a halt.[8]

Third, the historic system of small towns is not being altered merely because they are too small to provide people with opportunities for consumer goods and services. A more important reason is their failure to provide the oncoming generation with the career roles they need for becoming the creative productive personalities they feel obliged to be. Figures tell the tale:

> Graphs that indicate that population change in rural areas of the Great Plains States by 5-year age groups since 1950 give proof of the loss of population in the productive age range.[9]

And the loss is not a matter of numbers but of:

> . . . persons with higher educational attainment. In 1960, 8.9 percent of our urban population had 4 years or more of college compared to 5.3 percent of the rural nonfarm population and 2.8 percent of the rural farm population. One-third of farm-reared youths are college bound; one-half of urban reared youths are college-bound.[10]

There is thus a marked disparity between the capacity of organizations in the rural and urban sectors of our society to offer people career opportunities in keeping with their achievement potential. Rural people have never taken kindly to this disparity. Always it has been a sore point with them. To wipe it out has been one of their most persistent motivations since early times. This is very much the root of their present drive to reorganize the farm and town components of their society into fewer but larger units. This drive is not peculiar to the Great Plains. It is going on all over the United States.

C. *Technological advance in the Plains as expanding work space per capita.* But in the Great Plains it jams people up against an obstacle that they are relatively free of in most other regions. For the Plains are seemingly just wet enough to induce people to spread their job activities over nearly every foot of it. Were it drier, they likely would follow the example of their neighbors to the West who bunch up along the rivers and irrigated valleys, leaving the desert to the owl and rattlesnake. On the other hand, the Plains are not wet enough to support any larger population per square mile. It refuses to soak up any more gasoline, labor, and machinery per acre.[11]

In this way, it leads people to exploit the ever-increasing capabilities of their new technologies by increasing job space per town and farmworker alike. Thus, the merchant in a growing town spreads his service over an ever-broadening trade area hitherto serviced by merchants in presently declining towns. Similarly, the more successful farmer spreads his labor over acres hitherto tilled by his neighbors. And the same principle applies to the whole system of professional roles, including the doctor, the dentist, the implement dealer, the lawyer, the teacher, and the clergyman.

In this way, the Plains are thinning people off its surface at an astonishing rate. From 1940 to 1960, 270 (60 percent) of the 444 counties in the Plains proper had decreases in total population, and in 184 counties the decrease ranged from 10 to 20 percent (table 2).

In his poem, *Mending Wall,* Robert Frost penned their arresting lines:

> Something there is that doesn't love a wall,
> That wants it down.

Paraphrasing, we may say:

> Something there is about people the Great Plains doesn't love,
> And wants them out.

Table 2.—Percentage change in total population of counties of
Great Plains proper, 1950-1960

Change	Counties	
	Number	Percent of total
No change	15	3.4
Increase	145	32.6
Under 20 percent	88	19.8
20 percent and over	57	12.8
Decrease	284	64.0
Under 20 percent	237	53.4
20 percent and over	47	10.6
All.....................	444	100.0

Source: Derived from the U.S. Census of Agriculture.

By locating his tepees mainly along widely scattered rivers, the Red Man made peace with the preference of the Plains for buffalo. Then came the white man with his plows and fences, spreading over its broad expense a mantle of farms, small towns, townships, and counties which were indigenous to the humid regions to the East. Then in the 1930's the Plains answered his intrusion with gigantic dust storms that spread their debris as far eastward as ship decks in mid-Atlantic.

With uncommon courage, most people held on—some for lack of better opportunities elsewhere and some in the confidence that through their ingenuity and the help of agricultural researchers they could put together a new kit of farming practices that would conserve the limited moisture of the Plains, and in this way transform its fury into friendship for crops and cattle. This confidence was not a deceiving faith. They did achieve a new kit of practices that now enables them to do a fairly good job of conquering the weather hazards of the Plains.[1][2] The winds still blow, but the dust seldom chokes; the wheat and maize grains grow, and the cattle are content.

But one should never underrate the craftiness of the Great Plains. Conquer it from one direction and it expresses its distaste for people from another. For in requiring them to exploit the capabilities of their technologies by expanding the area of operation per worker, it is now thinning people out at a much faster rate than it could possibly do with its droughts and furious dust storms.

D. *Expanding area of operation per worker as increasing public service cost per capita.* In so doing, the Plains leads people to assume an increasing cost per capita of public services. For example, in North Dakota the cost of the services of a county school superintendent increases approximately $1.29 per capita if the population drops from about 18,500 to under 5,000 (table 3). The same principle applies to all other elective county positions. And it also applies to other local government units: townships, school districts, municipalities, and the like.

247

Since over 40 percent of counties in the Great Plains had from 10 to 20 percent decreases in population in the 1950's alone, it is apparent that people are either bearing a mounting per capita burden of local public service charges, or suffering a deterioration of the quality and quantity of such service, or both (table 3).

Table 3.—Per capita county costs in South Dakota by county population, 1961

(Dollars)

Population	Clerk of courts	Register of deeds	Auditor	Treasurer	Sheriff	State's attorney	Superintendent of schools
1,000 to 4,999 ..	1.88	1.36	1.98	1.99	0.15	1.05	1.76
5,000 to 8,999 ..	.69	.84	1.19	1.23	.17	.60	.98
9,000 to 12,999 ..	.50	.59	.93	.99	.12	.43	.71
13,000 to 16,999 .	.46	.47	.81	.91	.10	.35	.62
17,000 to 19,999.	.36	.38	.59	.73	.12	.35	.47
20,000 and over ..	.31	.35	.53	.70	.09	.17	.27

Source: Division of Taxation, Classified County Expenditures (Bulletin No. 62), Department of Revenue, Pierre, S. Dak.

E. *Offsetting mounting per capita public service costs through expanding size units of local governments:* But it seems apparent that they could easily offset this burden by restructuring their inherited system of local governments into fewer but more proficient size units, just as they are doing with their farms, small towns, and local business establishments.

To illustrate, consider the 19th century rule-of-thumb that a resident should be able to get to the county seat and back in the same day. In terms of present-day motor travel, this rule easily permits expanding from 3 to 4 times the service areas of local administrative organizations, which is in keeping with expanding sizes of farms and business organizations. This would increase the population base of county governments throughout most, if not all, the Plains to at least 20,000 people, which is the minimum below which overhead costs of government becomes disproportionately great.[13]

For example, a Nebraska study showed four adjacent counties with a population of about 1,500 to 2,000 families each. Merging them into a single county would rest local government on a population base of over 23,000. In this way, county services could be improved considerably at substantially less cost per capita and everyone would still be within an easy hour's drive of 45 miles from the county seat. And the same principle applies to other local administrative organizations. Thus, the very technologies which are generating mounting public service cost per capita, offer ample possibilities for offsetting this burden through converting small organizations into fewer but more proficient size units.

All studies lament the exceedingly small number of persons per unit of local government in the Plains. For the Nation, as a whole, the number is 1,280 as compared with only 133 in North Dakota, 146 in South Dakota, 166 in Nebraska, and 275 in Kansas. Concerning Kansas, a recent study declared:

> All Kansas has an over-abundance of such units; counties, townships, cities, school districts, and a variety of special districts, including soil conservation, cemetery, hospital, drainage, fire, and watershed. It is difficult to conduct government by units of low population for lack of specialized or even full time personnel; they overlap and duplicate, they don't have tax or population base to support them adequately; and their services vary—often from not good to worse.[14]

F. *Other ways of offsetting per capita costs of local governments:* Deserving attention are four other ways of offsetting mounting institutional per capita costs.[15] (1) First is combining municipal government with county government. Many incorporated villages have become too small to operate a full-scale program of local government, and may well find it to their advantage to have governmental functions performed by the county. (2) In many areas of declining population, per capita cost of public services might be reduced through cooperative administration of government functions, such as road maintenance, by neighboring counties or municipalities. (3) Another method is combining offices within counties. Iowa, for example, permits any combination of any one of these offices into: treasurer, auditor, recorder, clerk of court, and assessor. South Dakota is considering a constitutional amendment permitting a similar combination.[16]

(4) A fourth way of reducing mounting institutional costs per capita lies in altering the historic identity of farms as both places of residence and places of work and business. For example, as farms in a county decline from 2,000 to say 1,500 or 1,000, road costs per capita either skyrocket or else road service deteriorates badly, or both. As a result, maintaining good all-weather roads is already becoming prohibitive in some areas, and remaining farmers and ranchers are not fully enjoying the advantages of modern transportation.

This handicap could be largely overcome by shifting farm residences to towns or along strategic lines of communication between population centers. This is being done to a certain extent. For example, in some areas of Western Kansas, it is estimated that 30 to 40 percent of farmers and ranchers live in town and commute to work after the fashion of people in suburbia.[17] Town-farming and line-residence patterns along strategic highways are thus developing in the Plains, but they may need to spread to other areas and their potential benefits be realized more rapidly.

Increasing Conflict Between Proficiency and "Fundamentalist" Attitudes

The post-World War II shift to motorized technologies in rural America thus places a strain on the settlement era system of local governments which is no less severe than the strain it places on the older horse-and-buggy system of farms and small towns. But people share very different attitudes toward each of these facts. In line with historic proficiency concepts, they heartily embrace the requirements of their new technologies for radical change in their 19th century economic institutions. But, in line with "rural fundamentalist" attitudes, many seemingly stand as a wall against requirements of the same technologies for change in the 19th century system of social and political institutions.

For example, farmers are ceaselessly striving to expand their acreages to the point required for proficient use of their labor and management with high-powered equipment. And they are also uprooting the business structure of their older society. For, in driving on to the larger towns to do their shopping, they leave the smaller ones to wither on the vine. In the words of a recent Kansas study:

> Super market shopping has apparently become a way of life for the rural as well as the urban dweller.[18]

This does not mean that farm people fully approve of what they are doing. Researchers at Kansas State University found that farmers in Southwestern Kansas:

> ... were nearly unanimous (91 percent) in believing that the 'rural ways of life' should be preserved. Reasons commonly given were related to closeness to nature, advantages for bringing up children, more freedom, farmers could take care of business better by living on the land, and that farmers are needed to produce food.[19]

While these expressions are indeed the voice of affection for the older "ways of rural life," they are no check at all on economic action in line with historic proficiency directives. In this economic sphere of life, affections for the older order are so impotent that they arouse only momentary guilt twinges as people continue drastically to change their outdated horse-and-buggy system of farms and small towns.

But the reverse is true when it comes to reshaping the 19th century system of noneconomic organizations like schools, churches, and local governments. Over the past 40 years, marked progress has been made in restructuring the 19th century system of one-room rural schools into larger consolidated units. But the drive to preserve old ways has been a formidable obstacle, and the reorganizing job is far from complete. For example, in 1958, Kansas, Nebraska, North Dakota, South Dakota, Minnesota, Missouri, and Iowa had:

> less than 7 percent of the public school districts in the country, but over 80 percent of the nonoperating school districts, more than 50 percent of the one-room rural schools, and 55 percent of the districts with nine or fewer teachers. On the other hand, these 7 States accounted for only 7 percent of the districts with forty or more teachers.[20]

In the political sphere, preference for old ways has stood as a rock against restructuring local governments into more proficient sizes. For example, it has long been pointed out that townships are too small to make effective use of modern road machinery, employ a full-time highway administrator or a professionally trained assessor. Yet throughout the 15-year period of 1942-57, only 103 townships were abolished in the whole United States. Suggestions for county consolidations have met with even less success. And the same principle applies to proposals for consolidation of public offices within counties.

Rural America is thus caught in a distressing conflict between two diametrically opposite motivations. First are her historic proficiency directives to radically alter her 19th century system of farms and towns in line with the requirements of present-day technologies. The second are her directives that stoutly resist revising the older horse-and-buggy system of social and political institutions in line with requirements of the same technologies. How to get out of this bind—that is the central problem rural America is now up against, not only in the Great Plains but everywhere.

Area Economic Development as Bridging the Gap Between the Old and Emerging Rural Society

The way the country is tending to resolve the problem is called area economic development. The growth potential of economic areas stems from the fact that each contains (1) an indigenous labor force, (2) a supply of other resources, and (3) the demand of the indigenous population for goods and services. New industries are attracted into the area in direct proportion to the size and productive capabilities of the labor force, along with the availability of other resources needed by given industries, such as packing plants or milling establishments. New supermarkets, clothing stores, insurance agencies, automobile dealers, and the like are drawn into the area as a result of the demand generated by the purchasing power of the indigenous population.

The widespread need and desire for furthering area economic development raises a nest of questions. The most fundamental of these are conceptual, not administrative in nature. And they can be resolved only through seeking the help of able technicians and researchers to a far greater extent than we have up to now.

I do not have the competence to lay before you the answers to those questions. At this stage of the game, perhaps no one does. My hope is to treat the questions in a way that will help us see what a tremendous research job we have in fully mastering them, and in so doing become masters instead of puppets of the vast technological upheavals which everywhere are taking place. In this effort, I shall draw heavily upon the work of Professor Karl Fox of Iowa State University, who has done more imaginative and creative thinking on this subject than anyone I know.

A. *The definitional problem:* Professor Fox uses the concept of a "functional economic area" as a useful unit in discussing economic development. He defines such an area as the minimum unit of resources that has some growth potential. More fully stated, his concept is essentially this: An economic area is any chunk of geographic space which includes (1) the places or residences where a given population live, (2) the places where they work, and (3) the places where they do their shopping, get medical care, send their children to school, go to church, and the like. The roles of people as workers, consumers, parents, churchmen, citizens, and the like all fan out from the spots where they reside.

251

Professor Fox refers to this whole set of life roles as *"residentiary activities."* And he gives the name *"functional economic area"* to any chunk of space in which this whole set of activities (or "functions") is carried on.

In any such area, the population produce goods and services for people in other economic areas in exchange for goods and services they need for carrying on their own residentiary roles of home dweller, worker, shopper, and the like. Professor Fox estimates that the continental United States can be divided into approximately 400 to 500 "residentiary clusters," linked to each other by a vast production and exchange system that constitutes our national economy.

B. *Measurement problems:* This definition raises as yet unresolved measurement problems. For example, in terms of square miles and population, how large are these "residentiary clusters?" At this point, nobody knows. But four observations will help clear up what we are after and must get if we are to become guiders and masters of area economic development instead of being more or less run over by it.

(1) In the horse-and-buggy era, the geographic sizes of economic areas were roughly the same as counties. That is, each county not only included the places where people lived, but also the places where they worked, sent their children to school, did their shopping, went to church, had their recreation, and so on. This now is far from true. For example, in Jasper County, Iowa, there is a town called Newton. Significant numbers of workers daily go to work in a manufacturing plant at Newton from 10 or more surrounding counties. This means that the economic area, which used to be limited to Jasper County, now includes several times as much space as it did in the horse-and-buggy days. The same principle applies throughout the country. A rule-of-thumb is that the distance from the center of an economic area to its periphery is 1 to 1.5 hours of driving time. This is about as much time as people care to spend in going from where they live to where they work or where they do their shopping.

(2) Any economic area with a given population, say 50,000, may include a very small chunk of space, say 25 square miles. Or it may include a very big chunk, say 5 or 10 counties stretching over 100,000 square miles. What counts is not the precise number of people in the area but that the area must include not only the places where the population lives but also the places where they work and do their buying and selling.

This means that an economic area with a given population may be either a city or a rural area, depending on the density of population. To illustrate, Professor Fox took a city of 50,000 people and imaginatively spread its various sectors over the Corn Belt countryside. He found that in both cases the same 50,000 people had access to the same types and sizes of shopping centers and other services. In the center of the city was a business district covering one-half mile radius and employing about 10,000 workers. When deployed onto Iowa farms, this same labor force spread over 5 or 6 Corn Belt counties. To service this dispersed population, the little "convenience goods" stores and gasoline stations of the outer circle of the city fanned out into small villages and towns, many with less than 1,000 people. The supermarkets of the city spread out to the county seat towns. And its central business district was typically found to be the leading city of around 25,000 persons in the rural area.

(3) Now, what about the size of economic areas in terms of population? This question turns on both the density of people per square mile and the maximum distances they are willing to travel between their residences and their jobs and shopping places. If these variables balance off at approximately 50,000 people, they can have all advantages of large supermarkets and other services which require high volume for minimum cost per unit of service. Indications are that population density throughout the Corn Belt is sufficient to have a system of economic areas with each area having around 50,000 population, spread over 5 or 6 counties.

As a rule, a population of this size would cover a substantially larger area in the Plains. Thus, distances between residences and business places would be appreciably greater. As yet, we do not know whether Fox's concept of an economic area would limit size in the Plains to a population of less than 50,000 persons. And neither do we know whether proficient services actually require this large a population in the Plains, as seems to be the case in the Corn Belt.

(4) While research is still far from being able to delineate the newly developing system of economic areas in the Plains, investigations have already made clear that such areas are now much larger than counties. For example, preliminary studies by Nebraska researchers indicate that for planning purposes the 315 counties of the 4 Northern Plains States could be replaced by a mere 58 units. The same principle applies everywhere. As Professor Fox has observed:

> Each county now includes only a fraction of a functional economic unit, and many county officials are now groping blindly for significant and constructive things to do. Each county board is in the position of a blind man grappling with an unidentified portion of the anatomy of a multicounty economy.[21]

C. *Uses of system of economic areas in developing new productive opportunities:* There are six main ways a well worked out system of functional economic areas may be used as a guide in achieving improved social and economic order.

(1) It would give needed direction to the efforts of people trying to improve the productive opportunities of the indigenous labor force to the fullest extent possible. This amounts to fitting pegs into the correct holes, as well as forming new pegs to go into new holes. The "holes" in this analogy are the industrial plants and businesses. The "pegs" are the indigenous laborers having the specific skills required to do the jobs. New holes are developed as new industries and businesses are drawn into the area. New pegs are made as the indigenous laborers acquire new skills and education necessary to qualify for the new jobs. A functional economic area builds new pegs and finds new holes as it educates its people and draws in new or additional businesses and industries.

(2) A well worked out system of multicounty areas provides a useful framework for activities by voluntary citizens, even if county officers and State legislators indefinitely continue to be elected on the present basis. For, if voluntary groups organize for a study of problems affecting their whole area, they will almost certainly recognize educational and employment problems as

area-wide in scope. And they may seek to remedy them through use of State and local governments, or through federally aided programs.

The growing gap between the newly emerging boundaries of economic areas and the older horse-and-buggy boundaries of local governments has already led to transferring many coordinating and executive powers from county to State agencies, such as State boards of public welfare, State highway commissions, State boards of education. This same drift of local function to State and national government may be expected to continue unless and until the 19th century system of county boundaries and other units of local government are brought in line with the newly developing pattern of economic areas.

(3) This brings up a further use of a well worked out system of economic areas; it provides guidelines for eventual revision of the outmoded horse-and-wagon system of local governments in line with the requirements of present-day technologies. As previously explained, in the settlement era, the sizes of counties and economic areas were approximately the same, the upper size limit being fixed by the distance one could travel by horse and wagon to the county seat in a day. Thus, in the 19th century, the population of each economic area had a unit of government which:

> ... could deal in a coordinated way with the whole cluster of functions affecting people in the area in their capacity as residents, workers, consumers, and citizens.[22]

The need for such a unit of government is even greater today than in the settlement era, owing to the greater extent to which people now use government agencies in providing themselves with productive opportunities and social services. But, until we are able to determine realistic boundaries of the newly emerging economic areas, we have no reliable guide for restoring the historic similarity in the sizes of counties and economic areas. Such a guide will be provided as future research is completed.

(4) Again, a well worked out system of economic areas and a modernized system of counties is needed as a realistic basis for organizing the public school system. Throughout each area, teachers' salaries, curricula, and facilities should be of as nearly uniform quality as possible, so as to provide equal opportunities for all youth in the area. The elementary school system needs to be guided by the assumption that all pupils will move on into the junior and senior high schools of the area, and that a majority will go on to college. Acting on any other assumption perpetuates the separation of farm youth from others in the area—a separation that has always generated inequality of educational opportunity for farm and other youth in rural America.

(5) Again, well worked out system of economic areas and modernized county lines provides a means of coping with problems of low-income farms and underemployed farm people. In the main, job opportunities in an economic area are supplied by workers residing in the area. In fact, such a labor market is a necessary attribute of any economic area as previously defined. People on low-income farms are included in this labor market. The success with which they can enter nonfarm occupations in this market may be limited by their

educational backgrounds, specific vocational skills, aspiration levels, native endowments, and a sense of strangeness and fear of urban cultures. Thus, the problems of the labor force members on low-income farms can at least be analyzed on an economic area basis. And, in some cases, the area can provide needed solutions. For example, the leading city of the area would be the appropriate place for nonfarm vocational training programs and facilities.

If total job opportunities are expanding, the locational preferences of underemployed farm people may be met by training for expanding local job opportunities. However, vocational training should not be limited to training for local employment opportunities. In many areas, future possible expansion of such opportunities is limited to such an extent that not even the natural increase in population can be absorbed into local jobs. Many people will seek employment elsewhere. And it would be unfair to these people to deprive them of vocational training that will enable them to compete for well-paying jobs in other areas.

(6) Finally, without blueprints of the newly emerging economic areas in the Plains and elsewhere, there is actually little solid logical reason for upsetting the devotion to the present horse-and-wagon system of county areas. Put another way, in the absence of clear knowledge of the boundaries of present-day economic areas, the "rural fundamentalist" not only has a strong case, but his opposition actually owes him a debt of gratitude. Here is why.

There is widespread agreement that per capita costs of public services would be reduced if local government boundaries were stretched to include a larger area and more people—perhaps an entire economic area. There is also widespread agreement that the newly developing system of economic areas has run off and left the 19th century system of counties. And again most people agree that this disparity results in all manner of waste and cross purposes. From these facts, wise men often go on to urge that the older system of counties be brought more in line with the sizes of present day economic areas. But no one is yet wise enough to delineate the boundaries of the newly emerging system of economic areas. Therefore, in thus pressuring people to get on the band wagon for updating the outmoded 19th century system of counties, are we not in effect asking them to buy a pig in a poke? This is especially so since an outmoded system of county units is better than no system at all. As I see it, the clear deduction is that instead of being censored for his romance with the past, the "fundamentalist" deserves some thanks for keeping the rest of us from jumping out of the kettle into the fire.

Conclusions

In keeping with this thought, the present analysis leads to three major conclusions. (1) The kind of social and economic order which is needed in the Plains is already taking shape in a rapidly emerging system of new economic areas. This new system is also the logical basis for updating the 19th century system of local government units. (2) But at present this development is occurring more or less blindly for lack of information concerning the actual patterns of farms and various sizes of towns and trading areas which are coming to the fore. (3) This information can be developed only through well-coordinated efforts (a) to measure changes in population, farms, town sizes, and public service establishments since World War II, and (b) to project these trends into a pattern of future expectations. Much work of this nature is already underway in various State universities in the Plains States. But it may deserve an even higher priority than it now has, and also special emphasis on bringing together the entire findings into a systematic structure of the emerging economy of the Plains as a whole.

As this is done, people will have a much improved guide for reshaping their present organizations into ones more in keeping with their needs and aspirations. And my guess is that with such a guide, what has often been called "rural fundamentalism" will eventually reattach itself to a new and more efficient system of local governments with the same devotion it now has for the present system.

One final observation: Perplexity and concern over the kind of social and economic order most in keeping with the present-day needs is not peculiar to people of the Great Plains; it is shared by all America, urban as well as rural. Our country is all of one piece in having evolved ways of life and work that are in fundamental conflict with the carryover of 19th century forms of organization. Thus, no section of our population is exempt from anxieties over the shape of things to come, and the need of mutual support in the long and troublesome job of building new forms of community life that meet the organizational requirements of our new technologies.

CHAPTER 12. TRADITIONAL SOCIAL STRUCTURES AS BARRIERS TO CHANGE

In this chapter economic progress is equated with the steadily expanding power of a people individually and collectively to increase their total output of goods and services per capita. This expansion arises through changes in interlocking social structures, belief systems and values; in the numbers and quality of the population; in the relative proportions of goods demanded; in the combinations of production factors; and in technological innovations that continually upset accustomed ways of life and thought.

Agricultural progress is equated with the expanding capacity of farm people to play an increasingly effective part in accelerating the national output through supplying their total economy with foods and fibers appreciably faster than population growth adds new mouths to feed. Only as agricultures meet this test of proficient performance do they become capable of enabling an ever larger proportion of the total population to help expand the national output through engaging in nonfarm employments, including those which generate the increasingly productive farm technologies and related skills and knowledge, which in turn enable farmers to make steady increases in their productivity.

By this test, the best available quantitative data indicate that agriculture is definitely progressive in Western societies and Japan, but not in most Asiatic, Middle Eastern, and African societies recently achieving independence, nor in a number of Latin American countries *(Hendrix et al., 1965,* table 5).[1]

This question has two aspects. (1) Why are people in economically backward societies so reluctant to abandon age-old techniques and latch onto the gadgets of progress, such as higher yielding seeds, more productive animal breeds, contour farming, steel-beam ploughs, pesticides, chemical fertilizers, sanitary wells, and the like? (2) And why are they so reluctant to concert their individual behaviors into a national and international network of increasingly large-scale specialized units of collective action which are necessary for development and widespread use of increasingly productive technologies? In short, what are the central human (conceptual and attitudinal) barriers to the technological requirements of progress, on the one hand, and to the organizational requirements of increasingly productive technologies on the other?

By and large, the literature focuses mainly on the first of these questions, examining the barriers to the technological requirements of progress. Many divergent answers have been advanced. These answers fall into several main types. Some hold the barrier to increasing output is a high premium on leisure and a strong distaste for work *(Rottenberg, 1952, 99; Baran, 1952, 378; Spengler, 1954, 96; Baudin, 1954, 488-89; Weber, 1930, 59-67).* Others equate it mainly with an extreme lack of technological creativity, stemming principally

---

Note: Italicized items in parentheses are listed in the References on p. 281.

from the fact that the master-servant types of institutions of backward economies induce in the occupants of each status a spirit of dominance over those below them and a spirit of dependence and subservience toward those above them *(Hagen, 1962,* 65-83 and passim). Again, some researchers have gathered and analyzed massive volumes of data showing a high correlation between economic backwardness and a low-level achievement motivation *(McClelland, 1961,* 107-51 and passim). Again, an elaborate investigation recently has been carried out which equates the barrier to innovation with the lack of an independent, experimental frame of mind, the long-term cure for which is the gradual seepage of urban ways of thought and practice into rural ways *(Benvenuti, 1962,* 75-76, 123-34, 154-79, 383-400). Others hold that the central barrier to innovation is a fear people have that in attempting new practices, they may fail to produce as much as they know they can with their old methods, thus endangering their very survival *(Wiser and Wiser, 1963,* 117-18). So close is life to the bone that their impulse to take a chance on gaining a whole loaf from new and untried techniques is inhibited by anxiety over losing the crumb they feel sure of getting from their old practices. And this progress-blocking anxiety stems from sound economic sense. For innovations carry an immense risk for the uninitiated, and the risk is magnified by the very poverty they might escape by taking it. Operating at a bare subsistence level, a crop failure or a failure to cover the borrowed money by added harvests would be calamitous.

Still again, with impressive observations and logic, a noted analyst holds that the reason for lack of motivations for new technologies is that in backward societies the striving for high standing never becomes an "internal impetus" to technological progress. This is because social structures limit the scope of interpersonal bonds mainly to the family, clan, or tribe—primary groups which accord the individual his needed status without requiring him to earn it by growing two blades of grass where only one grew before *(Hsu, 1955,* 325-42).

Finally, with much evidence and logic, some reject all these versions of adverse motivations as constituting any significant barrier to technological innovations. The really formidable barrier, they hold, is people's lack of "cognition" (or knowledge) of improved methods of meeting their felt wants. Overcoming this lack of cognition requires an often extremely difficult teaching job of setting up gilt-edged "frequency associations" between new practices and desired benefits which can convince "unenlightened people" of a casual relationship between the two *(Erasmus, 1963,* 17-53). For example, even the wisest heads are hard put to devise ways of associating boiled drinking water and prevention of typhoid with such frequency and clarity as to lead the unenlightened to abandon their ancient conviction that if the patient dies, that is because Allah wills it, and if he gets well that also is because Allah wills it.

Finding out more precisely the nature of the human barriers to latching onto the gadgets of progress is indeed an important area of inquiry. However, our preference here is to bypass this usual line of investigation in favor of a discussion of the second, equally important question mentioned above: Why are people in economically backward societies so reluctant to concert their individual behaviors into increasingly broader networks of large-scale specialized units of collective action which are necessary for the development and widespread use of modernizing technologies?

Implicit in this question is the recognition that economic behavior is an interlock of three components: technological, organizational, and cultural. (1) The technological component is the techniques people use in carrying on a conquest of nature—turning physical and biological materials and forces into useable goods and services. In input-output explanations of economic development, this component is a residual variable called "improved technologies," which is assumed to explain all increases in total output that cannot be accounted for by changes in factor and product prices and in the use of factors or such unpredictables as weather. In these terms, the technological component of development includes the improved skills and knowledge of people as well as the improved materials, such as higher yielding seeds and animal breeds, fertilizers, telephones, and other hardware they work with. This means that investment for improving the technological component of behavior includes plowing savings into the formation of human as well as physical capital.[2]

(2) The organizational component of economic behavior is the capacity for concerting reciprocally helpful behaviors into a continually widening network of larger, specialized units of collective action necessary for enabling people to generate and put to use the improved technologies they must have in order to transform their physical and biological world into a place of ever-increasing goods and services. A simple example will serve to bring out the meaning of this statement. Today there are no flies in Taiwan. The new technology for this achievement was very simple: a small spray gun and some DDT powder, which nearly any child can operate. But the organizational requirement for generating and using this technology was an island-wide health association which, among other things, linked together the scientific behaviors of a few physicians with the household behaviors of a whole island. This linkage was accomplished through the intermediate actions of a small number of specialized nurses working with the physicians at the national level and with thousands of village (practical) nurses at the county level. These village nurses in turn worked with all the households of the island, explaining why it was to their advantage to rid the island of its flies and demonstrating how to do it with a spray gun.

The same principle applies to the many improved farm technologies which enable Taiwan farmers to achieve a progressive agriculture in the sense previously defined. For this progress has not stemmed primarily from a technical aptitude of the Taiwanese. Rather, it has grown out of an organizational talent for combining human behaviors in new ways that enable increasingly larger numbers of people to help each other in creating and putting to widespread use the more effective technologies. These technologies in turn have enabled Taiwan farmers to expand their total output at sufficiently rapid rates to enable a growing proportion of the total population to engage in nonfarm employments, including those which generate the technologies and related services that have enabled Taiwan farmers to steadily increase their productivity.

(3) The cultural component of behavior is the deep-seated feelings-convictions-belief systems which people hold (in varying degrees) concerning what rules of interpersonal (or intergroup) behavior deserve their allegiance, and which ones they feel obliged to distrust and oppose. This cultural aspect of any social system may include belief components which operate as a formidable obstacle to the restructuring of human behavior in ways necessary for faster rates of economic progress and fuller realization of each person's potentials. For example, in United States society it is well recognized that racially discriminatory rules have long operated as a formidable impediment not only to faster economic development, but more importantly to a much fuller realization of the democratic ideal to which this society, by and large, is strongly committed. Equally well recognized is the fact that this impediment to fuller growth stems from no lack of "cognition" of more productive nondiscriminatory practices, but from the deep-seated conviction of many that black skin is *prima facie* evidence of such inferior character as to deserve only subservient station.

These technological, organizational, and cultural components of economic behavior interlock in fostering or impeding development. The feelings-convictions-belief systems concerning appropriate rules of interpersonal behavior often operate as formidable barriers to the organizational requirements of modernizing the farm technologies of backward agricultures. It has already been explained that the development and widespread application of even the very minimum complement of technologies necessary for backward agricultures to become progressive is impossible except through the reciprocal services of far larger numbers of people than are contained in the family, village, clan, and tribe—the dominant units of collective action in relatively unmodernized societies. For example, the average American farmer produces enough food to feed himself and 27 others; but he is able to do this because large organizations of workers in hundreds of nonfarm industries make the implements and other materials he uses, and process and distribute his products, and a large staff of many experiment stations, extension services, and nonfarm businesses provide him with an ever-hastening stream of new production and marketing technologies.

There is another consideration behind our treatment of the organizational requirements of modern technologies. Within the whole network of increasingly larger and more specialized organizations necessary for meeting the technical requirements of progressive agricultures, the most strategic one is a progress-oriented government. Such a government is here recognized as one with sufficient (1) power, (2) perception of the felt wants of people, (3) determination, and (4) professional competence to conceptualize and implement interconnected institutional and organizational reforms necessary for achieving sustained economic progress. As a very minimum, such reforms presuppose governments capable of formulating and backing up rules that protect all individuals and their possessions against exploiters; rules that give agreements among individuals the dependability of legally enforceable contracts and protection against fraud or swindle; rules that shift resources and jobs from less to more efficient users, and reward people in line with their productive contributions; and tax and public investment rules that generate social overhead services like roads, schools, credit facilities, and power installations which people cannot provide for themselves, but which they must have for developing and using their capabilities as fully as possible. Without a whole nation of people being related to each other through such rules it is impossible for increasingly large numbers to combine their behaviors into reciprocally serving activities which are necessary for the creation and widespread use of increasingly productive technologies. And no generator of such large-scale organizing rules of life is conceivable without the emergence of progress-oriented, stable governments.

But a striking feature of most, if not all, economically backward societies is precisely the absence of such governments. Therefore, in accounts of successful take-offs in economic advance, we might expect to find clear identifications of the human barriers to the formation of stable governments, and also the conditions which transformed these barriers into positive motivations for meeting the organizational requirements of technological advance. But by and large, these identifications are precisely what one does not find.

For example, a recent book on the development of Japanese agriculture over the past 100 years asserts that the whole thing stems from the emergence in late 19th-century Japan of a strong, progress-oriented government *(Ogura, 1963)*. Yet the book is silent on conditions that explain *why* such a government emerged; the authors take for granted the very thing which most needs explaining. The same principle applies to accounts of the rehabilitation and progress in Taiwan agriculture since World War II *(Tang, 1957, 9-117; Hsieh and Lee, 1958)*. In discussions with able persons in foreign aid programs, this writer has repeatedly asked, What is the key requirement for getting agricultural development on the move? Invariably, the answer has been the emergence of a stable, progress-oriented government.

Still, all economic accounts of development thus far coming to our attention simply take for granted the presence of such a government. Given this presupposition, the way to launch the growth process is for social engineers to draw up the blueprint of measures for government to carry out. Very often there is consensus as to the appropriateness of the blueprints. But commonly little or nothing gets done because unmodernized social structures are so interlocked with convictions concerning appropriate rules of life as to render nonexistent and impossible for a long time to come the very kind of government required to implement the recommendations.[3] Lacking in such recommendations is any recognition that political development is a necessary precondition of economic development, and not the other way round.

These considerations give rise to the central concerns of this chapter. (1) Why are people in backward economies, by and large, so reluctant to gear their behaviors into increasingly large-scale governments, without which as previously explained, it is impossible for them to achieve the gadgets of progress? (2) How many this reluctance be transformed into positive motivations for meeting the organizational requirements of technological advance?

Three premises guide the handling of these questions. (1) In all cultures people (a) seek increases in physical comfort and freedom from anxiety about this comfort in the future, and (b) strive to earn (deserve) ever higher standing in their own respect and esteem, and the respect and esteem of others, including their posterity, their forefathers, their families, and their community, actual or imaginary. Few if any pains are so terrifying as the anxiety over being so devoid of meritorious qualities as not to deserve favorable valuation by anyone, including oneself.[4] (2) As no solitary individual can produce even a pin, these universal strivings for physical comfort and favorable images of personal and collective significance or worth can be met only through ways or rules of life and work which link people to each other in various statuses with approved claims to each other's services. As a reciprocity of rights and duties, these claims constitute a people's sense of justice—a system of rules that are viewed as giving each his due in virtue of his capabilities and contributions. (3) "Social structure" is the name sociologists use in referring to a people's total system of rules. And the components of the total social structure are called institutions. The social structure and institutions that exist within a country have a curcial bearing on the two central concerns mentioned above.

In line with these premises this chapter treats the causal relation between achievement of economic development and the organizational requirements of economic development. This is not intended as an exhaustive description of any specific country, much less of all underdeveloped countries. Rather, it is intended to provide a theoretical basis for better understanding and coping with barriers to economic development. Section I focuses on the fact that the class structure of relatively unmodernized societies deprives working people of power to achieve increasing control over both their social and physical environment by saddling them with primitive technologies. Section II deals with the way in which this felt impotence leads people to equate friends and helpers mainly with kinship groups, and outsiders with aggressors.

Section III focuses on how this primacy of local loyalties and distrust of outsiders operates as a formidable barrier to concerting individual behaviors into increasingly large-scale units of collective action, especially stable governments. Section IV turns to a second formidable barrier to progress—the equation of the just uses of sovereign power with maintenance of institutions that perpetuate technological backwardness. In Section V attention shifts to approaches to the development problem which offer promise of transforming these and other barriers to progress into positive motivations for economic and cultural growth. The concluding section briefly points up the underlying themes of the chapter and makes explicit an implied line of inquiry.

I. Social Structures and Technological Weakness of Backward Economics

Turn now to the first point: The way in which the class or power structure of unmodernized agricultural societies lead to extreme helplessness of rural people in altering either their social or physical environment.

Major Classes

The structures under consideration segregate the population into four major groupings: The elite, the simple folks, large-scale trader financiers, and cultural brokers.

The elite fall into primary and secondary groupings. The top elite typically is an economically and politically powerful landed aristocracy, usually residing in a few large towns and one or more central cities where the king's court, the national government, and main centers of commerce are located. This top elite is generated by social structures which in many societies combine into the same skin three statuses: landlord, lender, and sovereign. Occupants of these combined statuses hold the rule-making positions at all levels of the political hierarchy—local, provincial, and national. Around and under this hard-core landed elite are the secondary elite—the bureaucrats, the professionals (doctors, lawyers, writers, teachers, religious officials), and the military.

In terms of economic but not political power, most unmodernized societies include a class of large-scale trader-financiers. They are lenders to landlords, princes, and even peasants, although for the most part the peasant's landlord is also his creditor. In spite of their economic power, the trader-financiers are almost nowhere accepted by other elite groups as creatures of equal worth, or as occupying a natural or proper place in society.

Far below the landed elite in social distance are the simple folk: peasants, artisans, craftsmen, shopkeepers, and menials. By and large, peasants live in villages from which they go out each day to the fields to work. Typically, the village consists of a few dozen or few hundred houses clustered along a dirt street or group of intersecting streets. Along the street somewhere is a village pagoda, temple, or shrine. The village meeting place may be a religious abode or the village school, if there is one. In the center or at the edge of the houses may be the village well or tank, which holds the village water supply. Nearby may be the village threshing floor, grazing ground, and woodlot. Round about the village lie the fields. In such villages live approximately half the people of the world.

The vast social distance which separates the landed elite from simple folk stems from the conviction that the badge of meritorious qualities is exemption from economic work and that sure proof of inferior character is dependence on any employment having to do with fashioning the material means of life.[5] Guided by this conviction, the elite are persuaded that their superior status in life is justified, and feel repugnance to ways of the simple folk.

But the landed elite and the simple fork are not totally disconnected; they are hooked together by a lower-level elite which anthropologists variously call "the link," "the bridge," "the hinge," or "the cultural brokers." These brokers may be the local agent of the national government, the headman of the village, a monk or priest, the village school teacher, or a local member of the landed gentry. These small-gauge elite bring together what Redfield (1956, 70) has called "the little tradition of the village" and "the great tradition" of the central towns and cities. Through them the belief systems and values of the remote elite and the simple folk interact and influence each other.

263

Social Powerlessness of Farm Communities

Thus, peasant villages are not self-sufficient units, neither ideologically, politically, nor economically. The religious beliefs of the peasant, for example, come to him from outside his village and are not products of his own creation. And from times immemorial he has been governed from the city. The same applies to his material needs. For, while producing much of their own subsistence, villages nonetheless depend on distant town and city as outlet for much of their produce and as source for items they cannot make for themselves. Peasant villages thus form a class segment of a large unit of civilization. Kroeber *(1948,* 284) aptly characterizes these villages as "part-societies" with "part cultures."

A central feature of these part-societies is their powerlessness to alter the rules which are saddled onto them by outside centers of power. As Foster *(1961,* 47-48) has observed:

> . . . the basic decisions affecting . . . . villages are made from the outside and have always been so made. For generations the village has been able to show initiative only in the most limited areas.´. . . Moreover, not only does the villager have little or no control over the basic decisions made from the outside, but usually he doesn't even know how or why they are made. The orders, the levys, the restrictions, the taxes that are imposed from the outside have for him the same quality of chance and capriciousness as do the visitations of the supernatural world. And the peasant feels much the same toward both authorities of the city and the supernatural: he can plead, implore, propitiate, and hope for a miracle, but in neither case, can he expect by his own action to have any effective control.

This does not mean that the disappearance of village structures is a precondition for a sufficiently rapid degree of improved farm technologies to enable farm people in such structures to steadily increase their total farm output. But it does mean that widespread use of even simple technologies at rates sufficient to enable villages to make these steady increases in output has not hitherto been possible through village structures themselves but through the linkages of these structures with a network of outside specialized organizations. It is through these linkages that improved technologies are generated and brought into the villages, in the manner that DDT and spray guns were introduced in ridding Taiwan of flies. The same principle applies to improved seeds, fertilizers, irrigations facilities, multiple cropping practices, marketing technologies, related knowledge, and the like.

Social Structures As Leading to Technological
Weakness Of Peasants

In the relative absence of such linkages, peasant villagers feel a lack of any effective control over their wider social environment, and also a high degree of technological weakness or lack of effective control over their physical and biological environment. For in the absence of specialized organizations which link businessmen, government agents, landlords, researchers, and skilled and unskilled workers to each other in a nationwide chain or reciprocally serving activities, the only kind of gadgets which a few hundred souls at most can possibly generate are exceedingly impotent: aids for turning nature into an increasingly fruitful servant of human needs.

For example, the implement for carrying burdens is commonly a pan on the head or a sling of buckets over the shoulders. Digging is done more often with a board-bladed hoe than with a spade. In preparing the soil for planting, farmers tug and strain with a singleshare wooden plow, possibly with a steel tip, or a hand hoe, or a harrow consisting of a heavy log or board with wooden sticks projecting downward, and pulled by an ox, water buffalo, or camel. They harvest crops with a hand sickle or knife or pull up the plants by hand. To thresh grain straw they spread it over a spot of hard ground and drive animals over it to stomp out the kernels. They then winnow the grain by filling a bucket, raising it above the head, and pouring its contents to the ground so that the wind may blow the chaff away. Such primitive technologies are a necessary outcome of the social structures of relatively unmodernized societies.

II. Technological Weakness and the Primacy of Village and Kinship Loyalties

With such primitive techniques, the struggle for even minimal needs has long induced two deeply ingrained attitudes: village loyalties, and even stronger kinship bonds.

The primacy of village loyalties takes the form of scrupulous observance of reciprocity in exchanges of mutual help among members of the village or of clan groups among several villages. So helpless is the individual by himself alone that each would perish except for the help of the others in planting or harvesting, in maintaining irrigation ditches or paths, in house building, in conducting weddings, delivering the new born, burying the dead, and in all occasions in which disaster strikes.[6] With social structures thus limiting collective units of action to very small numbers of persons, the law of reciprocal dependence induces the common conviction that none are so deserving of ostracism as those who receive but refuse to return the help of fellow villagers in their hour of trouble.

In line with this conviction each family keeps track of the number of work days or pounds of grain they give others in order that it may receive a precise reciprocity of services when they are stricken. This buildup of a backlog of favors does not constitute a contractual exchange in the usual sense. For if a receiving family should fall into still greater need, it is not sued or censured for failure to repay its debts. On the contrary, fellow villagers feel obliged to give additional help, even to the point where the receiving family may feel an unbearable burden of obligations to the village.

But even this high premium on village loyalties is exceeded by a much stronger sense of family bonds—ties that usually include many more family members than the nuclear family of husband, wife, and children. For in a society so technologically weak as most peasant communities, the nuclear family is too small to meet even minimal needs. For example, in his study of a peasant village in southern Italy in which the nuclear family prevails, Banfield *(1958,* 148) observed that if both parents or even only the father dies before the children grow up, they usually become beggars. In a larger family, they would be cared for by grandparents, uncles, aunts and cousins.

With no group so important as his large family to turn to in all the hazards and difficulties of life, the individual in technologically backward peasant societies feels an allegiance to his kin that transcends all others. For example, the Wisers (*1963* 122-23) express the Indian villagers' sense of kinship loyalties in these sensitive words:

> No villager thinks of himself apart from his family. He rises or falls with it. . . . That man is to be pitied who must stand alone against dangers, seen and unseen, which beset him. Our families are our insurance. When a man falls ill, he knows that his family will care for him and his children until he is able to earn again. And he will be cared for without a word of reproach. If a man dies, his widow and children are sure of protection of a home.

III. Kinship and Village Loyalties as Barriers to Large-Scale Units of Action

Potentially, people are either reciprocators or exploiters; and which of these potentialities is actually realized evidently turns in great measure on the numbers of persons which given social structures link to each other in mutually servicing activities. When the structures limit the size of collective units of action mainly to the extended family, clan, or tribe, total helplessness of the individual to meet even his simplest needs without the helping hands of others induces a depth and richness and power of kinship bonds which is well-nigh incomprehensible to Western societies—societies in which large-scale units of collective action expand the scope of the helping hand to vast numbers of people in professional societies, in unions, in trade association, and in all levels of the nation-state. In thus enabling the individual to feel caught up in the concerns of vast units of humanity outside his kin, the social structures of technologically advanced societies inculcate a width of interpersonal allegiances which is incomprehensible in economically backward societies.

Fear and Distrust of Outsiders

Conversely, in mainly limiting helping hands to the small numbers in primary groups, the social structures of technologically backward societies induce the equation of outsiders with predatory intentions. This equation arouses a width of distrust and fear which is difficult for Western societies to comprehend. For example, based on their observations during the 1930's the Wisers (*1963*, 122) paraphrased the Indian villagers' fear and distrust of outsiders in these words:

> We do not trust the outside world, and we are suspicious of each other. Our lives are oppressed by mean fears. We fear the rent collector, we fear the police watchman, we fear everyone who looks as though he might claim some authority over us; we fear our creditors, we fear our partons,. . . we fear thieves, . . . and we fear the strength of our neighbor.

These beliefs seem to be quite prevalent even today, though perhaps to a lesser degree than earlier. This mentality of distrust and fear is embedded in the very architecture of dwelling sites. For example, in walking through either the best residential sections of the capital city of Taiwan or the poorest fishing villages on the island, one never sees a yard. For each living space is closed off from the others with high stone walls, 8 to 12 inches thick, with a row of jagged glass running along the top. In parts of rural India the walls are made of baked mud. And simple folk perfer dilapidated walls to well-kept ones because they provide a better shield against exploiters *(Wiser and Wiser, 1963,* 120):

> Dilapidation makes it harder for the convetous visitor to tell who is acutally poor and who simulates poverty. ... If the ordinary man suddenly makes his wall conspicuous, the extortioner is on his trail. You remember what a short time it was after Puri put up his imposing new veranda with a good grass roof, that the police watchman threatened to bring a false charge against him. He paid well for his show of progress. Old walls tell no tales.

Rural life is thus shot through with a mentality of mutual fear and distrust, even though survival as previously explained would be impossible without scrupulous observance of precise reciprocity in exchange of mutual help among villagers *(Lewis, 1951,* 294-429). And this mentality intensifies as the human circle expands to include the distant towns and cities. As expressed through the Wisers *(1963,* 124), this is how the country folk feel:

> In the cities they devise ways of exploiting us. We know how to drive bargains when we sell our wheat and sugar cane. ... But when we get our money and want to take home some cloth, the shopkeepers get out the pieces of cloth which they have been unable to dispose of and persuade us to buy them at exorbitant prices. But we want the cloth, and the next shopkeeper will cheat us as badly as the last. Wherever we go in the towns, sharp eyes are watching to tempt our precious rupees from us.

After expressing similar feelings toward courts, judges, lawyers, politicians, priests, missionaries, teachers, government hospitals and agents, postmen, landlords, and rental agents, the villagers summarized their fears and distrust of the whole world outside their kin in these bitter words *(Wiser and Wiser, 1963,* 127-29):

> You cannot know unless you are a villager, how everyone threatens us and takes from us. When .... a sophisticated town man goes anywhere, he demands service and gets it. We stand dumb and show our fear, and they trample on us .... There is no one outside our own group whom we dare trust. Everyone who comes to us or to whom we go, thinks of what he can get from us—be it money, or gain, or personal glory.

The Wisers' picture of the situation in India during the 1930's is admittedly too stark to be taken as representing all underdeveloped areas today. It portrays a degree of fear and mistrust which is not universal even in India. Nevertheless, it is still clear that the social structures we are here studying impart to people an extraordinary capacity for equating predatory intentions with most of humanity outside the primary groups. For example, in his study of a peasant village in southern Italy, whose culture is similar to that of "the Mediterranean and Levantine worlds," Banfield *(1958,* 9-10) documented many important expressions of this equation. Official positions and special training are viewed as weapons to be used by their possessors against others for private advantage. A young teacher from an artisan family expressed these attitudes this way *(Banfield, 1958,* 91):

> Study and education has helped some people to succeed. It has helped them by giving them an advantage over the ignorant. With their knowledge, they are able to exploit ignorance. They are able to cheat more dexterously.

Again, people interpret as fraud the claim of any person or institution to be motivated by zeal for public rather than private advantage *(Banfield, 1958,* 92). Again, since private citizens get no pay for busying themselves with public affairs, people deem anyone abnormal and even improper if he manifests any serious interest with public problems; they expect only politicians to have such an interest because only politicians are paid to bother themselves with public needs *(Banfield, 1958,* 98). And it also is taken for granted that, in addition to his pay, any public official will take bribes whenever he can get away with it, which he usually does. In the words of a teacher *(Banfield, 1958.* 96):

> Today one gets ahead only by bribes and recommendations. All of the examinations are infected by this disease and those who get ahead are the ones with the most drag.

In similar vein, a merchant after waiting months for a reply to his request for a permit to operate a cinema he was building had this to say *(Banfield, 1958,* 96):

> If I took an envelope with $160 and slipped it into the right pocket, I would have my permission right away. It's the little yellow paper that gets things done. Big and small, they all take bribes. Why don't you do it then? Because I don't have $160 to spare.

Distrust as a Barrier To Collective Action

In leading people to impute helpful attitudes to their primary groups and predatory intentions to outsiders, the social structure of relatively unmodernized farm societies erects a formidable human barrier to the formation of increasingly large-scale units of collective action which are necessary for achieving the gadgets of progress. Four observations will serve to develop the meaning of this fact.

(1) Large-scale units of action are impossible unless large numbers of people are able to bind themselves to each other as loyal leaders and followers. But the predatory image of the world outside one's primary group denudes people of this capacity. For under the guidance of this image no one can formulate a plan of action and persuade any others to follow it. And even if this were not the case, others would impute predatory intentions to him and reject him out of distrust *(Banfield, 1958,* 99-100). Malik *(1963)* has spelled out the organizational implications of this fact in these words:

> The people themselves do not know how to be led. . . . There is . . . not so much a dearth of leaders as a dearth of followers; public discipline is lacking. . . . There is no social or national responsibility; . . . that creative feeling of belonging to a larger enduring whole . . . is still to emerge. In short, the national human base, not as a clamoring mass, but as an organized whole, has still to be formed. . . . A responsible or at least intelligent following, a coherent whole on which and through which the leader can act, a structured body politic which can articulate and sustain the national will or this or that organization, or this or that social group—the creation of such a necessary

human base is one of the most formidable tasks challenging the leaderships of the new nations. Thus, a whole new, civilized national existence has to come into being if the new nation is to cope successfully with the strenuous demands of the present age.

(2) As Malik implies, the fear and distrust aroused by the equation of outsiders with predatory intentions is so potent that even in face of catastrophe people are commonly incapable of combining into national units of action necessary for staving off disaster. Consider South Vietnam, for example. For 9 years until his violent death in November 1963, Diem and his family exercised overwhelming influence *(Maffre, 1964,* E-1): "To be related to the family or to have won its favor meant preferment for most important positions."

Upon Diem's overthrow, authority shifted to a 62-member Military Revolutionary Council. Until the explosion of riots on August 27, 1964, the members of this junta spent as much—if not more—energy jockeying to further their individual family positions as against the Viet Cong. And the same principle still applies. Dominated by allegiances to narrow kinship groups, war with the common enemy is just a troublesome secondary matter *(Maffre, 1964,* E-1):

> To Vietnamese intellectuals particularly, the counterinsurgency effort is merely a bothersome topic compared with politics. This capital, which purports to direct the war effort, is largely populated by people profoundly uninterested in anything beyond Saigon.

(3) The equation of helpful attitudes with primary groups and predatory attitudes with outsiders leads people to feel they are acting quite properly in cheating strangers, making dishonest business comitments, and selling shoddy goods under false labels. By inducing this equation, the structures of economically backward societies erect a formidable inward barrier to the operation of the modern system of market exchanges involving unknown others. For the endless chain of reciprocally useful service exchanges is possible only for people with a large capacity for dealing as fairly with any other as with friends and relatives.

(4) And the same equation renders large numbers of people incapable of voluntarily concerting their behaviors into modern corporations and states through which the industralization of the West has been achieved. Thus in writing of pre-World War II China, Latourette *(1963,* 583) observed:

> Family loyalty is traditionally so strong that many a Chinese sees no turpitude in making sinecure positions for kinsmen in the company of which he is president or director—or in other ways doing what in the West would be regarded as defrauding the stockholders. Therefore, in spite of notable and probably increasing exceptions, in Chinese hands, unless it is in reality a family affair, the stock company is for some time to come likely to prove a failure.

The same principle applies to the pre-World War II Chinese government. As Hsu (*1955,* 346-47) has stated:

> The Chinese government . . . invested heavily in many lines of industrial endeavor . . . from mining and railroads to shipping and armaments . . . usually with borrowed funds from foreign powers. The trouble was that these funds soon found their way into private pockets. . . . The reason is not obscure. Since the Chinese government . . . is outside the primary groups, it becomes a

fair target for loyalists to family and community (village) at the expense of the former.

The same principle also applies, by and large, to all 19th century landlord civilizations except Japan. This exception is explained by the fact that in Japanese culture the Emperor was viewed as the divine heir of the progenitor of the Japanese race. This extension of the "primary group to include the relationship between the emperor and the people . . . gave the Japanese dynasty a stability which assured an unbroken rule over the Japanese people for at least fifteen hundred years." And this same extension rendered "bureaucratic corruption . . . as rare as corruption of the family and small community" *(Hsu, 1955,* 345-46).

Preference for Government by the Strong Hand

In all societies, the strongest political want or need of individuals is not the desire for a vote in selecting their rulers, but for rulers with sufficient power and will at least to protect their life and possessions against assault and seizure. In keeping with this fact, in economically backward societies, by and large, all classes "favor a regime that will maintain order with a strong hand" *(Banfield, 1958,* 96).

For example, in his study of southern Italy, Banfield *(1958,* 96-98) found this bias for the strong hand uppermost among peasants and others. When asked what the Fascists claimed to stand for, typical replies were as follows. Said a farmer:

> The Fascists wanted the peasants to have a better life. There was an eight-hour day and a standard rate of pay. If a proprietor made you work ten hours, you went to the employment office and they would force him to pay the right wage. Now it is everyone for himself, and everyone tries to get the most work for the least pay out of the peasant.

A merchant had this to say:

> Cloth was grade-labled and marked with a fixed price along the shelf edge. Everything was controlled. You knew what you were getting for your money. Now, unless you really understand cloth, a merchant can sell you inferior material at high prices. It was good for the customer and good for the merchant too. The customer knew what he was getting and the merchant could count on his twenty or thirty percent. Some people get one hundred percent today.

A teacher expressed her respect for the strong hand this way:

> During fascism, there was a great spirit of emulation among the pupils and good discipline. Today all this is gone; children grow up very rude and the teachers in school must always have sticks because the children are fighting among themselves, all the time.

This preference for the strong hand is commonly reinforced by repeated failures to achieve stable governments, necessary for progress, through use of Western multiple-party systems and parliamentary forms. This fact is well illustrated among the 37 new nations which have emerged in Africa since 1951. The main steps in their shift are substantially as follows.

First, in great measure the fuel that fed the popular drive to oust alien colonizers was the pledge of independence leaders to do more than the white man had done in building schools, clinics, and hospitals, securing more teachers and doctors, providing clean water for the village, building low-cost housing in the cities, and making it possible for everyone to have an adequate supply of consumption goods at prices people could pay. Second, having enlisted popular support through such pledges, the leaders of the new nations feel compelled to deliver on their promises on pain of otherwise being abandoned for other leaders who will. In the words of Nkrumah (*1958,* 53):

> We cannot tell our people that material benefits and growth and modern progress are not for them. If we do, they will throw us out and seek other leaders who promise more. . . . We have to modernize.

But leaders must have control of the army and police force and the budget-making process for a long enough period to get development plans and programs well under way. However, they soon found themselves defeated in this need by the carryover of colonial multiple-party systems and parliamentary forms in which the prime minister could be ousted by a vote of no confidence. Within African ways of life, this Western political machinery was simply a made-to-order means by which the opposition could make every conceivable appeal to dissident tribal, regional, kin, and class interests within the governing party itself.[7]

African leaders thus found themselves faced with a painful choice. They could hang on to their heritage of Western multiple-party systems and parlimantary forms, or they might junk this machinery in favor of strong one-party government—"mass party regimes" as Moore *(1966)* calls them. If they chose the first alternative, they would receive the accolade of Western societies for placing devotion to democracy above ambition for personal power and glory; in addition, they would run the danger of losing Western moral and material support if they did not do so (*Drake, 1964,* 115).

By and large, they chose the second alternative, holding that in so doing they are in fact exemplary agents of democratic aims and methods. Rubadiri (*1964,* 88) put the conviction this way:

> I for one do not believe that any institution or set of institutions can be identified with democratic ends, and there are none which, without reference to local conditions, can be said to be unique in securing democratic ends. . . . It has been gratifying to many of us to study how the tried institutions of the West are themselves different from each other. This can be only explained by the fact that different conditions prevail and call for different solutions for achieving ideal goals.

IV. Soverenignty of the Elite and Technological Backwardness

Attention now shifts to a second formidable barrier to the organizational requirements of progress—equation by the elite of the just uses of soveregin power with maintenance of institutions that perpetuate technological backwardness. The elite of the Chinese Republic on Mainland China before World War II will serve to illustrate the nature and potency of this equation.

Social Structures, Status, and Unprogressive
Convictions on Just Uses of Power

In historic Chinese culture, social structures segregated the population into two major classes: a relatively large class of poor tenants and a small elite class which commonly combined the three statuses of landlord, moneylender, and sovereign. As landlords, the elite collected rents from tenants. As lenders, they collected interest and principal on loans they extended to tenants. And as sovereigns, they occupied the decisionmaking positions at all levels of government, and thus prescribed the rules, including the tenure, credit, and tax rules, that maintained them as sovereigns, landlords, and lenders.

By and large, the rules they instituted induced in tenants negative production incentives—the fear of falling to an even lower status and income position if they did not work, rather than hope and confidence in their ability to gain an ever higher position through increasingly productive effort. For tenure rules called for approximately 50 percent of the total main crop yield, and might run up to 70 percent. In addition, tenants had to furnish their own fertilizers, farm equipment, and farm buildings. Leases were word-of-mouth deals with no definite time period; they had to be renewed each year, and might be terminated any moment the landlord saw fit (*Tang, 1957,* 13).

As Chinese farmers have long been competent operators (both on the Mainland and in Taiwan), the landed elite contributed little if any managerial inputs to farm operations. And in their capacity as lenders, they contributed few if any capital inputs. For they charged from 50 to 100 percent interest on loans they extended. Seldom is the return from any farm input enough to cover its purchase price plus an interest charge of 50 to 100 percent or more. Borrowing under these terms makes sense mainly as a means of staving off disaster, or of meeting such urgent personal needs as caring for the sick, discharging solemn religious duties, burying one's dead, or marrying off one's daughters in keeping with time-honored standards of decency and respect.

Although technological backwardness is a necessary outcome of such rules, the elite viewed them as establishing justice—a precise reciprocity or equivalence between service exchanges. The strength of this conviction stemmed not from selfishness in the usual sense, but from the anxiety people have over being so devoid of meritorious qualities as to deserve even lower standing, plus ample capacity for escaping this anxiety through attaching at least enough importance to their own deeds to convince themselves they have a natural or moral right to the statuses they hold by virture of the services they contributed. Neither did their convictions concerning the just use of power stem from any lack of professional ability to conceptualize reforms necessary to progress, or of power to implement them. For the essentials of land and other social reforms necessary to promote economic growth had been conceptualized by those who founded the People's Party in the early 20th century, and by those who founded the Republic of China in 1912. But aside from a relative few, these reform conceptualizations remained mainly a matter of paper-and-ink expressions. For their implementation required the elite to dislodge themselves from the landlord, lender, and sovereign statuses which they deemed their services deserved, and to hand their positions over to undeserving occupants.

Reform Through Catastrophic Learning Situations

For the reasons just cited, people's convictions concerning "what the social classes owe each other" are exceedingly powerful; so much so that rarely if ever are they able to shift to opposite ones without the aid of catastrophic learning processes. To illustrate: Essentially the same personalities were sovereigns of the Republic of Free China on Mainland China before World War II and on the Island of Taiwan after 1949. But their convictions concerning the just uses of power in the two periods were as opposite as the poles. Why?

A principal reason is that between the two periods lay a national catastrophe—loss of Mainland China to the Communists and the forced retreat of the Nationalist Government to Taiwan. Stripped of all their Mainland statuses, the elite of Free China reached the shores of the small island, sustained only by an army of 500,000 soldiers, needing rice above all else.

This catastrophe led them to ask why it all happened. Answers were substantially as follows: An important cause was their equation of institutional reforms necessary for progress with unjust use of sovereign power. Under the guidance of this conviction, they had aroused deep resentment within millions of Chinese tenant farmers—a hostility which commonly led them to transfer their allegiance to the Communists and turn in violence upon their former landlords and creditors (*Han, 1951,* 11). Moreover, Communist infiltrations among Taiwan tenants foreshadowed a similar disaster on the island. In this event, the sovereigns of Free China would go down in total ruin *(Tang, 1963,* 2).

In this way, the governing personalities of the Chinese Republic led themselves to three conclusions. First, in equating the just uses of power with the maintenance of institutions perpetuating technological backwardness, they themselves were a cause of the disasters which had struck them. Second, their last hope of survival turned on whether or not they had the capacity to earn the allegiance of all sections of the Taiwan population. Third, an indispensable first step to this achievement was a complete transformation of their older views and practices of social justice, and proving their new convictions through quick and resolute inauguration of a well-coordinated system of institutional reforms necessary for sustained cultural and material progress.

With an influx of approximately 100,000 trained civilians from the Mainland, the government on Taiwan had available ample professional competence to perceive the felt wants of peasants and others on Taiwan, and to conceptualize the specific reforms and programs necessary to release these wants into sustained increases in national output per capita. And thanks to 500,000 well-disciplined soldiers, they had sufficient power to carry out these reforms.

Basic steps taken to do this fell into three main categories: institutional measures, actions to improve knowledge inputs, and actions to improve physical inputs. Institutional measures included land rent reduction; a cadastral survey as a preparatory step to land tenancy reform; sale of public lands to operating families; a land-to-the-tillers program in which landlords sold rented lands to the government, which in turn resold them to hitherto tenant operators (*Tang, 1957,* 32-136); farmer associations and irrigation associations through which farmers manage their credit and marketing activities *(Hsieh, 1963b);* establishment and strengthening of township health associations; and measures to strengthen democratic governments at local levels *(Hsieh, 1963a).*

Within this new institutional framework, the new progress-oriented government spearheaded programs to enable farmers to latch onto increasingly productive technologies, such as extensive use of chemical fertilizers, improved crop varieties, new methods of controlling disease and pests, multiple-cropping systems, new irrigation construction, rotational irrigation practices, and groundwater development. To improve the technical knowledge of farmers, further measures were taken to establish well-staffed experiment stations, channeling their knowledge to farmers through a well-trained extension service working with farmers' associations at the local level; a nationwide system of public schools; a scientifically oriented national university; and a vocationally oriented system of secondary schools, heading up in a well-staffed agricultural college.

Thus translating into action their new concept of the just uses of power, the former governing personalities of Mainland China have enabled the people of Taiwan to increase their farm output at an average rate of 5.5 percent per year, and their per capita real total output at nearly 3.6 percent per year (table 1).

Table 1.—Rates of change in total farm output and real per capital total output, Taiwan, 1952-1962

Year	Total farm output		Real per capita total output	
	Index	Annual growth rate (%)	Index	Annual growth rate (%)
1952.	100		100	
1953.	113.82	13.82	107.20	7.20
1954.	115.03	1.06	107.49	0.27
1955.	117.27	1.95	112.59	4.74
1956.	126.55	7.91	113.47	0.74
1957.	136.92	8.19	116.51	2.68
1958.	148.76	8.65	119.56	2.62
1959.	151.17	1.62	124.24	3.91
1960.	151.37	0.13	131.32	5.70
1961.	166.14	9.76	138.76	5.67
1962.	169.30	1.90	142.04	2.36
Average	136.03	5.50	119.38	3.59

*Farm output data are from "Agricultural Production Index," complied by Rural Economic Development (RED), Joint Commission on Rural Reconstruction, Taipei, Taiwan (JCRR). The per capita total output estimates were compiled by RED, JCRR, based on data from "National Income of the Republic of China," DGBAS, Executive Yuan, Taipei, Taiwan.

V. Countering the Barriers

The question now arises as to the requirements for transforming the foregoing kinds of progress-blocking social structures, beliefs systems, and values into progressive ones. This transformation is already taking place more or less blindly. Thus the realistic question is not how to start economic and cultural growth from scratch, but how to initiate approaches to the development problem that can be relied upon to accelerate progress already taking hold. In line with this premise, three observations deserve mention.

Western Influences as Generators of Discontent With Progress-Blocking Social Structures and Values

In three distinct ways, Western influences are stirring up new felt wants and aspirations which are jarring people loose from allegiances to old ways of life and work in economically backward societies. Throughout Asia, the middle East, Africa, Latin America and on into the tiny islands of the sea, even the poorest of the poor have tasted the candy bars of progress and found them good. They like the Western bicycles that speed their legs; the TV's that bring them pictures and messages of faraway places; the pills that cool their fevers; the sprayguns that kill their flies, their mosquitoes, and the bugs that chew their cabbage. With Western trinkets thus stirring up their material wants, the rank and file cannot feel fully at peace with kinship and village structures and power elites that deprive them of the knickknacks of progress.

Again, in perceiving themselves stamped with technological impotence, poverty, illiteracy, and disease-ridden backwardness, people in unmodernized economies feel inferior to nations stamped with opposite badges. In leading them to this unfavorable comparison, Western affluence and power increasingly arouse a humiliating image of their individual and collective significance or worth. And this image further feeds their discontent with progress-blocking social structures and values which render them incapable of producing the technologies they need in achieving for themselves a dignity that even outshines the high standing of Western civilizations (*Rubadiri, 1964,* 85-88).

Finally, this discontent is further fed by a worldwide militant Communist movement which seeks to develop an indigenous leadership to organize and guide alienated peasants and others in a revolutionary takeover of sovereign power and use it for bringing to pass a world of plenty. From this movement stems, for example, a China that glowers as a sinister threat to her neighbors; an Indonesia that carries on a deadly vendetta with Malaysia; a Congo that seethes and festers with unrest; and a murderous struggle in Vietnam. Deep and implacable are the grudges and grievances which thus disturb the peace.

The Package Approach to the Development Problem

Channeling this discontent into constructive paths involves the hard job of conceptualizing new patterns of things to be done that appear feasible to developing societies. Soon after World War II and until quite recently, thinking mainly ran to singe-approach solutions, such as building many fertilizer plants

275

and hiring salesmen to sell farmers on the use of fertilizers; or setting up experiment stations and a well-rounded research program to accelerate development of new farm know-how, and a United States type of extension service to shovel the new knowledge out to farmers (*Johnson, 1964,* 2-7).

However, as anthropologists have long pointed out, all such single approach solutions are upended by the compatibility requirement of many activities which farmers must carry out in producing crops and livestock (*Foster, 1961,* 79-86). No significant yield increases stem from fertilizer applications alone; they arise only from an appropriate combination of fertilizer, improved seeds, pest control, water management, and the like. Thus, the one-shot fertilizer approach to the development problem can only wind up as so much wasted effort and resources, because it falsely imputes to fertilizer alone the entire yield response to the combination of improved technologies. The same principle applies to any other single-solution approach, including massive investments in the human agent designed to brighten the mind with Western sciences and infuse the muscles with a new host of technical skills.

As this fact became increasingly clear, thinking shifted to what Sherman Johnson has aptly called the package approach to the development problem. Johnson (*1964,* 7-19) has come to grips with spelling out the essential ingredients of this approach. Broadly speaking, the package divides in two main parts: a combination of improved technologies and related skills required for a more effective conquest of nature, and a set of organizations which make possible the improved technologies by linking rural villages and the outside world in a vast network of service exchanges.[8]

Kit of Improved Farm Technologies. There is no magic mix of improved technologies that can generate steady increases in farm output in all areas and conditions encountered in the less developed countries. But from basic research on the properties of soils, climate, and native plants and animals, and from deeper understanding of why people follow their present practices in different regions, we can learn a combination of improved farm technologies that will be suitable in each particular area.

Whatever the components of the combination may be, they must be generated and brought into rural villages by people from outside. For as previously explained, creation of even the simplest farm gadgets, together with the knowledge of how to use them, is far beyond the capabilities of such small units of collective action as the extended family, clan, tribe, or village. To achieve progress these small social units must be linked into much larger organizational units in which people have confidence and feel loyalty.

New Organizational Structures. This means that implementing any package of new technologies suitable to any area is impossible except as member of family and village structures are caught up in a new set of organizations that link them with the outside world in a vast network of service exchanges. This set of organizations includes two main sections: A set of intermediate organizations and a progress-oriented stable government.

Intermediate Organizations. The set of intermediate organizations constitute necessary linkages of farm villages and the outside world in an endless circuit of mutually servicing activities. To illustrate, the package may well include:

- Farm-supply market organizations that bring in from distant production points improved farm technologies: fertilizers, insecticides, implements, farm storage facilities, and the like.

- Farm-product market organizations that operate under standardized weights and measures and other trading rules necessary for fully protecting both buyers and sellers against swindle.

- Educational service organizations that are staffed with personnel equipped to bring in from distant experiment stations new knowledge of how to apply improved farm technologies, and who also have the knack of getting this new knowledge out of dust-gathering bulletins and into the heads of farmers without the farmers' having to read anything—or at least not much of anything.

- Irrigation associations that are staffed with personnel to allocate among individual farms water supplies brought in from central canals fed by reservoirs, constructed by the larger society beyond the local villages.

- Credit organizations that supply farmers with loan funds from remote depositors on reasonable terms for purchasing farm technologies and consumption goods.

Progress-Oriented Stable Governments. In addition to such a set of intermediate organizations, the total set of organizations necessary for implementing the package of improved farm technologies must include a progress-oriented stable government. As previously explained, such a government is a structure of sovereign personalities capable of setting up national targets and reaching them through a national framework of rules and agencies that: give private agreements the dependability of legally enforceable contracts; shift resources and jobs from less to more efficient users; reward increasingly productive effort in line with its contributions; collect revenues and allocate them to the development of social overhead services like school systems and research centers, roads and transportation facilities, water and power installations, which individuals cannot provide themselves but must have the use of it they are to develop and utilize their capabilities as fully as possible.

To say that any one component of the total package approach to the development problem is more essential to progress than any other is like quibbling over whether the heart is more essential to the operation of the body than the lungs, the liver, or the central nervous system. It can be said, however, that without precisely the kind of government just indicated, the whole package approach instantly collapses. For, without a progress-oriented stable government as their central anchor, the whole set of intermediary organizations evaporates, thereby cutting the service circuits between villages and the outside world. As this happens, the whole kit of improved farm gadgets falls apart, burying all hope of farmers ever achieving a more successful conquest of nature. For, as previously explained, only very primitive farm technologies can be generated and put to use by such small units of collective action as the extended family, clan, tribe, or village.

A Well-Rounded Research Approach to the 'Whys" and "Hows" of Development

The package approach to the development problem has been employed for some years with varying degrees of success in India and elsewhere—Taiwan, for example. This fact now makes possible a well-rounded research approach which might well lead to increasingly valid generalizations on "whys" and "hows" of development. The approach involves studies in depth designed to reach useful generalizations through four main steps.

In each area under consideration the study would first quantify the physical and human resources of the area, and the rates of economic advance that have been achieved over specified periods. The problem then becomes one of explaining why these growth events were (or were not) a necessary outcome of the particular way in which the developmental reforms and programs modified the older social system (community) under consideration.

To achieve this explanation, the study would next identify the components of the social system at the time the developmental reforms were initiated. These components include family (kinship), village, clan or tribal structures, property systems, power elites, and the connecting links between village structures and outside power centers. The components also include belief systems and values induced by traditional ways of life and work. These distinctly human variables would be segregated into the ones favorable to development, and the ones that operated as serious barriers to change. And these barriers in turn would be segregated into the ones that lead people to resist abandoning their age-old farming techniques and latching on to more productive gadgets, and the ones that lead them to resist concerting their behaviors into increasingly larger units of collective action necessary for creating and applying increasingly productive technologies. This segregation would shed needed light on the way both types of barriers feed on each other—a fact commonly obscured by the prevailing tendency to focus mainly on the first type of barrier, lugging in the second type principally as an afterthought. As the members of any social system vary widely with respect to the relative weights they attach to the competing claims of the various belief and value components of their culture, the study would quantify these variations to the extent possible.

Having thus delineated the components of the social system under consideration, the study would next give a breakdown of the total development program into (1) its package of improved farm technologies and (2) the set of reforms and program organizations through which the package was carried into rural villages.

The final step in the study would bring to a head the reasons why the satisfactory or unsatisfactory growth rates set forth in the first step of the study were a necessary outcome of the way in which the development reforms and programs (set forth in the third step) modified or failed to modify the social system delineated in the second step.

The stirring up of discontent with traditional ways of life and work by Western influences; the package approach to the development problem; and the well-rounded research studies designed to discover how achieved rates of economic growth stemmed from the package approach and how the progress-blocking social structures and interlocking systems of beliefs and values were overcome—these are important ways in which the barriers to progress can be and are being transformed into positive motivations for economic and cultural growth.

Summary and Conclusion

In most economically backward societies, the dominant units of collective action are the extended family, village, clan, or tribe. Such small social units are capable of producing and applying only very primitive farm (and other) technologies. This means that the requirements of economic progress are twofold. One is technological: the creation and widespread adoption of ever more effective gadgets for conquering nature. The other is the organizational requirements of the gadgets—the creation and operation of increasingly larger units of collective action, including progress-oriented stable governments, which are necessary for enabling a people to devise the more efficient gadgets they need for turning physical materials and forces into an ever faster flow of want-satisfying goods.

The literature mainly focuses on barriers to meeting the gadget require-ments of progress. To offset this imbalance, this paper has centered on the way in which the social structures of backward societies necessarily generate only primitive technologies, and also induce in people strong convictions concerning appropriate ways of life and work that commonly operate as formidable barriers to meeting the new organizational requirements of the gadget component of progress. However, at all steps in composing the paper, we have kept in mind the thought that the two types of barriers feed on each other, and also that both alike stem from the striving of people for proficiency in ways of life and work which are viewed as meriting increasingly favorable standing, in their own esteem and in the concerns and approbations of their human world. And we assume the same principle also applies to the positive motivations for progress, so typical of our own dynamic society. Although exploration of this theme could not be attempted here, we entertain the feeling that it might well lead to improved conceptualizations of social systems in relation to the process of economic and cultural growth.

REFERENCES

Banfield, 1958. E. C. Banfield, *The Moral Basis of Backward Society* (Glencoe, Ill.: Free Press, 1958).

Baran, 1952. P. Baran, "National Economic Planning," in B. F. Haley, ed., *Survey of Contemporary Economics,* vol. 2 (Homewood, Ill.: Richard D. Irwin, 1952).

Baudin, 1954. L. Baudin, "Irrationality in Economics," *Quarterly Journal of Economics,* 68:487-502 (Nov. 1954).

Benvenuti, 1962. B. Benvenuti, *Farming in Cultural Change* (Assen, Netherlands: Van Grocum, 1962).

Brewster, 1961. J. M. Brewster, "Beliefs, Values, and Economic Development," *Journal of Farm Economics,* 43:779-96 (Nov. 1961).

Drake, 1964. S. Drake, "Democracy on Trial in Africa," *Annals of the American Academy of Political and Social Science,* 354:110-21 (July 1964).

Embree, 1939. J. F. Embree, *Suye Mura: A Japanese Village* (Chicago: Univ. of Chicago Press, 1939).

Erasmus, 1963. C. J. Erasmus, *Man Takes Control: Cultural Development and American Aid* (Minneapolis: Univ. of Minnesota Press, 1963).

Foster, 1961. G. M. Foster, *Traditional Cultures* (New York: Harper, 1961).

Geertz, 1959. C. Geertz, "Form and Variation in Balinese Village Structure," *American Anthropologist,* 61:991-1012 (Dec. 1959).

Hagen, 1962. E. E. Hagen, *On the Theory of Social Change* (Homewood, Ill.: Dorsey, 1962).

Han, 1951. Lih-wu Han, *Taiwan Today* (Taipei: Hwa Kuo Publ. Co., 1951).

Hendrix et al., 1965. E. Hendrix et al., *Changes in Agriculture in 26 Developing Nations, 1948 to 1963,* U.S. Dept. of Agriculture, Foreign Agricultural Economic Report No. 27 (Washington, Nov. 1965).

Hsieh, 1963a. S. C. Hsieh, "The Role of Local Government in Rural Development," *Industry of Free China,* 20(1):2-7 and (2):10-19 (Taipei, July and Aug. 1963).

Hsieh, 1963b. S. C. Hsieh, "Farmers' Organizations in Taiwan and Their Trends of Development," *Industry of Free China,* 20(6):23-8 (Taipei, Dec. 1963).

Hsieh and Lee, 1958. S. C. Hsieh and T. H. Lee, *An Analytical Review of the Agricultural Development in Taiwan—An Output and Productivity Approach* (Taipei: Chinese-American Joint Commission on Rural Reconstruction, July 1958).

Hsu, 1955. F. L. K. Hsu, "Cultural Factors," in H. F. Williamson and J. A. Buttrick, eds., *Economic Development: Principles and Patterns* (Englewood Cliffs, N. J.: Prentice-Hall, 1955).

Johnson, 1964. S. E. Johnson, "Combining Knowledge, Incentives, and Means to Accelerate Agricultural Development," in Iowa State University Center for Agricultural and Economic Development, *The Economic Development of Agriculture* (Ames: Iowa State Univ. Press, 1965).

Kroeber, 1948. A. L. Kroeber, *Anthropology* (New York: Harcourt Brace, 1948).

Latourette, 1963. K. S. Latourette, *The Chinese: Their History and Culture* (New Haven: Yale Univ. Press, 1963).

Lewis, 1962. J. P. Lewis, *Quiet Crisis in India: Economic Development and American Policy* (Washington: Brookings Institution, 1962).

Lewis, 1951. O. Lewis, *Life in a Mexican Village: Tepositan Restudied* (Urbana: Univ. of Illinois Press, 1951).

Maffre, 1964. J. Maffre, *Washington Post* (Sept. 6, 1964).

Malik, 1963. C. H. Malik, "Developing Leadership in New Countries," address to the Plenary Session of the 13th CIOS International Management Conference, New York Hilton Hotel, Rockefeller Center, Sept. 19, 1963.

Marriott, 1955. McKim Marriott, ed., *Village India: Studies in the Little Community* (Chicago: Univ. of Chicago Press, 1955).

McClelland, 1961. D. C. McClelland, *The Achieving Society* (Princeton, N.J.: Van Nostrand, 1961).

Moore, 1966. C. H. Moore, "Mass Party Regimes," in H. J. Spiro, ed., *Africa: Primacy of Politics* (New York: Random House, 1966).

Nkrumah, 1958. K. Nkrumah, "African Prospects," *Foreign Affairs,* 37:45-53 (Oct. 1958).

Ogura, 1963. T. Ogura, ed., *Agricultural Development in Modern Japan* (Tokyo: Fugi Pub. Co., 1963).

Redfield, 1956. R. Redfield, *Peasant Society and Culture* (Chicago: Univ. of Chicago Press, 1956).

Rottenberg, 1952. S. Rottenberg, "Income and Leisure in an Underdeveloped Economy," *Journal of Political Economy,* 60:95-101 (April 1952).

Rubadiri, 1964. D. J. Rubadiri, "Africa: An African Evaluation," *Annals of the American Academy of Political and Social Science,* 354:84-90 (July 1964).

Spengler, 1954. J. Spengler, "Demographic Patterns," in H. F. Williamson and J. A. Buttrick, eds., *Economic Development: Principles and Patterns* (New York: Prentice-Hall, 1954).

Tang, 1957. Hui-Sun Tang, *Land Reform in Free China* (Taipei: Joint Commission on Rural Reconstruction, Jan. 1957).

Tang, 1963. Hui-Sun Tang, *Highlights of Land Reform in Taiwan* (Taipei: Joint Commission on Rural Reconstruction, 1963).

Weber, 1930. M. Weber, *The Protestant Ethic and the Spirit of Capitalism,* transl. by Talcott Parsons (New York: Scribner, 1930).

Wiser and Wiser, 1963. W. H. and Charlotte V. Wiser, *Behind Mud Walls, 1930-1960* (Berkeley: Univ. of California Press, 1963).

FOOTNOTES

Chapter 1. The Cultural Crisis of Our Time

[1] James, William, *The Principles of Psychology*. New York: Henry Holt & Co., 1890, vol. 1, pp. 293-294.

[2] Churchill, Winston, *Blood, Sweat and Tears*, New York: G. P. Putnam's Sons, 1941, p. 314.

[3] This I take to be the substance of Foster's statement that "the real essence of culture...lies in what we think and do, our attitudes, our social forms, and our religious beliefs." (Foster, George M., *Traditional Cultures: And The Impact of Technological Change*, New York: Harper & Bros., 1961, p. 68).

[4] For an especially able identification of major types of existential anxiety and an equally able differentiation between existential and pathological anxiety, see Tillisch, Paul, *The Courage to Be*, New Haven, Conn.: Yale University Press, 1952, pp. 32-63; 64-85.

[5] De Grazia, Sebastian, *The Political Community:* A study of Anomie. University of Chicago Press, Chicago, Ill., 1948, p. 48.

[6] Tillich, *The Courage to Be*, pp. 57-63.

[7] Nisbet, Robert A., *The Quest for Community: A Study in the Ethics of Order and Freedom.* Oxford University Press, N.Y., 1953, pp. 7, 12.

[8] *Op. Cit.*, p. 4.

[9] Aristotle, *Politics*, Book I, Chapter 5, p. 1254a. (Many editions and translations are available. The citation here is from Ross, W. D., *Works of Aristotle*, vol. 10, Oxford University Press, London, 1921.)

[10] Morrison, Samuel Elliot, and Commager, Henry Steele, *The Growth of The American Republic*, Oxford University Press, London, 1937, vol. 1, pp. 225-279.

[11] Jefferson, Thomas, Kentucky Resolutions, 1798. (Citation here is from *Documents of American History*, edited by Henry Steele Commager, Appleton-Century-Crofts, Inc., New York, 1949, p. 181).

[12] Hamilton, Alexander, *Works*, edited by H. C. Lodge, Houghton-Mifflin Co., N.Y., 1885, vol. 2, p. 51.

[13] James Bryce, *The American Commonwealth* (London; MacMillan and Co., 1889), vol. 1, p. 299.

[14] Cited by Frederick Brown Harris, "Spires on Barns," *The Evening Star,* editorial page Washington, D.C., Oct. 30, 1955.

[15] For a typical example of this caricature, see Mumford, Lewis, *The Condition of Man*, Harcourt, Brace & Co., N.Y., 1944, p. 199.

[16] For a startling expression of this bitterness by an artist, see Grant Wood's painting, American Gothic, owned by Chicago Art Institute and reproduced in Peyton Boswell, Jr.'s *Modern American Painting*, (New York: Dodd, Mead & Co.), p. 65.

[17] For a review of empirical studies of the psychological and organizational impacts of change-over from factory-automated processes on workers, see Dunlon, John T. (Ed.), *Automation and Technological Change*, Prentice Hall, Inc., Englewood Cliffs, New Jersey, 1962, pp. 45-65.

[18] Santayana, George, *Character and Opinion in the U.S.,* originally published in 1920, Charles Scribner's Sons, New York, 1924., p. 175.

[19] *Ibid.*

[20] DeTocqueville, Alexis, *Democracy in America*, Century Company, New York, 1898, vol. 2, pp. 2 & 3.

[21] For a summary of the operation of these work ethic concepts in the evolution of farm policy, see John M. Brewster's "Origin and Goals of Agricultural Policy and Programs," in *Farm Production Trends, Prospects and Programs*, Agricultural Information Bulletin No. 239, ARS, USDA, Washington, D.C., May 1961, pp. 21-26. For a similar summary of this operation in the Civil War Decade, see John M. Brewster's "The Farmer's Role in the Development of the National Economy," *Journal of Farm Economics*, Proceedings issue, December 1962, pp. 1301-1304.

[22] Gilpin, Robert, *American Scientists and Nuclear Weapons Policy*, Princeton University Press, Princeton, N.J., 1962, p. 10.

[23] *Ibid.*

[24] Cited by Gilpin, *American Scientist and Nuclear Weapons Policy*, p. 3.

[25] Cited by Niebuhr, Reinhold, *Moral Man and Immoral Society*, Charles Scribner's and Sons, N.Y., 1952 (copyright 1932) p. xvi.

[26] Dewey, John. Philosophy and Civilization, Minton Balch & Co., New York, 1931, p. 329.

[27] *Ibid.*, p. 328.

[28]*Leaves of Grass,* Christopher Morley (ed.) (New York, Doubleday, Doran & Co., Inc., 1940), pp. 268-9 and 272-3.

[29]Taken from J. W. Cunliffe, J. F. A. Pyre, and Karl Young (eds.), *Century Readings for a Course in English Literature* (New York: The Century Co., 1923), p. 766.

[30]Nicolay, John G. and Hay, John (eds.), *Complete Works of Abraham Lincoln,* Francis D. Tandy Company, New York, 1894, vol. 5., pp. 360-361.

[31]O. B. Frothingham, *The Religion of Humanity* (New York, 1873), p. 196, as cited by Henry F. May, *Protestant Churches in Industrial America* (New York, Harper & Brothers Publishers, 1949), p. 82.

[32]De Grazia, Sebastian, *The Political Community, Ibid.,* p. 70.

[33]Quoted by Arthur M. Schlesinger, Jr., *The Age of Roosevelt,* vol. 1, *The Crisis of the Old Order,* Houghton Mifflin Co., Boston, 1957, p. 120.

[34]Cited by May, *Protestant Churches in Industrial America,* p. 69.

[35]*Ibid.,* p. 94.

[36]Cited by De Grazia, *The Political Community,* p. 70-2.

[37]By the Economics Principles Commission of the National Association of Manufacturers, *The American Individual Enterprise System, Its Nature, Evolution and Future,* (New York: McGraw-Hill Book Co., Inc., 1946) vol. 2, p. 1019.

[38]Sumner, William Graham, *What the Social Classes Owe to Each Other;* (New Haven, Yale University Press, 1925, Chapter 1 and Conclusion. An essay first published in 1884, now reproduced in numerous readings; for example, Louis M. Hacker, (ed.), *The Shaping of the American Tradition,* Columbia University Press, New York, 1947, vol. 2, pp. 718-724.

[39]Charles C. Tansill (ed.) *Documents Illustrative of the Formation of the Union of the American States,* Government Printing Office, Washington, D.C., 1927, pp. 489-490.

[40]For documentation of this point, see John M. Brewster's *The Relevance of the Jeffersonian Dream Today: A Current Look at Griswolds's Farming and Democracy.* Prepared for Homestead Centennial Symposium, University of Nebraska, June 11-14, 1962.

[41]Madison, James, Federalist Paper No. 10, *The Federalist,* edited by Sherman F. Mittell, National Home Library Foundation, Washington, D.C., p. 55.

[42]For detailed documentation of this point, see pp. 20-32 of John M. Brewster's *The Relevance of the Jeffersonian Dream Today: A Current Look at Griswold's Farming and Democracy.*

[43]For an eye-witness account of this transformation, see John DeCrevecoeur's *Letters from an American Farmer,* first published in London in 1782, now available in Everyman's Library (No. 640) pp. 39-40, 53-56, 58-60.

[44]For a fuller account of the implications of this fact, see John M. Brewster's "Technological Advance and the Future of the Family Farm," *Journal of Economics,* Proceedings issue, December 1958, pp. 1599-1601.

[45]Webster, Daniel, "First Settlement of New England, 1820," address at the celebration of the two-hundredth anniversary of the landing of the Pilgrims at Plymouth Rock, reproduced in *Democracy, Liberty, and Property: Readings in the American Political Tradition,* edited by Francis W. Coker, Macmillan Co., N.Y., 1942, pp. 504-505.

[46]Benton, Thomas Hart, *Thirty Years' View: On A History of the Working of the American Government for Thirty Years, from 1820 to 1850,* D. Appleton and Company, New York, 1854, vol. 1, pp. 103-104.

[47]Cited by Arthur M. Schlesinger, Jr., *The Age of Jackson,* Little, Brown and Co., Boston, 1945, p. 293.

[48]I am aware these observations are quite contrary to reasoning in Reisman's *Lonely Crowd,* in Whyte's *Organization Man,* and the works of many other writers. Nonetheless, I am obliged to reject their thesis that our culture is disintegrating under the onslaught of a generalized status anxiety that is supposed to be generated by the pressure of increasingly larger organizations on individuals to follow the directives of others instead of their own.

[49]Cited in James E. Clayton, "Negro Making Himself Heard Across the Land," *Washington Post,* June 9, 1963, Section E, p. 1.

[50]Clayton, James E., "Negro Making Himself Heard Across the Land," *Washington Post,* Sunday, June 9, 1963, Section E, p. 1.

[51]Quoted by Dan Poole, "Realtors Attack U.S. on Housing Bias Ban," *The Evening Star,* Washington, D.C. June 6, 1963, p. A-1 and A-4.

[52]Lippman, Walter, "Point of No Return," *Washington Post,* June 11, 1963, p. A-15.

[53]Cawelti, John G., "Conformity and Democracy in America: Some Reflections Occasioned by the Republication of Martineau's Society in America," *Ethics,* an *International Journal of Social, Political, Legal Philosophy,* published by the University of Chicago Press, April 1963, vol. 73, p. 212.

[54]Lippman, Walter, "Strength to Govern Well," *Washington Post,* July 4, 1963, p. A-19.

[55]Lippman, Walter, *The Evening Star,* Washington, D.C., June 6, 1963, p. 1-A.

[56]Quoted by *Washington Post,* June 9, 1963, Section E, p. 1.

[57]Cited in Alan F. Westin, "The John Birch Society: 'Radical Right' and 'Extreme

Left' in the Political Context of Post World War II - 1962," reproduced in Bell, Daniel (ed.), *The Radical Right,* Doubleday & Co., Garden City, N.Y., 1963, p. 204. 206.

58*Ibid.,* pp. 206-207.

59*Ibid.,* p. 205.

60*Ibid.,* p. 208.

61 Duscha, Julius, "Birchers and Allies Out to Win the West," *Washington Post,* May 19, 1963, p. E-1.

62 Duscha, Julius, "Right Wing Radicals Active in Wyoming," *Washington Post,* May 2, 1963, p. A-2.

63 Martin Trow, "Small Businessman, Political Tolerance and Support for McCarthy," *The American Journal of Sociology,* vol. 64, November 1958, p. 274.

64*Ibid.,* p. 275.

65*Ibid.,* p. 275.

66*Ibid.,* p. 276.

67*Ibid.*

68 "Manpower Report to the President and A Report on Manpower Requirements, Resources, Utilization, Training" (U.S. Dept. of Labor,) U.S. Government Printing Office, 1963, p. 3.

69*Ibid.,* p. 3.

70*Ibid.,* pp. 27-28.

71*Ibid.,* p. xiii.

72 Sebastian De Grazia, *Of Time, Work, and Leisure* (New York: 1962, The Twentieth Century Fund), tables 1, 2, 3, pp. 441-444, interpretation of the data on pp. 63-139.

73 Reisman, David, "Work and Leisure in Post-Industrial Society," published in *Mass Leisure,* edited by Eric Larrabee and Rolf Meyersohn, Free Press, Glencoe, Illinois, 1958, p. 370.

74*Ibid.,* p. 367.

75 Sebastian De Grazia, *Of Time, Work, and Leisure* (New York: The Twentieth Century Fund, 1962), pp. 50; 273-274.

76 Niebuhr, Reinhold, *Moral Man and Immoral Society,* p. xiii.

77*Ibid.,* p. xii.

78*Ibid.,* p. xv.

79*Ibid.,* p. 1-2.

80*Ibid.,* p. 2.

81*Ibid.,* p. xxv.

82 Heilbroner, Robert L., "The Impact of Technology" in John T. Dunlop's (ed.) *Automation and Technological Change,* p. 25., Prentice Hall, Inc., Englewood Cliffs, N.J. 1962.

83 W. H. Auden, *The Age of Anxiety: A Barogne Ecolgne* (London: Faber and Faber Limited, 1948) pp. 24, 45, 47.

84 Tillich, Paul, *The Courage To Be,* pp. 146-147.

85 Snow, C. P., *The Two Cultures and the Scientific Revolution,* Cambridge University Press, New York, 1961, pp. 5-6.

86*Ibid.,* p. 7.

87*Ibid.,* p. 7.

Chapter 2. Views of Man and Society in the American Tradition

1 B. Jowett, translator, *The Works of Plato,* Four volumes complete in one, Tudor Publishing Company, New York, vol. 2, p. 212.

2 Abba P. Lerner, *The Economics of Control,* the Macmillan Co., New York, 1947, p. 40.

3 There is, of course, a conflict between maximizing the total satisfactions of the community by increasing the want-satisfying power per dollar (1) through equalizing incomes, and (2) through increasing the total number of dollars. For, while the assumption of equal "capacities to enjoy" may be awkward to deny, the assumption of equal "capacities to produce" is absurd. Some inequalities of income are necessary as incentives for each to do his best. Improving the general welfare through equalization of income cannot be carried to the point of destroying the incentives to improve welfare through producing a greater total income. But this fact does not disturb the main argument just set forth.

4 Lionel Robins, *The Nature and Significance of Economics and Science,* Macmillan and Co., Limited, St. Martin's Street, London, 1949, pp. 136-141.

[5]David Hume, *The Principles of Morals,* Section III, Part I, p. 17, LaSalle, Ill., The Open Court Publishing Company, 1946.

[6]Works of Aristotle, edited by W. D. Ross, Oxford University Press, London, 1921, vol. 10, p. 125a.

[7]Cyril Dean Darlington, *Conflicts of Science and Society,* Watts and Company, London, 1948, p. 28.

[8]Reinhold Niebuhr, *Moral Man and Immoral Society,* Charles Scribner's and Sons, New York, 1932, p. 118.

[9]Niebuhr, *ibid.* 118-119.

[10]Proceedings and Debates of the Virginia State Convention, p. 317. Cited by Russel Kirk, *The Conservative Mind,* Henry Regnery Company, 1953, pp. 143-144.

[11]Niebuhr, *ibid.,* pp. 135-136.

[12]*The Shaping of the American Tradition,* Columbia Univ. Press, New York, 1947, vol. 2, pp. 719, 723-24., Louis M. Hacker (ed.).

[13]The Economic Principles Commission of the National Association of Manufacturers, *The American Individual Enterprise System, Its Nature, Evolution, and Future.* McGraw-Hill Book Co., Inc. New York, 1946, vol. 2, pp. 1019.

[14]R. I. Nowell, "The Farm Land Boom," *Journal of Farm Economics,* vol. 29, No. 1, Feb. 1947, pp. 143-44.

[15]Francis W. Coker, *Democracy, Liberty and Property: Readings in The American Political Tradition,* New York, Macmillan Co. 1948, pp. 125-7.

[16]*Ibid.,* page 119.

[17]Charles C. Tansill, *Documents Illustrative of the Formation of the Union of the American States,* U.S. Govt. Printing Office, 1927, p. 781.

[18]Franklin F. Jameson, *The American Revolution as a Social Movement,* Princeton: Princeton University Press, 1940, p. 100.

[19]John Dewey, *et al, Creative Intelligence,* New York: Henry Holt & Co., 1917, pp. 208-9.

[20]For a highly original and comprehensive treatment of this subject, see George Herbert Mead's article entitled, "Scientific Method and Individual Thinker", in *Creative Intelligence,* by John Dewey and others, New York, Henry Holt & Co., 1917. Also see Mead's *Movements of Thought in the Nineteenth Century,* Chicago: The University of Chicago Press, 1936, pp. 264-7, 281-91, 405-11.

[21]George H. Mead, *op. cit.,* pp. 360-1.

[22]*Ibid,* p. 360-361.

[23]West Virginia State Board of Education vs. Barnette 319 U.S. 624.

[24]*Ibid,* p. 361.

[25]Thomas Jefferson, *Notes on the State of Virginia,* Univ. of North Carolina Press, Chapel Hill, 1955. Query 17, p. 159.

[26]*Ibid.,* Query 17, p. 159-60.

[27]*Ibid.*

[28]*Ibid.*

[29]*Ibid.*

[30]John G. Nicolay and John Hay, ed., *Works of Abraham Lincoln.* Francis D. Landy Co., 1894, vol. 3, p. 2.

[31]*Ibid.,* pp. 326-327.

[32]From a letter to A. G. Hodges, April 4, 1864, *ibid.,* vol. 10.

[33]*Ibid.*

[34]*Ibid.*

[35]Nicolay and Hay, *op. cit.,* vol. 8, p. 298.

[36]Ex parte Milligan, 71 U.S. (4 Wall.).

[37]Patterson vs. State of Colorado, ex rel. Attorney General, 205 U.S. 454.

[38]Meyer vs. State of Nebraska, 262 U.S. 390.

[39]Schenck vs. United States, 249 U.S. 47.

[40]Gitlow vs. people of New York, 268 U.S. 652.

[41]Henry David Thoreau, *Civil Disobedience.,* Fleming H. Pevell Co., Westwood, New Jersey, 1964, p. 17.

[42]Theodore Parker, Additional Speeches, (Boston: Little, Brown & Co.) 1855, vol. 2., pp. 209.

[43]Gunnar Myrdal, *An American Dilemma,* New York: Harper Brothers, 1944, pp. 1-6.

[44]George H. Mead, *op. cit.,* p. 409.

[45]*Ibid.*, p. 407.

[46]"The same data which are presented in the sensational press become scientific data when a competent social scientist studies them, examines them, gets them into such shape that they can be evaluated." (Mead, *ibid.* p. 407).

[47]Mead, George H., *Philosophy of the Act,* (Chicago: University of Chicago Press) 1938.

[48]Carl Sandburg, *Remembrance Rock,* New York, Harcourt, Brace and Co., 1948, pp. 19, 21-22.

[49]Cited by David L. Miller, "The Meaning of Evolution," *The American Scientist,* vol. 34, No. 2, Apr. 1946, p. 247.

[50]*Ibid.*, p. 246.

[51]Mead, *ibid.*,

Chapter 3. Additional Economic and Philosophic Aspects of the Spirit of Enterprise

[1] *The Autobiography of William Allen White,* The MacMillan Company, New York, 1946, p. 311.

[2] The Protestant Ethic and the Spirit of Capitalism, London, George Allen & Unwin, Ltd., Museum St., 1948 ed., p. 54.

[3] Thorstein Veblen, *The Theory of the Leisure Class,* MacMillian Co., London, 1912, p. 15.

[4] Essays in Our Changing Order, Augustus M. Kelley, 1964, p. 81.

[5] *Ibid.*, p. 80.

[6] The Place of Science of Modern Civilization, Russell and Russell, 1961, New York, pp. 296-297.

[7] *Absentee Ownership,* New York, The Viking Press, Inc., 1938, pp. 319-22.

[8] Cited by Roland H. Bainton, *Here I Stand: A Life of Martin Luther,* a Mentor Book, published by the New American Library, 1955, pp. 181-82.

[9] *Engineers and the Price System,* The Viking Press, New York, 1940, pp. 163-64.

[10] *Ibid.*, p. 165.

[11] *Ibid.*, p. 169.

[12] Ralph Barton Perry, *Puritanism and Democracy,* The Vanguard Press, New York, 1944, p. 81.

[13] Louis Boudin, "Irrationality in Economics," *Quarterly Journal of Economics,* vol. 68, Nov. 1954, pp. 488-89.

[14] "Income and Leisure in An Underdeveloped Economy," *Journal of Political Economy,* vol. 60, April 1952, p. 99. Also see Paul A. Baran, "National Economic Planning," in B. F. Haley, ed., *Survey of Contemporary Economics,* vol. 2 (Homewood, Ill., 1952), p. 378. Also, Joseph P. Spengler, "Demographic Patterns," in Harold F. Williams and John A. Buttrick (ed.), *Economic Development: Principles and Patterns,* New York, 1954, p. 96.

[15] T.S. Simey, "Welfare and Planning in the West Indies" (London, 1946), pp. 133-34, cited by Simon Rottenburg, *op. cit.,* p. 97.

[16] Vere Langford Oliver, "The History of the Island of Antigua," (London 1894), p. clviii, quoting C. W. E. Eves, "The West Indies (London 1891), cited by Rottenburg, *op. cit.,* p. 99.

[17] *Op. cit.,* p. 101.

[18] *Ibid.,* pp. 96, 101.

Chapter 4. Origins and Implications of the American Dream

[1] Cited by Reinhold Niebuhr, The Irony of American History, N.Y., Charles Scribner's Sons, 1952, pp. 24-25.

[2] Quoted passages cited by Niebuhr, *op. cit.,* p. 71.

[3] Cited by Niebuhr, *op. cit.,* p. 71.

[4] Cited by Niebuhr, *op. cit.,* p. 71.

[5] Alexis de Tocqueville, *Democracy in America,* translated by Henry Reever, Alfred A. Knopp, N. Y., 1960, pp. 136-137.

[6] Cited by Richard Hofstadter in *The Age of Reform,* Alfred A . Knopp, p. 277.

[7] *Ibid.*, p. 278.

[8] Cited by Charles W. Lowery: *Communism and Christ*, Morehouse-Gorham Company, New York, 1952, pp. 35-36.

[9] Cited by J. L. Talmon, *The Rise of Totalitarian Democracy*, Beacon Press, Boston, 1952, p. 195.

[10] Reinhold Niebuhr, *Beyond Tragedy*, New York, Charles Scribner's Sons, 1937, p. 29.

[11] *Ibid.*, p. 28.

[12] *Ibid.*, p. 30.

Chapter 5. The Place of American Agriculture in Mankind's Struggle Against Hunger

[1] See for example, Mead, G. H., Movements of Thought in the Nineteenth Century. Univ. of Chicago Press, Chicago, Ill., 1936, pp. 12-24.

[2] *Op. cit.*, pp. 25-50.

[3] There are many accounts of this; a highly able one is Charles W. Lowry's "Communism and Christ." Morehouse-Gorham Co., New York, 1952, pp. 1-38.

[4] Handlin, Oscar, *The Uprooted*. The Atlantic Monthly Press Book; Little, Brown & Co., Boston., 1951, pp. 33,37.

[5] *Op. cit.* pp. 35-36.

[6] *Op. cit.*, pp. 64; 82-89.

[7] *Op. cit.*, pp. 71-82.

[8] *Op. cit.*, p. 259.

[9] *Op. cit.*, pp. 243-244.

[10] For an excellent account of this transition and its political implications, see Samuel Lubell, "The Future of American Politics." Harper and Brothers, New York, 1951, chaps. 3 and 4.

[11] Letter to B. R. Sen, Director General of FAO.

[12] Statement on eve of his tour of the Far East.

[13] Address delivered to meeting of Magazine Publishers Association.

[14] From "The World Agricultural Situation 1961," U.S. Dept. of Agriculture, Foreign Agriculture Service, Washington, D.C., Dec. 1960, table 3, p. 3.

[15] Figures made available by Regional Analysis Division, Economic Research Service, U.S. Department of Agriculture. However, the idea was first developed by James T. Bonnen, "Adjustments in Agriculture, A National Basebook," edited by M. G. Smith and F. Christian, Iowa State University Press, Ames, Iowa, 1961.

[16] Smith, M. G. and F. Christian, "Adjustments in Agriculture," A National Basebook, table 3.5, p. 73. Iowa State Univ. Press.

[17] An hour of factory work on the average would buy 11 loaves of bread in 1958 but only 6.4 loaves in 1929, and the food packages it would buy in 1958 and 1929 compare as follows:

1958	1929
8.4 qts. of milk	3.9 qts. of milk
3.5 doz. eggs	1.1 doz. eggs
2.9 lbs. of bacon, or	1.3 lbs. of bacon, or
2.0 lbs. of steak	1.2 lbs. of steak

(F.V. Waugh and K. E. Ogren, "What Your Food Money Buys." Yearbook of Agriculture, 1959, U.S. Department of Agriculture.)

[18] Agricultural Outlook Charts, U.S. Department of Agriculture, 1961, figure 36, p. 18; table 16, p. 62.

[19] Trends in Output per Manhour in the Private Economy. U.S. Department of Labor, Statis. Bul. 1249, Dec. 1959, table 1, page 5.

[20] For a good account of the nature and economic significance of this fact, see L. M. Hacker and B. B. Kendrick, "The United States Since 1865." F. S. Crofts and Co., New York, 1932, pp. 174-175; 179-182.

[21] Bonnen, J. T., "The Nation's Present and Future Supply of Farm Products," in *Adjustments in Agriculture* - A National Basebook, p. 127.

[22] *Op. cit.,* p. 145.

[23] Daly, R. F., "Demand for Farm Products at Retail and Farm Level: Some Empirical Measurements and Related Problems." Jour. of the Amer. Statis. Assn. September 1958, pp. 667-68.

[24] Such an economy is here recognized as one which generates enough new jobs year by year to provide work opportunities (1) for all excess workers now in agriculture and industry; (2) for all workers now being displaced by rapid adoption of laborsaving technologies in both agriculture and industry; and (3) for all new workers entering the national labor force through population growth.

[25] Hendrix, W. E., "Problems of Low-Income Farmers," Farm Policy Forum, Iowa State College Press, Summer 1958, pp. 5-6; C. E. Bishop, "The Rural Development Program and Underemployment in Agriculture," Jour. Farm Econ., pp. 1199-1200.

[26] Bain, J. S., Industrial Organization. John Wiley and Sons, Inc., New York, 1959, pp. 430-439.

Chapter 6. Origin and Goals of Agricultural Policy and Programs

[1] See "The Machine Process in Agriculture and Industry," for a more complete discussion of this concept.

Chapter 7. Society Values and Goals in Respect to Agriculture

[1] "It is exactly this disagreement in value judgments that is the root cause of all social problems, both in the original definition of the condition as a problem and in subsequent efforts to solve it." R. C. Fuller and R. R. Meyers, "Some Aspects of a Theory of Social Problems," *American Sociological Review,* 6(1941):27.

[2] These traits are more fully considered in the author's paper, Value, Judgment and the Problem of Excess Capacity in Agriculture. Washington, D.C., U.S. Farm Economic Research Division, ARS, USDA, May 1960. [Ed. note: See ch. 1 of this book for discussion of this point.]

[3] William James, *Principles of Psychology,* Henry Holt and Company New York 1890, vol. 1, pp. 293-294.

[4] See p. 11-33 of the work cited in footnote 2 for a fuller discussion of these creeds than present space permits. [Ed. note: See ch. 1. In that discussion, these creeds are called "commitments."]

[5] The Economic Principles Commission of the National Association of Manufacturers. The American Individual Enterprise System, Its Nature, Evolution and Future. McGraw-Hill Book Company, Inc., New York. 1946 vol. 2. p. 1019.

[6] Hoover, Herbert, in acceptance of renomination, Aug. 11, 1932, Campaign Speeches of 1932, (N.Y. 1932) pp. 8-9.

[7] John C. Bennett, "How My Mind Has Changed," Christian Century Foundation, vol. 76, No. 51, Dec. 23, 1959, p. 1501. For an able economic analysis of the same point see John Kenneth Galbraith, *The Affluent Society,* Houghton Mifflin Company, Boston, 1958, esp. pp. 132-138.

[8] Bennett, *op. cit.* pp. 1501-2. For a fuller treatment of this point, see Arthur M. Schlesinger, Jr., "The Challenge of Abundance," *The Reporter,* May 3, 1956, pp. 8-11.

[9] On the central position of the exceptional experience of the individual in research, see George H. Mead, "Scientific Method and the Individual Thinker," in John Dewey and others, *Creative Intelligence,* Henry Holt and Company, New York, 1917, esp. pp. 206-209.

[10] Mead, George H., *Movements of Thought in the Nineteenth Century,* University of Chicago Press, Chicago, Ill., pp. 264-267; 360-362; 405-417. Also, Paul Tillich, *The Courage to Be,* Yale University Press, New Haven, 1953, pp. 104-105.

[11] For discussion of the Work-Imperative in Communism, see Dorothy Thompson's column, Evening Star, Washington, D.C., Oct. 17, 1957. Also pertinent are Kenneth S. Lynn's *The Dream of Success: A Study of American Imagination,* pp. 67-97, Little Brown and Company, Boston, 1955; and Sydney Hook's *Grim Report: Asia in Transition,* New York Times Magazine, Apr. 5, 1959.

[12] See observations of Gunnar Myrdal, *An American Dilemma. The Negro Problem and Modern Democracy,* pp. 1-6, Harper and Brothers Publishers, New York and London, 1944.

[13] See pp. 34-47 of reference cited in footnote 2. [Ed. note: See ch. 1 of this book.]

[14] For discussion of these exceptions see the author's paper, "Technological Advance and the Future of the Family Farm," proceedings issue, *Journal of Farm Economics,* vol. 40, No. 5, Dec. 1958, p. 1606-7.

[15] As explained elsewhere, this fundamental difference between machine industry and agriculture stems from the contrasting nature of materials handled in each case.

[16] Galbraith, *op. cit.,* pp. 112-118.

[17] Galbraith, *op. cit.,* pp. 112-118. Said Samuel Insull, the great utility magnate of the 1920's, "The greatest aid to the efficiency of labor is a long line of men waiting at the gate." Cited by Arthur M. Schlesinger, Jr., *The Age of Roosevelt,* Houghton Mifflin Co., Boston, 1957, p. 120.

[18] See reference cited in footnote 5.

[19] Glasgow, Robert B. and Hendrix, W. E., Measurements of Low Income in Agriculture as Problems of Underemployment and Economic Development, paper presented in Economic Section of annual meeting of Allied Social Science Associations, Washington, D.C., December 1959.

[20] The substance of this and the next 3 paragraphs have been worked out in detail by Wm. E. Hendrix, Income Improvement Prospect in Low-Income Areas, proceedings issue *Journal of Farm Economics,* December 1959; pp. 1065-1075; and Economics of Underemployment and Low Incomes, proceedings of Economics and Rural Sociology Section, Association of Southern Agricultural Workers, Birmingham, Ala., Feb. 5, 1960.

[21] Bonnen, James T., *American Agriculture in 1965,* in Joint Committee Prints, 85th Congress, 1st Session, on Policy for Commercial Agriculture, table 1 p. 147, Washington, D.C., U.S. Govt. Printing Office, Nov. 22, 1957.

[22] The logic of this section is of the same form as that first originated by John Dewey in his analysis of the "moral situation." See Dewey, John and Tafts, James H. *Ethics,* Henry Holt and Company, New York, 1908, pp. 205-211; and revised edition, 1932, pp. 173-176. On this point also see observations of Gunnar Myrdal on the moral nature of any social problem in *An American Dilemma, op. cit.*

[23] Dewey, John, *Freedom and Culture,* G. P. Putnam's Sons, New York 1939, p. 172.

[24] For excellent observations on the ethical neutrality of economic logic see Davenport, Herbert Joseph, *Economics of Enterprise,* The Macmillan Company 1943, pp. 126-127.

Chapter 8. The Relevance of the Jeffersonian Dream Today

[1] Griswold, A. Whitney, *Farming and Democracy,* New Haven, Yale University Press (published in 1948 by Harcourt, Brace and Co.,) pp. 19, 47.

[2] *Ibid.* p. 163, also see pp. 4-5, 14-16.

[3] Federalist paper No. 10. by Madison in *The Federalist,* ed. Sherman F. Mittell, National Home Library Foundation, Washington, D.C.

[4] Documents Illustrative of the Formation of the Union of the American States, Govt. Printing Office, Charles C. Tansill, ed. Washington, D.C., 1927, pp. 489-90.

[5] "First Settlement of New England," 1820, address at the celebration of the 200th anniversary of the landing of the pilgrims at Plymouth Rock, in the Works of Daniel Webster, vol. 1, pp. 5-6.

[6] From a speech by Thomas Hart Benton, *Thirty Years' View: A History of the American Government for Thirty Years, from 1820 to 1850,* (N.Y. D. Appleton and Co., 1854) vol. 1, pp. 103-104.

[7] Cited by Hacker, Andrew, The New York Times Magazine, Mar. 4, 1962, p. 84., "Voice of Ninety Million Americans."

[8] Jefferson, Thomas, "Notes on the State of Virginia," Query XIX, first published in 1782.

[9] *Ibid.*

[10] *Ibid.*

[11] Griswold, *Farming and Democracy, op. cit.,* p. 31.

[12] Jefferson, Thomas, *Notes on the State of Virginia,* Query XIX, first published in 1782.

[13] The pioneering works on this subject are: Weber, Max, *The Protestant Ethic and the Spirit of Capitalism,* Butler and Tanner Ltd., Frome and London, second impression, 1948, first published in 1930; Troeltsch, Ernst, *Protestantism and Progress,* Beacon Press, Beacon Hill, Boston, 1958; Tawney, R. H., *Religion and the Rise of Capitalism,* New York, Harcourt, Brace, and Co., 1926; Harkness, Georgia, *John Calvin: The Man and his Ethics,* Abington Press, New York, Nashville, 1958, see especially ch. 7.

[14] Cited by Tawney, *Religion and the Rise of Capitalism, op. cit.,* p. 240.

[15] *Ibid.,* p. 245.

[16] Cited by Perry, Ralph Barton, *Puritanism and Democracy,* the Vanguard Press, New York, 1944, p. 312.

[17] Cited by Max Weber, *The Protestant Ethic and the Spirit of Capitalism,* p. 261., New York, Scribner's Sons, 1958.

[18] *Ibid.,* p. 260.

[19] Cited by Perry, *Puritanism and Democracy,* pp. 314-315.

[20] Cited by Frederick Brown Harris, The Evening Star, editorial page, Washington, D.C., Oct. 30, 1955.

[21] See for example, Dempsey, David, "Myth of the New Leisure Class," The New York Times Magazine, Jan. 26, 1958; Abrams, Frank W., "The Dangers and Delights of Unlimited Leisure," The Saturday Review, Oct. 14, 1961.

[22] In the development of the following summary of Locke's theory of property, the author is especially indebted to two highly original and able interpretations of Locke's theory of property, C. B. MacPherson, "Locke on Capitalistic Appropriation," *The Western Political Quarterly,* 1951, pp. 550-566; and Leo Strauss, "Natural Right and History," Univ. Chicago Press, 1953, pp. 234-251.

[23] Locke, John, *Second Treatise on Civil Government,* first published in 1690, sec. 124.

[24] *Ibid.,* sec. 125.

[25] *Ibid.,* sec. 126.

[26] *Ibid.,* secs. 19 and 123.

[27] *Ibid.,* sec. 6.

[28] *Ibid.,* sec. 7.

[29] Cited by Leo Strauss, *Natural Right and History,* p. 227.

[30] *Ibid.,* pp. 226 and 227.

[31] Locke, John, *Second Treatise on Civil Government,* sec. 27.

[32] *Ibid.,* sec. 35.

[33] *Ibid.,* secs. 31 and 32.

[34] *Ibid.,* sec. 25.

[35] *Ibid.,* sec. 26.

[36] *Ibid.,* sec. 27.

[37] *Ibid.,* secs. 32 and 37.

[38] *Ibid.,* sec. 26.

[39] *Ibid.,* sec. 31.

[40] *Ibid.,* sec. 48.

[41] *Ibid.,* sec. 45.

[42] *Ibid.*

[43] *Ibid.*

[44] *Ibid.,* sec. 50.

[45] *Ibid.,* sec. 85.

[46] Locke, John, "Some Considerations of the Lowering of Interest and Raising the Value of Money," (1691), *Works* 1759 edition, vol. 2, pp. 22-23. Cited by MacPherson, *op. cit.,* p. 557.

[47] Locke, John, *Second Treatise on Civil Government,* first published in 1690, sec. 49.

[48] *Ibid.,* sec. 41.

[49] This fact is apparent in Perry's account of the waves of immigrants through the 18th century (Perry, Ralph Barton, *Puritanism and Democracy,* Vanguard Press, New York, 1944, pp. 62-81.)

[50] Griswold, *Farming and Democracy, op. cit.,* p. 41.

[51]Hacker, Louis M., *The Triumph of American Capitalism*, Simon & Schuster, New York, 1950, pp. 265-266.

[52]De Grazia, *The Political Community: A Study of Anomie*, Univ. of Chicago Press, Chicago, Ill., 1948, pp. 59-71.

[53]Morrison, Samuel Eliot, and Commager, Henry Steel, *The Growth of the Republic*, Oxford Univ. Press, New York, vol. 1, 1937, pp. 391-392.

[54]DeTocqueville, Alexis, *Democracy in America*, Tr. by Henry Reever, Century and Co., New York, 1898, vol. 2, pp. 163-164.

[55]Santayana, George, *Character and Opinion in the United States*, New York, Charles Scribner's Sons, 1924., p. 175.

[56]Federalist papers No. 10. by Madison in *The Federalist*, ed. Sherman F. Mittell, National Home Library Foundation, Washington, D.C.

[57]To be sure, "the abundance of land" was able to do this only through the assistance of Government land policies which did a fairly effective job of meeting the settlers' minimum request for first opportunities to acquire title to as much land as the usual family could handle with its own labor and the most productive technologies available.

[58]Nikolitch, Radoje, "Family and Larger Than Family Farms: Their Relative Position in American Agriculture," U.S. Dept. Agr., Agr. Econ. Rpt. No. 4, Washington, D.C., January 1962, fig. 6, p. 23, table 21, p. 40.

[59]*Ibid.*, table 16, p. 29.

Chapter 9. Role of the Researcher in the Formation of Public Policy

[1] On the nature and interdependence of pure and applied science, see Miller, David L., *Modern Science and Human Freedom*, University of Texas Press, Austin, Tex. 1959, pp. 121-157.

[2] I am indebted to J. Patrick Madden for assistance in developing this section.

Chapter 10. Philosophy: Principles of Reasoning Especially Applicable to Science

[1]Conant, James B., *Science and Common Sense*, Yale University Press, New Haven, Conn., 1951, p. 29.

[2]*Ibid.*, p. 25.

[3]*Ibid.*, p. 26.

[4]For lucid handling of distinction between cumulative and noncumulative knowledge, see Brinton, Crane, *Ideas and Men: The Story of Western Thought*, Prentice-Hall, Inc., New York, 1950, pp. 11-17; also Conant, *Science and Common Sense, op. cit.*, pp. 37-39.

[5]Conant, *ibid.*, pp. 38-39.

[6]*Ibid.*, p. 14.

[7]Cited by Conant, *op. cit.*, p. 43.

[8]Conant, *op. cit.*, p. 43.

[9]Cited by Morris R. Cohen and Nagel, *An Introduction to Logic and the Scientific Method*, p. 221.

[10]Galilei, Galileo, *Dialogues Concerning Two New Sciences*. Translated from the Italian and Latin into English by Henry Crew and Alfonso DeSalvio, Northwestern Univ.; with an introduction by Antonio Favaro, Univ. Padua, the MacMillan Co.

[11]*Ibid.*, p. 161.

[12]*Ibid.*, p. 169.

[13]*Ibid.*, p. 170.

[14]*Ibid.*, pp. 178-179.

[15]Cited by Cohen and Nagel, *Logic and the Scientific Method, op. cit.*, p. 108.

[16]"Posterior Analytics," book 1, ch. 4, in *Works of Aristotle*, W. D. Ross, ed., vol. 1, Oxford University Press, London, 1928, p. 101b.

[17]*Ibid.*, book 2, ch. 3, p. 90b.

[18]Eaton, Ralph M., *General Logic: An Introductory Survey;* Charles Scribner's & Sons, New York, 1931, Pt. 4, ch. 1, p. 483.

[19]Cohen and Nagel, *Logic and the Scientific Method,* p. 275.

[20]*Ibid.,* pp. 278-279.

[21]Northrup, F. S. C., *Logic of the Sciences and the Humanities,* ch. 11.

[22]Dewey, John, *Logic: A Theory of Inquiry,* ch. 21, esp. pp. 426-37, New York, Holt, Rinehart and Winston, 1960.

Chapter 11. What Kind of Social and Economic Order Do We Want in the Plains?

[1]This concept of the conflict between laborsaving technologies and increasing institutional costs per capita in the Great Plains is based on the penetrating analysis of the economic costs of "spaciousness" by Maurice M. Kelso, "Some Economic Dimensions to the Problems Growing Out of the Spaciousness of the West," paper prepared for meeting of American Association for the Advancement of Science, Denver, Colo., December 1961.

[2]Here, I have drawn heavily from Dwight G. Nesmith, "The Small Town," in *A Place to Live,* the Yearbook of Agriculture, 1963, Govt. Print. Off., Washington, D.C.; pp. 131-132.

[3]Fox, Karl A., "The Study of Interactions Between Agriculture and the Nonfarm Economy: Local, Regional and National." *Journal of Farm Economics,* February 1962, pp. 17-18.

[4]Voelker, Stanley W., *Economic and Sociological Trends Affecting Town and Country Churches in North Dakota,* the North Dakota Council of Churches, 13 Roxy Building, Fargo, N.D., p. 17.

[5]*Ibid.,* p. 16.

[6]*Ibid.,* pp. 15-16.

[7]Nesmith, Dwight A., "The Small Rural Town," Yearbook of Agriculture, 1963, Govt. Print. Off., Washington, D.C., p. 178.

[8]*Ibid.,* p. 178.

[9]*Ibid.,* p. 178.

[10]*Ibid.,* p. 178.

[11]This does not mean that land in the Plains is less "efficient" than elsewhere; a dollar's worth of it may produce as much or more profit as a dollar's worth of Corn Belt land. To suppose otherwise is to confuse productivity per acre of land with profitability per dollar of value of land.

[12]For a review and evaluation of this new kit of practices, see Warren R. Bailey, "The Great Plains in Retrospect with a View to the Future," *Journal of Farm Economics,* Proceedings Issue, December 1963, pp. 1094-1097.

[13]Farber, W. O., "Improving County Government: Reorganization and Consideration." Public Affairs, Governmental Research Bureau, University of South Dakota, Vermillion, S. Dak., p. 4. Shapiro, Harvey, "Economics of Scale and Local Government Finance," *Land Economics,* pp. 176-177.

[14]*Area Development,* Southwest Kansas Highlights, Kansas State University, Manhattan, Kan., January 1963, p. 29.

[15]The paragraphs that follow draw heavily from Fred D. Stocker, "Local Government Costs and Services Under Conditions of Sparse Population," paper prepared for meeting of Western Farm Economics Association, Laramie, Wyo., July 25, 1963, pp. 8-9; Clarence J. Hein, "Rural Local Government in Sparsely Populated Areas," *Jour. of Farm Econ.,* pp. 829-836.

[16]Farber, W. O., *op. cit.*

[17]Bailey, Warren R., "Land Problems in the Wheat Regions," *Land,* Yearbook of Agriculture, 1958, Govt. Print. Off., Washington, D.C., p. 153.

[18]See reference in footnote.

[19]*Ibid.,* p. 15.

[20]Knezeirch, S. J., "The Changing Structure of Public Education and Its Relation to the Educational Needs of Rural and Urban Areas," in *Urban Responses to Agricultural Change,* C. F. Kohn, ed., State Univ. of Iowa, 1961, p. 170.

[21] Fox, Karl A., "The Major Problem of Rural Society," paper presented at the third annual Farm Policy Review Conference, Ames, Iowa, Dec. 18, 1962, p. 11.

[22] *Ibid.*, p. 8., 664.

Chapter 12. Traditional Social Structures as Barriers to Change

[1] Available data did not permit Hendrix to segregate increases in total farm output due to increases in total inputs, especially land, from output increases due to improved technologies, including their implementing knowledge and skills. Were this segregation possible, his indicators of agricultural progress would be appreciably less rapid than the ones which available data permitted him to show.

[2] Since human and physical capital are thus simply aspects of the technologial component of behavior, is there need for the term "human factors?" I am unable to find any precise meaning ascribed to the term. And the same principle applies to the terms "social factors," "institutional factors," "political factors," "economic factors," and the like. May not this deluge of "factors" reflect a tendency to substitue verbal lumber for needed identification and analysis of basic structural and cultural concepts?

[3] For example, a writer recently identified the human factors leading to disappointing performance in the community development, service cooperatives, and national agricultural bureaus in India in recent years. Then he pointed out what the government should do to remedy these organizational breakdowns. But if I read his account correctly, the factors which led to the organizational failures he cites also rendered nonexistent the very kind of strong, competent, progress-motivated government required to implement his economic recommendations (*Lewis, 1962*).

[4] As William James observed, "No more fiendish punishment could be devised . . . than that one should be turned loose in society and remain absolutely unnoticed by all the members thereof. If no one turned around when we entered, answered when we spoke, or minded what we did, but if every person we met cut us dead, and acted as if we were nonexisting things, a kind of rage and impotent despair would ere long well up in us, from which the cruellest bodily torture would be a relief; for these would make us feel that, however bad might be our plight, we had not sunk to such a depth as to be unworthy of attention at all" Principles of Psychology, I, 293-94 (New York: Henry Holt & Co., 1898).

[5] How is one to explain the emergence of this equation of economic work with a badge of disrepute in virtually all unmodernized societies? This question has not received the attention it deserves. My own attempted explanation is included in *Brewster, 1961*, 782-91.

Editor's note: The article Brewester cited here is not included in the present volume of his selected works. Rather, his ideas on this concept are given in this volume in chs. 1 and 3.

[6] For variation in the organized forms of mutual aid from society to society, see *(Embree, 1939; Marriott, 1955; Geertz, 959)*.

[7] For further elaboration of this point, see *(Drake, 1964,* 118-20; *Rubadiri, 1964,* 89).

[8] Johnson *(1964)* refers to these intermediary organizations as field programs.